AMERICAN BAROQUE

American Baroque

Pearls and the Nature of Empire, 1492–1700

MOLLY A. WARSH

Published by the
OMOHUNDRO INSTITUTE OF
EARLY AMERICAN HISTORY AND CULTURE,
Williamsburg, Virginia,
and by the
UNIVERSITY OF NORTH CAROLINA PRESS,
Chapel Hill

The
Omohundro Institute of
Early American History and Culture
is sponsored by the
College of William and Mary.
On November 15, 1996,
the Institute adopted the present name
in honor of a bequest from
Malvern H. Omohundro, Jr.

Cover illustration: Baroque Pearl Boat Hatpin. Circa 1500. © Museum of London

Library of Congress Cataloging-in-Publication Data
Names: Warsh, Molly A., author. | Omohundro Institute of
Early American History & Culture, publisher.
Title: American baroque : pearls and the nature of empire, 1492–1700 / Molly A. Warsh.
Description: Williamsburg, Virginia : Omohundro Institute of Early American
History and Culture ; Chapel Hill : University of North Carolina Press, [2018] |
Includes bibliographical references and index.
Identifiers: LCCN 2017042775| ISBN 9781469638973
(cloth : alk. paper) | ISBN 9781469638980 (ebook)
Subjects: LCSH: Pearl industry and trade—Caribbean Area—History—
16th century. | Pearl industry and trade—Caribbean Area—History—17th century. |
Spain—Colonies—History—16th century. | Spain—Colonies—History—
17th century. | Pearls—Political aspects—History.
Classification: LCC HD9678.P42 C278 2018 | DDC 338.3/7140972909031—dc23
LC record available at https://lccn.loc.gov/2017042775

The University of North Carolina Press
has been a member of the Green Press Initiative
since 2003.

For Piotr Gwiazda

Rock, Star

ACKNOWLEDGMENTS

This book evolved over the course of much of my adult life thus far. As it grew up, so did I. The innumerable debts I have accumulated in research and writing seem to me like the squares of a quilt, stitched together to make a vast blanket of warm support. Without this support, I would not be the person I am. And this book would be a different book, or no book at all.

My beloved family: Hope Tompkins, David Warsh, Lucy McGowan, Mark McGowan, my starburst nieces Avery and Sloane, my heart is too full of love and gratitude for words. Jon Rosenfeld, you enrich all our lives. My grandmother Annis Content Meade, how I wish we could catch up and I could hear you laugh as we shared stories. My husband Piotr Gwiazda, whose mind captures and distills all the magic and absurdity of the world and whose steadiness keeps our ship upright in the stormiest of seas, this book is for you.

The friends and mentors I met as an undergraduate at Cornell University and a graduate student at Johns Hopkins University are many and extraordinary. Mary Beth Norton, my fearless leader, you set me on this path as a freshman in college and have helped me and inspired me at every step of the way. At Johns Hopkins, Phil Morgan is a model of academic integrity, rigor, and generosity. He and Barbara Morgan are also dear friends. Richard Kagan, *hispanista por excelencia,* is a mentor as demanding as he is warm and welcoming. He and Shreve Simpson threw more wonderful dinner parties than I can remember, from Baltimore to Florence to Philadelphia. In Phil and Richard, I was fortunate to work with two stellar people who also happen to be stellar historians. My deepest thanks to you both.

The bulk of the research for this book was made possible by the generous support of the Jacob K. Javits Fellowship and additional funding from Johns Hopkins University. A Fulbright grant enabled a transformative year in Portugal. The Scottish Society of Antiquaries funded a much shorter but similarly critical research trip to Scotland. In addition to my supervisors, I benefited immensely from the wisdom and kindness of Sara Berry, Toby Ditz, Lou Galambos, Michael Johnson, and the late John Russell-Wood. Chris Brown has been friend and mentor from the earliest days as well. Jack P. Greene and Amy Bushnell, towering figures each, never let a weak idea go unchallenged, and I am tougher and more exacting for their bracing encouragement. The early Americanist / Atlantic cohort taught me how to get through seminars and recover afterward, but the network of Johns Hopkins friends goes far beyond that weekly Monday night gathering: Joe Adelman, Sarah Mulhall Adelman, Rich Bond, Dirk Bönker, Teresa Cribelli, Sara Damiano, Andrew Devereux, Stephanie Gamble, Claire Gherini, Jonathan Gienapp, Katie Jorgensen Gray, Amanda Herbert, Cole Jones, Kimberly Lynn, Lars Maishak, Andrew Miller, Catherine Molineux, Kate Moran, Kate Murphy, Greg O'Malley, Nick Radburn, James Roberts, Justin Roberts, Jessica Roney, Erin Rowe, Leonard Sadosky, Carolyn Salomons, Katherine Smoak, Eran Shalev, Jessica Stern, Megan Zeller, and the late André Young. You have been cherished partners along this path.

My colleagues and friends at Texas A&M University gave me helpful feedback on this project as I was just beginning to transition from graduate school to being a professor. Andy Kirkendall, you are a great friend and DJ. Carlos Blanton, Cyndy Bouton, Walter Buenger, Glenn Chambers, Olga Dror, Kate Carté Engel, April Hatfield, Felipe Hinojosa, Angela Pulley Hudson, Priti Mishra, Ada Palmer, Jason Parker, Lisa Ramos, Jim Rosenheim, Rebecca Schloss, Adam Seipp, and Philip Smith, thank you for being so encouraging and kind. I am also grateful to Texas A&M for the grant from the Program to Enhance Scholarly and Creative Activities (PESCA), which enabled me to take a critical trip to Caracas, Margarita, Cubagua, and Coche in Venezuela. At the University of Pittsburgh, I have benefited enormously from my tireless and supportive chair, Lara Putnam, and the feedback and encouragement of my colleagues in the Department of History and beyond. In particular, Reid Andrews, Jonathan Arac, Olivia Bloechl, Molly Estes, Kathy Gibson, Laura Gotkowitz, Janelle Greenberg, Maurine Greenwald, Van Beck Hall, Diego Holstein, Holger Hoock, Patty Landon, Patrick Manning, Ted Muller, Tony Novosel, Marcus Rediker, Gayle Rogers, Rob Ruck, John Stoner, Gregor Thum, Grace Tomcho, Liann Tsoukas, and Bruce Venarde have gone out of their way to help and support me along the way. A Hewlett International Grant from the University Center for International Studies allowed my to deepen my engagement with the history of pearl fishing in Scotland and Sweden. Dean Cooper and Dean Knapp supported me and my work in more ways than one, including a generous grant from the Edwards Publication Fund for the book's illustrations and maps. The Humanities Center at the University of Pittsburgh gave me a critical semester away from teaching when I was finishing the first draft of the book. Lili Café in Polish Hill welcomes refugees and refugee writers: to Heidi, Mark, Catherine, and the whole neighborhood cast of characters, thank you for sharing your enchanted village. To the extended Pittsburgh crew: we sure hit the junior faculty sweet spot there for a

ments {ix}

minute. Pernille Røge and Vincent Leung, what a miracle to have landed in
Pittsburgh with you two. Raja Adal, Elizabeth Archibald, Rob Bland, Robin
Chapdelaine, Michell Chresfield, Niklas Frykman, Jennifer Josten, David
Luesink, Jamie Miller, Abigail Owen, James Pickett, Patryk Reid, Philipp
Stelzel, Mari Webel, Benno Weiner, Katja Wezel, Emily Winerock, you guys
are the best.

The undergraduate and graduate students with whom I have had the privilege to work at Johns Hopkins, Texas A&M, and the University of Pittsburgh
have challenged and inspired me. Their bright minds and spirits have often
saved me from the loneliness of writing.

Like most historians, I owe an enormous debt of gratitude to more archi-
vists than I could possibly name. I would like to extend particular thanks to
Isabel Aguirre for getting me started in Simancas and to David Beasley of
the Worshipful Company of Goldsmiths for his patience and generosity as
I was learning my way around London and its treasures. Hazel Forsyth at
the Museum of London introduced me to the Cheapside Hoard and the baroque pearl boat on the cover of the book. Edgar Samuel explained Sephardic London. In Lisbon, I learned so much from Nuno Vassallo e Silva at
the Museu Calouste Gulbenkian. In Caracas, the González-Silén family provided warm hospitality and many invaluable introductions. Tomás Straka at
the Universidad Católica Andrés Bello was a generous academic host; among
other things, he introduced me to Fidel Rodríguez Velásquez, in whom I
have found the fellow sixteenth-century Cubagua enthusiast I have long been
waiting for. In addition to the archival trips, the many conversations I have
had at seminars and conferences along the way have helped me think more
clearly about the project. I am very grateful to colleagues near and far for the
numerous opportunities to present works in progress at their universities.

I am deeply indebted to the Omohundro Institute of Early American History and Culture in Williamsburg, Virginia, where I spent two incredible
years as an NEH postdoctoral fellow. Presided over in those days by the incomparable Ron Hoffman and Sally Mason, the Omohundro Institute provided the time and space I needed to reconceive this project after finishing my
Ph.D. Kris Lane and Francesca Trivellato provided extensive early feedback
that informed my revisions to the very end. At a later stage, Jennifer Anderson and Daviken Studnicki-Gizbert were generous and influential readers of
the manuscript. I also made lasting friends while in Williamsburg. Alexandre
Dubé, Jonathan Eacott, Dan Livesay, Mary Livesay, Nick Popper, and Elena
Schneider, I smile just thinking about our funny times there. Chris Grasso
and Karin Wulf, you are such sharp, savvy, and supportive friends and col-

leagues. Kelly Crawford, Kim Foley, and Melody Smith, how we laughed! If I had failed to realize what an unusual place the Omohundro Institute is, Gil Kelly certainly reminded me. He was such a colorful character; I am lucky to have known him. The next time I am in town, I am looking forward to oysters with dear friends Beverly and Doug Smith. Jim Axtell, I treasure our catch-up conversations over pie at Charly's. Brett Rushforth, thank you for all the wonderful talks over tea. As Editor of the *William and Mary Quarterly,* Josh Piker helped me work through a major part of the book's argument in my article published in that journal in 2014.

The Omohundro Institute also saw this book into print. The editorial care and attention their Books team provides is unrivaled. Fredrika Teute, our conversations were an education in themselves. Your brilliant editorial insights opened windows in my mind and let in some much-needed fresh air. The book is more interesting because of you; thank you so much for the time you dedicated to this project. Paul Mapp, you took this project over when it was languishing in mid-revision doldrums and, with your trademark generosity and military precision, put some wind back into my sails. Thank you for bringing the project home alive, as you put it at the end of a memorable seven-hour discussion. Nadine Zimmerli, you are a wonderful, indefatigable friend and editor. I could not have done this without you. You worked miracles and kept me going when I thought I didn't have anything else left to give. I owe a similar debt of gratitude to Casey Schmitt, who combed through the tangle of footnotes, and to Ginny Chew, who is like a personal trainer for writers, taking a flabby manuscript and turning it into a stronger, sleeker book. Gerry Krieg did a wonderful job with the book's maps. I am humbled by the amount of work that my editors at the Omohundro Institute put into this book. Your generosity and rigor are an inspiration.

The networks of friends and family who made this book possible are, fittingly, overlapping and global. On the East Coast and in Poland, the extended Gwiazda family is an unfailing source of love and support. My love and thanks go to the Bailey-Minard family, particularly Sara Minard, my godsister; Mark Feeney, friend and editor extraordinaire; Hannah Allen, Annie Koehne de González, and Lisa Ahijevich Griffin, soulmates all. My Chicago family, Stephen Warsh, Ellen Adelman, Annie Warsh, Kathy Warsh, and Paul Gasparin, you make the Windy City cozy and welcoming. Laura Baccash, what a treat to catch up with you there, too. From the hallways of CRLS to Madrid to the peaks and perils of academia, Kate Burlingham has been my partner in crime for a long time. Alex White, you were funny and sharp at fifteen, and you are even funnier and smarter now. Your wit brightened a summer of copyedits. Talking with the world's hippest uncle and aunt, Tommy Amano-Tompkins and Karen Amano-Tompkins, about teaching, writing, reading, and life over amazing meals in a series of hidden SoCal gems has been one of the brightest spots of the last decade. Discussing history and politics with my sharp and passionate aunt Troy Ortiz keeps my academic perspective in check. Phoebe Tanner, you are a magician with family, food, and gardens. All my West Coast cousins made the last summer of this project full of love and fun.

My time in Madrid in the years between college and graduate school led to many lifelong friendships. Malena Bach, Almudena García, Alejandra Herrera, María José Mayor, María José Munguira, Natalia Zang: amigas de mi alma, os quiero mucho y agradezco de todo corazón todo lo que me enseñasteis y todo lo que hemos compartido a lo largo de los años. The incomparable Schvartzman family—Débora, Bernardo, Juanma, Dani, y Sara—no sé por dónde empezar. Mi familia adoptiva, me introdujeron a un mundo inmensamente generoso, acogedor, y sofisticado. En las innumerables comidas y sobremesas que compartimos en su salón, me abrieron universos. Gracias, desde el fondo de mi alma, por todo.

Many friends and colleagues have enriched my life and mind as I was writing this book. From various places I have called home: the Auspitz, Berger-Ripple, Cairns, King, Smith-Yerkins, and Turano families. For critical conversations along the way: Danna Agmon, Susan Baleé, Alison Bigelow, Jeffrey Bolster, Larissa Brewer-García, Kathy Burdette, Liam Brockey, Michael Bycroft, Myrta Byrum, Hugh Cagle, Beatriz Chadoor, Surkeha Davies, Topher Davis, Monica Dominguez Torres, Alejandra Dubcovsky, Sven Dupré, Kathleen DuVal, Pinar Emiralioğlu, Cécile Fromont, Alison Games, Mark Hanna, Scott Heerman, Daniel Hershenzohn, Steve Hindle, Javier Irigoyen-García, Alison Juozokas, Susan Juster, the late Michael Kammen, Diane Kane, Ryan Kashanipour, Christine Keiner, Anders Kloch, Jane Landers, Beverly Lemire, Michael Levin, Cici Malik, Lia Markey, Kevin McDonald, John McNeill, Luca Molá, Daniel Nemser, Marcy Norton, Peter, Sybil, and Zoë Pagnamenta, Gabriel Paquette, Rob Parkinson, Sarah Pearsall, Nathan Perl-Rosenthal, Carla Pestana, Rachel Price, Henriette Rahusen, Giorgio Riello, Susanah Shaw Romney, Neil Safier, Tatiana Seijas, Rebecca Shumway, John Soluri, Matthew Spooner, Christopher Taylor, Peter Thompson, Cécile Vidal, Elvira Vilches, David Wheat, Sophie White, and Anya Zilberstein.

Thank you all for helping me bring this project to completion. I couldn't have done it without you.

CONTENTS

ILLUSTRATIONS

ABBREVIATIONS AND SHORT TITLES

ACC	*Actas del Cabildo de Caracas*, I, *1573–1600* (Caracas, 1943)
AGI	Archivo General de Indias, Seville
AC	(Audiencia de Caracas)
IG	(Indiferente General)
SD	(Santo Domingo)
AGS	Archivo General de Simancas, Valladolid
AHN	Archivo Histórico Nacional, Madrid
AHU	Arquivo Histórico Ultramarino, Lisbon
ANTT	Arquivo Nacional da Torre do Tombo, Lisbon
ANTT/CC	Arquivo Nacional da Torre do Tombo, Lisbon, Corpo Cronológico
ANTT/LM	Arquivo Nacional da Torre do Tombo, Lisbon, *Livros das Monções*
BL	British Library, London
Californiana II	W. Michael Mathes, ed., *Californiana II: Documentos para la historia de la explotacion comercial de California, 1611–1679,* parts I and II (Madrid, 1970)
CC, I	Enrique Otte, *Cedulario de la monarquía española relativo a la Isla de Cubagua (1523–1550)*, I (1523–1534) (Caracas, 1961)
CC, II	Enrique Otte, *Cedulario de la monarquía española relativo a la Isla de Cubagua (1523–1550)*, II (1535–1550) (Caracas, 1961)
CMNAC, I	Enrique Otte, *Cedularios de la monarquía española de Margarita, Nueva Andalucía y Caracas (1553–1604)*, I, (Caracas, 1967)
CSP	Great Britain, Public Record Office, *Calendar of State Papers*, Colonial Series, ed. W. Noel Sainsbury et al. (London, 1860–): *East Indies, China, and Japan*, III, *1617–1621*, IV, *1622–1624; East Indies, China, and Persia*, VI, *1625–1629; East Indies and Persia*, VIII, *1630–1634*
CV	Enrique Otte, *Cédulas de la monarquía española relativas a Venezuela (1500–1550)* (Caracas, 1963)
HNM, II	Investigaciones H. Nectario María, tomo II, "Isla

	Margarita desde 1553 hasta 1604," Archivo General de Indias, Audiencia de Caracas, Seville
LM	Raymundo Antonio de Bulhão Pato, ed., *Documentos remetidos da India ou Livros das Monções* (Nendeln, Liechtenstein, 1976)
RAH	Real Academia de la Historia, Madrid
RBM	La Real Biblioteca, Madrid
RPCS	David Masson, ed., *The Register of the Privy Council of Scotland*, XII, *1619–1622* (Edinburgh, 1895); Masson and P. H. Brown, eds., *The Register of the Privy Council of Scotland*, 2d Ser., 8 vols. (Edinburgh, 1899–1908), I, *1625–1627*, IV, *1630–1632*, V, *1633–1635*
TNA	The National Archives, Kew, United Kingdom
E	(Exchequer)
HCA	(High Court of Admiralty)
SP	(State Papers, Foreign, 1509–1782)

AMERICAN BAROQUE

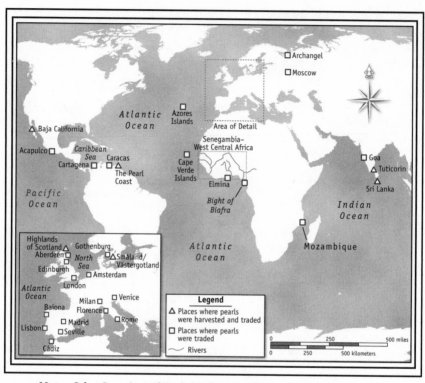

Map 1. Select Locations of Early Modern Pearl Production and Commerce.
Drawn by Gerry Krieg

INTRODUCTION
The Global Early Americas

The story of pearls in the early modern period could be told as a simple one: pearls mattered a lot at the start of the era and less so at its end. They were worn as jewelry in 1500; they were still worn as jewelry in 1700. But such a story would be misleading, just as the simple beauty of pearls obscures the complexity that produced them and moved them throughout global markets in the sixteenth and seventeenth centuries. The story of pearls is not, in fact, simple. It is baroque.

Today, pearls are predominantly associated with a modest adherence to rules of understated feminine beauty. Cheap or expensive, in pendant earrings or knotted ropes, pearls in the modern imagination convey an unassuming elegance to the woman who wears them, an air of unimpeachable and straightforward good taste. We think, for example, of a strand of pearls adorning a prim, feminine neck. Or of endless rows of the jewel sewn into hemlines and sleeves on extravagant costumes from a distant era. Or of a single luminous earring, enhancing the appeal of the bearer. They are an accommodating jewel: their simple, natural beauty presents no challenges and suggests that the woman who wears them will offer none herself. How did pearls shuck their earlier association with the riot of tastes and motivations that shaped their production and circulation four hundred years ago? *American Baroque* recovers this messier history of the jewel, seeking to restore complexity to our understandings of pearls.

The beginning of this story is a familiar one. Columbus set sail from the southern Spanish port of Palos in August 1492, having struck a pact with the Catholic Monarchs Ferdinand and Isabella for a share of whatever wealth he might find as he charted a new route to rich Asian markets. Less familiar, though, are the terms of that pact. Pearls topped the list of the items he sought; 10 percent of the same was to be his. The crown's explicit desire for this unusual maritime jewel put wind in the admiral's sails as he helped bring Spain's Atlantic empire into existence, and it was a prescient imagining of the wealth his wanderings would generate: pearls proved to be one of the most spectacular products of the New World Columbus stumbled upon. In the decades following his voyage, millions of them cascaded into Spanish crown coffers and beyond from the pearl-fishing settlements established off the Venezuelan coast.[1]

Why did pearls occupy such a prominent place in Columbus's sailing orders? How was it that this fragile little jewel, this organic product of a living creature, had the power to motivate and sustain visions of maritime empire? The pearl, a vehicle for both value and fantasy, had an appeal that was evident as a lustrous round white orb and, more subjectively, as an irregular baroque specimen, an ungainly excretion that could be transformed by the mind and hands of a skilled jeweler into the body of a dragon, the hull of a ship, or the torso of an enslaved boy (see Figures 1 [Plate 1], 27, and 29).

American Baroque tells the history of what people did with and thought about pearls in the aftermath of Columbus's accidental encounter with the Americas. The haphazardly established pearl-fishing settlements that emerged along the coast of Venezuela in the early sixteenth century embedded this early American export in global commercial circuits, transforming the market for the jewel and adding additional complexity to pearls' long-standing associations with the romance and danger of the sea. The profits and problems created along the Pearl Coast (as the region came to be known) drew this corner of the Atlantic world into an evolving geography of imperial jurisdiction, the contours of which reflected European dynastic concerns and the gradual integration of global markets as well as the demands of New World settlements.

Pearls themselves were not a product of the New World, of course. Pulled from river mussels or oysters, pearls were found the world over, although they were associated in the European imagination with the luxury markets of the Far East. In the Americas, European interlopers encountered pearl wealth through gifts and burial practices alike far beyond the north coast of South America. Pearls (produced by various species of bivalves) were fished in several places throughout the Americas, a valued natural resource from the rivers of Virginia to the Pacific coast of what would become Ecuador to the Caribbean, and many places in between.[2] Costa Rica (meaning "rich

1. Columbus's sailing orders, the *capitulaciones,* are translated and reprinted in Charles Gibson, ed., *The Spanish Tradition in America* (New York, 1968), 27–34.

2. For an overview of pearl worship in the pre-Columbus Americas, see Nicholas J. Saunders, "Biographies of Brilliance: Pearls, Transformations of Matter, and Being, c. AD 1492," *World Archaeology,* XXXI (1999), 243–257, esp. 248–249. Brilliance represented internal sacredness and could be found in many shiny objects—pearls as well as feathers, wampum, rainbows, and various metals, among other goods. The particular items of worship and cultural valences varied from culture to culture, but the association of luminescence with the sacred and spiritual world seems to have been widespread throughout the

Figure 1. Enameled Sea Dragon Pendant with Baroque Pearl.
Spain, late sixteenth century. Permission, The British Museum, London

coast") was said to be so named by the Spaniards because of its pearl wealth. With the exception of Panama and Venezuela, however, these sites of production would remain just that—periodically and moderately exploited arenas of natural resource cultivation. This circumstance reflected the geographic and demographic characteristics and restraints of the various locales. On the Ecuadorian coast between Atacames and the peninsula Santa Elena, for example, a combination of strong Pacific currents and the threats posed by foreign corsairs and sharks kept a larger industry from developing around the high-quality pearls found in its waters. (Other dangers are revealed by the remains of preceramic skeletons of Pacific coast divers buried near Huaca Prieta in Peru. These remains show extensive damage to the skeletons' eardrums, likely a reflection of the community's dependence on diving for bivalves.) As a result of existing indigenous practice and the serendipity of the geography of the Columbian encounter, it was the oyster banks along South America's north coast that became the site for a transformative experiment in early modern maritime empire.[3]

Although the Spanish overseas imperial mission is remembered largely for its violent and overweening Catholic unity of mission, uncertainty as much as certainty—disorder as much as order—shaped its first fifty years in the

Americas. On consumer demand for pearls in medieval European markets, see George Frederick Kunz and Charles Hugh Stevenson, *The Book of the Pearl: The History, Art, Science, and Industry of the Queen of Gems* (New York, 1908), 18–21. For a comprehensive overview of pearl production worldwide, see Elisabeth Strack, *Pearls* (Stuttgart, 2006).

3. On the Panamanian fisheries, see Alfredo Castillero Calvo, "El oro y las perlas en la economía colonial," in Castillero, ed., *Historia general de Panamá: El orden colonial* (Panama, 2004), II, 431–456. On Pacific coast pearl fishing, see Ann Marie Mester, "The Pearl Divers of Los Frailes: Archaeological and Ethnohistorical Exploration of Sumptuary Good Trade and Cosmology in the North and Central Andes" (Ph.D. diss., University of Illinois at Urbana-Champaign, 1990), esp. chap. 6, "Pearl Fishing during the Spanish *Colonia*." For an overview of other American pearl-fishing communities established or encroached upon by Spaniards, see R. A. Donkin, *Beyond Price: Pearls and Pearl-Fishing: Origins to the Age of Discoveries* (Philadelphia, 1998), chap. 10. On the skeletons of Huaca Prieta, see Ian Tattersall, "The Human Skeletons from Huaca Prieta, with a Note on Exostoses of the External Auditory Meatus," in Junius B. Bird, John Hyslop, and Milica Dimitrijevic Skinner, eds., *The Preceramic Excavations at the Huaca Prieta, Chicama Valley, Peru*, Anthropological Paper, American Museum of Natural History, LXII, no. 1 (New York, 1985), 59–76. This phenomenon of eardrum damage is known as aural exostoses. Given the high rate (33 percent) of exostoses among the Huaca Prieta people, researchers concluded that these individuals were regularly exposed to prolonged contact with the cold Pacific waters of the Humboldt Current in coastal Peruvian waters.

Americas. The pearl fisheries that developed along the coast of present-day Venezuela refract the familiar narrative of early Spanish Caribbean settlement in revealing ways. Their history sheds new light on how the components of a New World political economy were elaborated as unfamiliar places and people challenged approaches to the management of human and natural wealth. The history of these settlements underscores aspects of the origins of the Spanish Atlantic empire that are often overlooked: the remarkably early and chaotic imperatives that shaped its administrative bureaucracy and the critical importance of the maritime sphere in these formative decades. Often, the origins of Spain's American empire are traced to the major mainland conquests that came later in the sixteenth century and that differed in critical ways from the maritime and demographic realities of earlier Caribbean encounters. By emphasizing the importance of the maritime sphere to the emerging Spanish Atlantic economy, *American Baroque* challenges the long-standing historiographical emphasis on the terrestrial nature of the Spanish empire. It therefore speaks to a growing body of work within Atlantic world scholarship that pays attention to the geography of empire, especially the importance of the oceanic context.[4]

4. See Ida Altman, "The Revolt of Enriquillo and the Historiography of Early Spanish America," *Americas*, LXIII (2007), 587–614, for a discussion of the historiographical trend to ignore the Antilles in the wake of the first major mainland conquests of Cortés and Pizarro in the 1520s and 1530s. For a more recent example of the emphasis on the primacy of mainland developments, see John Tutino, *Making a New World: Founding Capitalism in the Bajío and Spanish North America* (Durham, N.C., 2011). A leading textbook on colonial Latin America follows this lead, opening with a discussion of the major mainland indigenous societies and offering a cursory overview of Caribbean encounters (Mark A. Burkholder and Lyman L. Johnson, *Colonial Latin America,* 8th ed. [New York, 2012]). An exception to the emphasis on the Spanish empire's supposed terrestrial nature is the work of Carla Rahn Philips and William D. Philips, who have worked on Spain's seaborne endeavors, including Pablo E. Pérez-Mallaína, *Spain's Men of the Sea: Daily Life on the Indies Fleets in the Sixteenth Century,* trans. Carla Rahn Phillips (Baltimore, 1998). Lauren Benton discusses the unique characteristics of the maritime sphere in *A Search for Sovereignty: Law and Geography in European Empires, 1400–1900* (Cambridge, 2010). April Lee Hatfield considers the unique geographies of rivers in *Atlantic Virginia: Intercolonial Relations in the Seventeenth Century* (Philadelphia, 2007). Marcus Rediker and Peter Linebaugh also argue for the sea as a distinct social and political climate in their classic work, *The Many-Headed Hydra: Sailors, Slaves, Commoners, and the Hidden History of the Revolutionary Atlantic* (Boston, 2000). For other scholars of the Atlantic world who have paid particular attention to labor, politics, and knowledge of the natural world in the maritime sphere, see Daniel Vickers, *Farmers and Fisherman:*

The Pearl Coast rose to early prominence as a site not just of profit but of struggles for control over resources. The fisheries achieved early infamy because of the brutal labor system of pearl diving that developed there amid intense debates about policy regarding the treatment of America's indigenous inhabitants. Furthermore, the single-minded focus on the harvesting of the region's pearls produced an extraordinary assault on the region's marine ecosystem, a sobering counterpoint to the abundant visual evidence of pearls' popularity in the period. The fisheries also revealed early on the interplay between global and local imperatives that would shape the history of the Americas from that point forward. The American pearl fisheries, intimately connected to distant markets through the commercial connections that helped distribute Caribbean pearls throughout Europe and beyond and yet profoundly influenced by site-specific practices and concerns, were a crucible of Spanish imperial administration and an early and enduring model of a global commodity trade.

Why has this story remained largely out of view until now? It was not just pearls' decreasing relative value to spices, gold, and, silver, although within decades of the Columbian encounter these and other global commodity trades eclipsed pearls as sources of imperial wealth. It was also the precise politics of mid-sixteenth-century Spain that led the history of pearls to be overshadowed by other narratives. The heyday of pearls corresponded with the earliest years of Atlantic experimentation, a violent and improvisational several decades. Over the course of this half century, the Caribbean pearl fisheries came to be understood as an egregious example of the mismanagement of human and natural wealth, an embarrassing product of ineffective royal policy. Early histories of the empire condemned this episode of natural and human resource mismanagement, and later accounts—establishing a precedent that would linger in the historiography over several centuries—began to emphasize stories of resource exploitation in which the apparatus of the state was more visible. Industries such as mining and sugar plantations

Two Centuries of Work in Essex County, Massachusetts, 1630–1830 (Chapel Hill, N.C., 1994); Vickers with Vince Walsh, *Young Men and the Sea: Yankee Seafarers in the Age of Sail* (New Haven, Conn., 2005); Michael J. Jarvis, *In the Eye of All Trade: Bermuda, Bermudians, and the Maritime Atlantic World, 1680–1783* (Chapel Hill, N.C., 2010); James Delbourgo, "Divers Things: Collecting the World Under Water," *History of Science*, XLIX (2011), 149–185; Christopher L. Pastore, *Between Land and Sea: The Atlantic Coast and the Transformation of New England* (Cambridge, Mass., 2014); and Christopher Parsons, *Cultivating a New France: Knowledge, Empire, and Environment in the French Atlantic World* (forthcoming).

required heavy capital investment that discouraged the type of individual engagement that was so common with pearl fishing. Instead, these later industries depended upon, and thus became subordinate to, larger and more complex sources of funding and oversight. The history of the Caribbean pearl fisheries — the lessons learned and ignored there and their impact on both the nascent Iberian imperial bureaucracy and the ambitions of Spain's rivals for dominance of the seas — shines a light on this largely forgotten period of trial and error. It reveals the protagonism of the maritime sphere in this formative era and the complex dynamics above and below the waves that influenced Spain's initial understandings of the Americas.[5]

Pearls posed specific challenges to the regulatory infrastructure intended to oversee the governance of the Indies' products and inhabitants. The Spanish crown's vision for the trade was both uncertain and contested. The pearl fisheries illuminate the often competing interests of individuals, large commercial networks, and the new imperial bureaucracy, all of which molded the global channels that would distribute pearls and manage the people and the places that produced them.

The American context of pearl production also informed the popularity of the jewel in the early modern period. Pearls' appeal reflected in part the maritime environment from which they came and in part a variety of more complex factors. Pearls were a sensual, enigmatic jewel linked to primal human impulses as well as many paradoxical binaries. Pearls were believed to be the product of intercourse, like humans; also like humans, they were endlessly diverse and subject to decay. Pearls were produced by nature, yet to desire them was unnatural, reflecting avarice and excessive willingness to engage

5. For Spain's censorship of mid-sixteenth-century historians and chroniclers, see Richard L. Kagan, *Clio and the Crown: The Politics of History in Medieval and Early Modern Spain* (Baltimore, 2009). For an overview of the Spanish crown's evolving approach to the governance of the Indies, see Ralph Bauer, *The Cultural Geography of Colonial American Literatures: Empire, Travel, Modernity* (Cambridge, 2003), 42–48. Even Enrique Otte, who seemingly compiled all archival data ever generated by the Venezuelan pearl fisheries, lost interest after Cubagua's profits faded. There is a growing interdisciplinary interest in historicizing the oceans and considering people as ecological actors who both observed and altered the changing sea. The January 2013 (XVIII) issue of *Environmental History* is a dedicated "Marine Forum"; see also W. Jeffrey Bolster, *The Mortal Sea: Fishing the Atlantic in the Age of Sail* (Cambridge, Mass., 2012). For interest in historicizing marine ecologies, see Loren McClenachan, Francesco Ferretti, and Julia K. Baum, "From Archives to Conservation: Why Historical Data Are Needed to Set Baselines for Marine Animals and Ecosystems," *Conservation Letters*, V (2012), 349–359.

in risky behavior. They were known for their simple beauty, but complex ecologies and commercial circuits produced them and made them available to consumers. Pearls could evoke purity as well as moral corruption. And they constituted a repository of value that itself was highly variable and subjectively determined. That the primary Caribbean pearl-fishing settlements were located on islands—long seen as sites of experimentation and aberration—further enhanced the drama and romance that attended the jewel in the European imagination.[6]

Over the course of six chapters, this book moves chronologically through the sixteenth and seventeenth centuries, tracing the history of these American settlements and the enduring appeal of pearls within a global Iberian imperial context. It further considers pearls' appeal and prominence in northern European experiments to expand the authority of centralizing governments on frontiers near and far. In doing so, *American Baroque* argues that the political economy of pearls gave rise to a productive tension between vernacular, small-scale understandings of wealth management (in which nature and expert labor played a major role, as did pearls' particular qualities) and developing imperial understandings of the same.

Pearls enabled a wide range of people to participate in the construction of and resistance to the regulatory state. The relationship between personal and imperial initiative was not one of constant antagonism but rather a mixture of intersection and divergence. Recognizable and successful elements of Iberian imperial identity existed alongside non-Iberian knowledge and praxis that were central to pearls' production and circulation. These semi-independent components included indigenous American knowledge of oyster reefs in Venezuela, enslaved Africans' practices of pearl harvesting and distribution, and the diversity of participants in Sri Lanka's booming pearl-fishery markets.[7]

6. For an overview of the romance and associations of islands in the European imagination, see Benton, *A Search for Sovereignty,* chap. 4. See also Elvira Pulitano, *Transnational Narratives from the Caribbean: Diasporic Literature and the Human Experience* (New York, 2016).

7. The small-scale and domestic uses of pearls echo the scholarly emphasis on the household as the place of elaboration of empire. See, for example, the articles in the forum "Centering Families in Atlantic Histories" in *William and Mary Quarterly,* 3d Ser., LXX (2013); Susanah Shaw Romney, *New Netherland Connections: Intimate Networks and Atlantic Ties in Seventeenth-Century America* (Chapel Hill, N.C., 2014); and Daniel Livesay, *Children of Uncertain Fortune: Mixed-Race Jamaicans in Britain and the Atlantic Family, 1733–1833* (Chapel Hill, N.C., 2017).

Pearls allow us to see the connections between the way empire was envisioned by monarchs, experienced at sea and on the ground by individuals, and enacted in law. The stories generated by this unusual, organic jewel range globally, crossing geographic and imperial boundaries and, perhaps more importantly, moving across scales, linking the bounded experiences of individuals to the legacy of imperial bureaucratic elaboration. They illuminate the intersection of these micro- and macrohistorical processes.

Around the globe, monarchs and merchants, enslaved African divers in the Caribbean and Scottish and Swedish yeoman living alongside cold northern European rivers, widows in Amsterdam and accused witches in Cartagena gathered, stole, sold, and wore pearls in ways that reflected the constraints and opportunities of the worlds they lived in. In an era when empires were creating their governing infrastructure for channeling human and material wealth, people used pearls in ways that helped to refine these imperial structures. The collected microhistories in this book reveal how a diverse body politic subjected the changing apparatus of imperial governance — to which they themselves were literally subject — to continual tests of utility.

The irregularity of pearls — their multiple shapes and sizes and the unpredictable appeal or use of any given one — underscored the related irregularity of subjects themselves, as it was the independent judgment of subjects that assessed pearls' quality and their independent actions that decided what to do with them, moving them neatly through imperial channels of taxation, hiding them for private trade, or transforming them into jewels. Qualitative, evaluative language would play a prominent role in crown officials' attempts to impose order on this irregularity. Of the vocabulary that circulated to describe pearls, intended to facilitate imperial control of the jewel, the distinct fate of two of these descriptive words illustrates well the enduring lesson of the American pearl boom, born of this early Spanish experiment in administering New World wealth. *Elenco,* first used by the central classical authority on pearls, Pliny the Elder, to describe an elongated pearl, came to mean in Spanish "catalog" or "index" — reflecting the very ordering impulse that pearls prompted. Another word employed in the early Caribbean fisheries for taxation purposes, *barrueca,* or "baroque" in English, which signified an irregular pearl, also lost its close association with the jewel but came to stand for the defiance of this imagined order, an extravagant expression of independence of imagination.[8]

---

8. The *Diccionario de la lengua española,* published by the Real Academia Española, http://dle.rae.es/?id=59UHRsI, defines *barrueco* as a word of unknown origin, meaning an irregular pearl. They offer the word for wart, *verruga,* as a possible source, as did the

In their reliance on language to bring precision to administrative approaches to the management of complex wealth, the Iberian monarchies drew on well-established nuanced vocabularies of color that were used to describe enslaved people in medieval Iberia. The cultivation of pearls and the exploitation of people, and the complexity posed by subjects and objects each, would be intertwined in the history of this unusual commodity trade as the independence of action and of taste helped create the settlements and the products derived from them.[9]

Throughout the sixteenth and seventeenth centuries, from the Pearl Coast of South America to English port towns to the shores of Sri Lanka, pearls traveled promiscuously from hand to hand, defying efforts at containment, from customs regulations to border patrols. On the Pearl Coast, pearls circulated as a result of the labor of increasingly large and autonomous crews of enslaved African divers, and their use on land reflected the assessments and needs of Pearl Coast residents rather than the fiscal imperatives and directives of the crown. In Europe and India, pearls greased the wheels of private financial transactions and diplomatic negotiations, providing ways for women to engage with a male-dominated marketplace and for men to affirm alliances of friendship that served to insulate them from the vagaries of political and economic fortune. In spite of a general consensus about the qualities that made a particular pearl better than any other (the larger, whiter, and more lustrous, the better), the appeal or worth of any particular pearl depended upon the context in which it was evaluated and the use to which it was to be put. These qualities made it impossible to standardize the use of pearls as currency and allowed subjects of distinct polities to use pearls as they saw fit.

In *American Baroque*'s discussion of locally elaborated political economies — shaped by ecologies, labor regimes, and real and imagined distances from commercial and political centers — the book reveals global webs of concerns and practices that shaped early modern empires. These vernacular customs limited the success of familiar early modern governing mechanisms to

---

sixteenth-century Spanish lexicographer Covarrubias. See Sebastián de Covarrubias Horozco, *Tesoro de la lengua Castellana o Española,* ed. Ignacio Arellano and Rafael Zafra (Pamplona, Navarra, Spain, 2006). For a scholarly overview of the various hypotheses regarding the word's origins, see "Baroque, New World Baroque, Neobaroque: Categories and Concepts," in Lois Parkinson Zamora and Monika Kaup, eds., *Baroque New Worlds: Representation, Transculturation, Counterconquest* (Durham, N.C., 2010), 2–3.

9. For an overview of terms for enslaved peoples in medieval Iberia, see Debra Blumenthal, *Enemies and Familiars: Slavery and Mastery in Fifteenth-Century Valencia* (Ithaca, N.Y., 2009).

extend control over wealth production, such as patents, monopolies, technology, and joint-stock companies. In the case of pearls, these mechanisms failed because of the expert human knowledge needed to mediate the interaction between nature and the state.[10]

The irregularity of many transactions involving pearls, as well as the irregularity of pearls themselves (embodied by the baroque pearl but represented by the jewel's immense natural variety), reveals the chaos of the practices and assessments that were central to early modern bureaucracies. The global pearl microhistories traced by *American Baroque* illuminate the tension between the imperial impulse to order and contain and the ungovernable motives and actions of independent subjects. These microhistories further suggest that it was practice with pearls, as well as the irregular beauty of the baroque pearl, that informed the potency of the word *baroque* as a metaphor for unbounded forms of expression.

Pearls did not emerge organically from the shells that contained them; they were pulled from their aqueous origins with varying degrees of violence. Their movement from river and ocean beds into individual hands and the swirl of global commodities markets and imperial coffers was a human production, dictated by subjective taste and fashion as much as by imperial edicts, the imperatives of tax officials, and the brutal greed of putative slaveowners. But the concept of the baroque—the association of the irregular shape of the baroque pearl with the unwieldy extravagance of art, literature, and early modern monarchy itself—was organic indeed. Pearls' enduring legacy, particularly in the long life of the term *baroque* as a metaphor for irregularity in form and function, was an unsurprising by-product of the jewel's similarly irregular early modern history. From heaps of shells on island beaches and rivers' edges to voyages large and small—in pockets, on jewelry, tucked into letters, and sewn into sleeves—*American Baroque* traces pearls' jagged global paths. In doing so, this book heeds Baroque scholar Irlemar Chiampi's call to rescue "that tired irregular pearl from such lengthy isolation."[11]

10. For a later consideration of the role of the natural world in political economic thought, see Fredrik Albritton Jonsson, *Enlightenment's Frontier: The Scottish Highlands and the Origins of Environmentalism* (New Haven, Conn., 2013).

11. See Chiampi, *Barroco y modernidad*, 43: "Cansada esa perla irregular de tan largo ostracismo." Unless otherwise noted, all translations from Spanish are mine. The literature on the concept of the baroque is enormous and spans multiple fields of study. The classic work is José Antonio Maravall, *Culture of the Baroque: Analysis of a Historical Structure,* trans. Terry Cochran (Minneapolis, Minn., 1986), originally published in 1975. Maravall argued that the baroque was a historical structure that was international in nature.

: 1 :

SEX, DEATH, AND THE SEA
Pearls in the Early Modern Imagination

"There may well be a strong alliance between the sea and our stomach,
but what connection is there with our backs? Are we not satisfied by feeding on
dangerous things without also being clothed by them? Do we get most bodily
pleasure from luxuries that cost human life?"
—*Pliny the Elder*

Pearls' appeal in the late Middle Ages and Spain's management of the extraordinary American pearl-fishing grounds and their products can be understood only by reconstructing long-standing, classically derived ideas about the geographic and marine origins of pearls and looking at pearls' particular Iberian legal and cultural contexts. Pearls had a sensual, mysterious, and risqué allure that would shape the jewel's evolving identity as pearls' European inheritance collided with distinct traditions governing pearl fishing and worship in the East and West Indies.[1]

Pearls were not an unfamiliar product of the New World, but the millions of American pearls produced in the Caribbean in the early years of the sixteenth century transformed the global market for them and their role in the imperial imaginary in Iberia and beyond. Furthermore, the particular circumstances of pearls' harvesting in the Americas posed new administrative challenges that existing Iberian legal precedents could not solve. With no clear body of laws regulating the treatment of pearls—were they treasure, a commodity and trade item, or a natural resource?—vernacular practice, elaborated on the ground and at sea in the new American settlements, would fill the void.[2]

---

1. Pliny the Elder's lengthiest consideration of pearls occurs in Book IX of his *Natural History*. See Pliny the Elder (Gaius Plinius Secundus), *Natural History: A Selection*, trans. John F. Healy (London, 1991), 135.

2. A similar upheaval would not occur again until Mikimoto Kōkichi learned to cultivate pearls in the early twentieth century; and even then many continuities in the trade remained. For the recent history of the pearl trade, see Stephen G. Bloom, *Tears of Mermaids: The Secret Story of Pearls* (New York, 2009); and Keith Bradsher, "Pearls, Finer but Still Cheap, Flow from China," *New York Times*, Aug. 1, 2011. For an early and influential

"The Decay of Morality Is Caused by the Produce of the Sea": Pearls and Unnatural Encounters in Pliny the Elder's Natural History

No single source on the nature and origin of pearls was more important to late medieval European understandings of the jewel than the first-century writings of Pliny the Elder in his *Natural History*. Pliny's treatment of pearls laid the groundwork for ideas about the jewel that would persist for millennia, including pearls' association with the Far East. In his *Natural History*, Pliny identified "Taprobane," "Stoidis" (probably Sri Lanka and an island in the lower Persian Gulf), and "the Indian promontory of Perimula" as major sources of pearls. The best "specially praised" specimens were "the pearls from the islands around Arabia and in the Persian Gulf and Red Sea." Pliny also underscored the natural variety that characterized pearls — those from the Red Sea were "bright," he explained, "while those in the Indian Ocean are like flakes of mica and exceed others in size." This inherent diversity of form was central to pearls' appeal: "The longer ones have their own intrinsic charm," he noted, while "the greatest praise is for pearls to be called alum-coloured." In an assessment of the factors contributing to any particular pearl's valuation, Pliny explained that "their value lies in their brilliance, size, roundness, smoothness and weight." The same physical qualities would shape perceptions of pearls' worth for thousands of years, but Pliny went on to note how the sheer range of types of pearls made any standard assessment of them very difficult to enforce. After providing the list of criteria for assessing pearls, Pliny noted that they had "such uncommon qualities that no two pearls are found exactly alike." Pliny explained that this inherent uniqueness was why the Romans called pearls *uniones* (whereas foreigners called pearls *margaritae*). The etymological emphasis of the word *uniones* on oneness reflected any given pearl's unique qualities, and the word's plural form (as opposed to *unio* for a single pearl) thus conjures a collective of distinctive specimens.[3]

----

study of maritime commodity trades that introduced the notion of "vernacular practices," see Peter E. Pope, *Fish into Wine: The Newfoundland Plantation in the Seventeenth Century* (Chapel Hill, N.C., 2004).

3. Pliny the Elder, *Natural History*, trans. Healy, 134, 135, 136. See María M. Portuondo, *Secret Science: Spanish Cosmography and the New World* (Chicago, 2009), 28, for Renaissance reliance on Pliny, Strabo, and Pomponius Mela. See also David A. Lupher, *Romans in a New World: Classical Models in Sixteenth-Century Spanish America* (Ann Arbor, Mich., 2006). For an overview of pearls and pearl myths, including their medieval popularity, see R. A. Donkin, *Beyond Price: Pearls and Pearl-Fishing: Origins to the*

In Pliny's consideration of the jewel's origins and appeal, he emphasized the generative and destructive powers of the sea and the mysteries of death and sex. Pearls evoked physical intimacies — sex and mortality — as they occurred in the sensual and savage context of the ocean. His discussion opened with a general critique of decadence and its link to unnatural engagement with the products of the sea, writing that "shellfish are the prime cause of the decline of morals and the adoption of an extravagant lifestyle." In Pliny's holistic treatment of the jewel, the desire for pearls could not be separated from the life-threatening work it took to obtain them. Humans' desire for pearls was unseemly in light of the costs of procuring them, the wish for such costly adornment an even more grotesque reflection of human hubris in the face of the power of the sea than the desire to eat fish. Pliny contrasted fishing — a risky activity but one that provided necessary sustenance — with the equally hazardous pursuit of pearls. "As if it were not enough for the produce of the seas to be stuffed down our throats," he lamented, "it is also worn on the hands, in the ears, on the head and all over the body of women and men alike!" The notion that humans would seek to embellish themselves with the products of a body of water into which men dove naked perplexed him. Pliny wondered, "What has the sea to do with clothing, the water and waves to do with wool?" It was a perversion to seek to cover oneself in the products of an element that demanded nudity: "The sea receives us in a proper way only when we are without clothes. There may well be a strong alliance between the sea and our stomach, but what connection is there with our backs? Are we not satisfied by feeding on dangerous things without also being clothed by them? Do we get most bodily pleasure from luxuries that cost human life?" This macabre and somewhat salacious spectacle — to risk death, unclothed, to adorn the mortal body — infused pearls' appeal.[4]

Pearls' association with death and decay — and thus their utility for thinking about the nature of the fragile human body — remained powerful for centuries. Their link with death was twofold: first, the desire for pearls often claimed the lives of those who sought them, and, second, pearls themselves were delicate, susceptible to destruction and decay (when dehydrated or exposed to corrosive elements).[5] "There is no doubt that pearls are worn away

Age of Discoveries (Philadelphia, 1998); and George Frederick Kunz and Charles Hugh Stevenson, *The Book of the Pearl: The History, Art, Science, and Industry of the Queen of Gems* (New York, 1908).

4. Pliny the Elder, *Natural History*, trans. Healy, 134–135, 136.

5. Pearls are primarily composed of calcium carbonate, which is very sensitive to acids

by use and that lack of care causes them to change colour," Pliny noted. Pearls' dual link with death and the sea reached perhaps its most famous expression in Shakespeare's *Tempest,* which drew heavily on news of Caribbean explorations. In the play, death by shipwreck is described by Ariel with invocations of submarine luxury: "Full fathom five thy father lies; / Of his bones are coral made; / Those are pearls that were his eyes." Death was the price of proximity to maritime wealth.[6]

But it was not just the sea's destructive power that informed Pliny's treatment of pearls. The ocean's procreative power—in particular, the poorly understood union of the elements believed to be involved in pearls' creation—and the perceived female identity of the oyster also played a central role in his discussion. Pliny's account placed sex (particularly notions of female reproduction) next to death at the heart of pearls' appeal. The connection of oysters with sexuality lingers in our modern views of them as an aphrodisiac as well as with the occasional suggestion that cultured pearls are the product of the rape of a bivalve.[7]

Although Pliny noted that men as well as women wore pearls, his treatment of the jewel—its genesis and circulation—underscored pearls' evocation of traits believed to be female. In his telling, pearls were the product of a sexualized encounter deep beneath the waves. Although he misunderstood pearl formation, Pliny noted correctly that pearls emerged from living creatures—the erotic oyster, its shells and slippery flesh evocative of female genitalia. The shells that produced pearls, Pliny explained, "when stimulated by the season for procreation, they open up, as it were, and are impregnated with dew, so the story goes." "Then these pregnant shells give birth, and their offsprings are pearls of a quality corresponding to the quality of the dew they have received."[8]

(such as those contained in perfume). In the right conditions, however, they can last for ages, hence the survival of some pearls from the ancient world. See Neil H. Landman, Paula M. Mikkelsen, and Rudiger Bieler, eds., *Pearls: A Natural History* (New York, 2001), 26, 42.

6. Pliny the Elder, *Natural History,* trans. Healy, 136. Marcia Pointon discusses pearls' association with death and decay in *Brilliant Effects: A Cultural History of Gem Stones and Jewellery* (New Haven, Conn., 2009), chap. 4, esp. 107. She describes pearls as existing at the intersection of the "visceral and the aesthetic" (117). The insight about pearls' role in *The Tempest* (1.2.398–400) is hers (107).

7. On cultured pearls as the product of sexual violence against the oyster, see Victoria Finlay, *Jewels: A Secret History* (New York, 2006), 98.

8. Pliny the Elder, *Natural History,* trans. Healy, 135.

Pliny's notion of pearls as a product of dew penetrating an oyster shell did not approximate the actual process by which pearls are created. When pearls are reduced to their chemical composition—mineralized deposits within soft tissue—many different living animals produce them. According to this definition, even kidney stones could be considered pearls. But the luminous, lustrous, iridescent, round specimens that consumers around the globe desire today as they did two thousand, one thousand, and five hundred years ago are predominantly produced by a reduced number of mollusk species that tend not to be edible. Most pearl producers are bivalves and feed in a way known as passive filter feeding. Filter feeding increases the likelihood of stray detritus or small creatures becoming lodged in the tissue of the mantle of the bivalve, the mantle being the soft tissue that lines the shell. When the mantle experiences a disruption, it coats the foreign substance with shell material, or calcium carbonate. The item that prompts this process—the famed grain of sand, for example (though that is rare)—becomes the nucleus of the pearl.[9]

Pliny's explanation of the genesis of pearls was less precise but more compelling. Pliny portrayed oysters as both fragile and fierce heroines in the drama of pearl creation, easily intimidated but also ferocious in their attempts to protect their hidden jewels. In his telling, oysters were highly sensitive to changing weather; thunder, for example, caused them to "take fright and close up so suddenly that they produce what are called 'wind' pearls, which are inflated and have a light and empty form: these are the oysters' miscarriages." These sensitive creatures could also respond to perceived threats to their precious cargo: "Whenever a shell sees a hand, it closes up and hides its wealth since it knows that this is the object of the search. If a hand is inserted, the shell cuts it off with its sharp edge—no other punishment is more just." Pearls were a pathology of nature, a beautiful if anomalous creation that provoked pathologies of behavior, leading covetous humans to risk death in their pursuit.[10]

This characterization of pearls contained elements of accuracy and inaccuracy. In reality, bivalve mollusk populations contain a mixture of male, female, and hermaphrodite members, but the mollusks can change gender many times over the course of their life span. They also can react extremely rapidly to perceived danger, in spite of having no brain and being composed of no more than a few organs and a shell. Both factors are critical to the bivalves' survival—river mussels, for example, can change into hermaphrodites

9. On pearl formation, see Elisabeth Strack, *Pearls* (Stuttgart, 2006), 96–97. For kidney stones as pearls, see Landman, Mikkelsen, and Bieler, eds., *Pearls,* 26–27.

10. Pliny the Elder, *Natural History,* trans. Healy, 135.

to produce the sexual organs that will allow them to fertilize their own eggs. It was only in the twentieth century that scientists came to fully understand pearls' creation and mutable oyster biology.[11]

The gendered elements of pearls' supposed origins would endure long after Pliny's account. Indeed, his discourse on the sexual, female nature of pearl production and their profligate use by women in particular laid the groundwork for the paradoxical and enduring linkage of the jewel with both feminine virtue and feminine vice. In Pliny's view, it was not just that oysters were female but also that female desire for pearls led men to dive for them. Noting that oysters were protected from pearl-seeking predators not just by their sharp shells but also by the rocks, deep water, and sharks that tended to surround them, he complained that, "nevertheless, these things do not safe-guard pearls from women's ears!" Pliny went on to recount stories of profligate pearl consumption by wealthy women, including the tale of Cleopatra dissolving a precious pearl in vinegar to impress Antony. He further noted that "now even poor people desire pearls, saying that a pearl is like an attendant for a lady when she is out and about." The pearl was an expression of female identity through its (re)production and its consumption, a duality that would long be evoked in art and discourse concerning pearl use. Pearls could not be separated from the nature (physical and moral) of the human bodies that wore them and died for them.[12]

Pliny's writings established an additional critical characteristic of pearls, their mutability. In his account, pearls' physical qualities changed depending on the circumstances of their creation. (This susceptibility to environmental influence would have particular resonance in the context of the Americas and Europeans' preoccupation with how the New World environment might alter their physical nature.) As Pliny explained it, the quality of any given pearl depended on both the purity of the dew and the weather at the time of the pearl's conception: if the dew that impregnated the oysters was "pure," then the pearls are "brilliant"; but, if it was "cloudy," they are "a dirty colour." Ideas about pearls' color corresponding to their waters of origin persisted throughout the early modern period and beyond. Some experts believed that a pearl's color matched the inside of the mollusk that produced it; in reality,

11. On bivalves' response to danger, see Strack, *Pearls*, 94–95.

12. Pliny the Elder, *Natural History*, trans. Healy, 135–136. Pointon, in *Brilliant Effects*, considers Pliny's treatment of pearls, noting the degree to which Pliny's discussion of the jewel, its origins and use, was tied to social critique of consumption and gendered (even sexual) practices (117–118).

a pearl's color is determined by constantly shifting variables, such as the minerals in the water where the mollusk resides, making it nearly impossible to deduce origin based on a pearl's appearance (though many early modern pearl vendors made their money by asserting otherwise).[13]

An additional paradox was the jewel's association with light and thus life, even as pearls emerged from the dark and often deadly depths of the sea. Before complex faceting techniques were developed to craft hard gemstones into numerous glittering surfaces, pearls represented an immediate, shining beauty that needed no alteration in order to catch light and represent illumination. Their reflective brilliance thus represented perfection without any need for manual artifice; they were a gift from nature whose potency rivaled the absolute power of night and day and the seasons. Furthermore, this brightness reflected their perceived origins in an encounter between opposite elements: the sky (the producer of dew) and the sea. Pliny emphasized this unusual mixing and its effect on pearls' appearance: "For it is certain that pearls are conceived from the sky, with which they have more connection than with the sea, so get from it their cloudiness, or, if the morning is bright, a clear colour." The notion that pearls were a result of an irregular coupling persisted for millennia and would give particular potency to their utility in exploring perceived binaries and contrasts.[14]

All these ideas imbued pearls with powerful and titillating notions of sexual reproduction, the penetration of a slippery, enclosed space by a foreign intruder, and unlikely pairings. Pearls' association with a thing and its opposite — the highest (dew from the heavens) and the lowest (the depths of the sea), nature (the ocean and its marine life) and the unnatural (humans' wish to plumb the ocean's depths and consume its products), light (the sky and pearls themselves) and dark (deep waters and, later, dark bodies) — would long inform their symbolic power. The frisson generated by this type of unnatural mixing would linger throughout the early modern period, as the influx of new American pearls made this luxury jewel available to consumers of tremendously varied backgrounds.

13. Pliny the Elder, *Natural History,* trans. Healy, 134. The scholarship on European fears of physical degeneracy in the Americas is immense. For a discussion in the Spanish American context, see Ralph Bauer and José Antonio Mazzotti, eds., *Creole Subjects in the Colonial Americas: Empires, Texts, Identities* (Chapel Hill, N.C., 2012).

14. Pliny the Elder, *Natural History,* trans. Healy, 135. On the power of darkness, see A. Roger Ekrich, *At Day's Close: Night in Times Past* (New York, 2005). On innovation in hard-stone faceting, see David Mitchell, ed., *Goldsmiths, Silversmiths, and Bankers: Innovation and the Transfer of Skill, 1550 to 1750* (Oxford, 1995).

Pearls' popularity as adornment and the enduring European influence of Pliny's text ensured that pearls would loom large in visions of seaborne success as Spain and Portugal began to extend their Atlantic exploration in the fifteenth century. Long-standing symbols of the riches as well as the dangers of the high seas, pearls represented all that could be gained and lost through these maritime forays. They emerged from the watery depths of an ocean that sustained life but also threatened and delivered destruction; they required a willingness to court death in maritime journeys to faraway lands and in dives to the bottom of the sea.[15]

Pearls in Iberia: The Cultural and Legal Contexts

In addition to classical understandings of pearls, there were also unique Iberian cultural and legal contexts that informed how people thought of pearls and how they were governed as both a product of the natural world and as a source of wealth immediately before and in the wake of Columbus's voyages. Certainly Iberian ideas about pearls located the jewel in the context of rich and exotic markets of the East. A rosier picture of pearl diving than that conveyed by Pliny is seen in the fourteenth-century *Catalan Atlas,* which depicts nude male pearl divers gathering precious stone-like, oysterless pearls and describing the spells they used to ward off dangerous fish (Figure 2, Plate 2). The atlas suggests that Spaniards were at least somewhat familiar with the labor of pearl diving. The fantasy of pearls existing underwater alongside other gems, however, with no hint of the ecosystems that produced them, indicates the lack of clear knowledge about pearls' origins. It reveals the jewel's place in the public imagination as a treasure rather than as a product of a living marine ecology. The atlas also points to Baghdad as a major pearl market; medieval Spanish pearl consumers sourced their pearls from many distant locales, going so far as to purchase specimens from merchants in Tunisia. Indeed, it was easier access to the opulent markets of the East — with pearls chief among their riches — that informed the decision of the *Reyes Católicos* (the Catholic Monarchs, Isabella of Castile and King Ferdinand of Aragon) to fund Columbus's far-fetched proposal in the final decade of the fifteenth century.[16]

The desire for pearls and other lucrative commodities was not, of course,

15. On the enduring mystery of the ocean, see Joyce E. Chaplin, "Knowing the Ocean: Benjamin Franklin and the Circulation of Atlantic Knowledge," in James Delbourgo and Nicholas Dew, eds., *Science and Empire in the Atlantic World* (New York, 2008), 73.

16. On the demanding pearl tastes of medieval Spanish consumers, see Robert A. Carter, *Sea of Pearls: Seven Thousand Years of the Industry That Shaped the Gulf* (London, 2012), 58, 63-64.

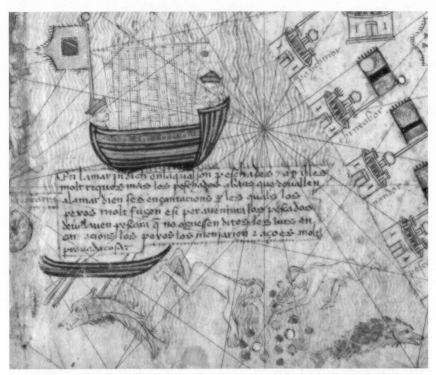

Figure 2. Detail of Pearl Diving from Catalan Atlas. *Circa 1375. Permission, Bibliothèque nationale de France. The cartouche describes spells used to warn off dangerous fish. Note that the pearls are depicted as bright precious stones.*

the only motivatation for the partnership between Queen Isabella, King Ferdinand, and the ambitious sea captain. The Monarchs were flush with the success of recent battles in their quest for religious homogeneity within the peninsula, and by some measures it is true that Columbus sailed west at a moment of unprecedented Iberian religious pride and political unity. Sponsored by zealous, powerful Catholic rulers, the admiral embarked on his voyage armed with the conviction of his own deep faith as well as that of his monarchs. With Spain's two most powerful kingdoms, Castile and Aragon, newly united thanks to the marriage of Isabella and Ferdinand, Iberia found itself at the vanguard of political and religious unity — unity that the rest of Europe was far slower to obtain in the wake of centuries of warfare and plague.[17]

17. On Columbus's faith, see William D. Phillips, Jr., and Carla Rahn Phillips, *The Worlds of Christopher Columbus* (Cambridge, 1993).

In spite of this apparent religious unity of mission, circumstances on the peninsula were not quite so settled. Although Iberian cultural and legal customs alongside a crusading Catholicism played critical roles in shaping Spaniards' earliest encounters in the New World, so, too, did the hum of uncertainty and flux that emanated from the peninsula. This destabilizing undercurrent reflected momentous transformations that were reshuffling royal policies and populations within Spain and Portugal. Even the powerful union of Castile and Aragon was recent and contentious, a political merger that yoked together independent regions with vastly differing customs.[18]

At the end of the fifteenth century, Spanish law remained complex, diverse, and powerfully rooted in local practice. The Iberian peninsula consisted of a conglomeration of kingdoms, and the notion of one "Spain" did not exist. Columbus himself addressed Ferdinand and Isabella as "king and queen of the Spains." Furthermore, the political and religious turmoil convulsing the peninsula meant that the requirements for subjecthood were shifting rapidly. These shifts had devastating consequences for the Jewish and Muslim inhabitants affected and for the crown, deprived of a large segment of its tax base and of productive workers. The perceived need to enforce distinctions among subjects would shape approaches to sumptuary legislation, including the use of pearls, in the aftermath of Columbus's discovery. As the Spanish crown hardened the lines it drew among categories of populations at home and abroad, pearls' ability to skitter effortlessly across borders and among diverse vassals proved particularly frustrating.[19]

The fateful year 1492 marked several turning points within the period of this general Iberian transition. Columbus's voyage is the most famous of these, but no less significant were the fall of the last independent Muslim kingdom on the peninsula, Granada, to royal forces, the expulsion of Spain's Jewish population in the name of a crusading Catholic faith, and the publication by Antonio de Nebrija of the first Spanish grammar, the *Gramática sobre la lengua castellana*. Each of these events would have deep implications for the evolution of the Spanish New World and royal attitudes toward the incorporation and governance of subjects. The least obviously momentous of

18. Beyond Iberia's borders, factional divisions throughout Europe challenged Spain's claims to sovereignty on the Continent. For three classic overviews of the late medieval and early modern Iberian political landscape, see J. H. Elliott, *Imperial Spain, 1469–1716*, 2d ed. (New York, 2002); John Lynch, *Spain under the Habsburgs, 1516–1598*, 2 vols., 2d ed. (New York, 1981); and Teófilo F. Ruiz, *Spanish Society, 1400–1600* (New York, 2001).

19. Richard Kagan, "The Spain of Ferdinand and Isabella," in James R. McGovern, ed., *The World of Columbus* (Macon, Ga., 1992), 22.

these events—the publication of the grammar—would prove to be perhaps the most potent symbol of the extension of Castilian authority and the centrality of vernacular language (*castellano*, Castilian, as opposed to Latin) and custom to that process. In his prologue to the work, Nebrija expressed his conviction that "language had always been the companion of empire," offering several examples from the ancient world and noting that Castillian would be critical to the spread of Spain's power over enemies and allies alike.[20] Nebrija's endorsement of the significance of Castilian over Latin reflected a growing acceptance within Europe of vernacular language as an acceptable vehicle for the elaboration of art and the expression of power. The vernacular (both language and practice) would take on additional significance in the New World, where it would play a complex role in both extending and undermining imperial governance. This transition became evident early on in the Venezuelan pearl fisheries, where the lexicon of the settlements—from the words describing the terrestrial and marine geography of the region to the names for laborers, practices, and pearls themselves—evolved in response to local custom far more than imperial edicts.[21]

Nebrija's definitions of pearls (offered in his Latin-Spanish dictionary, also published in 1492) are worth noting as a point of departure from which to measure all that would be learned in years to come. He explained the jewel in terms of color and shape, making clear that the designations employed by Pliny—*margarita* and *uniones* (for perfectly matched specimens)—remained in circulation in Castilian Spanish and in Latin along with a term of Arabic origin, *aljofar,* meaning seed pearl. Nebrija offered several related definitions for the Latin word *margarita,* which he explained was a synonym "for aljofar or pearl" *("por el aljofar o perla").* He defined the word *margaritifer* as "that which produces aljofar" *("lo que cria aljofar"),* hinting at pearls' origin in living creations. Another term employed by Pliny surfaced in Nebrija's grammar: *elenco,* described by Pliny as pearls that are "of a long, tapering shape . . . ending in a full bulb." Nebrija defined the Latin word *elenchus*

20. "Que siempre la lengua fue compañera del imperio," in Antonio de Nebrija, *Gramática sobre la lengua castellana,* ed. Carmen Lozano (Barcelona, 2011), 12. On Nebrija's *Grammar,* see Thomas Paul Bonfiglio, *Mother Tongues and Nations: The Invention of the Native Speaker* (New York, 2010), 82. See also Tzvetan Todorov, *The Conquest of the Americas: The Question of the Other,* trans. Richard Howard (New York, 1984), 123.

21. Roland Greene, in *Five Words: Critical Semantics in the Age of Shakespeare and Cervantes* (Chicago, 2013), emphasizes the importance of practice in the creation of meaning. The five words he deems "engines" (10) of cultural elaboration in the Renaissance are *invention, language, resistance, blood,* and *world.*

as an "elongated pearl" *("por la perla prolongada")*. The term *elenco* would undergo a profound transformation in meaning over the course of the next century, coming to stand for the notion of indexing and the related impulse to categorize — a reflection of the challenges posed by the Pearl Coast settlements and their ungovernable mixture of pearls and people.[22]

Classical tradition met Iberian antecedents in law as well as in the language that would influence approaches to pearls in the post-Columbus era. No legal precedent was more instrumental in shaping the *capitulaciones* — that is, the sailing orders Columbus agreed upon with the Catholic Monarchs in April 1492 — than the Siete Partidas (or Seven-Part Code). Elaborated under Alfonso X, the thirteenth-century ruler of Castile, the Siete Partidas reflected his desire to impose order on the immense medieval complexity that characterized the kingdoms during his rule. This medieval code of law provided the legal model for the capitulaciones's terms concerning wealth distribution as well as the relationship between lords and vassals. The Siete Partidas would inform not only these early instructions to Columbus but also centuries of legislation throughout Spain's global empire.[23]

A close consideration of the Siete Partidas's treatment of pearls sheds light on the Iberian legal traditions that would combine with pearls' classical associations to shape approaches to pearls in the post-Columbus era. The jewels' maritime origin remained key to their mystery as it had in classical times. Pearls' watery origin and their genesis within living creatures distinguished them from mineral deposits. In the late fifteenth century, the questions of how to produce, cultivate, and tax pearls remained largely unanswered. No accumulated body of knowledge had produced administrative paradigms analogous to those that had developed for governing precious metals. A long tradition of mining (dating from Roman times) existed in Castile — a reflection of deposits of gold, silver, zinc, lead, sulfur, coal, iron, and mercury — as well as a knowledge of metallurgy. There was no such systematic, practical expertise in pearl cultivation. The mechanisms for controlling pearls' circulation remained similarly opaque. Unlike precious metals, pearls did not require much, or any, modification in order to be transformed into tradable goods or used as money. They did not need any sort of refining, nor could

22. Elio Antonio de Nebrija, *Diccionario Latino-Español,* ed. Germán Colón and Amadeu-J. Soberanas (Barcelona, 1979); Pliny, *The Natural History,* trans. John Bostock and H. T. Riley (London, 1855), 435.

23. See Robert I. Burns, ed., *Las Siete Partidas,* trans. Samuel Parsons Scott, 5 vols. (Philadelphia, 2001).

they be marked to register any kind of taxation. These unique qualities, however, did not keep pearls from being considered alongside precious metals, in spite of their differences, as emblematic of overseas imperial wealth and frequently treated as products of underwater mines. Over time, unique circumstances of pearl cultivation and circulation demanded some regulatory concessions. Whereas mid-sixteenth-century legislation transferred ownership of all mines and precious metals to the crown (justified by noting metals' ready conversion into revenue that could be used for various purposes, from war to the support of the royal household), no such sweeping legislation occurred regarding pearl fisheries.[24]

The critical guidelines that would shape Spanish legal approaches to pearls can be found scattered throughout the many sections of the Siete Partidas. In Title XXVI of the second Partida devoted to material spoils taken in war, Law VI acknowledged the tradition of assigning a victorious king a fifth of all movable property gained. This tradition of the fifth of all spoils was taken into the New World and instituted as the royal fifth tax *(quinto)* on total production. But applying a policy designed to govern war booty to assessing products of the natural world would prove quite difficult in the case of pearls. Title XXVIII in the third Partida touched upon ownership in various contexts, but again treated pearls as objects disconnected from the environment that produced them. The sea remained mysterious; its products also.[25]

The regulations that pertained to pearls in the Partidas allowed a great deal of leeway to those who came across pearls but did not touch upon pearls' renewability or exhaustibility as products of living creatures and complex habitats. Law V specified:

> Men find gold, pearls, and precious stones in the sand of the sea shore. For this reason we decree that where a man finds any of the things aforesaid and is the first to take possession of them, they shall belong to him. For, as whatever is found in a place of this kind is not part of the property of any individual, it is but proper and right that it should belong to him who first discovers it or takes possession of it, and that no one else should dispute this, or place any impediments in his way.

It was easier to legislate pearl ownership when they were removed from the watery contexts that produced them. Because pearls were often harvested

24. See Daniela Bleichmar et al., eds., *Science in the Spanish and Portuguese Empires, 1500–1800* (Palo Alto, Calif., 2008), 313.

25. Burns, ed., *Las Siete Partidas,* trans. Scott, II, 478–479.

only when the oysters (or mussels) bearing them were unloaded on the shore or riverbanks, pearls could be deemed the product of shoreline explorations and thus subject to the law of first come, first served. Law IX in the third Partida further recognized "the sandy beaches on the banks of rivers" as "the Common Property of Every City and Town," whereas Law XI stated that "the income from salt-wells, fisheries, and works in iron and other metals, and the taxes and tributes paid by men" belonged to emperors and kings. The latter measure was justified because it allowed the rulers "to pay their expenses, protect their dominions and kingdoms, and wage war against the enemies of the faith," and thus "they might avoid imposing many pecuniary burdens upon their people, or oppressing them in other ways." The distinction made in the Partidas between wealth found on seashores — the property of those who came across it — and the products of cultivated fisheries set the stage for conflicts over pearl fishing. In the Caribbean, it became increasingly clear that pearl fishing was an arena of natural resource husbandry that demanded careful attention and that neither laws governing mines nor those governing treasure or booty could effectively govern.[26]

As laid out by the Partidas, pearls existed in limbo, understood more as treasure from a mysterious and ungovernable realm than as a product of a fragile natural ecosystem. Legal precedent guaranteed a great deal of independence to individuals who worked the shores and fishermen who needed to land and dry their catch. The sea remained beyond the bounds of jurisdiction. As Law III ("What Those Things Are Which Belong in Common to All Creatures") in Title XXVIII of the third Partida specified:

> The things which belong in common to the creatures of this world are the following, namely; the air, the rain-water, and the sea and its shores, for every living creature can use each of these things, according as it has need of them. For this reason every man can use the sea and its shore for fishing or for navigation, and for doing everything there which he thinks may be to his advantage.

This legal precedent for approaching the sea and its products as a common resource would profoundly shape the emergence of American pearl-fishing grounds.[27]

26. Ibid., III, Title XXVIII, Laws III, IV, V, IX, XI, 820, 821, 822.

27. Ibid., Law III, 820. For general perspectives on legal ambiguity and oceanic space, see Lauren Benton, *A Search for Sovereignty: Law and Geography in European Empires, 1400–1900* (Cambridge, 2010); and Philip E. Steinberg, *The Social Construction of the Ocean* (Cambridge, 2001).

Born of a desire to simplify Iberia's tangle of laws, Alfonso X's initiative was only partially successful, however. By the time of Columbus's voyage, an immense diversity of practices and regulations characterized the many kingdoms of Spain, varying from region to region and from city to city. This complexity reflected Spain's history of political (and, to some degree, cultural) fragmentation. One of the products of the kingdoms' legal multiplicity was an unusually strong tradition of customary law, a legacy of pre-Roman days as well as Roman and Visigothic law. The legacy of Moorish rule, the *fueros* (regional and local charters unique to Spain), the influence of the church, and the law books of later Christian kings also played influential roles.[28]

The legal diversity within Spain found an echo in its cultural diversity, a vexed issue at the time of Columbus's voyage. Pearl's popularity in Iberian dress from the days of the Catholic Monarchs, through the introduction of elaborate, austere Burgundian court ritual under Charles V, to the ruff-collared excesses of the seventeenth century was deeply tied to expressions of political and cultural identity (see Figures 3 and 4).[29]

Sumptuary laws of the late medieval period focused largely on differentiating Christians from Spain's Jewish and Muslim inhabitants, and, in particular, stigmatizing Moorish ways of dressing. Even as Christians considered Andalusian Moorish dress (particularly textiles) as the height of luxury (and the popular equestrian sport known as the *juego de cañas,* or game of canes, involved all participants dressing as Moors), they were suspicious of its cultural and religious associations. As the Catholic Monarchs elaborated Columbus's *capitulaciones* in the kingdom of Granada, shortly after the fall

28. This paragraph characterizing Spanish law by the late fifteenth century summarizes E. N. Van Kleffens, *Hispanic Law until the End of the Middle Ages: With a Note on the Continued Validity after the Fifteenth Century of Medieval Hispanic Legislation in Spain, the Americas, Asia, and Africa* (Edinburgh, 1968), 17–18. On Spanish law's fragmentation, see from 120.

29. See Priscilla E. Muller, *Jewels in Spain, 1500–1800* (New York, 1972), for an overview of taste in adornment. On the evolution of Spanish court ceremonial in the sixteenth and seventeenth centuries, see J. H. Elliott, "The Court of the Spanish Hapsburgs: A Peculiar Institution?" in Phyllis Mack and Margaret C. Jacob, eds., *Politics and Culture in Early Modern Europe: Essays in Honour of H. G. Koenigsberger* (Cambridge, 1987). The extravagant dress that drew contemporary critics' scorn is perhaps another example of baroque expressionism most frequently identified as "decorative excess"; see David R. Castillo, "Horror (Vacui): The Baroque Condition," in Nicholas Spadaccini and Luis Martín-Estudillo, eds., *Hispanic Baroques: Reading Cultures in Context* (Nashville, Tenn., 2005), 87.

Figure 3. Alonso Sánchez Coello, The Infantas Isabel Clara Eugenia and
Catalina Micaela. *1575. © Museo Nacional del Prado. Two young princesses
(daughters of Philip II of Spain) are wearing double-stranded ropes of
pearls and elaborate pearl headdresses.*

of the last Moorish kingdom on the peninsula, they were surrounded by the
material expressions of Moorish wealth that played a foundational role in
Spain's distinct, hybrid culture.[30]

Aesthetic tastes certainly played a role in the Monarchs' interest in spon-
soring Columbus's proposed voyage to the East. Queen Isabella was famously

30. See Barbara Fuchs, *Exotic Nation: Maurophilia and the Construction of Early Modern Spain* (Philadelphia, 2009). Javier Irigoyen-García discusses medieval sumptuary
legislation intended to control Muslim Iberians' sartorial practices in *"Moors Dressed as
Moors": Clothing, Social Distinction, and Ethnicity in Early Modern Iberia* (Toronto,
2017), esp. 5-12 . On the popularity of Moorish jewels, and Queen Isabella's fondness for
them, see Muller, *Jewels in Spain,* 22-25.

Figure 4. Diego de Velázquez, Isabella of Bourbon, First Queen of King Philip IV. *Circa 1632. Permission, Statens Museum for Kunst, Copenhagen*

fond of ornamentation: in the words of royal chronicler Hernando de Pulgar, "She was a woman who was very ceremonious in her dress and adornments, in the choice of her daises and thrones, as well as in the service of her person." Financial concerns, however, weighed more heavily still. At the time of the admiral's voyage, the Spanish crown needed additional sources of funding. Royal revenue came largely from the prosperous kingdom of Castile's *alcabala,* a long-standing sales tax dating to Muslim rule and first instituted in Castile in the fourteenth century (the alcabala varied as a duty levied on a percentage of the value of all goods sold). In spite of the relative health of the economy in 1492, the Monarchs' significant spending added urgency to the search for new sources of income. Isabella might not have pawned her jewels to pay for the trip, as a popular legend tells it, but the king and queen cast their nets widely in search of financial support. The war with the Islamic Nasrid kingdom of Granada had been won just a few months earlier (in January 1492) with monetary support from the church. A papal dispensation further allowed the Monarchs to retain the money gained from the sale of indulgences and put it toward Columbus's voyage. His trip, it was hoped, would bring significant returns.[31]

Ferdinand and Isabella drafted their agreement with Columbus, the *capitulaciones,* in two parts, each with a distinct purpose and each distinctly medieval in its approach to the distribution of political and material power. The first of the two documents identified Ferdinand and Isabella as "Lords that are of the said oceans," and in that capacity they were able to grant Columbus whatever they saw fit in return for "all those islands and mainland" discovered by "his hand and industry." The rulers named Columbus "Admiral of the Ocean Sea, viceroy, and governor" of all new lands to be encountered, granting the titles in perpetuity and permitting them to pass to his descendants. They also granted him significant influence in shaping the governance of any new territories, such as the power to nominate individuals to administrative positions. In addition to these concessions, the Catholic Monarchs allowed Columbus significant rights to any material wealth he might find. The third clause of the first capitulación specified that a tenth of "all and whatever merchandise, whether it be pearls, precious stones, gold, silver, spices, and other things whatsoever," would belong to the admiral, "the other nine parts remaining for your Highnesses." The second capitulación, drafted fewer than two weeks later, dealt with the administrative and judicial hierarchies undergirding the trip, particularly the relationship between God, the Monarchs, and the admiral.[32]

31. Pulgar is quoted in Kagan, "The Spain of Ferdinand and Isabella," in McGovern, ed., *Worlds of Columbus,* 24; on the papal dispensation, see 27. For the religious context that informed Queen Isabella's ambitions, see Peggy K. Liss, *Isabel the Queen: Life and Times,* rev. ed. (Philadelphia, 2004), esp. chap. 9.

32. The capitulaciones are translated and reprinted in Charles Gibson, ed., *The Spanish Tradition in America* (New York, 1968), 27–34. The first agreement was signed on April 17, 1492, and the second on April 30, 1492. On the terms of Columbus's agreement

The thinking behind the inclusion of pearls in the capitulaciones almost certainly reflected their treatment in the Siete Partidas. The governing precedents established in the law code affected pearls in their identity both as a product of the natural world and as a commodity that fell into the category of treasure. As the former, pearls seem to have become increasingly incorporated into definitions of the patrimony *(realengo)* of the state, which included forests and salt mines. As treasure, they were mentioned in conjunction with gold in the context of movable goods and the spoils of war. The elaboration of this approach to treasure unfolded over many centuries (beginning with the Romans) and from the Middle Ages to the early modern period grew to encompass the idea that all people who found treasure owed a portion to the king as tribute. The American context, in which these precedents took on new import, would transform the practical implementation of these laws. Spanish law overseas was followed in the breach, and the strong Iberian precedent of granting authority to local customary practice would prove as powerful in the New World as it had long been in the Old.[33]

Cloaked in the authority granted by the capitulaciones, Columbus sailed from the port of Palos in southern Spain in early August 1492, carrying classical knowledge and medieval legal precedent into unknown waters. These earliest associations of pearls — these fragile, quasi-animate objects of desire, products of a fraught maritime world — persisted even as they were transformed by the Columbian encounter. Pearls took on new meanings over the course of the next two centuries as colonial expansion, shifts in approaches to the natural world and its products, and the growth of imperial ambition shaped the global contexts in which the jewels were harvested and consumed.

---

with Ferdinand and Isabella, see Phillips and Phillips, *The Worlds of Christopher Columbus,* 133–135.

33. For the role of two natural commodities — salt and timber — in state building, see David Goodman, *Spanish Naval Power, 1589–1665: Reconstruction and Defeat* (Cambridge, 1997). For more on salt and the Castillian understandings of crown patrimony, see María Rosario Porres Marijuán, *Las reales Salinas de Añana (siglos X–XIX)* (Bilbao, Spain, 2007). On *realengo,* see Colin M. MacLachlan, *Spain's Empire in the New World: The Role of Ideas in Institutional and Social Change* (Berkeley, Calif., 1988), 15–18. On Spanish law being followed in the breach, see Van Kleffens, *Hispanic Law until the End of the Middle Ages,* 264–265. Tamar Herzog also considers Iberian precedent and practice in administering land and natural resources in *Frontiers of Possession: Spain and Portugal in Europe and the Americas* (Cambridge, Mass., 2015).

PEARLS AND A
POLITICAL ECOLOGY OF EMPIRE,
1498-1541

The hum of news and excitement buzzed through the port towns of southern Spain and Portugal in the waning years of the fifteenth century as ships, sailors, and the tales and treasure they carried sailed into Iberian harbors. It was not until Columbus's third crossing into the unfamiliar Caribbean archipelago that he encountered pearls. On this 1498 voyage, as he and his crew wended their way along the South American coastline through the Gulf of Paria, the admiral made contact with pearl-wearing Indians (likely Guayquerí from neighboring islands). A shared appreciation for the jewel presumably facilitated communication: in contrast to New World commodities such as chocolate and tobacco, pearls' luminescence and their sensual associations with fertility and the mysterious and generative power of the sea linked indigenous American and European approaches to the jewel.[1]

Upon the mariners' return to Spain in the wake of this encounter, word of the region's rich oyster beds spread quickly. Scattershot settlement and plunder began and rapidly increased along the Venezuelan coastline, focused largely on the trade in pearls, without generating major crown intervention or any sustained set of administrative privileges. In these early haphazard years

1. On tobacco and chocolate, see Marcy Norton, *Sacred Gifts, Profane Pleasures: A History of Tobacco and Chocolate in the Atlantic World* (Ithaca, N.Y., 2008). On pearls in the Americas and indigenous conceptions of them, see Nicholas J. Saunders, "Biographies of Brilliance: Pearls, Transformations of Matter and Being, c. AD 1492," *World Archaeology,* XXXI (1999), 243-257. Despite the commonalities of European and indigenous views of pearls, however, pearls were not exempted from the European instinct to dismiss indigenous ability to assess worth. Columbus wrote of his encounter with native peoples off the coast of Venezuela, "There wasn't anyone on board who knew gold from pyrite or pearl from chrysoberyl" (ibid., 243). Ann Marie Mester, *The Pearl Divers of Los Frailes: Archaeological and Ethnohistorical Exploration of Sumptuary Good Trade and Cosmology in the North and Central Andes* (Ph.D. diss., University of Illinois at Urbana-Champaign, 1990), provides an overview of the role of light worship in American indigenous societies.

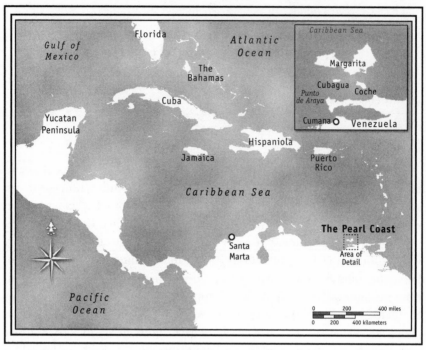

Map 2. The Pearl Coast in the Greater Caribbean. Drawn by Gerry Krieg

of raiding and encounters, confronted by chaotic novelty and unprecedented challenges of all types, the Spanish crown struggled to make sense of this New World, seeking to impose administrative order upon it without a clear blueprint of how to do so. Embedded in global Iberian merchant networks, populated by indigenous peoples from the circum-Caribbean as well as Africans and Europeans of all origins, the teeming waters and contested territories of this corner of the evolving Atlantic world would provide enduring early lessons in the importance of intricate ecosystems that bound the natural world to local practice and to imperial coffers. Over the course of the first four decades of the sixteenth century, the inhabitants of the coast would work together in an often brutal and coerced fashion to produce extraordinary pearl wealth. In doing so, they put forth their vision of an American political economy, one that had a living ecology at its heart. In the pearl fisheries, the vocabulary of imperial administration evolved in dialogue with practices on the ground, as subjects from three continents labored under wildly varying conditions to build lives on land based on riches from the sea. De facto practices of wealth generation and management informed emerging de jure approaches to imperial control over the region's resources.

A "Pearl Coast" Political Economy

As the Spanish crown and its servants struggled to assimilate the import of recently encountered lands in the Americas and their riches, pearls gave form and vocabulary to this evolving corner of a new imperial geography. Columbus, inspired by the pearls he and his crew received in exchange for various goods—and, according to a later account by Bartolomé de Las Casas, by the abundant dew Columbus saw throughout the region (which recalled Pliny's explanation of the genesis of pearls as the product of dew falling upon open oysters)—invoked the jewel in his names for the waters and islands around which he had sailed. He baptized the stretch of water between the small island of Cubagua and its larger neighboring island the "Golfo de las Perlas," or the Gulf of Pearls. In a similar vein, he christened the large island "Margarita." In 1500, the map of Juan de la Cosa, a mariner who traveled with Columbus during the pearl-producing third voyage, labeled the entire adjacent coast as the "Costa de Perlas," or Pearl Coast. These early monikers proved predictive: pearl-fishing operations would expand along the coast throughout the century as profit-hunters sought undisturbed oyster banks.[2] The region figured prominently in early Spanish administrative engagement with this unfamiliar world; it was not only depicted on early maps but also explicitly mentioned in the charter decree of Seville's Casa de Contratación

2. Bartolomé de Las Casas, *Historia de las Indias* . . . , ed. Agustín Millares Carlo, with preliminary study by Lewis Hanke, 3 vols. (Mexico and Buenos Aires, 1951), II, 20, 26. See also Pablo Ojer, *La Formación del Oriente Venezolano* (Caracas, 1966), 14. Las Casas claimed to have used Columbus's own diary as his source for the retelling of the admiral's voyages. On Las Casas's and Hernando Colón's biographies of Columbus, see William D. Phillips, Jr., and Carla Rahn Phillips, *The Worlds of Christopher Columbus* (Cambridge, 1993), 9. For a discussion of the Juan de la Cosa map, see Ricardo Cerezo Martínez, *La cartografía náutica española en los siglos XIV, XV, y XVI* (Madrid, 1994), chap. 7. On Columbus's imagined riches and the creation of an "economy of the marvelous" upon his return to Spain, see Elvira Vilches, *New World Gold: Cultural Anxiety and Monetary Disorder in Early Modern Spain* (Chicago, 2010), 53. Antonello Gerbi discusses Columbus's turning to Pliny to shore up his hopes for the pearls to be found in the New World in *Nature in the New World: From Christopher Columbus to Gonzalo Fernández de Oviedo,* trans. Jeremy Moyle (Pittsburgh, 1985), 13.

(House of Trade), which included distinct clauses addressing the trade and exploration of "the islands where pearls are found."[3]

Pearls—never the oysters from which they were drawn—inflected the vocabulary of life and labor in these settlements for centuries. The Pearl Coast became alternately known as the "Costa de Aljófar" (Seed Pearl Coast); the humble dwellings in which Spaniards lived during pearl-fishing seasons were known as *rancherías de perlas,* or pearl settlements. Often the region's specific place-names were entirely ignored: after Cubagua and the adjacent islands of Margarita and Coche became centers of pearl fishing, they were often referred to simply as the "Islas de Perlas," or the Pearl Islands, or simply the *pesquerías de perlas,* or pearl fisheries.[4]

From the region's earliest days as a site of imperial experimentation, its simple pearl-focused nomenclature belied the diversity and complexity of these rough-and-tumble communities. European settlement and exploration of the Pearl Coast reflected from the beginning a mixture of individual and royal initiative, an uneasy if necessary partnership that underlay life and commerce in the pearl fisheries. With no fixed policy for settlement of the Pearl Coast, Spanish king Ferdinand continued to try to gain control of the region

3. For the Jan. 20, 1503, decree establishing the Casa de Contratación, see *Colección de documentos inéditos relativos al descubrimiento, conquista y organización de las antiguas posesiones españolas de Ultramar* (Madrid, 1890), V, 29–42, esp. 39, doc. 9 (quotation). For a discussion of the influence of early pearl-hunting voyages on the genesis of the Casa de Contratación, see Carl Ortwin Sauer, *The Early Spanish Main: Carl Sauer's Classic Account of the Land, Nature, and People Columbus Encountered in the Americas* (Berkeley, Calif., 1966), 161. For a detailed treatment of the Casa de Contratación and its early history, see Kenneth R. Andrews, *The Spanish Caribbean: Trade and Plunder, 1530–1630* (New Haven, Conn., 1978), 54–57; and Antonio Barrera-Osorio, *Experiencing Nature: The Spanish American Empire and the Early Scientific Revolution* (Austin, Tex., 2006), 35–37. The founding of the Casa marked the beginning of the crown's campaign to regain some of the prerogatives they had bartered away in their initial agreements with Columbus. For a discussion of the Spanish crown's evolving approach to the governance of the Indies, see Ralph Bauer, *The Cultural Geography of Colonial American Literatures: Empire, Travel, Modernity* (Cambridge, 2003), 42–48.

4. The German historian Enrique Otte, a prolific scholar of the pearl fisheries and colonial Venezuela, wrote the classic history of the Caribbean pearl fisheries in the early sixteenth century and compiled innumerable royal decrees and correspondence pertaining to the colonial history of the South American Pearl Coast. This book owes an immense debt to his labors and would have been impossible without his pioneering scholarship. Otte discusses the naming of the coast by explorers and the crown in *Las perlas del Caribe: Nueva Cádiz de Cubagua* (Caracas, 1977), 93.

through piecemeal contractual concessions. In 1500 and 1501, five additional voyages, all financed privately, sailed for the region, along with one crown-financed expedition.[5] Spanish settlers and sojourners on the larger Antillean islands (particularly Puerto Rico and Hispaniola) also played a critical role in redirecting the flow of money and people to the Pearl Coast from around the Caribbean. In 1504, in recognition of this steady traffic, the king ordered the governor of Hispaniola, Nicolás de Ovando, to build a fortress on the mainland to provide protection for pearl traders and *rescate* (forced trade or barter) expeditions. In 1512, the crown authorized private pearl-trading voyages to Cubagua and adjacent territories from Hispaniola. Subsequently, the crown began to receive modest pearl payments from Cubagua in the form of the *quinto*, a tax on a fifth of the total pearl haul. Pearls were to be assessed by weight and grouped into units called *marcos*, equivalent to roughly half a pound. Payment to the crown from the region averaged one hundred marcos in weight (or roughly fifty pounds) of pearls per year from 1513 to 1520. It was at the start of this period, in 1513, that the new governor of Hispaniola, Diego Colón, received royal permission to build a fort in *las perlas* ("the pearls," an ambiguous phrase that likely referred to the Venezuelan mainland near the island of Cubagua). Overall, the relative royal neglect that facilitated a chaotic evolution of pearl-fishing settlements reflected the crown's preoccupation with the larger Antillean islands. Royal attention was firmly fixed on Hispaniola, its gold mines and political and religious disputes.[6]

5. For details on King Ferdinand's various attempts to establish an asiento approach (meaning a contract, or individual license, granted to an individual or company by the crown) for the Costa de Perlas from 1504 to 1511 and on the triumph of *rescate* (forced trade or barter) instead, see Otte, *Las perlas del Caribe*, 96–97, 102–107, 127–128. Cerezo Martínez, in *La cartografía náutica española*, discusses the years of plunder that followed Columbus's 1498 voyage (80–86). See also Otte, *Las perlas del Caribe*, 100–102; and Sauer, *The Early Spanish Main*, 108–114, 190–191. Sauer discusses these voyages as leaving the Pearl Coast "without provision of government" (114). For an additional discussion of the early-sixteenth-century Pearl Coast, see Michael Perri, "'Ruined and Lost': Spanish Destruction of the Pearl Coast in the Early Sixteenth Century," *Environment and History*, XV (2009), 132–133.

6. Perri, "'Ruined and Lost,'" *Environment and History*, XV (2009), 129–161, esp. 150. Otte discusses both the introduction of the quinto into the fisheries and the pearl payments it generated in its first years in *Las perlas del Caribe*, 52–54. For an overview of early political struggles in Hispaniola, see Patricia Seed, "How Globalization Invented Indians the Caribbean," in Eva Sansavior and Richard Scholar, eds., *Caribbean Globalizations, 1492 to the Present Day* (Liverpool, 2015), 58–82. Frank Moya Pons also discusses Hispaniola's primacy in the first decades of the sixteenth century in chaps. 1 and 2 of *His-*

Meanwhile, a distinct regional political economy developed on the Pearl Coast. As the pearl-fishing settlements along South America's northeastern littoral and adjacent islands grew, they transformed the area's political economy, its ecology, and its demographic makeup. Pearls were only one component of the Venezuelan coast's natural wealth, which included copper, gold, rocks, and various semiprecious stones. However, the hunt for pearls soon eclipsed interest in these other resources. Although indigenous inhabitants of the Venezuelan littoral had long harvested oysters—*Pinctada radiata*—for their meat and pearls, the scale of exploitation changed dramatically with the arrival of Spaniards in the early sixteenth century. The lasting impact of this unswerving focus on pearls had less to do with a new European valuation of the jewel than with the changing scale of their pursuit and the complex related costs.[7]

European incursions along the Pearl Coast also transformed local ecology in ways that Spaniards could not have predicted based on their prior experiences in Iberia, taking a toll not only on the oyster beds but also on the flora and fauna on land. On the islands of Margarita, Coche, and Cubagua, for example, livestock multiplied and began eating young plant shoots, allowing cacti to proliferate. The frenzied "greed they [the Spaniards] had for getting pearls, even if the oyster banks were destroyed," wreaked havoc not only on the waters and lands adjacent to the pearl-fishing settlements but also on places and peoples within striking distance of European profit-seekers hunting for laborers.[8]

Regional transformation was rapid but uneven, with Europeans' pearl ava-

_____

tory of the Caribbean: Plantations, Trade, and War in the Atlantic World (Princeton, N.J., 2007). B. W. Higman writes in *A Concise History of the Caribbean* (Cambridge, 2011) that "Santo Domingo served for a generation as the centre of administration for the whole of Spanish America" (82).

7. For a discussion of Pre-Columbian patterns of resource use on the Venezuelan coast, see Neil L. Whitehead, *Lords of the Tiger Spirit: A History of the Caribs in Colonial Venezuela and Guyana, 1498–1820* (Dordrecht-Holland, 1988); and Louis Allaire, "Archaeology of the Caribbean Region," in Frank Salomon and Stuart B. Schwartz, eds., *The Cambridge History of the Native Peoples of the Americas,* III, *South America,* part 1 (New York, 1999), 668–733.

8. See Neil L. Whitehead, "The Crises and Transformations of Invaded Societies: The Caribbean (1492–1580)," in Salomon and Schwartz, eds., *Cambridge History of the Native Peoples of the Americas,* III, part 1, 864–903; *CC,* II, 172 (Mar. 10, 1540). The original quotation reads: "cudiçia que tenían de sacar perlas, aunque se destruyesen los ostiales."

rice checked by their dependence upon local peoples for sustenance. For example, although European mechanisms of commercial exchange and the place for precious stones and metals within them might have indeed been different from those that existed in the pre-contact Americas, evidence suggests that pearls continued to be exchanged and valued in ways that reflected concerns beyond the purely economic. This kind of cultural continuity might well have been particularly true along the Pearl Coast of Venezuela, where the particulars of population distribution and social organization meant that these coastal peoples maintained their relative autonomy until the mid-seventeenth century. The Warao, Guaquerí, and Arawak (Lokono) peoples of the northern South American coast critically influenced the region's evolving character in the aftermath of the arrival of Europeans. Initially, Spanish interlopers exchanged plates, bells, wine, and foodstuffs for pearls gathered by groups of indigenous divers. This kind of trade activity might not have been a disruptive innovation—local native economies revolved in part around the exchange of food surpluses and were influenced by ideological concerns as well as economic ones. Along the northern coast of what is now Venezuela, the inhabitants relied on shellfish gathering, and the conch *Strombus gigas* was used to make tools as well as prized as food. The tools made from Strombus shell, for example, such as axes and adzes, were likely employed in the manufacture of canoes. (The name *Warao* meant "canoe maker" or "canoe owner.")[9]

Even as the settlements dedicated to pearl fishing developed along the coast and on outlying islands, European sojourners could ill afford to anger their trading partners, depending on them as they did for most essential items, from food, fuel, and water to clothing and canoes. Most notable

9. Neil L. Whitehead, "Native Peoples Confront Colonial Regimes in Northeastern South America (c. 1500-1900)," III, part 2, 382-442 (quotation on 394), and Whitehead, "Crises and Transformations," III, part 1, 864-903, both in Salomon and Schwartz, eds., *Cambridge History of the Native Peoples of the Americas*. On Spanish contact with the indigenous inhabitants of Margarita, see C. S. Alexander, "Margarita Island, Exporter of People," *Journal of Inter-American Studies*, III (1961), 548-557. For a description of pearl-fishing operations and increasingly aggressive behavior by Spaniards on Margarita circa 1520, see Otte, *Las perlas del Caribe*, 173-176. For more on the Spanish presence and indigenous labor in the early sixteenth century, see Morella A. Jiménez G., *La esclavitud indígena en Venezuela (Siglo XVI)* (Caracas, 1986), 162-199; Otte, *Las perlas del Caribe*, 120-150; Perri, "'Ruined and Lost,'" *Environment and History*, XV (2009), 129-161. Bartolomé de Las Casas described the enslavement and sale of Lucayans in Las Casas, *Historia de las Indias*, ed. Carlo, II, 353. See also William F. Keegan, *The People Who Discovered Columbus: The Prehistory of the Bahamas* (Gainesville, Fla., 1992), 221-222.

was the Spaniards' reliance on manioc flour *(aru)* and fresh water supplied largely by the Arawaks on the Guayana coast, among other native peoples. The Arawak peoples of the Atlantic coast would remain essential trading partners for decades. As violence and disease took their toll on coastal populations, however, European settlers extended their predatory raids in search of a labor force to dive for oysters. These *rescate* forays brought violence and dislocation to the native populations of the Greater Caribbean and the South American mainland.[10]

Guaranteeing a regional labor supply revealed itself to be a problem early on in the decades following the Spaniards' arrival in the Caribbean. In the wake of Dominican friar Antonio de Montesinos's 1511 condemnation of Spanish crimes against Indians on Hispaniola, the crown issued the Leyes de Burgos in 1512, prohibiting the enslavement of Indians in the New World. A few years later, Ferdinand's grandson and successor Charles I and V (who ruled from 1516 to 1556 and became Charles V when he was elected Holy Roman emperor in 1519) authorized several religious missions to the Pearl Coast, hoping to maintain peaceful relations with its indigenous inhabitants. These forays met with only moderate success, and enslavement continued by other means and names, as the flood of indigenous peoples forcibly transported to the pearl fisheries attests.[11]

As the settlements along the Pearl Coast grew, relative local indigenous power meant that European sojourners had to look elsewhere for their workforce. Spaniards carried on slave raiding in Carib and Arawak settlements in the Lesser Antilles and along the Caribbean coast up to the Yucatán. Some populations in particular suffered greatly because of the perceived needs of the fisheries: Spaniards believed Lucayan inhabitants of the Bahamas to be

10. Even as livestock multiplied and pearl-fishing settlements expanded along the mainland coast during the sixteenth century, residents of the pearl fisheries continued to rely on importation (often from Spain as well as the Greater Antilles) to supply some of the fisheries' most essential needs, such as tar, ropes, sails, and clothing used for the operation of the pearl canoes, and even pine from the Canary Islands for the boats' construction. For examples of requests for foodstuffs and other goods, see *CV*, 114 (May 5, 1519), 311 (Sept. 12, 1528); and *CC*, I, 72 (Aug. 17, 1538), 89 (Sept. 12, 1528), 178 (Oct. 15, 1532); *CC*, II, 188 (Feb. 26, 1541). See also Allaire, "Archaeology of the Caribbean Region," in Salomon and Schwartz, eds., *Cambridge History of the Native Peoples of the Americas*, III, part 1, 668–733, esp. 670, 673, 683.

11. For the crown's evolving Indian policy and its effect on the Pearl Coast, see Francisco Domínguez Compañy, "Municipal Organization of the Rancherías of Pearls," *Americas*, XXI (1964), 58–68.

adept divers and brought them into the pearl fisheries in increasing numbers, leaving those islands nearly depopulated by the end of the 1520s. Estimates for the number of indigenous people enslaved and transported in the region vary wildly, from six thousand taken from the Pearl Coast, Trinidad, and Curaçao to between thirty and forty thousand Lucayans removed from the Bahamas. Not all of these people went to the pearl fisheries, of course, and the pearl fisheries contained diversity beyond these populations.[12]

Caribbean peoples could be enslaved if they were designated *caribes,* defined in the first decade of the sixteenth century as any native peoples who resisted Spanish authority. Those classified as *taíno* (also *aruaca* or *guatiao*) were treated as subjects. Unsurprisingly, the designations were political. Even in 1520, when the labor needs of Spanish residents of Hispaniola led the crown to sponsor a formal reevaluation of the region's inhabitants (leading to new designations of caribe to justify slave raiding), the indigenous residents of Margarita (among a handful of other islands in the vicinity of the pearl fisheries) were exempted, a reflection of Spaniards' reliance on their indigenous neighbors. Neither the *encomienda/mita* system (the two paradigms of coerced indigenous labor that came to dominate colonial settlements in the Spanish Americas) nor the epidemic disease devastation that transformed the larger Caribbean islands in the first few decades of the sixteenth century characterized Venezuela's coast, which meant that native labor remained, for the most part, under the control of local indigenous leaders.[13]

In the context of the search for laborers for these New World settlements, in 1512 the king consented to a request from the secretary of the Real Audi-

12. Sauer, *The Early Spanish Main,* states that 30,000 to 40,000 Lucayans were enslaved and transported. Nancy van Deusen estimates that more than 650,000 indigenous people (a number she says is likely low) were enslaved and forcibly relocated throughout the Iberian world in the sixteenth century, beginning in the 1490s. She acknowledges that exact figures are hard to arrive at given widespread illegal slave raiding and the scarcity of accurate records. Van Duesen also cites Karen F. Anderson-Córdova, "Hispaniola and Puerto Rico: Indian Acculturation and Heterogeneity, 1492–1500" (Ph.D. diss., Yale University, 1990), which estimates that 34,000 "foreign" slaves, including Lucayans, were transported to Hispaniola and Puerto Rico. Otte estimates 6,000, which Van Deusen deems low. See Nancy E. Van Duesen, *Global Indios: The Indigenous Struggle for Justice in Sixteenth-Century Spain* (Durham, N.C., 2015), 2 n. 5.

13. For the significance of the terms *caribe* and *taíno,* see Whitehead, "Crises and Transformations," III, part 1, 864–903, esp. 869–870, 879–880, and Whitehead, "Native Peoples," III, part 2, 382–442, esp. 407–408, both in Salomon and Schwartz, eds., *Cambridge History of the Native Peoples of the Americas.*

encia de Santo Domingo (royal court) on Hispaniola to send more *esclavas blancas,* or white female slaves, to the Indies. Just a few years later, however, Spanish residents of the West Indies put pressure on the crown to provide enslaved laborers directly from Africa. In a 1518 petition, Spaniards on Hispaniola argued that enslaved Africans would be less likely to be rebellious than slaves brought over from Castile. That same year, Charles I indicated his support of this proposed change in the workforce by licensing Lorenzo de Gouvenod, comte de Bresa, to deliver four thousand black slaves to the Spanish Americas over seven years (de Gouvenod then resold the license to four Italian business partners). The crown also authorized Dom Jorge, the illegitimate son of Portuguese king João II, to send four hundred African slaves to Hispaniola. These early royal experiments in supplying the region with enslaved Africans underscore the conundrum posed by the New World. On the one hand, the unfamiliar territories represented a new arena in which to pursue European alliances; on the other, the labor demands of these American settlements gave rise to innovation and experimentation with many unintended consequences, such as the political and moral dilemmas posed by the growing trade in enslaved Africans and indigenous peoples.[14]

14. For the 1512 petition for esclavas blancas, see Otte, *Las perlas del Caribe,* 122 n. 589. The 1518 petition is discussed in Esteban Mira Caballos, "Las licencias de esclavos negros a Hispanoamérica (1544–1550)," *Revista de Indias,* LIV, no. 201 (May–August 1994), 273–297, esp. 275. As late as 1527, *blancos ladinos* (acculturated whites, likely orthodox Christians from the eastern Mediterranean) worked alongside enslaved indigenous and African laborers in the Caribbean, and one resident received a royal license to bring a woman and a boy identified as such (in addition to "twelve black slaves") to Hispaniola. The two ladinos were later referred to as "slaves" as well; see "Real Cédula a Francisco de Frías vecino de Salvatierra de la Sabana, dandole licencia para pasar doce esclavos negros y dos blancos ladinos," July 12, 1527, AGI, IG: 421, legajo 12, fol. 168r (quotations). Debra Blumenthal, *Enemies and Familiars: Slavery and Mastery in Fifteenth-Century Valencia* (Ithaca, N.Y., 2009), provides excellent background on patterns of late-medieval Iberian slavery. For more on the influence of Iberian paradigms of slavery on the early Spanish Caribbean in a slightly later period, see David Wheat, "Mediterranean Slavery, New World Transformations: Galley Slaves in the Spanish Caribbean, 1578–1635," *Slavery and Abolition,* XXXI (2010), 327–344. For the early African slave trade into Spanish America (including the Gouvenod license and the concession to Dom João's bastard son), see António de Almeida Mendes, "The Foundations of the System: A Reassessment of the Slave Trade to the Spanish Americas in the Sixteenth and Seventeenth Centuries," in David Eltis and David Richardson, eds., *Extending the Frontiers: Essays on the New Transatlantic Slave Trade Database* (New Haven, Conn., 2008), 63–94. See also José Luis Cortés López, "1544–1550: El período más prolífico en la exportación de esclavos durante el s. XVI. Aná-

As a result of these initial experiments in administering new Atlantic territories, the Pearl Coast became ever more deeply embedded in networks of commerce and alliance that spanned the Atlantic and extended into the Indian Ocean and Asia. The pearl wealth beginning to come from the Caribbean gave the Spanish crown hope that these western Indies would allow them to compete with their peninsular rivals, the Portuguese, recently enriched by the charting of new maritime paths to eastern markets. Just as pearls from both eastern and western fisheries mixed and mingled as they traveled the globe (for example, prominent pearl merchant Lazarus Nürnberger procured pearls for sovereigns from Iberia to Turkey, including the pope, from both the East and West Indies), so, too, did many of the networks that competed for and distributed them.[15] It was not only the commercial circuits that connected these distant pearl-producing locales. Just as the Caribbean pearl fisheries drew immediate attention from the most prominent religious figures of the day, so, too, did the Indian Ocean pearl fisheries (located on the so-called Fishery Coast). While famed advocate for the indigenous population in the Americas Bartolomé de Las Casas represented the Dominicans on the Venezuelan Pearl Coast, in the Indian Ocean fisheries none other than Francis Xavier, the founder of the Jesuit order, played a prominent role in the conversion of the Fishery Coasts' Tamil-speaking pearl fishers, the Paravas, in the 1540s. In the Indian Ocean, the Paravas remained at the center of negotiations surrounding pearls' production and circulation for the next two centuries, navigating among the competing interests of regional Hindu and Muslim powers as well as rival Europeans.[16]

----
lisis de un interesante documento extraído del Archivo de Simancas," *Espacio, tiempo y forma*, Serie 4, *Histora moderna*, VIII (1995), 63–86.

15. On the simultaneity of these Iberian forays into pearl fishing, see Agnelo Paulo Fernandes, "The Portuguese Cartazes System and the 'Magumbayas' on Pearl Fishing in the Gulf," *Liwa*, no. 1 (June 2009), 12–24, esp. 5–6. Otte discusses the international networks of pearl merchants and Lazarus Nürnberger's eastern and western pearl dealings in *Las perlas del Caribe*, 74.

16. Caught in a series of violent regional conflicts with Muslim rivals, the Paravas decided to seek the protection of the Portuguese king in return for mass conversion to Christianity. On the Paravas and the Fishery Coast, see S. Arunachalam, *The History of the Pearl Fishery of the Tamil Coast* (Annamalai Nagar, Tamil Nadu, India, 1952). On the Paravas and their relationship with the Jesuits and Christianity, see S. B. Kaufmann, "A Christian Caste in Hindu Society: Religious Leadership and Social Conflict among the Paravas of Southern Tamilnadu," *Modern Asian Studies*, XV (1981), 203–234; Stephen Neill, *A History of Christianity in India: The Beginnings to AD 1707* (Cambridge, 1984),

Although overlapping networks linked the history of eastern and western pearl fisheries, a major difference between the two sites of resource exploitation was the labor system. The enforced servitude and slavery that came to characterize the American Pearl Coast early on did not have a parallel in the Indian Ocean. The enslaved laborers along the Pearl Coast worked in appalling conditions to harvest the oysters whose pearls enriched the sundry merchants and officials with investments in the fisheries. One of the most vocal critics of the Caribbean settlements' regime of pearl diving was Las Casas, who in 1517 successfully lobbied in Spain for permission to join the missions in the fisheries, where he hoped to bring an end to Spanish encroachments in the region. It was during his time there that he formed his enduring impressions of the danger and suffering that accompanied the pursuit of pearls.[17] His account characterized the fisheries as violent and lawless, a hotbed of nefarious practices that flourished in the absence of good governance. Indeed, a central aspect of Las Casas's critique was the lack of an effective administration for dealing with the abuses perpetrated in the Indies. In his blistering condemnation of Spanish behavior, Las Casas laid the blame for the state of affairs squarely on the shoulders, not of the king, but of the Council of the Indies, a weak body with no powers of enforcement "with whom principal fault and great sin lies."[18]

141–150, 163–184; and, for a later period, Markus P. M. Vink, "Between the Devil and the Deep Blue Sea; The Christian Paravas: A 'Client Community' in Seventeenth-Century Southeast India," *Itinerario*, XXVI, no. 2 (July 2002), 64–98, esp. 70–75. For an overview of Jesuits in India, see Dauril Alden, *The Making of an Enterprise: The Society of Jesus in Portugal, Its Empire, and Beyond, 1540–1750* (Stanford, Calif., 1996), 49, 91–95, 538–544. On the political organization of southern India in the period, see Maria Augusta Lima Cruz, "Notes on Portuguese Relations with Vijayanagara, 1500–1565," in Sanjay Subrahmanyam, ed., *Sinners and Saints: The Successors of Vasco da Gama* (Oxford, 1995), 13–39.

17. For a short history of Las Casas, see Lawrence A. Clayton, *Bartolomé de Las Casas and the Conquest of the Americas* (Chichester, U.K., 2011). For a brief discussion of the types of labor indigenous residents of Cubagua performed, see also Otte, *Las perlas del Caribe*, 360–361.

18. The Council of the Indies was established in 1524 to oversee all government activity in the Americas. Las Casas's condemnation of the Council is: "Muchas veces lo ha mandado remediar el Consejo con cédulas del rey e no ha aprovechado nada, pero la culpa principal y el pecado muy grande tiene el mismo Consejo, porque no parece sino que lo proveen solamente por cumplir e para que no se cumpla lo que en favor de los indios mandan, pues no castigan rigorosamente los que no cumplen lo que en favor de aquellas gentes han proveído y proveen, ha sido la causa principal de estar aquel orbe asolado, lo

Las Casas's lengthy *History of the Indies,* which he began drafting in 1527, described pearl fishing as a monstrous labor regime that transformed the Indian divers into terrifying otherworldly creatures. Laboring from sunrise to sundown, the divers would repeatedly descend three or four fathoms (eighteen to twenty-four feet) to gather oysters. They were beaten upon returning to the canoe by a brutal Spanish overseer if they took too long between dives, and they were frequently bitten or killed by sharks and other marine predators. The salt opened sores on their backs, and seawater caused their naturally black hair to appear burnished, making the divers look like "sea wolves." Las Casas observed that these enslaved Indians, disfigured by their labor, looked like a "different race of men or monsters." The life of these divers was no life at all, he asserted, but rather an "infernal death," characterized by violence as well as terrible ailments, such as dysentery, brought on by spending so much time in cold water. The pressure on divers' chests from the depth of the water frequently caused them to hemorrhage blood from their mouths, and many died after only a few days in the fisheries. In his *Brief History of the Destruction of the Indies,* Las Casas wrote of pearl fishing that "no hellish and hopeless life on this earth that may be compared with it, however hard and terrible taking out the gold in the mines may be." The many extractive and productive industries of the Americas would produce suffering of innumerable varieties and magnitudes for those who labored in their mines, fields, plantations, and fisheries. It seems clear that pearl diving was indeed one of the many ways to live and die in agony in the wake of the Columbian encounter.[19]

Royal chronicler Gonzalo Fernández de Oviedo y Valdés's account of the pearl-diving regime in the fisheries during the heyday of the 1520s echoed that of Las Casas. By the 1520s, the small, unwelcoming island of Cubagua had become the center of Spanish-controlled pearl-fishing operations. Miniature and desolate, Cubagua was an unlikely base. Located ten miles off the Venezuelan coast and just fifteen square miles in size, the island had no

cual se pedirá a ellos principal y aspérrimamente." See Las Casas, *Historia de las Indias,* ed. Carlo, III, 404.

19. Bartolomé de Las Casas, *An Account, Much Abbreviated, of the Destruction of the Indies with Related Texts,* ed. Franklin W. Knight, trans. Andrew Hurley (Indianapolis, Ind., 2003), 62–63 ("no hellish"). For an extended description of the horrors of pearl diving, see Las Casas, *Historia de las Indias,* ed. Carlo, III, 402–403. For an overview of changes in Pearl Coast pearl-fishing practices and crew composition during the sixteenth century, see Molly A. Warsh, "Enslaved Pearl Divers in the Sixteenth Century Caribbean," *Slavery and Abolition,* XXXI (2010), 345–362.

sources of fresh water, few sources of food on which humans can survive, and little shelter from a relentless, blazing sun. The first Spanish settlements on the island were little more than seasonal shelters (Oviedo later referred to them as "huts and shacks"), impermanent dwellings for the residents of Santo Domingo and San Juan who made regular seasonal forays to the island and the adjacent mainland to barter for pearls harvested by large clans of Guayquerí divers working under the command of a chief. Oviedo described crews of six to seven pearl divers who sailed at daybreak for the oyster banks, where they worked in shifts for hours on end. At night, they would return to the islands, where overseers would seize their hauls and lock them into jails. In his *General and Natural History of the Indies* (1526), Oviedo marveled that this grueling labor regime had turned Cubagua, a "very small and extremely sterile" island, "without a drop of water from a river or any other source . . . nor any place to plant or maintain anything in support of man," into the source of riches exceeding those of any other settlement in the Spanish West Indies.[20]

They were astonishing riches indeed. During the 1520s, climbing quinto payments sketch the outlines of the growth of the slave trade and the aggressive oyster harvesting that supported its rise. In 1521, the number of Cuba-

20. Charles V appointed Oviedo official royal chronicler of the Indies, a post he held from 1532 to 1557. Oviedo composed the two-thousand-page *General and Natural History of the Indies* between 1514 and 1549 while living on Hispaniola. In 1535, the first nineteen books were published (of an eventual fifty); the first part of the *History* was reprinted in 1547 and translated into French (1555) and Italian (1556). The full work was not published until the mid-nineteenth century. His text provided the most comprehensive coverage of the Indies and was based on primary sources, giving it the authority of an eyewitness account. Fellow chronicler López de Gómara referred to it and to Peter Martyr's histories as the only true accounts of Spain's early experiences in the Indies. See Kathleen Ann Myers, *Fernández de Oviedo's Chronicle of America: A New History for a New World,* trans. Nina M. Scott (Austin, Tex., 2007), 1–5. Oviedo estimated the yearly value of the pearls received by the crown from the island to be fifteen thousand ducados and more. He describes Cubagua as "muy pequeña y esterilísima e sin gota de agua de río, ni fuente, ni lago o estaño; y con esta y otras dificultades, sin haber en ella donde se pueda sembrar ni hacer mantenimiento alguno para servicio del hombre, ni poder criar ganados, ni aver algún pasto, está habitada y con una gentil república que se llama la Nueva ciudad de Cádiz, y ha sido tanta su riqueza, que tanto por tanto no ha habido en las Indias cosa más rica ni provechosa en lo que está poblado de los cristianos." See Gonzálo Fernández de Oviedo, *História General y Natural de las Indias,* II, ed. Juan Pérez de Tudela Bueso (Madrid, 1959), 187–188 (quotation on 188). For his characterization of the settlements as a handful of huts and shacks *(toldos y chozas),* see 195.

guan pearls sent to the crown in payment of the quinto rose dramatically to more than two hundred marcos (approximately one hundred pounds of pearls), double the average yearly payments of the preceding seven years. This figure more than tripled the following year, and from 1522 to 1526 the average annual quinto payment totaled more than seven hundred marcos of pearls. The following year, the crown's pearl haul reached its peak, with quinto payments producing twelve hundred marcos, or six hundred pounds, of the jewel.[21]

The profits of the Pearl Coast's boom years reflected a rapid rise in Cubagua's population. In 1520, the island's European population totaled roughly three hundred, and the following year Spanish denizens of Santo Domingo on Hispaniola founded the small city of Nueva Cádiz on Cubagua. By the mid-1520s, Cubagua's European residents numbered close to one thousand, and the island was home to almost one hundred rancherías de perlas. By the 1530s, as many as fifteen hundred people lived on the island. These residents were a mixture of indigenous peoples from around the Caribbean, New Christians from Spain and Portugal, German commercial factors and their associates, Italian merchants, and Spaniards from all over the peninsula in addition to Moriscos (Christian converts from Islam) *esclavos blancos* (white slaves) from the eastern Mediterranean, and enslaved Africans brought to the fisheries by privateers or licensed ships directly from Africa or via the Iberian Peninsula.[22]

The numbers of indigenous and African inhabitants of these settlements

21. For quinto figures, see Otte, *Las perlas del Caribe*, 52–54. Cubagua's output fell markedly in the years following 1527, to an average of six hundred marcos from 1528 to 1531, to a quinto of slightly more than three hundred marcos in 1532, to an average of two hundred from 1533 to 1536, followed by quinto payments of fewer than one hundred marcos from 1537 to 1540. These numbers reflected the depletion of the oyster banks closest to Cubagua; pearl harvests from the region remained large because of the discovery of new oyster beds near the neighboring island of Coche. For a discussion of the value of pearl imports, see Huguette Chaunu, Pierre Chaunu, and Guy Arbellot, *Séville et l'Atlantique, 1504–1650* (Paris, 1957), esp. VII, 613–624.

22. For population statistics, see Perri, "'Ruined and Lost,'" *Environment and History*, XV (2009), 135. On Margarita, the Indian population dropped from seven hundred in 1528 to four hundred in 1537; see R. A. Donkin, *Beyond Price: Pearls and Pearl-Fishing: Origins to the Age of Discoveries* (Philadelphia, 1998), 322. For individual pearl shipments and the diversity of these private entrepreneurs, see Otte, *Las perlas del Caribe*, 64. *Las perlas del Caribe* focuses on the commercial circuits that pearls traveled from Cubagua and includes a discussion of the various merchants who did business in the area (66–78). For an overview of the island's inhabitants, see also Otte's section on early Cubaguan society (337–391).

remain elusive, as do their precise origins, although occasionally the latter can be glimpsed. In 1527, the paymaster of Hispaniola received permission to carry "to the island of Cubagua and the pearl fisheries twelve black slaves from Cape Verde or from Guinea or from wherever you want . . . they must be good swimmers and divers." Preferences could work in the opposite direction, as well: in 1534, royal correspondence concerning a cargo of one hundred slaves being brought to the region included an order not to import any "blacks from Gelofe [Wolof]." It seems likely that these enslaved laborers were believed to be particularly rebellious, perhaps a reflection of the region's long-standing integration into Iberian trade networks as well as its particular linguistic and religious characteristics.[23]

As the king and royal officials in Seville worried about the glut of pearls depressing prices for the jewel, the cost of enslaved laborers in the fisheries rose to new heights: by 1526 and 1527, at the peak of pearl production on Cubagua, Spanish pearl canoe owners were paying between 100 and 150 *pesos de oro* (with each peso worth slightly more than four grams of twenty-two-carat gold and equivalent to 450 maravedis) for each Lucayan diver. The prices for male divers—of unspecified origin—remained high more than a decade later, at 144 pesos de oro in 1540. Occasionally, Pearl Coast residents paid slave traders for their human cargo in the same currency that the enslaved

23. *CV*, 231 (Aug. 2, 1527). Linda A. Newson and Susie Minchin suggest, in *From Capture to Sale: The Portuguese Slave Trade to Spanish South America in the Early Seventeenth Century* (Leiden, 2007), that Africans were brought in to replace Indian divers because they were believed by Spaniards to be stronger and better suited physically to the demands of pearl diving (5). Kevin Dawson explores this possibility in "Enslaved Swimmers and Divers in the Atlantic World," *Journal of American History*, XCII (2006), 1327-1355. On the centrality of slavery to the emergence of Spanish colonial governance, see Sherwin K. Bryant, *Rivers of Gold, Lives of Bondage: Governing through Slavery in Colonial Quito* (Chapel Hill, N.C., 2014). Estimates of the total slave importation to Spanish America for the period between 1505 and 1599 suggest an annual arrival between 1,000 and 2,000 Africans, with an approximate total (accounting for both aborted legal voyages as well as unrecorded smuggling) of 132,000 slaves by 1595. See Almeida Mendes, "Foundations of the System," in Eltis and Richardson, eds., *Extending the Frontiers*, 17, 19-22. Research by Alex Borucki, David Eltis, and David Wheat suggests that the numbers might well have been higher. See Borucki, Eltis, and Wheat, "Atlantic History and the Slave Trade to Spanish America," *American Historical Review*, CXX (2015), 433-461. For inventories of Cubaguans' possessions, including slaves, see Otte, *Las perlas del Caribe*, 508-514. The inventories are reprinted there. On the "jelofe" or Wolof region of Senegambia and its integration with Iberian trade networks, see Toby Green, *The Rise of the Trans-Atlantic Slave Trade in Western Africa, 1300-1589* (Cambridge, 2012), 70-71.

would then be expected to harvest: pearls. The two industries — pearl harvesting and the transatlantic slave trade — were deeply intertwined from their earliest days.[24]

The enslaved workers came from far-flung places of origin and performed diverse tasks as part of their bleak lives. When Spaniard Pedro de Barrionuevo died in 1528, he left among his possessions one *morisca* slave, Ana, age thirty; two *indias de servicio* (service Indians) named Beatriz and Juana; one "india *naboría*" (*naboría* was a term of Arawak origin whose meaning varied in different time periods and regions but commonly referred to a permanent Indian dependent of a Spaniard); and twelve Indians "in a jail." In 1533, Pedro de Herrera left one black slave, Isabel, with two children; one Indian woman from the Yucatán, Isabelica; one Indian girl from Margarita, Luisica; six naborías belonging to the governor Diego de Ordás (suggesting that individuals residing elsewhere sent Indians to the fisheries to obtain pearls, a practice that would become increasingly common later in the century); one "Indian woman" and "2 sick Indian men" with no geographic identifier and "1 Indian man from the Yucatán"; and Juanico "from the pearl fisheries." Miguel de Gaviria owned in 1533 "one little black boy, 'Andresico'"; one enslaved Indian woman "in chains," Catalina; one Indian from Trinidad, "Perico"; and three Indian boys obtained through rescate known as Perito Carioco, Juanico, and Periquito. The same year, Pedro Ortiz de Matienzo left behind an estate including four Indian women (Isabel, Catalinilla, Elena, and Leonor), two canoes, and twenty-three "pearl Indians." The names of a number of these "pearl Indians" suggest their distant origins: Perico Darién, *El cacique* ("the chief"), *el muco* (meaning unclear), Juan Lucayo, Panagua,

24. Las Casas offers this price for Lucayan divers in Las Casas, *Historia de las Indias*, ed. Carlo, II, 353. For the price of male divers in 1540, see the sale of a pearl-fishing business in appendix II in Otte, *Las perlas del Caribe*, 533–544. The price for each male diver was significantly more than the cost of a female enslaved Indian, who, along with her daughter and a canoe and its various equipment was sold for the same price as a single man. For the worth of pesos de oro in gold, see Kris E. Lane, *Pillaging the Empire: Piracy in the Americas, 1500–1750* (Armonk, N.Y., 1998); and Paul E. Hoffman, *The Spanish Crown and the Defense of the Caribbean, 1535–1585: Precedent, Patrimonialism, and Royal Parsimony* (Baton Rouge, La., 1980), 255. For slave traders' being paid in pearls, see, for example, AGI, SD: 1121, legajo 2, fols. 65v–68r (Jan. 22, 1536); *CMNAC*, I, lvii. This phenomenon is also discussed in John K. Thornton and Linda M. Heywood, *Central Africans, Atlantic Creoles, and the Foundation of the Americas, 1585–1660* (Cambridge, 2007), 6, 18–19. On "blacks from Gelofe," see Otte, *Cédulas de la monarquía española relativas a la parte oriental de Venezuela (1520–1561)* (Caracas, 1965), 171 (Jan. 6, 1534).

Francisquillo Ranaburi, Francisquillo Bihón, and Gil de Paria. Spaniard Francisco Portillo, who also died in 1533, claimed ownership of "7 Indian women and men who worked in the home"; "a black man who goes in a boat"; "a new canoe"; "16 old pearl indians that use it [the new canoe]"; and "2 *chapetónes* [meaning unclear] Indians." The names and occupations of these laborers reveal the wide-ranging origins and statuses of the inhabitants of the pearl fisheries. The simplicity of the descriptors of their perceived ethnicities and labors belie both the complex world of various types of work that sustained the fisheries and the immense dislocation and hardship of those forced to toil there against their will.[25]

The most obvious products of these settlements—the millions of pearls harvested—served to put this corner of the Americas on actual maps while also solidifying pearls' place in imagined geographies of the New World, a symbol of the wealth maritime empire could bring. Pearls' prominence as adornment and their utility as ready cash obscured their origins: the circumstances of their production were invisible to their consumers. Pearls' ubiquity as much as their plain, fragile beauty—they brooked no more human alteration than a drilled hole—obscured the violent maelstrom of commerce and labor that produced them. On a hem, around a neck, traded for food or wine or passage, pearls bore no traces of the lives altered and lost through enslavement or the submarine pillaging of the reefs that brought them to light. Pearls bore no marks of origin, leaving room for their consumers to imagine one as they saw fit.

Pearls in Private and Imperial Hands

It is impossible to track the precise quantities of pearls that flowed from the Americas into Iberian markets and beyond. Not only was the official mechanism for registering and taxing pearls flawed (as will be discussed in more detail below), but the majority of the pearls traveled through private channels. Nonetheless, abundant—if eclectic—evidence from the time period attests to the immense influx of Caribbean pearls and their importance to individuals and to the crown as adornment, money, and sources of imperial funding.[26]

25. These inventories are held in the AGI in Seville and reprinted in Otte, *Las perlas del Caribe,* 508–514. For royal decrees concerning working conditions of divers and prohibiting the importation of inland slaves, see *CC,* II, 106 (Dec. 7, 1537), 145 (Mar. 21, 1539), 194 (May 1, 1543).

26. Otte discusses the patchy records of pearl shipments in *Las perlas del Caribe* in his note on sources, 555–556; see also 57 for pearls' importance to the imperial policies of Charles V. On the use of jewels for political purposes and to offset royal expenses in the

With pearl harvesting and circulation embedded in religious, commercial, and political networks that spanned the globe, pearls from all over traded hands among humble and enterprising individuals, facilitating the fortunes of small-scale businessmen (and women) of varying profiles, even as they were used by rulers to arrange marriages, pay for armies, and convey status and spectacular wealth. In Seville, pearls generated their own specialists within the larger jewel trade—at least six pearl drillers and twenty-two silversmiths who specialized in working with pearls lived in the Andalusian port town from 1517 through the close of the 1540s. The ability to drill a pearl without shattering it was a valuable one; in 1525, one Andrés de Carmona, identified as a "seed-pearl driller," bought an enslaved woman and her son in exchange for 15,000 maravedis, or 40 ducados (maravedis are coins that served as the base unit of accounting, with 375 equaling 1 ducado) and the promise to drill twenty-four marcos (or roughly twelve pounds) of aljofar, or seed pearl, for clothing.[27]

Not all the pearls arriving in Iberian port towns came on official ships. The distribution of Caribbean pearls was not necessarily chaotic, but it certainly obeyed a different, privately determined order from the vision the monarchy held for the controlled distribution of this source of New World wealth. Individuals, royal officials, and the crown did not often act in concert when it came to moving wealth around the Atlantic, and pearls were particularly susceptible to personal rather than royal fiat, small and easily hidden as they were. Records of small-scale pearl transactions reveal how the jewel facilitated personal aims, alliances, and fortunes. An early example comes from 1522, when French corsairs attacked the ship of one Alonso de Algaba just off the Portuguese coast as it was returning to Spain from the Indies loaded with many items of value. A Portuguese ship came to the rescue only a short time later, but the crew then seized all precious items from the Spanish ship. This double piracy generated a series of exchanges between the Spanish and Portuguese monarchs and their ambassadors, as the Spanish king attempted to recover the fruits of his overseas domains on behalf of the merchants who had claims to the ship's cargo. The Portuguese king finally relented and ordered

---

late fifteenth century, during the reign of Ferdinand and Isabella, see Priscilla E. Muller, *Jewels in Spain, 1500–1800* (New York, 1972), 7–14.

27. For the rise of Seville as a port town, see Stanley J. Stein and Barbara H. Stein, *Silver, Trade, and War: Spain and America in the Making of Early Modern Europe* (Baltimore, 2000), 10–14. For pearl jewelers and drillers, see Otte, *Las perlas del Caribe*, appendix A II, 403. On Andrés de Carmona, see *Catálogo de los fondos americanos del Archivo de Protocolos de Sevilla*, V, *Siglos XV y XVI* (Seville, 1937), 259.

the return of the confiscated merchandise, pearls included—only to have the Spanish officials in charge of redistributing the recovered jewels to their original owners withhold a portion of the valuable cargo.[28]

Some years later, a similar case unfolded involving the jewels carried aboard the ship of one Alonso Delgado, on his way to Spain from Hispaniola on a ship whose cargo included pearls from Cubagua. After a forced landing on the island of Faial in the Azores, he transferred his goods to a Portuguese ship and sailed into the Portuguese port of Viana. Upon arrival, port officials seized all his cargo. When Delgado sued for the return of his goods in court, he won back nearly all of his possessions—but a tenth of his pearls remained with the port officials. Delgado lodged a complaint with the Spanish ambassador to Portugal, who then relayed the incident to Charles V, who demanded that the pearls be returned to Delgado, employing language that explicitly stated that the wrong to the individual was a wrong perpetrated against the crown and its control of the Indies trade. It is unclear whether Delgado received his pearls. In these early decades of overseas imperial administration, however, the success of laws governing the management of overseas wealth depended as much upon individuals' assessment of their utility as official enforcement. The dialogue between individual imperative and imperial directive was not entirely antagonistic but rather often mutually reinforcing, with privately assessed value intersecting with imperially dictated approaches to wealth management. The experiences of both Algaba and Delgado attest to how possession could challenge and legitimatize formal claims to jurisdiction.[29]

Another glimpse of the interplay between private approaches to wealth management and the nascent imperial regulatory infrastructure is offered by the case of Hispaniola resident Antonio Meléndez. In 1526, at the height of Cubagua's pearl boom, Meléndez sent pearls from the West Indies to his wife in Spain via a cleric and friend. When the ship on which the cleric was traveling docked in Lisbon, the cleric disembarked with the pearls, whereupon Portuguese port authorities promptly seized them, claiming that he had lost the right to keep them by carrying them into foreign territory. In an attempt

28. AGI, IG: 420, legajo 9, fols. 24v–26v (May 23, 1522).

29. AGI, IG: 420, legajo 9, fols. 24v–26v (May 23, 1522), legajo 10, fols. 316v–317r (Apr. 28, 1526), IG: 423, legajo 10, fols. 286r–286v (Sept. 19, 1539) (". . . y porque desto nro. subditos reçiben daño y es en perjuyzio del trato de nras yndias porque como sabeis por el asiento q tenemos hecho con el Serenisimo rey nro. hermano no se puede llevar dezima alguna a nros subtidos asi de perlas como de otra cosa ninguna . . ."), legajo 19, fols. 286r–286v (Feb. 2, 1539), IG: 1092, no. 255 (July 28, 1540).

to regain the jewels, the intended recipient of the pearls, Inez de la Fuentes, wrote directly to the crown. Charles V in turn wrote to king João III of Portugal and asked him to restore the pearls. By this time, the pearls had made their way into the possession of a resident of Lisbon, who presumably had bought them from an enterprising port official. Individuals could easily bypass rules that were not yet hard and fast; defending his decision to carry the pearls off the ship, the cleric claimed his only crime was ignorance of the "law and custom" of Portugal. Whether or not the cleric knew the rules, it seems likely that he carried the pearls off the boat hoping to sell one or two on the Lisbon market and to keep the profit as payment for serving as a courier.[30]

Nor was it only Europeans who put pearls to private uses: in spite of stringent measures intended to control divers' movements in the settlements and their contact with pearls, they frequently managed to keep many for themselves. As a result, Charles V issued a decree in 1527 detailing punishments for slaves who absconded with pearls. Later in the century, slaves were permitted to purchase their freedom, but only by paying with gold, not with pearls—presumably because pearls were too easy to come by.[31]

The crown issued regular measures intended to cut down on the number of pearls that disappeared from official sight as soon as they were pried from the oysters that produced them. The attention the crown gave to these failures of accounting suggests a deep concern with the proliferation and promiscuous circulation of the jewel. If only residents would store pearls properly (in iron chests with three keys specified by the crown) and send the court the requested varietals of pearls, the Casa de Contratación could keep track of them, and the crown could rest assured that proper oversight of this resource prevailed. But these mechanisms did little to achieve their intended purpose. The series of royal decrees invoking the power of storage protocols, official pearl evaluators, and proper counting houses and warehouses mark the at-

30. AGI, IG: 420, legajo 10, fols. 319r–319v (Apr. 29, 1526).

31. The decree specified that no free person, Indian, or slave was to leave the island of Cubagua with any undeclared pearls. First-time offenders, if Indian or African slaves, were to be given one hundred lashes in public; if second-time offenders, they were to have both ears cut off and be expelled from the islands. A free person caught smuggling pearls was to forfeit the jewels and pay the town council a fine of twenty thousand maravedis. See RBM, Ordenanza, II/2892, fols. 143r–153v (Dec. 13, 1527). This royal edict also prohibited the drilling of pearls on the island. For slaves' buying their freedom with gold, see Report by Pedro Luys de Vargas y el tesorero Balthasar Perez Bernal, n.d., AGI, IG: 1805. IG: 1805 corresponds largely to ship registers; randomly included in this legajo are several separate reports (with a range of dates or undated) on the pearl fisheries.

tempt to hold some beachhead of royal authority against the relentless tide of actual practices. In a world of rapidly evolving laws and customs, individuals acted independently in their assessments of risks and rewards. They worried about government response only if necessary.[32]

This type of independently determined action involving pearls characterized their circulation at court as well as on the high seas and in bustling harbor towns. Throughout the 1520s, jewelers employed by the royal household bought pearls from individual merchants; female members of the royal households of Spain and Portugal arranged pearl purchases directly from one another; agents of the Portuguese crown bought Caribbean pearls in Seville. In spite of the quantity of pearls (or perhaps because of it: it was very easy to remove a single pearl, or handful of pearls, from a large pile of them, their absence barely detectable yet their new owner enriched) and royal efforts to count and tax the jewel, the flow of pearls remained unpredictable and difficult to track.[33]

Spanish attempts to draw the Pearl Coast, its products and inhabitants, into an imperial fiscal and administrative orbit would require a new approach to the region's resources. However, officials first tried to institute familiar mechanisms for managing wealth. For example, the introduction of the quinto into the governance of Pearl Coast wealth reflected familiar practices such as those laid out in the Siete Partidas, but it fell short in revealing ways. Pearls posed particular accounting problems. The crown attempted—and largely failed—to fiscalize this irregular jewel by treating it as bullion and seeking to impose the weight-based tax of a fifth of production, the quinto. The unit into which pearls were gathered, the marco, was ill suited to capturing the worth of any particular pearl or batch of pearls. The marco was the same weight-based measure used to assess silver bars, but pearls bore little resemblance to precious metals. First, they were very small. Many contemporary sources, Gonzalo Fernández de Oviedo y Valdés among them, described Cubaguan pearls as tiny, from two to five carats (with five carats equivalent to one gram). Second, pearls exist in tremendous natural variety, and the worth of any particular specimen reflects its shape, luster, and color in addition to

32. On the need for a customs house and a chest with three keys in which to store pearls, see *CC*, I, 177 (Oct. 15, 1532).

33. For pearl purchases by a Portuguese factor in Seville, see ANTT/CC, Parte 1, maço (mç.) 31, no. 79 (Oct. 29, 1524). Portugal's Queen Isabel authorized payment for pearls purchased from the marquess of Dénia, ANTT/CC, Parte 1, mç. 32, no. 48 (May 29, 1525), no. 2 (Oct. 3, 1525).

its size. A weight-based measure failed to account for the quality of any given pearl; it reflected ideas about the nature of wealth born of experience with gold and silver rather than an organic maritime product.[34] Furthermore, the tax was easy to avoid at sea or on land by skimming the best pearls off the top of the harvest before the quinto was assessed. The private, hidden nature of diving as well as pearls' small size and immediate accessibility (they did not need to be altered in order to be rendered valuable) made them a very difficult commodity to supervise. At sea and on land, inhabitants of all origins traded pearls for sundry items. Merchants committed fraud by sending unregistered shipments back to European markets alongside registered ones. The regular arrival of pirates and foreign corsairs, who called on the fisheries to do welcome or unwelcome business at predictable intervals throughout the sixteenth century, further contributed to Caribbean pearls' untaxed circulation. Finally, even if the pearl quinto had been assessed without fraud of any sort, which was highly unlikely, the quinto represented at its most ambitious and frictionless just 20 percent of the pearl harvest. Thus, at least 80 percent of the pearls harvested from the Caribbean oyster beds moved through private channels into markets on both sides of the Atlantic and beyond.[35]

34. The marco was a common measure for silver bars based on the mark of Cologne. For a discussion of pearls' physical qualities and assessments of their worth, see, for example, Neil H. Landman, Paula M. Mikkelsen, and Rudiger Bieler, eds., *Pearls: A Natural History* (New York, 2001). For a classic older work, see George Frederick Kunz and Charles Hugh Stevenson, *The Book of the Pearl: The History, Art, Science, and Industry of the Queen of Gems* (New York, 1908). On the size of Pearl Coast pearls, see Fernández de Oviedo, *Historia general y natural*, ed. Tudela Bueso, II, 204.

35. For early piracy on Cubagua, see Otte, *Las perlas del Caribe*, 80-81. The *Cedularios* he compiled of documents pertaining to the Pearl Coast's early years are also littered with references to corsairs and fears of pirate attacks. The presence of Spain's imperial rivals in the pearl fisheries shaped the circulation of people as well as the flow of pearls. For residents of Cabo de la Vela (in present-day Colombia) buying black slaves from two men who had ejected French corsairs from the fisheries (and for royal concern about the profits from their sale), see "Real Cédula," Sept. 21, 1546, AGI, AC: 1, legajo 1, fol. 111r. In the 1550s, the Spanish crown banned residents of Margarita from buying Brazilian Indians from Portuguese merchants. See Richard Konetzke, *Colección de documentos para la historia de la formación social de Hispanoamérica, 1493-1810*, I *(1493-1592)* (Madrid, 1953), 297 (Dec. 17, 1551), 339 (Sept. 21, 1556). Another sign that the circulation of pearls was related to the presence of non-Spanish rivals in the fisheries is the Council of the Indies' decision to reward the treasurer of Cabo de la Vela with sixty marcos of pearls for his successful defense of the settlement from French predators; see "Sumario de Consulta del Consejo de Indias," post-1550, AGI, IG: 737, no. 63.

Figure 5. Quentin Metsys, The Moneylender and His Wife. *1514.*
Oil on wood, 70.5 × 67 cm. Musée du Louvre, Paris, France.
© RMN-Grand Palais / Art Resource, N.Y.

Where did the pearls that traveled along independent paths end up? Who
were the people and what were the practices that facilitated their movement
from hand to hand? The picture of pearls sitting on a small black cloth in the
1514 painting by Quentin Metsys, *The Moneylender and His Wife,* is sugges-
tive of the way a pearl, or pearls, functioned as currency and how pearls could
blend unremarkably with similar specimens once sold (Figure 5, Plate 4).
While the moneylender and his wife carefully weigh and separate the assorted coins lying on the table in a jumble, the pearls sit apart. They are part

of the panorama of liquid wealth from which the couple makes their living, but they cannot be weighed and categorized like the coins. Resting invitingly on what appears to be a small black cushion, their provenance and future remain a mystery. The pearls' simple beauty reveals nothing about their origin. There is no hint of what purpose they might be put to in the future: they do not seem to have been drilled for use in jewels. The pearls simply lie in wait for the infinite possible fantasies and paths that potential consumers may project upon them.

In the hands of monarchs, pearls functioned to further imperial goals through diplomatic alliances and large-scale financial transactions. During his nearly forty-year reign, Charles V made liberal political use of the jewel, granting large numbers of pearls to trusted advisers or potential dynastic allies. In 1518, the king granted the wife of a courtier that year's entire royal pearl allotment. On numerous occasions throughout the early 1520s, he promised his sister Leonor, the wife of King Manuel of Portugal, all the pearls from the Indies, perhaps laying the groundwork for his own 1526 marriage with Isabel of Portugal. It is no wonder that pearls figured prominently in the emperor's political negotiations: over the course of his reign, Charles V received a total of fifteen thousand marcos of pearls—34.5 million pearls (nearly eight thousand pounds)—two-thirds of them from the pearl fisheries along the Pearl Coast and the remainder from pearl-fishing ventures along the South American coast and in Panama.[36]

The king further influenced the distribution of American pearls across global markets through his use of administrative concessions that tied non-Spanish merchants to the wealth of the Pearl Coast. German merchants, jewelers, and bankers figured prominently in the Caribbean fisheries' early years thanks to the particular diplomatic alliances that the Spanish crown pursued in the name of securing powerful European supporters. The king's willingness to grant the Welser family administrative control of Venezuela from 1528 to 1556, the height of the fisheries' production boom (a concession that recognized the Welsers' support of his successful bid for the title of Holy Roman emperor), reflected the influence of European concerns on the initial administrative approach to the New World. The Welsers were also crucial in

36. For Charles V's sending all pearls to Isabel of Portugal, see AGI, IG: 420, legajo 9, fols. 40r–40v (Nov. 11, 1522). Otte, *Las perlas del Caribe,* also discusses these early *mercedes* (or royal grants) of pearls on 57–58, in addition to the total number of pearls received during Charles V's rule.

the development of the slave trade in the region: they solidified their commercial ties to the Pearl Coast when Charles V granted them the slave trade asiento (or contract) in 1528.[37]

Welser-affiliated merchants as well as the factors of other German and Flemish commercial houses such as the Fuggers and Herwarts also became major distributors of pearls from the Pearl Coast beginning in the 1520s, placing pearls at the heart of the networks of resource distribution that launched the Atlantic imperial economy and spanned the global Iberian world. Representatives of the Herwart family and Seville-based merchant Lazarus Nürnberger were charged with receiving all pearls delivered to Seville from Cubagua and seeing them safely to the Casa de Contratación. Nürnberger worked as a factor for the Hirschvogel firm in India in 1517 and, as noted earlier, sold pearls from both the East and West Indies to German and Turkish clients. These men became Seville's principal pearl merchants for the duration of Charles's reign.[38] By drawing these northern European merchants into the trade in New World pearls, Charles V set in motion the globalization of the trade in one of the Spanish crown's flagship Atlantic imports, positioning the Americas in global context from their earliest post-Columbus days.[39]

37. For the circumstances of Charles I's ascension to the throne, see J. H. Elliott, *Empires of the Atlantic World: Britain and Spain in America, 1492–1830* (New Haven, Conn., 2006), 120–122. The Welsers' commercial connections facilitated the important German involvement in the Atlantic pearl trade in the sixteenth century. For more on the Welsers, see Alberto Armani, *La genesi dell'Eurocolonialismo: Carlo V e i Welser* (Genoa, 1985). On Charles I's Roman imperial ambitions, see David A. Lupher, *Romans in a New World: Classical Models in Sixteenth-Century Spanish America* (Ann Arbor, Mich., 2003), 45.

38. Between sugar and slavery, these German merchants played a critical role in the development of the two trades that would come to define the Atlantic world. That pearls were present—and highly profitable—in these earliest post-encounter decades is largely forgotten. On the Fugger family, see Mark Häberlein, *The Fuggers of Augsburg: Pursuing Wealth and Honor in Renaissance Germany* (Charlottesville, Va., 2012); and Hermann Kellenbenz, *Los Fugger en España y Portugal hasta 1560* (Castilla y León, 2000), 497–498.

39. Many of the most prominent German jewel merchant families (the Welsers and the Herwarts among them) played a large role in loaning money to the Portuguese crown and controlling a variety of the most lucrative commodity trades to emerge from Portugal's Asian voyages, in particular the spice trade and, later, the jewelry and pearl trade. The Herwart family from Augsburg were major players in Lisbon's pearl and jewel market from the late fifteenth century onward, with an important *feitoria* (trading factory) in Antwerp, which dealt in pearls from both Portugal and Spain. On German and Flemish communities in Portugal, see Walter Grosshaupt, "Commercial relations between Portu-

The movements and uses of pearls, then, in these earliest years of Atlantic empire reveal the numerous imperatives shaping patterns of transoceanic commerce and administration in the initial decades of the sixteenth century. Produced by an unfamiliar habitat, harvested by indigenous Americans and, increasingly, Africans, and moved throughout global markets by Europeans of various provenances, pearls illuminate the myriad small- and large-scale interests molding the contours of this New World and the infrastructure intended to govern it.

Aware of the failings of the quinto as a taxation mechanism, royal administrators turned to the nuances of language to counteract its inefficiencies, introducing elaborate categories in which to place pearls depending on their perceived quality. The taxonomy of pearls was from its inception intimately tied to the administration of imperial wealth and stands as a striking example of language intervening to add precision and efficacy to power structures. By the 1520s, these terms for pearls aimed to better capture the inherent variety of the natural jewel and the resulting profound variation in any individual specimen's perceived worth. Intended to separate pearls into useful subcategories within the marco, the descriptors in circulation (there were at least twenty-one different qualitative classifications in use during the decade) could capture a pearl's form or its function. A *perla barrueca* (baroque pearl) was a bulbous, irregular pearl; a *perla chata,* a flat pearl; an *asiento* pearl was flat on one side and round on the other. One of the chief determinants of a pearl's worth was its *oriente,* or orient, referring to a pearl's general luster and reflecting the jewel's historic association with the Far East. These categories changed over time and in part reflected the common uses to which pearls were put. The employment of this subjective, evaluative language reflected the mixture of fantasy and reality informing the regulatory infrastructure intended to govern the New World's products and people. On the one hand, the terms assigned to the Pearl Coast and the people who lived and labored there effaced realities on the ground, emphasizing the product (pearls) over the processes that produced them. On the other hand, the ever-changing range of words employed to describe the pearls themselves reflected the crown's fiscal aims (the descriptive categories were intended to

gal and the Merchants of Augsburg and Nuremberg," in Jean Aubin, *La decouverte, le Portugal et l'Europe: Actes du colloque, Paris les 26, 27, et 28 mai 1988* (Paris, 1990), 362–383; and Eddy Stols, "Os mercadores flamengos em Portugal e no Brasil antes das conquistas holandesas," *Anais de história,* V (1973), 9–54. On Nürnberger's pearl dealings, see Otte, *Las perlas del Caribe,* 61, 74–75.

facilitate taxation of pearls) but also reflected the uses to which people put pearls in the fisheries and beyond.[40]

If the vocabulary for pearls was rich and nuanced, the opposite was true of the language to describe the settlements and their inhabitants. The simple pearl-centered descriptors belied the rough-and-ready, hodge-podge, and violent nature of the island settlements, which relied on the labor of a variety of people employed in different capacities. The diversity of the region's inhabitants and European reliance on indigenous partners and Europe alike for necessary food and supplies was elided by regional nomenclatures that suggested that pearls were the sole purpose of the settlements and their inhabitants. This perception was both true and misleading. Not only was the region called the Pearl Coast, or the Seed Pearl Coast, the region's residents were also defined by their involvement with the pearl fisheries. Owners of oyster boats were called *señores de canoas,* or "lords of canoes," "canoes" being the term for the (increasingly large) vessels used to arrive at the oyster banks. Indian and later African laborers were also frequently referred to as *buzos de la pesquerias de perlas,* or "pearl fishery divers." Although residents complained to the crown about the stench of large piles of rotting oysters in the pearl-fishing settlements, references to oysters were conspicuously absent elsewhere.[41] The phrases used to describe the enslaved divers suggested that they did not fish for oysters but for pearls themselves: they were known as *esclavos de perlas, or* "pearl slaves"; *negros de concha,* or "conch blacks"; or *sacadores de perlas,* "pearl extractors." Only the terms for the settlements themselves —*granjerías* (from *granja,* farm)— evoked general cultivation rather than the extraction of pearls.[42]

40. For a discussion of categories in circulation in the 1520s and the changing descriptive vocabulary for pearls over the next several centuries, see also Otte, *Las perlas del Caribe,* chap. 1, esp. 36–41. He notes that all attempts to categorize pearls according to these descriptors were ultimately unsuccessful.

41. According to Gonzalo Fernández de Oviedo, there were "so many oysters that the excess becomes an annoyance and they are no longer prized as food"; see Fernández de Oviedo, *Natural History of the West Indies,* ed. and trans. Sterling A. Stoudemire (Chapel Hill, N.C., 1959), 115–116.

42. It does not seem that the term *negro* was also assigned to indigenous divers, as they are frequently identified as "indios." The origin of the term "conch blacks" (in circulation at the end of the sixteenth century) is uncertain; it might have reflected slaves' use of conch shells to collect pearls that they removed from oysters. Another possible source for the term comes from an illustration of a conch shell in the "Histoire naturelle des Indes," known as the Drake Manuscript (circa 1590), in which the anonymous author asserts that

Just as the predominance of "pearls" in the toponymy of the region elided the range of needs and activities of the residents, the vocabulary of administrative structure imposed an imaginary order on the chaos of flux and impermanence that characterized the island. As the population of Cubagua grew, its changing legal status brought with it the development of municipal organization, with mayors, councils, and deputies all structured and governed by Spanish law. Granting the island's settlement of Nueva Cádiz the title of *villa* (town) in 1526 and *ciudad* (city) in 1528 revealed royal and residential aspirations for the incorporation of Cubagua into a European-based fabric of empire and carried powerful and long-standing associations with paradigms of Spanish civic and governmental control. However, the imperatives of local governance proved more influential on both regional patterns and crown approaches to the management of Cubagua and the entire Pearl Coast. As these formal Spanish terms bestowed notions of civic incorporation upon these pearl-fishing settlements, the reality of those who lived and labored in them stood in stark contrast to the order that the familiar terms implied. In fact, they were new settlements with new types of relationships being forged in them, relationships among subjects and between subjects and the environment.[43]

Pearls' abundance and the crown's reliance on them for all sorts of purposes made manifest early on the difficulties of managing the jewel, posed primarily by their range in quality and kind. The qualitative language for pearl assessment proved critical to officials back in Spain charged with managing the jewel's distribution. Because of the subjective nature of these categories (one man's baroque pearl might be another man's asiento pearl; the gem's irregular shape assessed differently), pearls also served as a reminder of the confounding independence of individual assessments of worth. Fiscalizing pearls depended upon the judgment of those subjects charged with assessing them, which was highly variable and beyond control.

----

a hair "like human hair" was found and used by black divers to alleviate the pain in their eardrums caused by diving (see also Figure 7, in Chapter 3, below). Or the term might have reflected the use of *concha* to mean generally "shell," thus loosely describing the slaves' involvement with oysters. See also AGI, IG: 1805, fol. 2 (circa 1590).

43. For Cubagua's shifting legal and administrative landscape, see Perri, "'Ruined and Lost,'" *Environment and History*, XV (2009), 136; and Domínguez Compañy, "Municipal Organization," *Americas*, XXI, no. 1 (July 1964), 58–68. Otte also discusses the changing legal status of Cubagua in *Las perlas del Caribe,* 87. For the significance of the terms *villa* and *ciudad,* see Richard L. Kagan, *Urban Images of the Hispanic World, 1493–1793* (New Haven, Conn., 2000).

The frustration caused by this reliance on individual acumen is evident in the king's negotiations about pearls with customs officials in the Casa de Contratación. In 1525, 416 undrilled pearls that the Casa officials had sent to the court needed to be weighed again upon arrival: the king chastised officials of the Casa for sending him pearls from Seville without "seeing, counting, and weighing them." Six months later, the king again ordered the Casa to auction all gold and silver arrived from the Indies and to sell all pearls except for 15 marcos "of the largest barrueca pearls and of all types," which he needed at court. Why he needed them is unclear, but it is noteworthy that he wanted these irregular specimens for a particular use. In November, he ordered the sale of 170 marcos of pearls and requested that a particularly large pearl from Cubagua be sent to the court. Every royal request or rebuke involving pearls pointed to the essential role played by subjects' independent judgment in their assessment of the jewel.[44]

Employing the various terms in circulation to describe pearls of distinct qualities, Charles V and customs officials in Seville often differed over how to evaluate and dispose of the pearls delivered from the Pearl Coast. Whereas unusual or particularly valuable specimens were usually sent to the court for incorporation into the royal wardrobe, the king also used pearls as a source of cash, selling large numbers of them to finance his mounting military campaigns throughout Europe. These latter appropriations forced the king to confront the adverse effects of rising pearl harvests on their price as well as the inadequacies of the existing administrative bureaucracy charged with channeling pearls between the monarchy's expanding realms. Presumably motivated by concerns about the price of pearls, in 1525 Charles V ordered that Casa officials maintain absolute secrecy about the arrival of pearls from the Indies. No one was to see them, and, if possible, their mere presence in the Casa was to be kept a secret until the king himself gave the order. After the monarch asked officials what pearls were selling for, Casa officials warned the king that a surfeit of pearls had brought the price down, and a marco of pearls was selling for just thirteen *ducados* (or ducats, each worth 375 maravedis). In need of cash, Charles V nonetheless ordered the bulk of the shipment sold and the proceeds sent to court—along with particular

44. For additional documents concerning the handling and sale of pearls in Casa custody, see AGI, IG: 1961, legajo 3, fols. 61v–63r (Sept. 13, 1533), IG: 420, legajo 10, fols. 263v–264r (Feb. 10, 1526). These instances are also discussed in Otte, *Las perlas del Caribe,* 58–59.

types of pearls (large ones and those with varied shapes) that he intended for personal use.[45]

In 1527 — Cubagua's peak year of production, with a quinto of nearly 1,300 marcos — the king again drew on pearls to finance the costs of his expanding empire and in his haste bypassed the directives of his own administrators. Six ships bearing 505 marcos of pearls arrived in Seville at the end of that summer, and the impending glut of pearls threatened to bring their price down. The king's counselors advised him to hold off on the sale, but the monarch could not afford to wait: he ordered that the pearls be sold at the highest prices possible "because due to the need we have here we cannot wait any longer as you say." Ignoring the advice of his administrators, the king turned directly to a private merchant to dispose of the jewels. The Casa learned that the king had arranged for the sale of the pearls to Burgos merchant Cristobal de Haro, at 10.5 ducados per marco, for which de Haro paid in specie directly to the court.[46]

The single-minded focus on the pursuit of pearls in the fisheries belied the complexity that characterized the settlements, their inhabitants, and the multiple uses — in the Caribbean and far beyond — to which the jewel was put. The patterns of pearl circulation (highly variable, determined privately, and difficult to control) reveal the central element of the political economy of the jewel to have been independent judgment. It was independent judgment that determined not only the nature of the pearl in question (its type and worth) but also the risks and rewards involved in moving, selling, or buying the pearl. The detailed and shifting qualitative vocabulary for describing pearls in the pearl fisheries in these early decades found an echo in the similarly diverse judgments that individuals made when deciding how best to use the pearl to further their own aims.

Technology and Ecology in the Pearl Fisheries

The pearl bonanza carried many costs, some that became immediately visible and some that took decades of dialogue between Pearl Coast residents and the crown to come to light. It was not until the 1520s that the lessons of the pearl fisheries began to become clear, as the haphazard settlement of the

45. This episode is discussed in Otte, *Las perlas del Caribe,* 58–59.

46. AGI, IG: 421, legajo 12, fol. 208 (Oct. 22, 1527). The king needed pearls in anticipation of his military expedition in Rome and of armed conflicts with France and England; see Otte, *Las perlas del Caribe,* 60.

early years gave way to a brutal, if lucrative, regime of natural and human resource exploitation and a host of related problems of governance. Over time, the region's astonishing pearl hauls laid bare the contingent components of wealth creation in the New World, such as the role of ecology and expertise in the cultivation and assessment of this natural resource. New, site-specific approaches to the management of natural and human resources resulted from this maelstrom of maritime destruction and terrestrial transformation, although they developed after much trial and error. Even as news of the extraordinary conquests in Mexico in the 1520s (and, later, in the 1530s, in Peru) reached Spain, the American pearls flowing throughout Caribbean markets and into Seville served to remind people of the wealth being produced along the Pearl Coast. Indeed, the sharpest price inflation under Charles V occurred during the fisheries' heyday of the 1520s, and it is hard to imagine that observers of Seville's dockside hustle and bustle did not associate the proliferation of these iridescent gems with the perplexingly painful consequences of this newfound, American wealth.[47]

The numbers of oysters it took to produce the record pearl hauls of the 1520s are difficult to comprehend (see Figure 6). Later arrivals to the Caribbean noticed the lack of birdsong owing to deforestation, but equally stunning, if less immediately obvious, was the alteration of the submarine ecosystem of this corner of the Americas. The estimates of marine biologists who have studied the Venezuelan fisheries suggest that on average a single pearl was found for every ten oysters opened. Using these estimates as a guide, it would have taken an annual harvest of approximately 40 million oysters during the Cubaguan fisheries' most lucrative decades to produce the pearls reported in official tax records. These numbers indicate an estimated harvest of 1.2 billion oysters in fewer than three decades.[48]

47. On prices under Charles V, see J. H. Elliott, "The Decline of Spain," in Elliott, *Spain and Its World, 1500–1700: Selected Essays* (New Haven, Conn., 1989), 217–240, esp. 235.

48. For more on the ecological transformations along the Pearl Coast, see Molly A. Warsh, "A Political Ecology in the Early Spanish Caribbean," *William and Mary Quarterly*, 3d Ser., LXXI (2014), 517–548. For a scientific consideration of these early pearl harvests and their effects on the oyster population, see Landman, Mikkelsen, and Bieler, eds., *Pearls*, 17, 21. Marine biologist Aldemaro Romero is more conservative in his estimates (assuming the highest possible productivity and lowest number of oysters extracted per pearl), but he also comes up with an estimated harvest of more than a billion oysters in less than thirty years; see Romero, "Death and Taxes: The Case of the Depletion of the Pearl Oyster Beds in Sixteenth-Century Venezuela," *Conservation Biology*, XVII, no. 4

Figure 6. Modern Middens (shell mounds), Isla de Coche, Venezuela.
Photograph by Molly A. Warsh

The ecological consequences of these immense oyster harvests were not immediately visible to royal officials, but the corresponding depression of pearl prices as the result of excessive pearl availability drew people's attention, as did the continual complaints about abuses of all sorts in the fisheries. Perhaps the most dramatic royal failure to impose order on the settlements came in the form of its controversial and futile sponsorship of technology intended to eliminate the need for the labor force that was causing such problems. The Spanish crown backed various oyster-harvesting devices over the course of the sixteenth century, only to meet with repeated failure on the Pearl Coast. In their rejection of these technological intrusions, fishery residents

(August 2003), 1013–1023, esp. 1019; as well as Romero, Susanna Chilbert, and M. G. Eisenhart, "Cubagua's Pearl-Oyster Beds: The First Depletion of a Natural Resource Caused by Europeans in the American Continent," *Journal of Political Ecology*, VI (1999), 57–78. See also Clyde L. MacKenzie, Jr., Luis Troccoli, and Luis B. León, "History of the Atlantic Pearl-Oyster, *Pinctata imbricata*, Industry in Venezuela and Colombia, with Biological and Ecological Observations," *Marine Fisheries Review*, LXV (2003), 1–20.

put forth an understanding of the maritime realm as a shared commons where resource control could be established through demonstrated expertise.

The first extant license for mechanized pearl fishing dates to 1520, granted to one Juan de Cárdenas, a pilot and resident of Seville. The terms of his agreement with the crown reflect the lingering influence of ideas about pearls as booty and treasure—wealth to be taxed, rather than cultivated—that informed the royal approach. The challenges that would prompt later mechanical proposals once the full social and environmental costs of the pearl fisheries' operation became clear (deadly and heavily criticized labor regimes, unorthodox on-island dynamics, and reduced oyster hauls) were not yet apparent. Cárdenas's license permitted him to arm two caravels (sailing ships) to travel to the coast of Paria (present-day Venezuela) in search of various types of material wealth: gold, silver, precious stones, and slaves as well as pearls. Although the license identifies Coche and Cubagua by name and alludes to rumors of pearl wealth in the vicinity, neither island had emerged as a clear center of pearl-fishing operations.[49]

Several aspects of Cárdenas's contract suggest that crown hopes for the region already reflected Pearl Coast realities. Cárdenas was explicitly instructed to conduct peaceful trade with the area's native inhabitants in exchange for goods. This directive spoke to rising concerns about Spanish treatment of the New World's indigenous inhabitants and the harmful persistence of violent rescate practices. Indeed, the autonomy of the Pearl Coast's indigenous residents was recognized in the crown's description of "the people who come to fish for pearls." Already, it appears that part of the appeal of Cárdenas's device was its promise to facilitate independent Spanish action by introducing technology, allowing oyster harvesting to proceed without a reliance on these autonomous indigenous pearl harvesters. Cárdenas claimed to have "had word" of pearls that could be found in depths beyond the reach of human divers—his technology would deliver the otherwise inaccessible riches of these waters. Cárdenas's invention (which his contract described only generally as a "certain device with which you're confident you will be able to retrieve" pearls) disappeared from the historical record; it could not compete

49. "Licencia a Juan de Cárdenas para armar carabelas," 1520, AGI, IG: 420, legajo 8, fols. 253v–255r. Cárdenas received his patent even before the 1524 establishment of the Council of the Indies, the official body intended to oversee all government activity in the Americas. For a discussion of Castile's patent practices in the sixteenth century, see Nicolás García Tapia, *Técnica y poder en Castilla durante los siglos XVI y XVII* (Salamanca, Spain, 1989), chap. 9.

in the face of the demographic transformations that swept the pearl fisheries in the years immediately following his proposal.[50]

In their rejection of the similar proposals that followed Cárdenas's, fishery inhabitants pointed not only to their own experience but also to that of indigenous and African divers in their defense of the unique approach to the management of the area's human and natural resources. Even amid the immense oyster harvests of the fisheries' first decades of operation, Spaniards realized they were dealing with a renewable, living resource and that oyster banks recovered when they were left alone for a time.[51] Residents' careful attention to their sustaining habitat surfaced in the 1529 debates over a dredge proposed by an Italian resident in Seville named Luis de Lampiñan. As soon as Lampiñan arrived on the Pearl Coast, Cubaguan residents protested his intervention, and just nine months after the original grant the king responded to their petition by revising the depths at which Lampiñan could operate his dredges. Realizing that the new depth restrictions would limit his potential profits, Lampiñan fought back, taking his case to the Audiencia de Santo Domingo in late January 1529. In their opposition to Lampiñan's device, Pearl Coast inhabitants offered their own understandings of how the region's marine ecosystem functioned in relationship to circum-Caribbean patterns of commerce and labor. While the crown continued to turn to non-Spanish concessionaires who promised mechanical solutions to maritime wealth exploitation, free residents of the fisheries advocated for their own understandings of resource husbandry.[52]

Lampiñan's case caught the Spanish crown at a crossroads, torn between the demands and interests of its European territories and subjects and the challenges of a far less familiar New World empire. On the one hand, the

50. "Licencia a Juan de Cárdenas para armar carabelas," 1520, AGI, IG: 420, legajo 8, fols. 253v–255r (quotations); Manuel Luengo Muñoz, "Inventos para acrecentar la obtención de perlas en América, durante el siglo XVI," *Anuario de estudios Americanos*, IX (1952), 55.

51. As Antonio Barrera-Osorio has argued, inhabitants of the pearl fisheries were "administrators" of nature as well as consumers of its products, and this active engagement shaped their relationship with a distant crown. See Barrera-Osorio, *Experiencing Nature*, chap. 3, esp. 73–74 (quotation on 74). He makes the point that even unsuccessful experiments provided the crown with useful knowledge about the nature of the New World and helped to develop empirical procedures for evaluating new proposals.

52. For negotiations between Luis de Lampiñan and the Spanish crown, see *CC*, I, 50–52 (Jan. 10, 1528), 63–64 (Apr. 4, 1528), 64–65 (Apr. 4, 1528), 81–83 (Sept. 12, 1528), 90 (Sept. 19, 1528), 97 (Jan. 22, 1529), 99–101 (Feb. 7, 1529).

crown's concession to Lampiñan reflected its established willingness to engage non-Spaniards in the exercise of empire—from contracting out the administration of new territories to granting individual merchant concessions. These contracts were themselves tools of empire, but they would not work as well in the crown's new Atlantic domains as they had in the Old World. The expertise of new subjects—even enslaved and indigenous ones—would prove to be a more powerful ordering principle in the fisheries.

Lampiñan was a minor noble with influence in a region at the center of Spain's Italian ambitions, and it is possible that the crown thought the royal grant to the Milanese nobleman (and his two Italian partners) would potentially build allegiance within powerful factions in Spain's ever-fragile Holy Roman imperial territories. Yet the terms of Lampiñan's contract also reflected the crown's growing desire to reclaim the prerogatives it had ceded in the early years of administering unfamiliar territories. Granted a six-year monopoly on fishing for pearls in the vicinity of Cubagua, Lampiñan promised to deliver a third of the haul to the crown. This was a higher proportion than the standard fifth and perhaps reflected an awareness of just how much wealth the fisheries could produce in light of the decade's pearl bonanzas. Nonetheless, the terms of his agreement adhered to a vision of crown prerogative based in the administration of metals rather than maritime wealth.[53]

In spite of these lingering European influences on Lampiñan's contract, the appeal of the Italian's invention undoubtedly reflected the realities of the pearl fisheries. The debates surrounding his dredge occurred at the apex of the settlements' most lucrative and destructive decade and in a moment of growing concern about both the depletion of the oyster banks and the toll of these profits on the pearl divers. Just a year before the crown granted Lampiñan's contract, Bartolomé de Las Casas began composing his *History of the Indies* in which he assailed the labor regime of the pearl fisheries. The fisheries had already become a symbol of New World mismanagement, and Lampiñan's device spoke directly to these concerns. Writing several decades later, royal chronicler Antonio de Herrera y Tordesillas noted that the Italian's dredge (which he described as so large it had to be "pulled by one or two caravels") was appealing because of its promise to retrieve "larger and

---

53. On Spanish politics in Italy, see Michael J. Levin, *Agents of Empire: Spanish Ambassadors in Sixteenth-Century Italy* (Ithaca, N.Y., 2005); Thomas James Dandelet and John A. Marino, eds., *Spain in Italy: Politics, Society, and Religion, 1500–1700* (Leiden, 2007); Stefano D'Amico, *Spanish Milan: A City within the Empire, 1535–1706* (New York, 2012).

more" pearls "without there being a need for Indians or slaves to dive to the bottom of the sea" to get them. The machine's successful introduction would spare the crown the headache of dealing with this controversial labor system without sacrificing pearl profits. In this context, the crown's desire to introduce mechanical devices into the fisheries cannot be interpreted as a reflection of uncertainty over how and where to harvest oysters, as had been the case with Cárdenas. Instead, Lampiñan's license reflected an attempt to address a problem in a profitable but problematic part of the empire.[54]

The uproar over Lampiñan's proposed dredge underscored how futile such attempts would be if they failed to consider local practice and knowledge. During the trial generated by Lampiñan's intrusion into their maritime domains, Spaniards parsed the political ecology of the region into its interdependent parts. The Spaniards who sought to discredit Lampiñan and his device carefully monitored the effects of tides, temperatures, and water currents on oyster reproduction and growth. Witnesses called to testify in the trial illuminated the relationships among different subjects and between these subjects and the environment from which they and the crown profited. Residents' responses indicate that Spanish inhabitants of the pearl fisheries, predatory and extractive though their practices were, also paid attention to maritime ecology even at the height of their oyster-harvesting frenzy.[55]

The case also revealed the autonomy of Cubagua within a Spanish Caribbean whose administration was increasingly consolidated on Hispaniola. In particular, the case highlights the tension between the mandate of the regional court—the Audiencia de Santo Domingo, located on Hispaniola—and the power and independence of the residents of Cubagua. Though Lampiñan concentrated his appeal efforts on Hispaniola, it was on Cubagua itself where the case was most fully discussed, overseen by the island's council and prominent residents. Distinct claims to authority, rooted in knowledge of place and particular practice, persisted within the changing geography of

54. Lampiñan's device was described by Antonio de Herrera [y Tordesillas], *Historia general de los hechos de los castellanos en las islas y tierrafirme del mar oceano*, ed. Mariano Cuesta Domingo (Madrid, 1991), II, 645–648 ("larger," 648). Luengo Múñoz also discusses Lampiñan's device in "Inventos," *Anuario de Estudios Americanos*, IX (1952), 56.

55. For the original transcript of the Lampiñan trial, see "Don Luis Lampiñan y consortes vecinos de la ciudad de Sevilla con la Justicia y vecinos en la Nueva Ciudad en cadiz en la Isla de Cubagua, sobre la forma en que aquel havia en hazer la pesqueria en perlas; en 2 piezas," 1530, AGI, Justicia: 7, no. 4. For an overview and partial transcript of the trial, see Enrique Otte, "El proceso del rastro de perlas de Luis de Lampiñán," *Boletín de la Academia Nacional de la Historia*, XLVII, no. 187 (July–September 1964), 386–406.

overseas imperial administration. The preeminence of local practice was in many ways a reassertion of customary law over imperial law, of tradition as much as innovation.[56]

As the trial unfolded, Spaniards familiar with pearl-fishing practices on the Pearl Coast justified their jurisdiction over a large swath of Caribbean waters through their demonstration of knowledge about the coast's land and seascapes—knowledge generated in large part by the labor of New World subjects. The witnesses made the case to the crown that free and unfree residents of the Pearl Coast were the region's essential administrators and that its productivity depended upon their practices, rather than some Italian interloper's. Spaniards did not point solely to indigenous wisdom to make their case; they bolstered their claims by citing their own experience on both sides of the Atlantic Ocean. All the men called to testify had been in the American pearl fisheries for some time, and many also referenced knowledge of dredges gained while working in Iberia.

Even as the Spaniards in their testimony invoked the European context to bolster their claims to authority, they emphasized to the crown that the pearl fisheries were a new setting that demanded innovation and the skills of new subjects. Indeed, the witnesses' attention to the region's marine ecology focused on the indigenous divers' critical role in exploiting and caring for the oyster banks. Only the divers could hear the noises the oysters made, Spaniards claimed, sounds likened to "hogs rooting for acorns"—likely the snapping shrimp or other marine life that flocked to the rich waters where pearl fishing took place. From the sonic landscapes of oyster reefs to the centrality of sea grass to oyster reproduction patterns, to the deleterious effects of raking the ocean floor and the care divers took to harvest only full-sized specimens, trial testimony revealed that Spaniards relied on divers' expertise. Spaniards' incorporation of indigenous knowledge was further demonstrated in witnesses' employment of the Taíno term *xaguey,* meaning the deep underwater depressions where good pearl-bearing oysters were found. The success of the pearl fisheries and the regional economy they sustained depended

---

56. For an overview of Spain's evolving New World administration, see Elliott, *Empires of the Atlantic World,* 120–127. On the enduring power of local law in Spain, see E. N. Van Kleffens, *Hispanic Law until the End of the Middle Ages: With a Note on the Validity after the Fifteenth Century of Medieval Hispanic Legislation in Spain, the Americas, Asia, and Africa* (Edinburgh, 1968), 256. Van Kleffens discusses the limitations of the attempts by Charles V and his successors to centralize administration and public law, emphasizing the endurance of Spanish "particularism."

upon skilled labor. The oyster habitat required careful, knowledgeable custodianship, as did the divers, who, Spaniards observed, needed rest days if
they were to be productive.[57]

When the trial's judges finally sent all testimony to the Council of the
Indies in Spain, they included a damning assessment of the proposed
dredge's potential impact on the region's political economy. Their statement linked pearl fishing and the pearl trade with regional commerce and
the wealth of the empire: "[The dredge] would destroy the said island, its
householders [veçinos] and residents, and the trade and fishing of pearls
would cease, which would cause great damages to his Majesty's revenue and
royal dues [derechos reales] and to the said householders, residents, and
traders on the said island, and not only to them, but also to those islands with
which they trade, because commerce and trade between them would cease."
In this explanation of their rejection of the Italian's dredge, Cubaguan residents identified themselves as the crucial administrators of the wealth of empire; his "Majestys revenue and royal dues" were inseparable from their own
locally determined practices.[58]

Throughout the trial, witnesses spoke to the proposed dredge's effects on

57. "Don Luis Lampiñan y consortes," 1530, AGI, Justicia: 7, no. 4, fol. 66. For a
lengthier discussion — and accompanying sound clip — of the noisy biodiversity of healthy
oyster banks, see Warsh, "A Political Ecology," *WMQ*, 3d Ser., LXXI (2014), esp. 535. An
extended description of oyster reproduction, its relationship to currents and depths, and
the dissemination of oyster spat is quoted in Otte, "El proceso del rastro perlas," *Boletín
de la Academia Nacional de la Historia*, XLVII, no. 187 (July–September 1964), 395, 401.
For the meaning of *xaguey*, see Manuel Alvar Ezquerra, *Vocabulario de indigenismos en
las Crónicas de Indias* (Madrid, 1997), 216. See also William F. Keegan and Lisabeth A.
Carlson, *Talking Taíno: Essays on Caribbean Natural History from a Native Perspective*
(Tuscaloosa, Ala., 2008).

58. For a clear transcription of this explication, see Otte, "El proceso del rastro perlas,"
Boletín de la Academia Nacional de la Historia, XLVII, no. 187 (July–September 1964),
386–406 (quotation on 405–406): "Sy el dicho rastro oviese de pescar e pescase en los
límites, mares y comarcas de la dicha ysla que por el dicho conçejo e vesinos della en el
dicho proçeso están espresados en an pescado e pescan e pueden pescar, que sería des-
truyr la dicha ysla y veçinos e avytantes en ella, y el dicho trato y pesquería de perlas
çesaría, de que vernía mucho daño a las rentas e derechos reales de su magestad e a los
dichos veçinos e moradores e contratantes en la dicha ysla, y no solamente a ellos, pero a
estas yslas que con ella contratan, porque çesaría el comerçio y contratación que con ella
tienen, por ser como es la dicha ysla la segunda destas yslas e de donde se a avydo e cada
día a y espera aver mucho provecho, e questo hera e es su paresçer, para que sobre todo
su magestad mande y provea y aclare lo que fuere servydo."

tax revenue as well as to its impact on the region's trade. Each witness was asked to confirm that "the interest and benefit that accrues to the crown from these realms if their villas and towns are inhabited, paying the taxes they owe to his majesty, are far greater than the profits *[provecho]* that would result from dredging in the said island and surrounding areas *[comarcas]*." The representatives of the councils of Santo Domingo and Salvaleón de Higüey on Hispaniola added their voices to the chorus of complaints about the device, stating that inhabitants of the surrounding region came to Cubagua to sell their food products in exchange for pearls. Their testimony was followed just days afterward by statements from residents of Cubagua and San Juan, all of whom asserted that their livelihoods depended on their commerce with Cubagua, a commerce that would cease if the islands were to be abandoned because of the introduction of the Italian's dredge.[59]

Although there were multiple claims for jurisdiction over the region's human and natural wealth, these regional opinions prevailed in their explanation of the region's political economy.[60] Cubagua residents successfully defeated the interloper. Charles V revoked his agreement with Luis de Lampiñan and went on to pass several protective measures that reflected the information generated by the Italian's case. In the Pearl Islands, the local *cabildo*, or council of governing men, were the most important arbiters in local mat-

59. See "Don Luis Lampiñan y consortes," 1530, AGI, Justicia: 7, no. 4, fol. 74; Otte, "El proceso del rastro perlas," *Boletín de la Academia Nacional de la Historia*, XLVII, no. 187 (July–September 1964), 386–406 (quotation on 398): "Yten sy saben que es mucho más el ynteresse e provecho que se sygue a la corona real de estos reynos que las dichas villas e pueblos estén pobladas, pagando como pagan los derechos a su magestad devidos, que el provecho que se puede seguir de rastrear en la dicha ysla e comarcas con los dichos rastros, e digan los testigos lo que çerca desto saben."

60. Jurisdiction on the Pearl Coast would remain divided for centuries, with ecclesiastical authority emanating from the mainland, judicial authority from Hispaniola, and administration from Seville. The role of the larger Antilles in the settlement of the Pearl Coast, combined with fierce indigenous resistance on the mainland, kept Cubagua and adjacent islands in the orbit of the Caribbean and Spain more than of Caracas for nearly two centuries; it was not until the late seventeenth century, when the Pearl Islands were at last incorporated in the Audiencia de Santa Fé, that the coast finally achieved greater administrative integration with the mainland, or Tierra Firme. On the split nature of different kinds of jurisdiction, see Manuel Luengo Muñoz, "Notícias sobre la fundación de la ciudad de Nuestra Señora Santa María de los Remedios del Cabo de la Vela," *Anuario de estudios Americanos*, VI (1949), 757–797. On the pearl islands' gradual integration with the mainland, see Perri, "'Ruined and Lost,'" *Environment and History*, XV (2009), 132–133, esp. 150.

ters. A number of laws aimed at protecting pearl divers addressed the depth
of dives and the maximum duration of shifts in the pearl canoes. Furthermore, in the 1530s, the crown passed a series of preventive bans intended to
protect the oyster banks. These included a system of rotation whereby different oyster banks were fished for a period of time and then left dormant;
pearl fishing was also prohibited in particular months, presumably to protect
breeding and young oysters during the rest of the year. The crown additionally prohibited the seizure of divers in the case of their owners' debt; their
labor was deemed too essential to the fisheries' operation.[61]

As pearl-fishing operations expanded along the coast of the mainland,
fishery residents' reliance on ever-larger boats manned by increasing numbers of enslaved divers prompted additional prohibitive legislation. In 1537,
Charles V tried to address the destruction of young oysters by banning the use
of big pearl-fishing boats (known as *canoas grandes* or *piraguas*), capable of
holding more than six divers. Addressing Cubaguan officials, the king urged
a return to the use of "canoes with a single oar" with smaller crews, since
the practice of using "big canoes" and catching "new and old oysters" indis-
criminately "has greatly diminished the oyster beds." Free and unfree residents of the Pearl Coast, rather than the crown, which only passed reactive
legislation, remained the imperfect custodians of the region's resources.[62]

61. For examples of early awareness of the depletion of oyster banks in the wake of
Lampiñan's trial, see *CC*, I, 218 (Dec. 30, 1532); *CC*, II, 94 (Sept. 5, 1537), 172 (Mar.
10, 1540). For more on the reproduction cycles of pearl-producing mollusks, see Elisabeth Strack, *Pearls* (Stuttgart, 2006), 96; MacKenzie, Troccoli, and León, "History of
the Atlantic Pearl-Oyster," *Marine Fisheries Review*, LXV (2003), 3. These seasonal pro-
scriptions might have been misguided in any event: the female pearl oyster sheds her eggs
when the water temperature is highest, but, when water temperatures do not fluctuate
dramatically, as is the case in the Caribbean, several breeding seasons may take place during one year. For regulations issued in the late 1520s, see Domínguez Compañy, "Municipal Organization," *Americas*, XXI, no. 1 (July 1964), 67–68. The success of Cubagua's
residents in defeating Lampiñan and the passage of laws in the wake of the trial suggests
that Spanish officials did, in fact, pay attention to knowledge being generated in the New
World. For an opposing characterization, see Alison Sandman, "Controlling Knowledge:
Navigation, Cartography, and Secrecy in the Early Modern Spanish Atlantic," in James
Delbourgo and Nicholas Dew, eds., *Science and Empire in the Atlantic World* (New York,
2008), 31–52. She emphasizes how cosmographers were not interested in local knowledge
earned through experience. In contrast, my findings echo Susan Scott Parrish's emphasis
in the same volume on the role of colonial subjects in knowledge production ("Diasporic
African Sources of Enlightenment Knowledge," 281–310).

62. See *CC*, II, 94 (Sept. 5, 1537).

In the meantime, the laborers at the heart of these negotiations over jurisdiction in the fisheries continued to endure exposure to extreme violence,
their bodies thrown overboard by canoe owners when the divers died in the
boat from exertion. Those pearl divers still in the water were then further en-
dangered by the sharks drawn to the jettisoned corpses. The crown became
aware of these practices and attempted to deter them by establishing fines for
such behavior in a 1538 decree. The fines suggest that Christianity served as a
somewhat useful distinction in the fisheries among enslaved or semi-enslaved
Indians and Africans, many of whom bore Christian names in addition to a
surname consisting of some ethnic identifier. Although this apparent conversion to Christianity did not protect them from the brutal labor of diving for
pearls, it might have afforded them a slightly more dignified death. The fine
for throwing "Christian" slaves overboard was twice as much for slaves referred to solely as "black and Indian," without any religious modifier.[63]

Even as the crown attempted to reclaim some of the prerogatives it had
ceded in its earliest concessions to Columbus and his successors, the proliferating mechanisms for trying to control subjects and objects along the Pearl
Coast came to limited effect. Pearls' promiscuous movement from hand to
hand on the Pearl Coast and beyond continually frustrated royal attempts to
harness New World productivity to political power. The crown could no more
control the harvesting, use, and circulation of pearls than it could control the
social relations that developed from the practice of pearl fishing. Pearls could
not be controlled as either natural resource or commodity, a blurry distinction in the fisheries. In the absence of specie, residents used pearls as currency and also transformed them into jewelry. The crown targeted both of
these practices by establishing in 1531 a marco's equivalency in pesos de oro
and also by continually prohibiting pearl drilling on the islands. Facilitating
the orderly transfer of pearls between the Costa de Perlas and Spain proved
equally difficult. In 1535, royal officials in Cubagua reported to the king that
the Casa had failed to acknowledge the receipt of pearl shipments for more
than four years. The monarchy responded with a decree ordering the Casa
to provide receipt of pearls in the future and to write an account of the types

63. *CC*, II, 129 (Feb. 26, 1538). The 1538 decree ordered canoe owners to cease throwing
the bodies overboard and instead to bury them outside city limits in a well-protected grave
to prevent dogs and other animals from digging up the corpses. Failure to obey carried one
fine if the dead slaves were black or Indian and a different penalty if the deceased diver
was deemed "Christian" with no racial modifier. These regulations could mean two things:
European pearl divers (that is, "Christians") sailed in pearl canoes alongside African and
Indian enslaved divers, or some black slaves were recognized as Christian.

and quantities of pearls that they had received from Cubagua over the previous ten years.[64]

In the fisheries themselves, enslaved workers in the settlements continued to respond to their captivity and treatment in numerous ways. In the 1530s, the crown specified the punishment (one hundred lashes delivered in public and the amputation of the right hand if a weapon was involved) for any black slave who assaulted a "christian." Flight from the settlements was another option for the enslaved, an indication of the inadequacy of Spanish authority on the pearl-fishing islands and the mainland. In 1538, local officials enumerated the financial responsibilities of any island resident wanting to own more than two black slaves—he had to contribute to a common fund from which search parties for runaways could be paid, among other things. By the end of the 1530s, the issue of black slaves' fleeing both Cubagua and Margarita was serious enough to warrant a royal decree determining the punishments to be meted out to slaves who escaped and were caught, which ranged from one hundred lashes to the amputation of the right foot and both ears, to death. On the larger island of Margarita, laborers could flee to the mountains or the remote Macanao Peninsula; the mainland also saw the growth of Maroon communities that would endure for centuries in many iterations. Rough socializing among pearl-fishery inhabitants characterized these settlements as much as the violence and coercion that sustained their labor regime. Spaniards bought and sold and beat the Indian and African laborers who worked on the island, but they also drank and consorted and formed long-term unions with them. If they survived the day's labors, at night these free and semifree laborers moved about the island with considerable autonomy; they traded and socialized with their putative masters. The crown objected but could do little to alter these realities. These prohibitions paint a picture

---

64. A marco of pearls was declared to be worth twelve pesos de oro when used as payment for goods and supplies, but, when using pearls to purchase gold, the exchange rate was to be determined by the parties involved. For an early attempt to stop pearls from being used as currency, see *CC*, I, 135 (Nov. 4, 1531). For more on the use of pearls as currency in the early years of the fisheries' operation, see Otte, *Las perlas del Caribe*, 35–36, 54–55. For an early prohibition of pearl drilling, see *CC*, I, 188 (Dec. 14, 1532). In 1532, Charles V passed the first of these laws prohibiting the drilling of pearls on the island: AGI, IG: 420, legajo 10, fols. 263v–264r (Feb. 10, 1526). For Queen Isabel and Cubaguan officials, see AGI, IG: 1962, legajo 4, fols. 1–2 (Nov. 13, 1535). For additional documents concerning the handling and sale of pearls in Casa custody, see AGI, IG: 1961, legajo 3, fols. 61v–63r (Sept. 13, 1533), IG: 1963, legajo 7, fols. 160v–1633r (Aug. 14, 1544), IG: 1963, legajo 9, fols. 116v–117r (Sept. 13, 1544).

of a chaotic and fluid society where people — much like the pearls that united
them in a common, if coerced, purpose — moved fluidly and without de facto
regard for de jure categories. What happened at sea could not be separated
from the relationships that obtained on land.[65]

Meanwhile, because pearls could be used to import anything, their abundance discouraged the growth of other industries along the coast. This dependence on a single natural resource molded inhabitants' relationship with
the crown in a number of ways. Fishery residents ignored crown directives
when they did not suit them but sought royal intervention if it promised to
be beneficial. Cubaguans continually pled poverty and asked for exemptions
from import duties. In 1532, the crown responded to a petition from the officials and residents of the city of Nueva Cádiz on Cubagua stating that, because of the regular importation of woolen and cotton clothing, there were no
artisans, and women had nothing with which to occupy themselves or from
which to earn a living. The crown ruled in the residents' favor and prohibited
the importation of the specified items in order to encourage the presence of
"artisans, tailors, and seamstresses." But, although the crown could bestow
the lofty titles of villa and ciudad upon the rapacious settlements and attempt
to summon civic occupations such as tailors and seamstresses into existence
through decrees, the pearl fisheries continued to be communities dominated
in character and labor by one goal — pearl extraction. The singular focus on
pearls was pursued by a multitude of people in cacophonous, violent collaboration.[66]

Crown encouragement of new professions notwithstanding, the region's
political economy continued to revolve around pearls and the human and

65. See *CC,* II, 128 (XXIII, Feb. 26, 1538), 129 (XXVII, Feb. 26, 1538), 231 (Nov. 10,
1550). This mention of "Christians" without a racial modifier again raises the issue of
whether black and Indian slaves could be deemed as such or only as Europeans. For Spanish men and Indian women, see, for example, *CC,* II, 28 (Aug. 17, 1535). A 1538 decree
prohibited the giving of wine to any "black slave nor Indian of any color" (item XXI in the
decree), and the penalties for this offense varied depending on whether the wine had been
given for free (that is, in a social setting) or for payment of any sort (*CC,* II, 126). The fine
for sharing wine socially was more severe than for engaging in trade or barter. The decree
also ordered that blacks and Indians (either slave or free) were not to leave their owner's
house after dark unaccompanied, suggesting that both groups did regularly move about
the islands of their own accord.

66. For sample requests for exemptions from the *almoxarifazgo* (a customs tax on merchandise), see *CC,* I, 121 (Apr. 4, 1531), *CC,* II, 32 (Oct. 17, 1535), 40 (Dec. 8, 1535), 202
(May 1, 1543). For the importation of seamstresses, etc., see *CC,* I, 199 (Dec. 30, 1532).

natural resources that went into producing them. In 1535, the crown ordered that Margarita Indians be permitted to work for Spaniards in the fisheries "because this was the only way they could eat." Perhaps the crown was responding to fictitious claims from Spanish residents, who were hoping to force the crown to approve Indian labor. Even if such assertions were spurious, however, they reflected the degree to which the pearl fishery impoverished the region's economy and inhabitants. In 1536, the queen prohibited the practice of buying land from the Indians because it left them "with nowhere to plant cassava and corn," prompting them to move off the island and threatening the viability of the settlement. In a phrase that attests to the degree to which the basic needs of fishery inhabitants vied with their desire for wealth, the crown lamented in 1538 the damage caused by Spaniards who left the Pearl Islands for the mainland in search of *"oro, ropa y maíz"*: gold topped the list, but clothing and corn immediately followed.[67]

Pearls set the tone for economies of exchange, coercion, and negotiation on the Pearl Coast, but they also existed within commercial networks that extended far beyond this corner of the Caribbean and that revolved around other goods. Indeed, pearls' ability to move seamlessly from place to place, embedded in multiple overlapping commercial networks, made it almost impossible to track and tax them. Furthermore, pearls' variegated pathways point to the numerous concerns, people, and contexts that drove their movement beyond imperial directives. In 1540, for example, Charles V ordered the royal court of Hispaniola to take great care to register all items being traded to slave-bearing Portuguese ships because too often these ships failed to declare the merchandise they received from Spanish settlers in return for slaves. As a result, most of the "passengers, gold, silver, and pearls that [Portuguese captains] leave on the Azores islands or in Portugal" remained unregistered and untaxed. The king went on to complain that only a couple of token ships ever returned to Seville in compliance with the law that Portuguese slave traders report all imported goods to the Spanish Council of Trade. These were not

67. *CC*, II, 18 (Aug. 7, 1535), 61 (Nov. 3, 1536); *CC*, I, 86 (Apr. 20, 1538). For licenses to conduct rescate for corn and canoes, see *CC*, I, 72 (Aug. 17, 1528); for the need for a well on Cubagua, see *CC*, I, 220 (Dec. 30, 1532). A royal decree issued by Charles V in 1538, dealing with the administrative and logistic problems facing residents of Cubagua, highlighted in passing the Spanish residents' dependence on Indian pearl divers' specialized skills. Because fortune-hunting governors of the islands were so frequently departing on exploratory trips and taking provisions from Cubagua, the "Indians who know how to [dive for pearls]" were left without food and provisions, which forced the fisheries to cease operation and caused the royal treasury to suffer. See *CC*, II, 65–66 (Feb. 16, 1538).

isolated incidents: Charles V communicated regularly with the officials at the Casa de la Contratación about the illegal unloading of pearls and other items in the Azores and how to put an end to this independent trade.[68]

After the extraordinary first four decades of exploration and exploitation in pearl fisheries east and west, the Caribbean heyday came to a close in a fittingly spectacular and destructive fashion. In 1541, a tsunami wiped out the city of Nueva Cádiz de Cubagua, likely destroying the island's remaining oyster banks as well. New mainland conquests reaped human and material rewards for the crown that overshadowed the profits from pearls — even though the jewel still drew attention from Spanish explorers with an eye for New World wealth, as Hernando de Soto's accounts of mainland pearl wealth during his 1539–1542 travels attest. French corsairs attacked what remained of the settlement in 1543, carrying people and pearls to Panama and even Peru.[69]

The early history of these settlements illuminates the mutually constructive nature of the regulatory mechanisms of the global Iberian empires. These mechanisms in theory governed the pearl fisheries, but their efficacy depended upon the movements of pearls and people within and beyond the Pearl Coast. Early royal visions of wealth management failed to encompass the realities of life in the pearl fisheries, where residents produced distinct understandings of the relationship between economies on land and ecologies at sea as well as between the labor of diverse subjects and the wealth of the empire. Thus it was in this context, with multiple people pursuing profit with distinct understandings of what that meant and how to create it, that recent arrivals and longtime inhabitants of the Americas argued in word and deed about the nature of a New World empire. Together they debated how to govern its diverse subjects and how to cultivate, harvest, and tax its products.

68. AGI, IG: 1963, legajo 7, fols. 160v–163r (Aug. 14, 1540); AGI, SD: 868, legajo 1, fol. 269v (Sept. 7, 1540). On more than one occasion, the Casa was accused of deliberate mishandling of the precious commodity, if not outright theft. In 1544, the king issued a royal order demanding that the officials of the Casa refrain from withholding private shipments of pearls that rightfully belonged to Seville merchants — illegal behavior that prompted merchants to bring lawsuits and write many letters of complaint to the king. See AGI, IG: 1961, legajo 3, fols. 61v–63 (Sept. 13, 1533), IG: 1963, legajo 9, fols. 116v–177r (Sept. 13, 1544).

69. For Garcilaso de la Vega's account of Hernando de Soto's pearl findings in southern North America from 1539 to 1542 and for effects of storms on pearl mussels, see Landman, Mikkelsen, and Bieler, eds., *Pearls,* 125, 186. For corsairs' carrying people and pearls to elsewhere in the Americas, see Otte, *Las perlas del Caribe,* 394–395.

Pearls' identity at the intersection of natural resource and commodity forced a rethinking of approaches to wealth management, one the precedents established in the Siete Partidas could not address. The conflicting approaches to wealth husbandry that shaped Europe's New World political economy are glimpsed with clarity in the vocabularies and practices that characterized the pearl fisheries.[70]

70. My findings are in keeping with Tamar Herzog's work on the nature of early modern citizenship, particularly as explored in *Defining Nations: Immigrants and Citizens in Early Modern Spain and Spanish America* (New Haven, Conn., 2003), in which she argues that the exercise of rights (as opposed to legal or political declarations) shaped the boundaries of early modern communities. On the elaboration of different types of authority in distinct geographic settings, see Lauren Benton, *A Search for Sovereignty: Law and Geography in European Empires, 1400–1900* (Cambridge, 2010). John Lynch, in *Spain, 1516–1598: From Nation State to World Empire* (Oxford, 1991), discusses taxation as a key component of the processes that were transforming ruling powers in this period and helping to establish the dominance of a central governing authority.

: 3 :

"EVEN THE BLACK WOMEN
WEAR STRANDS OF PEARLS"

*Assessing the Worth of Subjects and Objects
in a New Era, 1540–1600*

Cubagua's 1541 destruction shifted but did not end pearl fishing along the Venezuelan littoral. The tsunami that brought a dramatic end to the Pearl Coast's most lucrative years also coincided with the dawn of a new era of Spanish imperial control, one in which the reins of overseas empire began to be more tightly (if still imperfectly) held by the crown. In the aftermath of Cubagua's devastation, settlements moved down the coast and to the larger island of Margarita, and pearl fishing continued to draw private and royal investors.[1]

In the decades that followed, the pearl fisheries continued to be the site of conversations about wealth creation. The crown, seeking to draw this corner of the colonial world closer to the imperial administration, took an approach to the fisheries' governance that combined concessions to and rejection of the political economy advanced by the fisheries in the previous decades. Meanwhile, the conquests and profits of Tierra Firme (the American mainland, in particular the major silver deposits found at Potosí in upper Peru in 1545 and Zacatecas in New Spain in 1547) soon eclipsed the profits drawn from the Caribbean's underwater mines and turned attention away from the Caribbean islands. The immense riches and challenges produced by this new stage of colonization drew the American mainland into the heart of the empire's domestic identity in a way that had not occurred previously. Even as the crown tightened the mechanisms in place for governing the human and natural wealth of its domains, the Pearl Coast remained a thorn in the crown's side

---

1. The continual refining of the crown's approach to the administration of the New World was further illustrated midcentury by Charles V's decision to found an archive in Valladolid to house the records generated by the imperial enterprise. Ralph Bauer, *The Cultural Geography of Colonial American Literatures: Empire, Travel, Modernity* (Cambridge, 2003), 26, discusses the founding of the archive at Simancas. The archive was completed by Philip II in 1559.

because of its continually evolving and violent labor regime, its quicksilver product—pearls—and the challenging relations that developed among the settlements' free and unfree inhabitants.

The most explicit contemporary reflections on the pearl fisheries' early history and their significance came from within the Spanish empire itself, penned by royal chroniclers who considered the nature of this early experiment with wealth generation and management. Throughout the sixteenth century and beyond, chroniclers and natural historians exercised enormous influence in shaping Europe's understanding of the Atlantic explorations— of the physical nature of this new land and of the metaphorical nature of distinct parties' claims to control over it. In the context of the Counter-Reformation and Spain's continuing quest for religious orthodoxy, these critical reflections on the early pearl fisheries threatened to provide fuel for Spain's enemies and drew censorship. In 1556, the crown passed a law ordering that all books touching upon the history of the Indies must first be seen and approved by the Council of the Indies before publication. This order came too late for Bartolomé de Las Casas's *Short Account of the Destruction of the Indies,* however, which appeared in Seville in 1552 and Antwerp in 1579. The *Short Account* provided Spain's Protestant enemies with an invaluable critique of Spain's imperial misdeeds.[2]

2. Official chronicles reflected a long-standing tradition of narrative construction of authority, and these lengthy histories represented a far more refined and practiced idiom of reportage than the uneven, imperfect archival record of personal disputes and fiscal battles preserved by the incipient overseas bureaucracy. As decades passed, however, the crown feared the possible political and religious backlash of unfavorable accounts more than ever, particularly as the debate between Las Casas and Ginés de Sepúlveda unfolded in Valladolid in 1550–1551. For a discussion of the Spanish crown's anxiety about the circulation of information related to the Indies, see Richard L. Kagan, *Clio and the Crown: The Politics of History in Medieval and Early Modern Spain* (Baltimore, 2009), 110, 156–160, 172; and Kagan, "History," in Evonne Levy and Kenneth Mills, eds., *Lexikon of the Hispanic Baroque: Transatlantic Exchange and Transformation* (Austin, Tex., 2013), 150–152. Juan Pimentel calls these chronicles some of "the classical products of Iberian science . . . the genre in which the first great contributions of the scientific knowledge of the New World appeared." See Pimentel, "The Iberian Vision: Science and Empire in the Framework of a Universal Monarchy, 1500–1800," in Roy MacLeod, ed., *Nature and Empire: Science and the Colonial Enterprise, Osiris,* 2d Ser., XV (2000), 17–30. María M. Portuondo discusses this trend toward censorship in *Secret Science: Spanish Cosmography and the New World* (Chicago, 2009), 104–106. The crown began banning books that provided troubling accounts of Spanish behavior in the Indies in 1527, just as Las Casas

One of the chroniclers to suffer the crown's displeasure was Francisco López de Gómara, historian and archrival of Las Casas. As Spain entered into a period of soul-searching regarding the adverse economic and moral consequences of the sudden influx of wealth from the New World, López de Gómara offered frank assessments of the crown's initial mismanagement of the empire, emphasizing the misdeeds of rogue conquistadors and the havoc they wrought. From the perspective of the monarchy and the Council of the Indies, such an account was at odds with the mission of defending the legitimacy of the Spanish presence in the New World. Both López de Gómara's personal enmities and various complaints about the content of his work (largely having to do with his vilification of Francisco Pizarro and critique of the conquest of Peru) led the crown to prohibit the sale and distribution of his wildly successful *Historia general de las Indias* in 1553, just two years after its initial publication (the *Historia* appeared in nine editions during this period). Clandestine editions of the *Historia* continued to appear after the official ban, however, both within and beyond Spain. By the end of the sixteenth century, ten Italian editions, nine French editions, and two editions in English had been published. The crown could do nothing to suppress the appetite for such critiques of Spain's imperial endeavors and little to prevent the circulation of accounts such as López de Gómara's.[3]

López de Gómara's criticisms of particular aspects of Spain's early engagement in the Americas revealed his understanding of the hierarchy of influences and actors at play in the settlements' earliest days. In his account of the pearl fisheries, he condemned Las Casas and pointed to the issues raised by the mismanagement of the region. López de Gómara implied that it was only after failing as conqueror that Las Casas became a Dominican friar. In doing so, López de Gómara continued, he "failed to augment royal revenues, ennoble workers, or send pearls to the Flemish." These were indeed the roles envisioned for the pearl fisheries in these critical exploratory years: they were expected to contribute to royal revenues, to exemplify the crown's governance of subjects, and to further Spain's European alliances. But in their

began to write his monumental *Historia* and less than a decade before Fernández de Oviedo would publish the first volumes of his *Historia general y natural.* On the Spanish crown's midcentury tightening of censorship rules, see Kathleen Ann Myers, *Fernández de Oviedo's Chronicle of America: A New History for a New World,* trans. Nina M. Scott (Austin, Tex., 2007), esp. the introduction and chapter 7.

3. See Kagan, *Clio and the Crown,* 159–160, for more on López de Gómara.

unchecked production of pearls, they served principally to undermine order, rather than to embody it.[4]

Many observers marveled at the proliferation of pearls and the social consequences of their abundance. López de Gómara remarked, "Now everyone wears pearls and seed pearls, men and women, rich and poor; never in any province in the world did so many pearls enter as in Spain, and in such a short period of time." Another chronicler, Garcilaso de la Vega, marveled in the 1560s that there were so many pearls entering southern Spanish ports that they were sold "in a heap in the India house at Seville just as if they were some kind of seed." Along the same lines, José de Acosta observed with a degree of shock that pearls were so abundant that "hasta las negras traen sartas"—or even black women wear strands of them. The profusion of pearls upended traditional hierarchies; the use of this luxury object now muddied distinctions among subjects that the possession of pearls had heretofore helped to mark.[5]

Why were pearls so highly sought after? Reflecting on pearls' popularity, López de Gómara captured the jewel's association with the struggle at the heart of the imperial project: the extension of control over distant places and people. Echoing Pliny's reflections on the relationship between pearls' appeal and their dangerous provenance, López de Gómara wondered whether so many people sought pearls "because they are brought from another world, and before they were discovered they were brought from very far away, or perhaps it is because they cost the lives of men." Pearls brought their bearers a piece of the imperial drama: proximity to exotic peoples and places and the violence and death inherent in the quest for overseas wealth.[6]

4. Francisco López de Gomara, *Historia general de las Indias,* 2 vols. (Madrid, 1941), I, 186.

5. Ibid., II, 206. Garcilaso de la Vega, *Royal Commentaries of the Incas, and General History of Peru* (1609), ed. and trans. H. V. Livermore (Austin, Tex., 1966), I, 532; [José] de Acosta, *Historia natural y moral de las Indias,* ed. Edmundo O'Gorman (Mexico City, 1962), book 4, chap. XV, 168. The proliferation of wealth of various types from the New World raised concerns about the relationship between New World wealth and Spain's economic and moral decay. See Elvira Vilches, *New World Gold: Cultural Anxiety and Monetary Disorder in Early Modern Spain* (Chicago, 2010), for a discussion of Spain's moral and material crisis.

6. López de Gomara, *Historia general de las Indias,* II, 207: "Quizá es porque se traen del otro mundo, y se traían, antes que se descubriese, de muy lejos, o porque cuestan hombres."

It was not only pearls that challenged the Spanish crown's midcentury push to regain royal prerogative in the New World and implement procedures for categorizing and managing its people and products. An inherently destabilizing diversity remained at the heart of the expanding empire. By the mid-sixteenth century, the Spanish crown had gone to great lengths to forge or force alliances with (and claim sovereignty over) peoples from the Americas to the Philippines. Throughout these varied domains, the crown confronted the question of how to husband human and material capital as new resources were discovered and new combinations of subjects were brought together under a single ruler. On the eve of Philip II's marriage to Mary Tudor in 1554, Spain ruled over an empire of unparalleled size. Yet, even as the crown expanded its jurisdiction around the globe, within Iberia and Europe more broadly it faced profound challenges to its rule and religious orthodoxy.

As tensions within Spain's Holy Roman imperial possessions grew, the monarchy's European holdings fractured (seen most spectacularly in the outbreak of violence in the Netherlands in 1566 (an early episode in Spain's eighty-year conflict with the Dutch). Castile was left at the center of the monarchy's administrative identity even as its global imperial claims reached unprecedented size. Fissures also appeared within Iberia, where lingering questions of religious and cultural identity and subjecthood came to a head in the Morisco Revolt of 1568–1570. Philip II's brief union with Mary Tudor of England (1554–1558) and Spain's annexation of Portugal in 1580 underscored the powerful influence of dynastic concerns on the shape and range of emerging overseas empires. A popular song from the time captured the pervasive sense of anxiety about Spain's unexpected alliances and the accompanying cultural upheaval. The singer yearned for home, free of complex commitments abroad: "I don't want any love affairs in England / I have better ones in my homeland / Oh God of my homeland / Take me away from here / Ay, England is no longer for me." The song expressed a prevailing sense of discomfort with the possibility of intimate alliances with strangers; although the ditty was ostensibly about a love affair, it seems to have channeled collective wariness of Spain's political bedfellows.[7]

The challenges posed by a heterogeneous subject base at home and abroad coincided with the onset of severe financial crises that compelled new fiscal relationships with the monarchy's far-flung territories and inhabitants. The

7. Carta de Lorenzio de Castro, Dec. 29, 1557, RBM, II/2186, doc. 32: "Yo no quiero amores en Ynglaterra / Pues otros mejores tengo yo en mi tierra / Ay Dios de mi tierra / saqueísme de aquí / Ay que Ynglaterra ya no es para mí."

crown suffered its first bankruptcy in 1557, and to raise money Philip II (who had succeeded his father as king in 1556, ruling until his death in 1598) turned not only to taxation but also to unusual measures such as seizing money from America, issuing royal favors and patents in exchange for payment, and taking costly loans—measures that contributed to the lingering tension between the crown's desire to reassert its control over its New World territories while also delegating its administration. In Portugal's overseas territories in Brazil and the Estado da Índia (as Portugal's eastern empire was known), the union of the crowns (1580-1640) largely left administrative practices in place, out of necessity more than principle.[8]

Amid these sea changes in Iberian imperial power, subjects throughout Iberian territories sought to ascertain what this changing shape of the empire would mean for them as the crown wrestled with the form and structure of its rule. Pearls offer a window into the negotiations at the heart of this process, as individuals and centralizing states refined their understandings of the creation and assessment of value. In the pearl fisheries, perceptions of expertise shaped hierarchies of worth. Beyond the fisheries, the paths traveled by pearls reaffirmed the value of networks of alliance over imperial regulations intended to channel the flow of objects and subjects between realms.

As the crown sought to husband the wealth of empire, pearls skittered across borders and between hands, finding their place with moneylenders and diplomats, enslaved divers and Jesuit priests. In these multiple global exchanges involving pearls, we see the intersection of personal imperatives and private judgments about wealth with the emerging imperial bureaucracy that sought to order and contain people and products. In patterns of both production and circulation, the independence of action and of judgment by subjects played a critical role.

"All in Confusion and Together": *Chaos and Control in the Fisheries*

The demands for labor and the complexities posed by the indigenous and African labor force continued to be at the center of the profits and problems of the pearl fisheries throughout the second half of the sixteenth century. In the 1540s, in the wake of Cubagua's destruction, profit-seekers established fisheries in Cabo de la Vela, and, three years later, the inhabitants of the new settlements petitioned for the license to import one hundred black slaves

---

8. For more on the financial crises of these years, see John Lynch, *Spain, 1516-1598: From Nation State to World Empire* (Oxford, 1991), 134-135.

for "the farms and pearl fisheries." This expansion occurred concomitantly
with renewed royal attention to the issue of abuses of indigenous inhabitants
of the Americas. A significant element of the crown's move to tighten oversight of its overseas holdings was the publication of the *Recopilación de leyes
de los reinos de las Indias* (Laws of the Indies) in 1542, a compilation of rules
governing all matters concerning Spain's New World territories. Among its
many specifications, the *Recopilación de leyes* ordered that no free Indians be
forced to work as divers and that the bishops and judges of Venezuela oversee the decent treatment of the slaves in the fisheries. If the risk of death in
the fisheries could not be avoided, then pearl fishing in the area was to cease.
Unsurprisingly, the laws had limited effect on the Pearl Coast. In 1546, the
bishop of Santa Marta had to be reminded to obey the laws and to assure
that Indians and blacks in the fisheries be given proper care. In the 1550s, the
crown prohibited settlers from including blacks in their *encomiendas* (grants
of native labor or tribute) or from buying Brazilian Indians from Portuguese
merchants on Margarita—the law itself suggesting that both practices persisted. In spite of such regulations, inhabitants in these settlements continued
to deal with the demands of life and labor in the fisheries as they saw fit and
to blur the lines the crown hoped to draw among subjects.[9]

The crown hoped to solve the problems of the fisheries' heterogeneous
labor force by replacing it. Royal experts traveled to the settlements to report
on best and worst practices, and the monarchy continued to support the proposals for pearl-fishing devices that might remove the need for human divers.

9. For requests for slaves and their presence (both African and Indian) in the pearl
fisheries, see *CC*, II, 205 (June 30, 1543) (quotation), 230 (Feb. 12, 1548); AGI, AC: 1,
legajo 1, fols. 108r–111r (June 5, 1546); and Richard Konetzke, *Colección de documentos para la historia de la formación social de Hispanoamérica, 1493–1810*, I *(1493–1592)*
(Madrid, 1953), 297 (Dec. 17, 1551), 339 (Sept. 21, 1556). Although one slave merchant
complained in 1548 that he could not sell his brother's black slaves on Margarita because
of the poverty of the residents (*CC*, II, 230 [Feb. 12, 1548]), his claim seems suspicious;
given inventories of slave holdings of Margarita residents and reactive legislation designed
to curb illegal slave-trading practices in the 1550s, it is more likely that he hoped to find
higher prices in newer settlements where residents would pay more. For a history of the
early years of the Cabo de la Vela fisheries, see Manuel Luengo Muñoz, "Notícias sobre
la fundación de la ciudad de Nuestra Señora Santa María de los Remedios del Cabo de la
Vela," *Anuario de estudios Americanos*, VI (1949), 757–797. Eduardo Barrera Monroy considers the origins and experiences of Indian divers in the mainland pearl fisheries in the
last half of the sixteenth century in "Los esclavos de las perlas: Voces y rostros indígenas
en la granjería de perlas del Cabo de la Vela (1540–1570)," *Boletín cultural y bibliográfico*,
XXXIX, no. 61 (2002), 3–33.

In the context of Spain's recent bankruptcy and general financial distress, the pearl-fishing devices proposed in the second half of the century were often cloaked in terms of recovery and restoration: obtaining pearls as a form of lost wealth alongside items lost in shipwrecks. This conceptualization of pearls as treasure belied the knowledge produced over the previous half century of pearls as the product of a living ecosystem; however, the new proposals did not entirely fail to incorporate the lessons of the previous fifty years. Much as the crown tried to separate indigenous and African subjects from the exploitation of this resource, those hoping to profit from the fisheries could not ignore the abundant evidence about how expertise shaped the harvesting of pearls. Thus, the new pearl-fishing machines no longer attempted to replace human labor altogether. Instead, they promised to substitute one kind of subject for another.

In the crown's concessions to pearl-fishing entrepreneurs in the 1550s and 1560s, European approaches continued to coexist alongside a recognition of New World realities. Royal contracts continued to license Europeans (both Spaniards and non-Spaniards) to manage the wealth of the Indies while acknowledging that these new outposts of empire often depended upon the skills of unfamiliar peoples. Investors and inventors who ignored New World realities were destined for failure. For example, in 1565 the crown sponsored Pedro de Herrera, who received a license from the Council of the Indies, to employ his invention to get "from under water anything silver gold pearls that might have fallen into the sea." His patent did not describe the device in any detail, nor did it make any mention of a labor force, which likely hastened its failure.[10]

Roughly ten years after Herrera received his license, the king granted a license to a Portuguese merchant, Captain Antonio Gómez de Acosta, to introduce "a number" of canoes and "up to 100 black slaves" into the pearl fisheries. The terms of Gómez de Acosta's license addressed the link among different types of labor, expertise, and the subjecthood of various actors involved in pearl fishing. The contract specified that no one was to interfere with the merchant's venture because of his Portuguese origin, and, although he was prohibited from employing Indians against their will, he was allowed to employ anyone who "understood" about pearl fisheries. This was a remarkable recognition that knowledge of pearl fishing conveyed authority to the people who possessed it. Gómez de Acosta's license stopped short of

10. For Pedro de Herrera, see "Licencia para poder sacar oro de devajo del agua," 1565, AGI, IG: 425, legajo 24, fol. 228.

recognizing explicitly what fishery residents had been saying for more than fifty years: people who best understood the industry were the pearl divers.[11]

A year later, in 1568, amid concern over the treatment of Indians in the pearl fisheries along the Venezuelan coast, the crown granted permission to a trio of men (Antonio Luis de Cabrera, Diego de Lira, and Antonio de Luna) to introduce into the fisheries a new "device to fish for and retrieve from underwater pearls gold and silver and things from sunken ships." Their grant from the council also included a license to bring with them one hundred black slaves, though the labor they were to perform was not specified. It is unclear what their device looked like or why it failed, though it is clear the three men anticipated trouble; in their contract, the crown stipulated that no resident of the Indies was to interfere with the operation of their equipment *(yngenio)* under penalty of a large fine. The partners' innovation failed to take hold along the Pearl Coast, like others before it. The promise of these mechanical approaches to harvesting underwater wealth was clearly no match for the existing system of exploited labor that prevailed along the Pearl Coast, in which residents were deeply invested and which produced profits.[12]

In spite of Pearl Coast residents' rejection of crown-sponsored technologies intended to mechanize the central labor of pearl fishing, their attitude to imperial governance was not uniformly hostile. Communication between inhabitants and the crown reveal ambivalence and a willingness to turn to royal authority when it made sense to do so. In residents' continual requests for concessions of all sorts—including permission to import everything from pitch and tar for the pearl-fishing boats to wine, cloth for clothing and sails, and enslaved Africans—they engaged with and reaffirmed the potential utility of the emerging overseas bureaucracy. Moreover, they cleverly manipulated the crown's desire for pearl profits by requesting various types of tax exemptions in order to encourage investment for the discovery of new oyster banks and the preservation of the settlements. When it suited them to do so, residents located the pearl fisheries within a hierarchy of imperial possessions by claiming that pearl fishing entailed "more work and risk" than silver mining and thus deserved to be taxed less stringently.[13]

11. For Gómez de Acosta's license and the reference to people who "understood" about pearl fishing, see "Real Cédula," 1567, AGI, IG: 427, legajo 30, fols. 186v–187v: "Traer las demas personas q entienden a las dha. pesquería."

12. For de Cabrera, de Lira, and de Luna's grant, see "Capitulación," 1568, AGI, IG: 425, legajo 24, fols. 424v–427v.

13. On at least one occasion, royal officials lauded residents who "unburdened their consciences" by paying overdue taxes on their harvested pearls, but more often than

Further evidence of the centrality of expertise to shaping hierarchies of wealth distribution in the Venezuelan pearl fisheries came to light in the 1570s, following the recovery of oyster banks near Margarita and the development of new pearling grounds near the small island of Coche. Crown-sponsored officials sent to observe and chronicle practices along the Pearl Coast created a series of reports that described an active and complex arena of resource exploitation and management. According to these reports, significant numbers of people and material resources were employed in the pursuit of pearls—many more, in fact, than those recorded during the fisheries' heyday or suggested by renditions of a single pearl boat, no matter how big it was or how large the crew. One written account estimated that there were six thousand people doing business in the pearl fisheries; another estimated that twenty-one canoes were operating on Margarita, though the numbers occasionally rose to twenty-six or thirty, and between sixteen and eighteen at Rio de la Hacha. (The term *canoe* by the late sixteenth century referred to all the associated laborers and supplies as well as the boat; one observer described pearl-boat crews consisting of thirty black slaves—twenty-four divers, plus a crew of six "service" slaves—who provided the divers with food and water from a base on shore.) Although a Spanish overseer was supposed to accompany the divers to ensure that no tumult broke out in the boat (presumably because of competition for promising oyster reefs or harvested pearls), the reports suggest that these supervisory measures were followed in the breach and, even then, posed little threat to customary practices.[14]

Traders looking to exchange goods for pearls sought out the divers at sea (and their supply crew on land). One report claimed that many *piraguas* (or smaller boats) carrying provisions needed by the island settlements would travel from all over the mainland directly to "wherever they are fishing for pearls," where they would trade "with the blacks of the canoes or the people who remained as guards in the settlement." In considerable detail, these re-

---

not they complained about the crown being cheated of its due. See HNM, II, unpaid quintos, 1580, doc. 71, Gaspar de Peralta, 1580, doc. 68, license for a caravel, 1580, doc. 69, Peralta petition, 1581, doc. 73, Margarita requests merced, 1586, doc. 98, commerce with *indios aruacos*, 1588, doc. 117, wood from mainland, 1586, doc. 100, pearl fishing compared to silver mining, 1586, doc. 101, no seizure of pearl fishing materials, 1588, doc. 119.

14. HNM, II, pearl fishing to begin on Coche, 1575, doc. 15; Ricardo Ignacio Castillo Hidalgo, *Asentamiento español y articulación interétnica en Cumaná (1560–1620)* (Caracas, 2005), chap. 4; Report of Pedro Luys de Vargas y el tesorero Balthasar Perez Bernal, n.d., AGI, IG: 1805.

ports revealed a rich tapestry of actors who controlled the distribution of pearls in the fisheries, largely beyond the jurisdiction of royal officials. In these rough-and-tumble communities, power on land and expertise and knowledge at sea were intimately intertwined, and access to pearls was the source from which influence flowed.[15]

The reports in their entirety amounted to a single, critical lesson: living wealth lay at the heart of the region's profitability. The reports provided extensive detail on the habitats of the two central pillars of the region's economy, the divers and the oyster banks. The reports reaffirmed the divers' humanity even as they detailed the measures intended to limit their freedom. Furthermore, the reports outlined a volatile political economy in which an enslaved diver controlled access to a good whose value—contained in quantities so small they could easily fit into the palm of his hand—would, in theory, buy his freedom fifty times over (in reality, enslaved residents were prohibited from buying their liberty with pearls).

The crown visitors detailed the regimes intended to keep these highly skilled laborers in top physical form as well as the autonomy their skill afforded them. The reports noted that successful divers abstained from sex because it caused weight loss and also from excessive food, which inhibited their ability to hold their breath. Additionally, the observers also attempted to explicate (in surprisingly accurate terms) the process by which oysters reproduced and (less accurately) that by which pearls were created. The observers focused most of their attention, however, on the difficulties of controlling the circulation, taxation, and use of pearls in the fisheries. Of particular concern was enslaved divers' control over the pearls they harvested and the jewel's rampant circulation throughout the region. Pearls circulated "dizzily from hand to hand," the Spanish visitors wrote, and the slaves themselves "spend [pearls] and distribute them casually," using them to obtain "what is necessary for their houses and haciendas from merchants." Just a few pearls could make an enterprising resident—free or enslaved—a fortune: one report estimated that a small packet "the size of 4 fingers" could carry pearls worth one thousand *ducados* (ducats). When an enslaved African man could be sold for twenty-four ducados, this sum was a fortune. To put these sums in perspective, a contemporary account of pearl profits in the Caribbean fisheries at the turn of the century claimed that a pearl canoe operated by a particularly

15. Another report in AGI, IG: 1805, by Francisco Freile de Zamora, n.d., gives different estimates about how far out to sea the pearl canoes went in search of oysters as well as a description of how the oysters reproduced (quotation on [3]).

talented crew could harvest pearls worth three hundred ducados in a week, and a less-adept boat, two hundred ducados a week. A three-carat pearl was worth more than fourteen pesos, or nearly seventeen ducados. The destabilizing abundance of pearls and the way in which they concentrated economic power and conveyed political power to those who held them—enslaved or free—upended social hierarchies and underscored the inadequacy of numerical appraisals of value in the fisheries.[16]

The officials' reports confirmed that the production and harvesting of pearls shaped the infrastructure and social dynamics of the settlements far more than crown initiative. Spanish administrators residing on the Pearl Coast were among the targets of the observers' criticism. Charged with upholding royal directives, their own investment in pearls and pearl-fishing operations (including canoes and enslaved divers) led them to embrace the innovations that these settlements demanded, such as arming their enslaved crews in order to compete with rival pearl-fishing crews as well as to fend off corsairs. They further exploited their privilege to secure enslaved divers for their own pearl-fishing operations. Portuguese slave traders accused one Margarita governor in the late 1580s of defrauding them in his purchase of slaves from the "rivers of Guinea"; they cursed him as a heretic and lamented that they had not gone "to Guinea in order to bring blacks to the devil." The same governor came under fire for permitting excessive interaction between "the blacks he has for pearls" and the Indians in his employ. Just as in Seville, where the sight of black women wearing strands of pearls threatened perceived hierarchies of color among subjects, the reality of life on the Pearl Coast made a mockery of rules and regulations: the governor's accuser said that such permissiveness was "like making a free person slave and the slave free because the blacks that are captives command the Indians that are free." Once again, pearls were associated with topsy-turvy pairings of opposite elements; the best pearls circulated with the least powerful subjects de jure, who were simultaneously the region's de facto most powerful residents. The free

16. Report of Pedro Luis de Vargas y el tesorero Balthasar Perez Bernal, n.d., AGI, IG: 1805. For the price of an enslaved African man, see HNM, II, Alvaro Mendez de Castro, 1589, doc. 121. For comparative boat hauls, see AGI, IG: 1805, which contains a report labeled "Memorial ansi de la cria de las perlas en la concha como de la manera de pescarlas y beneficiarlas y de los generos que dellas ay del precio y balr de cada onza del genero," received in 1578 (the only report with a date contained within this file). The report suggests a wonder at "natural" powers, of the oyster, the sea, and the black slaves. For units of currency and their equivalencies, I am following Kris E. Lane, *Pillaging the Empire: Piracy in the Americas, 1500–1750* (Armonk, N.Y., 1998), 31.

mixed with the unfree, the African and indigenous residents of the coast re-versed roles, and Europeans were left at their mercy.[17]

However shambolic they appeared in the eyes of the crown, these unruly settlements continued to provide profits and prompt investment. In 1581, the crown received 1,908 *marcos* of pearls (approximately 950 pounds of the jewel) from Margarita and 2,015 marcos (more than 1,000 pounds) in 1587. The pearl *quinto* from the fisheries near Rio de la Hacha were not as grand but still significant, delivering 248 marcos (roughly 120 pounds of pearls) in 1581 and 878 marcos (nearly 450 pounds) in 1587. These immense pearl har-vests recalled Cubagua's heyday some sixty years earlier, in which the small island sent more than 600 pounds of pearls to the crown in a single year. A cycle of smaller booms and larger busts—as measured by the quinto—would continue for the rest of the century.[18]

What kinds of investment and hardship went into the rising quinto ship-ments of pearls in the last few decades of the century? These renewed pearl harvests required more than just new oyster banks or the recovery of ex-hausted ones. The political ecology of the region, as inhabitants had long known, was a more complex affair, depending on a delicate balance of cul-tivation and exploitation. A half century of protective measures intended to prevent the ill-treatment of the Indies' indigenous inhabitants and continu-ing crown attempts to sponsor pearl diving did little to alter prevailing pat-terns of human and natural resource management in the fisheries. An official *visita* (inspection) in 1570 to the Cabo de la Vela settlements produced hor-rifying tales of the enslavement and abuse of indigenous pearl divers whose uprooted lives and suffering made possible the fisheries' survival. A woman identified as Inesica, or "little Ines," testified that she had been brought to the fisheries as a small girl; all she could remember of her journey from the Val-ley of Upar (present-day Valledupar, Colombia) to the fisheries was that she cried a great deal along the way. Women and men recounted dreadful beat-ings and privations, and a man named Dominguito affirmed that he said the

17. "Memoria de las cossas que don Luis de Rojas governador por su magd de la governacion de Veneçuela y su muger e hijo deon Juan de Rojas an hecho en la dha go-vernacion," circa 1587, AGI, SD: 203, ramo 1, no. 32, fols. 19–30 (my thanks to David Wheat for bringing this document to my attention). See HNM, II, "Título de tesorero para el dicho Juan de Vargas Marques," 1579, doc. 64, item XLIIII, prohibits royal cus-toms officials (the *contador, factor,* and *veedor,* or accountant, factor, and inspector) from conducting pearl fishing.

18. R. A. Donkin offers these figures in *Beyond Price: Pearls and Pearl-Fishing: Ori-gins to the Age of Discoveries* (Philadelphia, 1998), 325.

Christian catechism at night for his soul and that all pearl divers prayed because they were "losing their souls beneath the water." This visita testimony might not have circulated widely, but, coming in the wake of the publication of Bartolomé de Las Casas's *Account, Much Abbreviated, of the Destruction of the Indies* in 1552, it likely sharpened royal concerns about the pearl fisheries while doing little to ameliorate the lives of those who suffered in them.[19]

The desire for laborers for these settlements sustained a wide-ranging slave trade. Spaniards supplied materials for (ever-larger) pearl canoes from Spain, while "Indians from Brazil" and "blacks from Guinea" continued to be brought to the Pearl Coast by various bearers.[20] By the 1570s, 1580s, and 1590s, canoe owners repeatedly justified their requests for goods necessary for the "sustenance of the blacks" by claiming that these residents were absolutely essential to the settlements' survival. Brought to the Pearl Coast from Iberia or, increasingly, directly from Africa and delivered legally or illegally by Spanish or Portuguese contractors (or contrabandists), these enslaved Africans were identified in the last three decades of the sixteenth century as being from the "Rivers of Guinea" or Cape Verde.[21]

The Flemish author of a 1590s travelogue about the Gold Coast of Guinea,

19. Bartolomé de Las Casas, *An Account, Much Abbreviated, of the Destruction of the Indies with Related Texts,* ed. Franklin W. Knight, trans. Andrew Hurley (Indianapolis, Ind., 2003), esp. 62–64. The testimony of various indigenous pearl divers of diverse origin is quoted and discussed in Barrera Monroy, "Los esclavos de las perlas," *Boletín cultural y bibliográfico,* XXXIX, no. 61 (2002), 3–33 (quotation on 24). Complaints about the treatment of Indians in the fisheries at Río de la Hacha on the Guajira Peninsula generated a royal visita in 1540. A major investigation into the ill-treatment of Indians in the pearl fisheries at Río de la Hacha followed in the mid-1560s; see "Tratos a los indios," 1564, AGI, Patronato Real: 195, ramo 27. A second visita to Cabo de la Vela took place in 1570 (Barrera Monroy, "Los esclavos de las perlas," *Boletín cultural y bibliográfico,* XXXIX, no. 61 [2002], 3–33, esp. testimony on 13, 18, 23).

20. On the changing contours of the transatlantic slave trade to the Spanish Americas, see David Wheat, *Atlantic Africa and the Spanish Caribbean, 1570–1640* (Chapel Hill, N.C., 2016). For "blacks from Guinea" working alongside "Indians from Brazil," see HNM, II, "Bernardo Ramírez: Al gobernador de la Isla Margarita . . . ," doc. 147. For the prices of slaves from Cabo Verde and Guinea sold on Margarita, see HNM, II, "La acordada de factores . . . ," doc. 121.

21. AGI, AC: 2, legajo 1, fols. 81r–81v (Mar. 27, 1584). For petitions to supply fisheries (including "clothing for the blacks"), see AGI, AC: 2, legajo 1, fols. 67r–68v (Feb. 15, 1580), legajo 1, fols. 71r–71v (May 1, 1580). The town's general representative complained that, without supplies from Spain, the canoes could not go out in search of pearls: AGI, AC: 2, legajo 2, fol. 177v (Feb. 13, 1598).

Pieter de Marees, suggested that the region was known for its swimmers and divers and that many were sent to the Pearl Coast:

> As it is customary for children, from their earliest youth onwards, to spend their time in the water every day, girls as well as boys . . . the Inhabitants here, especially those living in the coastal towns, are very good Swimmers. . . . They are very fast swimmers and can keep themselves under water for a long time. They can dive amazingly far, no less deep, and can see under water. Because they are so good at swimming and diving, they are specially kept for that purpose in many Countries and employed in this capacity where there is a need for them, such as on the Island of St. Margaret in the West Indies, where Pearls are found and brought up from the bottom [sea-bed] by Divers, as is more elaborately told in the Histories written about that subject.

De Marees also raised the possibility that it was these laborers — as well as the pearls they harvested — that linked the global Iberian world from the Caribbean to the Indian Ocean: "In the East Indies too, in places such as Goa and Ormus, where they dive no less than 20 fathoms deep into the salt water in order to bring up from below fresh water which the people drink because it is free of certain diseases and Worms, they often use Negroes or blacks for this purpose on account of their great expertise in swimming and diving" (see Figure 7). Once again, the notion of expertise was invoked to justify the role played by certain types of subjects in certain types of labor.[22]

A glimpse of what the laboring reality on the Pearl Coast looked like is offered by one artist's rendition of a large pearl-fishing boat in the 1590s (Figure 8). By the end of the century, it was not uncommon for African crews to sail the increasingly large pearl-fishing vessels — capable of carrying between eighteen and twenty men — with minimal or no white supervision. The illustration reveals that the name "pearl canoe," with its connotations (in English, at least) of small size, was highly misleading. Perhaps most interesting about this depiction of a pearl boat is the absence of a white overseer. An account by French explorer Samuel Champlain, who traveled through the region at the end of the 1590s, echoes the image in certain ways. Champlain described Margarita as "very fertile in corn and fruits" and possessing a large pearl-fishing fleet:

22. Pieter de Marees, *Description and Historical Account of the Gold Kingdom of Guinea (1602),* ed. and trans. Albert van Dantzig and Adam Jones (Oxford, 1987), 186–187.

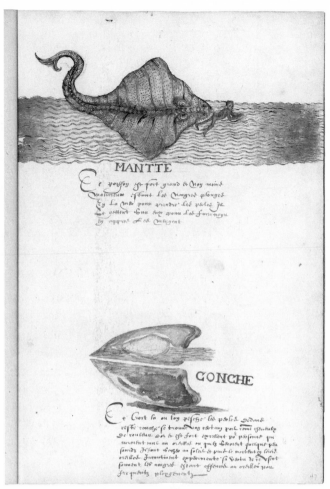

Figure 7. *"Mantte" and "Conche." From "Histoire naturelle des Indes" (circa 1586), fol. 47r. The Morgan Library and Museum. MA 3900. Bequest of Clara S. Peck, 1983. The "Histoire naturelle des Indes" is an anonymous guide to the New World and is known as the Drake Manuscript. It was likely composed by a French Huguenot traveling with Francis Drake in the 1590s. The translation of the accompanying text of the illustration is: Mantte: "This fish is very large and no less vicious. When the negroes dive in the sea for pearls it jumps on them to make them drown and afterwards eats them"; Conche: "It grows where one fishes for pearls. In this conch is found a certain hair like human hair the color of gold and it is very excellent for people who have an earache or who are somewhat deaf. They dry it in the sun and then put it in their ears and immediately feel its benefit. The negroes often use it, their ears being hurt by frequent dives." See the Morgan Library and Museum, http://www.themorgan.org/collection/Histoire-Naturelle-des-Indes /47#overlay-context=collection/Histoire-Naturelle-des-Indes/47.*

Figure 8. Pearl-Fishing Canoe with Black Divers.
From "Histoire naturelle des Indes" (circa 1586), fol. 57. The Morgan
Library and Museum. MA 3900. Bequest of Clara S. Peck, 1983.
The translation of the accompanying text is: "Canoe for Pearl-Fishing:
Pearls are being fished in the ocean between the main-land and Isla de Margarita,
approximately ten leagues, in three or four fathoms of water by the negroes who dive
into the sea, holding a hoop-net to descend to the bottom where they scrape the soil where
the oysters are, in order to find the pearls. And the deeper they descend in the water, the
larger are the pearls they find. Not being able to hold their breath longer than a quarter
of an hour, they come up again and pull their hoop-net. The fishing from morning to
evening having been completed, they return to La Rancheria where they live. Pearls
are being fished in three places, namely, on Isla de Margarita, in Riohacha, and at
the Cabo de la Vela." See Patrick O'Brian et al., eds., Histoire Naturelle des Indes:
The Drake Manuscript in the Pierpont Morgan Library *(New York, 1996).*

Every day more than three hundred canoes leave the harbour of the said town, which go about a league to sea to fish for pearls, in ten or twelve fathoms water. The said fishing is done by negroes, slaves of the king of Spain, who take a little basket under their arm, and with it plunge to the bottom of the sea, and fill it with ostrormes [meaning unclear], which resemble oysters; then go up again into their canoes, and return to the port to discharge them, in a spot designed for that purpose, when the officers of the king of Spain receive them.

Champlain was clearly impressed by the size of the fishing fleet, and his description also seems to contain a sense of admiration for the efficacy of the divers and their system of gathering oysters in baskets. He makes no mention of Spanish overseers in the pearl-fishing boats—indeed, he casually refers to the canoes as belonging to the divers ("their canoes"). Implicitly, Champlain describes a labor regime in which enslaved divers operated independently at sea, with Spanish royal authority coming back into view on shore in the figure of the "officers of the king of Spain."[23]

In practice, pearl distribution did not function so smoothly, with the pearls delivered directly by the divers to waiting Spanish officials. In the American pearl fisheries, life was a jumble, with indiscriminate mixing of people and pearls. The royal response was to seek to reorder the settlements, mandating discrete categories of pearls and discrete responsibilities for each type of subject, but vernacular practices of wealth cultivation and distribution prevailed. Royal officials contributed to these alternate practices by being absent from the fisheries at critical moments, such as when oysters were brought ashore from the pearl-fishing boats and disappeared into private hands and houses. In response, the crown mandated that the officials be present in the fisheries for the duration of the pearl-harvesting season to ensure that the oysters were brought ashore "without opening or hiding any" and delivered to the officially designated locales. Once deposited in these safe houses, officials would keep careful watch over workers who were to open the shells. Even the punishments for breeches of these laws emphasized the importance of these distinctions, varying in severity depending on the identity of the perpetrators. Categories of people, as of pearls, proliferated in the New World. As with pearls, these categories of subjects served as a guide to measuring their

23. Samuel Champlain, *Narrative of a Voyage to the West Indies and Mexico in the Years 1599–1602, with Maps and Illustrations,* ed. Norton Shaw, trans. Alice Wilmere (London, 1859), 7.

worth when it came to punishing transgressions. A canoe foreman *(canoero)* or diver who was "black, mulatto, or Indian" who opened shells anywhere other than the officially designated storehouse was to receive two hundred lashes and serve ten years laboring in the galleys. If the accused was Spanish or mestizo, the punishment was one hundred lashes and the forfeiture of all goods. Repeat offenders were to be given two hundred lashes and sent to labor in the galleys for life.[24]

The movement of pearls pointed to the failures of attempts at categorization and specialization. Whether in Europe or in the Americas, the private nature of pearl movement drew attention to the degree to which people evaded imperial control, making independent judgments not only about the value of the pearls concerned but also about the alliances and networks that gave order and meaning to their lives. In the Caribbean pearl fisheries, there was nobody more essential to the circulation of pearls than the divers themselves. Their centrality to the region's identity gave them a degree of power over the circulation of the jewel that the crown sought in vain to arrest. As report after report from the Pearl Coast attests, enslaved divers escaped frequently, colluded with neighboring Indians as well as foreign corsairs, socialized with nonenslaved residents of the fisheries, and to a large degree controlled the distribution of the pearls they harvested. Crown decrees concerning these problematic subjects oscillated between attempts to ameliorate their working and living conditions and measures designed to reduce their influence and autonomy in the settlements. Some of these measures were common throughout Spain's New World holdings, such as the 1570 royal injunction that settlers were not to bring married slaves from Iberia without also bringing their wives and children. But others reflected more precisely the reality of the Pearl Coast, such as the lengthy 1579 decree that sought to tighten the administrative infrastructure (as well as the physical structure) of these settlements.[25]

It was this promiscuity of people and pearls, this chaotic intermingling, that posed a source of great concern to the crown. The 1579 decree overwhelmingly emphasized containment, of people as well as of the jewel. Pearls were to be categorized and taxed according to quality and type, the imperfect prototype for processing pearls that was first put into place earlier in the

24. HNM, II, "Título de tesorero," doc. 64, items XXI–XXIX, deal with various aspects of procedures in the pearl fisheries.

25. The documentary collections *(Cedularios)* compiled by Enrique Otte are full of accounts of the difficulties that characterized the pearl fisheries. See, for example, *CC,* II.

century. Royal observers singled out practices that challenged crown prerogative, such as drilling pearls (which was forbidden) and, in a noteworthy
linguistic recognition of the related anxieties between the mixing of subjects
and the mixing of objects, "marrying" pearls of different categories by stringing together mismatched varieties. The precision and efficacy of these qualitative categories (such as *granzones,* or "big grains," and *amarillas redondas,*
or "yellow round ones," among others) were variable and subject to rampant
fraud. Once categorized, pearls were then to be further contained, placed in
elaborate locked boxes and stored in "strong houses" to be built by "Indians
and slaves," spaces in which residents (and pearls) could take refuge from
corsairs. In spite of these measures, the movement of pearls and people in
these settlements defied regulation. Pearls moved according to locally determined imperatives, whether in negotiations at sea, among traders from the
mainland and enslaved pearl canoe operators, or on shore as the fisheries'
motley residents forged the de facto boundaries of their community.[26]

Observers of the fisheries in the late 1570s and 1580s also provided a window onto the enduring relationship between vernacular practices, language,
and the contextual worth of pearls. Although there seems to have been a general consensus on which pearls were the best (the largest, the whitest), the
worth of any particular pearl was determined in the moment by the person in
a position to do the evaluating—whether it was the enslaved diver opening
the shells in the fishing boat or the buyer and seller determining the worth of
a pearl versus a piece of meat in a store in Caracas. The names for different
types of pearls in circulation illustrates the relationship between the worth

26. HNM, II, "Título de tesorero," doc. 64, item XXIIII: on separating the pearls
into their proper categories and giving the best fifth to the crown; item LVII: on the need
for security houses to protect "indios y esclavos" from being robbed by corsairs and to
dissuade them from coming. In this case, the terms "indios" and "esclavos" are used as
though the two categories do not overlap. Francis Drake's 1585–1586 raids on Cartagena and Santo Domingo are among the most famous of these plunder-driven missions,
but there were many more—not just on major cities but also on Spanish treasure ships,
island fishing settlements, and regional pearl storage warehouses. See AGI, Audiencia de
Panamá: 30, no. 16 (Apr. 15, 1577). This letter to Philip II from residents of Panama clearly
states the level of threat that the *cimarrón* communities of escaped slaves posed to the
fisheries. See Donkin, *Beyond Price,* 330; Lane, *Pillaging the Empire,* 41–43. The interplay among English privateers, African pearl divers, and Spanish pearl-fishery operators
and slaveowners is also discussed briefly in John K. Thornton and Linda M. Heywood,
Central Africans, Atlantic Creoles, and the Foundation of the Americas, 1585–1660 (Cambridge, 2007), 6.

of pearls and their social context within the local political economy. In the fisheries, networks of production were intimately linked to networks of distribution, and subjective judgment was an essential ingredient in assessing a pearl's value.

The vocabulary of pearl use and circulation also reflected practices in the fisheries, those that were unremarkable and those that were deeply challenging. While the term *ave maría,* for example, referred to pearls suitable for rosaries, other terms reflected practices elaborated by the enslaved divers. One report described as customary the practice that every Sunday the "blacks of the canoe" gave to the overseer and captain of their canoe "two or three marcos" (or between a pound and a pound and a half) of pearls for the canoe owner. This generated the name *topos domingueros,* or "Sunday pearls." *Topos* was one of eight categories into which double-washed pearls were to be separated by enslaved divers, who, according to one observer, would sit in a circle around the oysters they gathered, opening them and placing them in conch shells while supervised by a Spanish overseer. Pearls of seven to eight carats were the most valuable, "the biggest to be taken out of the sea in our time," and were worth more than four hundred ducados. If a pearl that size had a mate (a match), then the two were worth more than fifteen hundred ducados. Those of least value were to be given to pharmacists for medicinal use. Of these various and valuable specimens, the report's author noted that the slaves managed to keep the best pearls for themselves.[27]

The most worrisome of the vernacular practices chronicled by these official reporters were the remarkable auctions called *caconas* (a word that came to be used to refer to the highest-quality pearls), a type of distribution network that defied crown channels. Once or twice a month, "depending on how the fishery is doing," a boat owner would call all the enslaved divers to his house. There he would display an array of goods ranging from imported clothing and shoes to wine and cards and tell the gathered divers to take whatever they most desired. In return, he would ask for all the pearls that the divers had retained for themselves over the previous two weeks or so, "which experiences shows are the best." According to the author, the pearls gathered from this cacona were often "worth more than the fishery [haul] of twenty or thirty days." He concluded that the pearls obtained from the cacona were

27. For the report, see AGI, IG: 1805, fol. 3 (circa 1590). Jane E. Mangan cites the term *topo* as meaning "dress pins" in late-sixteenth-century Peru in "Moving Mestizos in Sixteenth-Century Peru: Spanish Fathers, Indigenous Mothers, and the Children in Between," *William and Mary Quarterly,* 3d Ser., LXX (2013), 292.

"the principal source of profit of the lords of the canoe because they are best and most oriental that are extracted."[28]

What is striking about the caconas is not so much the relatively common colonial practice of masters' offering inducements to their enslaved laborers but the subjectivity and range of the value given to pearls that they revealed. Moreover, the cacona, characterized by one author as an "Indian word, from when the Spaniards bartered with them just as they now do with the blacks of the canoes," also stands as a fascinating example of how indigenous vocabularies (and perhaps customs) evolved in the changing circumstances of early colonialism. Pearls were the heart of the region's economy, and the divers were the indispensable skilled laborers who produced them and shaped their circulation at the most critical moment, immediately after they were harvested. It is unsurprising that they used this power to keep the best pearls for themselves, dispensing them via the cacona in exchange for other sundry items.

In this context, the crown yet again sponsored a device (seemingly a type of dredge, invented by one Domingo Bartolomé and named the *tartana*) that promised to do away with the labor of pearl fishing; indeed, it explicitly promised that it would replace black divers. The device failed. Cubagua's residents insisted that no machine could manage this natural resource as skillfully as their enslaved divers did. Perhaps they were reluctant to cede the power that this volatile labor system allowed them; an enslaved labor force that they nominally controlled was an instrument for maintaining some independence from a royal bureaucracy.[29]

In spite of the continual exclamations about the unregulated flow of pearls within the fisheries, there also existed a recognition among local officials that, in the absence not only of basic goods but also the specie to procure them, pearls were needed as a medium of exchange. In the 1580s, officials in Caracas noted that pearls were the obvious choice to facilitate and enable basic commerce, "especially for the purchase of food items and clothing" in the region. The municipal council noted that the lack of minted money or gold was the source of much suffering and want "among rich and poor" in the city

28. For a description of the cacona, see AGI, IG: 1805, fols. 4–5 (circa 1590). Eduardo Barrera Monroy offers a transcription of this particular report in "Los esclavos de las perlas," *Boletín cultural y bibliográfico*, XXXIX, no. 61 (2002), 3–33.

29. On Bartolomé, see HNM, II, docs. 149–152. See also *CMNAC*, I, 218–221 (June 29, 1592). His device is also discussed in Manuel Luengo Muñoz, "Inventos para acrecentar la obtención de perlas en América durante el siglo XVI," *Anuario de estudios Americanos*, IX (1952), 68–72.

and inland, a situation that might be remedied by "dealing and contracting with pearls, the item of which there is most." The council's directive stands as an unusually explicit recognition of the potential benefits (as opposed to the costs to the settlements' social and economic order) to be had from pearls' abundance. Because the jewel was so accessible, pearls could ease the hardships caused by the lack of specie experienced by rich and poor alike.[30]

The subjective nature of pearls' appeal, however, made it very difficult to regulate their use as an official form of payment. In 1589, the governing council of the city of Caracas acknowledged the frequency with which inhabitants used pearls as cash and appointed a committee to consider the worth of certain quantities and qualities of the jewel. Pearls' viability as currency was compromised by fluctuations in supply. In 1590, the pearl supply in the region spiked following the discovery of new oyster banks on the mainland, and the prices of pearls dropped in response, rendering previously fixed pearl currency ratios invalid. The council's attempts to standardize the use of the jewel met with resistance: store owners refused to accept pearls as payment or requested greater numbers of them or better-quality specimens than the established ratios called for.[31] In 1595, the council again ordered that pearls be accepted as payment "in the butcher's shop just as in the rest of the grocery stores, taverns, and for other items that are sold often in small quantities, and in all other deals." No one was to "dare to ask for more" than the established amount. Again, inhabitants resisted the council's attempt to standardize the subjective judgments embedded in pearl transactions; they lamented that "some store keepers and bakers that sell bread will not and do not want

30. *ACC,* 99 (Sept. 9 1589): "Por no aver en esta çiudad y governaçion moneda acuñada, sino que en el comerçio de la tierra se trata con oro, y porque al presente en esta çiudad y su término no se saca oro, de cuya caussa en la república se padece nescessidad, así entre ricos como pobres, y que esta nesçessidad se podría evitar tratando y contratando con perlas, por ser género de que hay más cantidad, especialmente para el comerçio de la ciudad."

31. After two days of debate, the council determined that the problems caused by the lack of specie were so acute that pearls were to be allowed to circulate as money in the province of Caracas "at the prices that circulate on Margarita." The council determined that sixteen reales of pearls would be worth one *peso de oro fino* (peso of fine gold): *ACC,* 101 (Sept. 19, 1589). A year later, the council reaffirmed the decree to allow pearls to circulate as currency "as they do in Margarita and Cumana" and noted that these declared equivalencies were not always obeyed; the council sought to address the "many problems and debates and differences among the householders and residents regarding governance and inequality in payments" (*ACC,* 142 [Mar. 23, 1590]).

to receive pearls [as payment]." Perhaps in an effort to allay merchants' fear of fraud, the council ordered that a silversmith make precise pearl-measuring weights to be distributed to all small vendors throughout the city. This measure does not seem to have helped: a few years later, merchants continued to pick through the pearls offered them as payment and to choose the specimens they deemed superior, rather than accept payment by weight.[32]

Similar problems plagued Margarita. Store owners would accept only a higher quality of pearls than the one legally deemed acceptable for payment, and black pearl divers hid "a great part" of the pearls they gathered—in addition to those they brought to the caconas—and used "the best and the most valuable" of them "to come and buy things to eat and other things they need." These practices, vexatious though they were to crown officials, were central to the equilibrium that prevailed on the Pearl Coast.[33]

Contained within the singular dominance of this one commodity—pearls—were ways of expressing the diversity of needs of the region's inhabitants. Enslaved divers demanded their own concessions through the cacona, and Spaniards continued to sidestep the regulatory provisions intended to divert the best pearls to the crown. In 1591, Philip II once again noted the frequency with which pearls continued to evade the quinto and the amount of fraud perpetrated in the fisheries. The king blamed all residents of these settlements ("merchants, traders, contractors and all residents and inhabitants of the island and province") for their complicity in depriving him of his due. He also remarked on the continuing failure to sort pearls into their designated categories and the tendency to place them "all in confusion and together."[34]

At the close of the sixteenth century, enslaved pearl divers had successfully carved out private lives beyond the fisheries and took advantage of any opportunity to pursue their own interests. Royal officials in Cumaná, on the mainland, complained that a new law prohibiting Indians from fishing for pearls "of their own free will and for payment" had the effect of making the black slaves ("those lazy bastards") unwilling to work as well, preferring instead

---

32. The full quote fixes "11 grains of *rostrillo* (a lesser-quality type of pearl) for every real, up to the quantity of half a peso . . . in the butcher's shop just as in the rest of the grocery stores, taverns, and for other items that are sold often in small quantities, and in all other deals," and that no one "dare to ask for more than 16 reales per peso." See *ACC*, I, 398 (Jan. 7, 1595), 400 (Feb. 6, 1595).

33. AGI, IG: 1805.

34. *CMNAC*, I, 179, 180 (May 18, 1591).

to "tend their gardens and plantings and spend time with black women." In 1600, the crown again complained, noting the "games" and "raffles" of pearls that went on among the crews of the pearl-fishing boats. The crown sought to outlaw transactions between the boats' crews and slaveowners, who, the crown alleged, invented reasons to spend time near the boats, where they demanded their "caconas and pearls" and traded for valuable pearls with *negros ajenos,* or black divers in other peoples' employ. In spite of these complaints, that same year the crown recognized the centrality of the enslaved divers to the region's identity and their role within the imperial political economy by placing them in the center of the coat of arms the king granted the island of Margarita in 1600 (Figure 9). The king described the coat of arms as a shield with a partially blue background, "with a canoe in the middle and the blacks of the fishery, and on the bottom the depths of the sea . . . and on top of the said shield a crown, from which a pearl is suspended."[35]

Enslaved Africans and the pearls they harvested posed continual challenges to imperial control, yet they were also critical symbols and sources of the natural and human wealth of the empire's overseas domains. Margarita's coat of arms stands as yet another attempt by the crown to subsume a deeply challenging set of social and economic relations and place them—through a visual metaphor of political power—under the aegis of the crown.

Promiscuous Circulation of Pearls and People

As the Iberian crown struggled to impose order on the circulation of people and products within and beyond the fisheries, Spain and Portugal's rivals looked upon pearls and the settlements that produced them as potent symbols of what maritime empire could bring, both extraordinary wealth and wanton destruction. Pearls were embedded in narratives of maritime expansion, their complex multiple associations evidenced in art and writing alongside imperial initiatives to establish pearl-fishing operations around the globe.

35. AGI, SD: 190, 1590–1690; HNM, II, "New (old) decree, 1600," doc. 226 (this decree refers to the lengthy 1591 decree and laments that many of the same activities are still occurring); *CMNAC,* I, 301 (Nov. 30, 1599), 322 (Nov. 27, 1600): "y por la presente hago merçed a la dicha çiudad de la Asumpçión de la dicha isla Margarita de que agora y de aquí adelante aya y tenga por sus armas un escudo, la mitad del campo açul, con una canoa en medio y los negros de la pesquería, y en el hueco hondas de mar, y en lo alto del escudo a los dos lados dél San Felís y San Adaut, que son avogados de la dicha çiudad, y ençima del dicho escudo una corona, de la qual penda una perla que llegue hasta el campo azul, y por los lados unas letras que digan Sicut Margarita preçiosa, segund ba pintado en esta escudo, las quales doy a la dicha çiudad de la Asumpçión por sus armas."

*Figure 9. A Modern Rendition of the Coat of Arms Granted in 1600
to Margarita. Held in the Museo de Nueva Cádiz en Asunción, Margarita.
Photograph by Molly A. Warsh*

Figure 10. Elizabeth I, 1533–1603 (the "Armada Portrait"). Circa 1588. Oil on oak panel, 1,105 mm. × 1,270 mm. © National Maritime Museum, Greenwich, London

In the 1570s, French essayist Michel de Montaigne reflected on pearls as symbolic of the avarice and destruction that characterized accounts of the Americas. Pairing the jewel with a popular spice as chief motivators of the destructive encounters that Columbus's fateful trip engendered, he wrote: "So many cities razed, so many nations exterminated, so many millions of people put to the sword, and the richest and most beautiful part of the world turned upside down, for the traffic of pearls and pepper!" He was far from unusual in singling out the jewel as a symbol of the violence and glory of maritime empire. Pearls similarly evoked wealth, power, and violence in Elizabeth I's "Armada Portrait," painted shortly after England's defeat of Spain, in which the victorious monarch, situated against a backdrop of the naval battle, her hand jauntily perched on a globe she promises to dominate, is adorned in a headdress and ropes of the jewel (Figure 10). The portrait was painted in the wake of Sir Francis Drake's raids on Caribbean settlements, many of which produced pearls for the queen.[36] Drake was hardly the only source of pearls in England. Fellow privateer John Hawkins promised pearls to the queen from his raids in the 1560s; ship captains sold them to jewelers; royal jewelers bought them from individuals in a variety of conditions; and a prominent London goldsmith and the jeweler to Queen Elizabeth employed a ne'er-do-well West Country agent to supply him with pearls purchased from prize ships brought into West Country ports.[37]

Pearls' symbolic potency as emblems of maritime prowess was invoked in the jewel Elizabeth I gave to Francis Drake in recognition of his services to the crown in the late 1580s. The so-called Drake Jewel suggests that it was not pearls and pepper—as Montaigne suggested—that people thought of when empire came to mind; rather, it was pearls and enslaved Africans, at least in an Atlantic context. The pendant contains an image of the queen with her symbol, the falcon, on one side, and, on the reverse, the image of a black slave.[38]

36. Michel de Montaigne, "Of Coaches," in Donald M. Frame, trans., *The Complete Essays of Montaigne* (Stanford, Calif., 1958), 695. For a receipt of pearls delivered by Drake, see SP 46/17, fol. 198, TNA. As hostilities resumed between England and Spain in 1585, Spanish settlements in the Indies endured seventy-six different hostile expeditions by Elizabethan privateers over the next two decades. The surge of assaults against Spain's settlements and treasure ships, spearheaded by English West Country slave traders and privateers such as John Hawkins and Francis Drake, included devastating attacks on Cartagena. See Lane, *Pillaging the Empire*, 49.

37. Hawkins's 1567 letter to Elizabeth promising pearls is in SP 12/44, fol. 16, TNA. For a ship captain selling pearls to a jeweler in 1594, see Additional Manuscripts 14027, TNA. For examples of similar purchases of pearls by Spanish royal jewelers, see AGI, Contaduría: 196A, 1561–1649, no. 1, "Real Cédula" (Apr. 24, 1576), no. 2, "Real Cédula" (Feb. 24, 1578); AGI, IG: 426, legajo 26, fols. 125v (Oct. 6, 1578), 132v–133r (Nov. 10, 1578), IG: 739, no. 208 (Aug. 16, 1579), no. 371 (Oct. 7, 1581), IG: 740, no. 32 (Mar. 24, 1582); AGI, Contaduría: 5, nos. 1–3, "Perlas, esmeraldas y otras cosas que se entregaron al guardajoyas de Su Majestad," 1584–1597; Lane, *Pillaging the Empire*, 33–35, 49–50. These privateering hauls were quite lucrative: between 1585 and 1604, the annual value of goods (pearls among them) brought back to England from the Spanish Main by privateers was one hundred thousand pounds. See Philip D. Morgan, "Virginia's Other Prototype: The Caribbean," in Peter C. Mancall, ed., *The Atlantic World and Virginia, 1550–1624* (Chapel Hill, N.C., 2007), 349. For more on the port agent, see Molly A. Warsh, "Pearls and Plunder: The West Country Contact of a Jeweller to Queen Elizabeth," *Jewellery History Today*, no. 7 (February 2010), 5–6.

38. For the image of the Drake Jewel, see H. Clifford Smith, *Jewellery* (London, 1908), plate 34. On the jewel's history, see David S. Shields, "The Drake Jewel," *Uncommon Sense*, no. 118 (Spring 2004), http://oieahc.wm.edu/uncommon/118/drake.cfm.

If reflections on empire in art and prose employed pearls to evoke the violent complexities of maritime expansion, in practice pearls were used to shore up and maintain alliances amid the tumult caused by the era's shifting borders. Pearls, then, were associated not solely with destruction and dominance but also with custodianship—of both personal material wealth and also of ties among associates. Pearls reveal many different kinds of people debating in word and deed the question of how value (material and human) was to be assessed and regulated. These private political economies were simultaneously embedded within, and independent of, an imperial political economy that sought to monopolize wealth husbandry.

Though their calculations of risk and reward and the contours of their networks remain just beyond our view, we see traces of these alternate, intersecting economies in the records of individuals who shipped pearls on Spanish fleets from the Caribbean to varied recipients and destinations. For example, ships' registers documenting cargo leaving Santo Domingo in the 1550s include private shipments of pearls belonging to *particulares* (individuals), and the terse descriptions of these various pearl owners hint at an intricate and broad web of consumers. These records suggest that there was no fixed path along which pearls traveled. Perhaps some remained in the hands of the person recorded in the register, but some were destined for further distribution once they arrived in Europe. Even in the cases in which just the names or official titles of the owners are given—for example, "the king," "the judges and officials," and, remarkably, "the Bishop of Morocco"—we cannot know what these individuals intended to do with the pearls once they received them. The occasional vocational qualifiers of the pearls' owners ("the merchant brothers Diego and Alvaro Beltrán," "the silversmith de Mendoça," "the precious stone broker Francisco López") suggest that the imported pearls would not linger in the possession of these men. On an even larger scale, Caribbean pearls continued to travel far beyond the Atlantic waters from which they were fished and the Iberian hubs that received them to Charles V's northern European allies: in 1549, the Fuggers bought ten thousand American pearls, and Flemish merchants obtained a new license to control the circulation of Cubaguan pearls under Charles V's son and successor Philip II.[39]

A glimpse of one of the extra-imperial networks that delivered pearls throughout Spanish diplomatic networks appears in a peculiar 1567 case of customs evasion by Sephardic merchants at the London port of Gravesend.

39. "Registros de oro, plata y mercancias," 1554–1556, AGI, IG: 1802; Hermann Kellenbenz, *Los Fugger en España y Portugal hasta 1560* (Castilla y León, 2000), 496–497.

The extant trial testimony suggests that Margaret of Parma, the Spanish regent of the Netherlands, asked the Spanish ambassador to England, Diego de Guzmán de Silva, who had access to a network of Portuguese pearl merchants, to arrange for a shipment of pearls on behalf of herself and the duke of Alba, skirting customs duties and political sensitivities. Incomplete but tantalizing, the case illuminates the connections between private assessments of wealth and risk and larger political and commercial circuits.[40]

The clandestine nature of the transaction likely reflected the tense political climate: the Spanish crown's 1557 bankruptcy and resulting tax increase in the Dutch provinces threw the Spanish Netherlands into turmoil. The conflict in the Netherlands coincided with mounting hostility between Spain and England throughout the 1560s as well as England's own commercial and political disputes with the Dutch. Antwerp merchants quarreled with the English officials over trading rights and customs duties. Meanwhile, the Spanish rulers of the Netherlands were increasingly irritated by the activities of English Channel pirates (such as those whose prize ships produced Venezuelan pearls for the crown) and the English government's interference with Spanish shipping.[41]

40. For the trial testimony, see E/133/1/84, TNA.

41. Ambassador Guzmán de Silva, the diplomat at the heart of the clandestine pearl trade, began his four-year tenure in London in the midst of these diplomatic wrangles. Just a few months before his arrival in London, the English Privy Council had closed all English ports to shipping from the Netherlands and imposed penalties on ships that violated the embargo. As soon as Guzmán de Silva assumed his post, he began negotiating an end to this embargo with Sir William Cecil, Queen Elizabeth's chief advisor and secretary of state, and trade was reopened on January 1, 1565. (These dealings likely confirmed his connections with major players in the commerce of both countries.) Nonetheless, economic and diplomatic problems continued to interfere with commerce between the two nations for the rest of Guzmán de Sliva's tenure in England, and in 1569 tensions once again brought trade to a halt. In 1563, Spanish authorities in the Netherlands closed Low Country ports to English merchants, and merchants from the Netherlands were prohibited from exporting goods on English ships. These actions provoked retaliatory measures from England, many designed to hurt Antwerp's business market. On commercial problems between England and the Netherlands, see Vincent Ponko, Jr., "The Privy Council and the Spirit of Elizabethan Economic Management, 1558–1603," American Philosophical Society, *Transactions*, New Ser., LVIII, no. 4 (1968), 1–63. Robert Brenner argues that this period of troubled commercial relations in the 1560s and 1570s led English merchants to break their reliance on Antwerp and to begin searching for their own direct access to Eastern goods. See Brenner, "The Social Basis of English Commercial Expansion, 1550–1650," in Sanjay Subrahmanyam, ed., *Merchant Networks in the Early Modern World*,

Given the strained relations between Antwerp merchants, Spanish bureaucrats, and English customs officials at the time of the pearls' seizure, it was the commercial and political connections at the heart of the deal, and the preeminence of private over official channels, that came under scrutiny when two Gravesend officials discovered the pearls.[42] The questions asked of the merchants focused entirely on the networks responsible for moving the pearls from place to place. Court officials attempted to ascertain the precise nature of the transaction (for example, whether the pearls were being transported as merchandise or as a gift) as well as the geographic range of the participants in the affair and the logistics that enabled its execution. Witnesses were asked if they did "directly or indirectly speak and persuade" with customs officials in Plymouth or elsewhere, revealing an anxiety about sub-rosa circuits that undermined official channels. How many people had been privy to the deal, and for how long had it been planned? Had one of the merchant's connections to the Spanish ambassador enabled him to "make [frende] and labour to the Courte or to Any other place" with the goal of arranging further movement of the pearls? Had letters between Antwerp and England played an important role in arranging the deal, and, if so, who had served as couriers? Interrogating officials betrayed a pronounced concern about the permeability of the kingdom's borders and the power of extra-imperial networks that facilitated the movement of goods and people between realms.[43]

How the case was resolved is unclear. That the merchants were of Por-

---

1450–1800 (Aldershot, U.K., 1996), 284. These troubles in Antwerp marked the beginning of the end of the city's commercial dominance.

42. Details about Ambassador Guzmán de Silva's life are not abundant, but before being named ambassador he was a cleric from Ciudad Rodrigo, associated with the archbishop of Toledo, Cardinal Don Juan Talavera. In 1563, the Spanish Council of State named him ambassador to England. The skill he employed in solving the problem of halted commerce between England and Flanders made this one of the most notable successes of his career. On Guzmán de Silva, see Manuel Fernández Álvarez, *Tres embajadores de Felipe II en Inglaterra* (Madrid, 1951), 137–139; and Michael J. Levin, *Agents of Empire: Spanish Ambassadors in Sixteenth-Century Italy* (Ithaca, N.Y., 2005), 30–42. Guzmán de Silva — who would move to Venice as ambassador in 1571 — served as ambassador in London from 1563 to 1567. On Guzmán de Silva's tenure in Venice, see Levin, *Agents of Empire*, 8, 30, 160–165, 190–196.

43. E/133/1/84, TNA. Where the pearls originated remained unclear and indeed appears to have been of no interest to the interrogators; given the parties involved and the contours of the pearl trade in the late sixteenth century, though, it is very likely they came from either Lisbon or Seville and were from either the East or the West Indian pearl fisheries.

tuguese origin—likely New Christian—heightened the intrigue around the case. Alongside a growing trend toward specialization among artisans, including those working with jewels, there was a perception that outsiders controlled the jewel trade. Many of Lisbon's and Seville's goldsmiths and lapidaries were of New Christian origin or foreign-born (often from non-Catholic lands to the north). Religious tension, combined with the natural intrigue generated by products of great monetary value, rendered suspect the gem trade and those who took part in it, as did the growing formal recognition of these artisans.[44]

In Spain, royal recognition of silversmiths and goldsmiths as *artífices,* or artist-craftsmen (which implied a knowledge of science and the arts as opposed to mere mechanical mastery) was achieved in 1552 with an order by Charles V. Lisbon was also home to numerous specialists. By the mid-sixteenth century, a survey conducted at the behest of the archbishop of Lisbon (who wanted to chronicle the growth of the city) recorded at least 32 *lapidários,* or precious-stone dealers, and 430 goldsmiths, many of whom (if not most) likely also worked with precious stones of all types. In a 1566 petition, Lisbon's lapidaries requested royal recognition and regulation of their profession, and by 1572 they appeared as a separate category in Lisbon's official guide to the rules governing mechanical trades. Like the Sephardic network discovered at Gravesend, merchants' and jewelers' social and business networks often spanned contentious borders, and they employed a variety of strategies that enabled them to range widely and deal effectively with the risk and trust issues inherent to long-distance trade in highly valuable goods. Although merchant nations (as communities of foreign-born merchants living abroad were known) had long benefited from protected status in the cities in which they traded, as allegiances splintered throughout the sixteenth century the perception of these foreigners at the heart of the kingdom became more fraught. Foreign merchants became associated with external challenges to orthodoxy and sovereignty over the empire's wealth.[45]

44. On immigration and industry, see Lien Bich Luu, "Aliens and Their Impact on Goldsmiths' Craft in London in the Sixteenth Century," in David Mitchell, ed., *Goldsmiths, Silversmiths, and Bankers: Innovation and the Transfer of Skill, 1550 to 1750* (London, 1995), 43–52.

45. Priscilla E. Muller, *Jewels in Spain, 1500–1800* (New York, 1972), 3–5. For more on merchant nations and the particular problems they faced in Iberia, see Daviken Studnicki-Gizbert, *A Nation upon the Ocean Sea: Portugal's Atlantic Diaspora and the Crisis of the Spanish Empire, 1492–1640* (Oxford, 2007); Walter Grosshaupt, "Commercial Relations between Portugal and the Merchants of Augsburg and Nuremberg," in Jean Aubin, ed.,

Although the particular associations with foreigners and suspect religions likely intensified the anxiety surrounding the Gravesend case, it was not just jewelers and merchants who depended upon sub-rosa networks of allies and associates. No matter the origin of their erstwhile owner, pearls followed nearly ungovernable paths from market to owner and from owner to market again. Even the Spanish royal household continued to receive pearls through many channels. Arnão Vergel, the jeweler to Philip II's third wife, Isabel de Valois (from 1559 to her death in 1568), often mended humble pearl jewelry for assorted and frequently anonymous clients—pearls that had fallen off military epaulets, for example, or pearls that needed to be re-enameled or re-drilled. Vergel also purchased batches of pearls of undeclared provenance from a jeweler's assistant; on another occasion, he recorded his own purchase of a single *asiento* pearl that he must have needed for some item. Vergel did not bother to record the name of this seller of a single pearl. Once, a surname-less Santiago brought Vergel a relatively large pearl, weighing thirty carats, whose drilled hole had been blocked. (This particular pearl Vergel seems to have kept for his own use.) A pearl of uncertain origin and indeterminate value could, in a different setting, be incorporated with ease into an entirely new jewel, altering its worth and significance.[46]

Pearls were a mobile and easily hidden source of cash, and their abundance and range of quality made them an ordinary, everyman's jewel. They could be reattached, restrung, and repurposed in any number of ways, their provenance erased as they were dropped into a pile alongside similar specimens. Pearls trickled through and around ports and markets on scales small and large, worth great sums and barely anything at all. They proved nearly impervious to royal regulation even as they commanded the monarchy's steady attention. Philip II corresponded regularly with royal officials both within Spain and beyond about the arrival and distribution of pearls. In 1576, in a letter that touched upon the arrival in Lisbon of unregistered pearls destined for Seville, the king ordered an inquiry into the merchant networks involved. Not only were Seville's officials to look into "the people with whom [the recipient of the pearls] does business," the king additionally requested a thorough investigation into smuggling in Lisbon, embedding pearls in a com-

La découverte, le Portugal et l'Europe (Paris, 1990), 362–383; Kellenbenz, *Los Fugger,* 496; and Eddy Stols, "Os mercadores flamengos em Portugal e no Brasil antes das conquistas holandesas," *Anais de história,* no. 5 (1973), 9–54.

46. AGS, Inventario no. 39, Sección X: Casa Real, Obras, y Bosques, "Cuentas de Arnao Vergel, platero de oro," fols. 1–107.

plex world of illicit commercial dealings. Much like the interrogators in the case of pearl smuggling in London a decade earlier, Philip II wanted to know as much about the makeup of the networks of unlawful trade and traders as possible. Find out, he wrote, "what ships they traveled on, what their names were and to whom they belonged and from where they came, and the quantity of gold, silver, leathers, sugars and other things that they have unloaded, and what parts of our kingdom they live in, and with whom they correspond and do business." Pearls moved undetected with particular facility, thanks to their material qualities, but they illuminated a much larger world of exchange and alliance that continued to operate semi-independently of the imperial bureaucracy intended to track and contain it.[47]

The motivations of people dealing in pearls were as varied as pearls themselves. Moving untaxed pearls across borders did not always point to large networks of clandestine smugglers; sometimes the unregistered trades served far more humble personal needs. In the southern Iberian port of Sanlúcar de Barrameda in 1579, one Captain Alonso Forero returned from the Indies carrying two ounces of undeclared pearls. When the pearls were discovered, he explained that he had brought the jewel "for his personal expenses along the way, and to cover his time at court, and so that if the [courier] ship were to come in he could go for the post." Forero sought to use the jewels as his hedge against future uncertainties, but instead they were seized and fell into the hands of a greedy port agent, whom the captain unsuccessfully sued in the hope of seeing his pearls returned. Forero was unusual only because he got caught.[48]

The union of the Spanish and Portuguese crowns in 1580 made controlling goods in transit through peninsular ports even more difficult: pearls (among other items) often disappeared amid the confusion of competing and often

47. The king sent a royal decree to the House of Trade in Seville, asking officials there to send to his ambassador to Portugal, Don Juan de Silva, copies of certain laws and ordinances relevant to the case of a Portuguese vessel that had sailed from Portugal to Margarita and had returned to Portugal with unregistered pearls (AGI, IG: 1956, legajo 2, fols. 1r–1v [July 24, 1576]). A month later, the king wrote again to the ambassador, this time thanking him for a report on another parcel of unregistered pearls that had been seized in Lisbon (AGI, IG: 426, legajo 26, fols. 6–7 [Aug. 22, 1576]). Ambassador de Silva knew the name of the man in Lisbon for whom the latest recovered jewels were destined, and the king ordered that the information about these pearls be passed on to the officials in Seville, who were to look into the matter of the Lisbon contact's associates in that city.

48. AGI, IG: 739, no. 218 (Nov. 4, 1579), IG: 1956, legajo 3, fols. 50–50v (Nov. 13, 1579).

contradictory regulations and the increasing specialization and organization of those who dealt with them.[49] In 1583, Seville's royally appointed driller of pearls complained to the king that the majority of pearls that entered the city did so illegally, unregistered and untaxed. Far from the peninsula, pearls continued along their varied paths to market. For example, Dutch traveler Jan Huyghen van Linschoten in the early 1590s encountered a Spanish ship captain in the Azores who offered to sell him pearls that he carried on board worth fifty thousand ducats.[50]

Pearls captured peoples' imaginations on scales small and large. They symbolized the romance of maritime empire and the ambitions of those who sought to stake a large claim to the wealth it produced; they could be used concretely to finesse financial matters of personal importance or to reaffirm personal alliances. Evidence of pearls' prominence in both arenas emerge from the courts of Italy in the second half of the sixteenth century, where wealthy and ambitious Medici rulers in Florence collected pearls and commissioned reflections on their origins, and where in Venice high-ranking Spanish diplomats conducted furtive pearl trades in a climate of political uncertainty and financial precariousness. Pearls' power in action and in art thus extended from the sandy shores of the Pearl Coast to the corridors of European courts.

The Medici rulers of Florence were intensely interested in the Americas and sponsored artwork exploring the New World and its implications in addition to amassing large collections of exotic objects of American provenance.

---

49. For a succinct discussion of the impact of the union on border controls, taxes, and trade between the two nations, see Miguel Ángel Melón Jiménez, *Hacienda, comercio y contrabando en la frontera de Portugal (Siglos XV–XVIII)* (Cáceres, 1999), 41–57. An example of the tricky situations that arose in regulating the pearl trade during the period of the union is seen in the lengthy process that accompanied the evaluation and sale of some unregistered pearls that had been recovered from a Portuguese ship in 1597. The case reveals the complicated relationship between the Lisbon customhouse (Casa de Alfândega), Spanish officials, and the hired lapidary, silversmith, pearl borer, and auctioneer who were in charge of selling the pearls and delivering the profit to the Spanish royal consejo. See AGI, Contaduría: 45, 1591–1599, ramo 15 (1597); AGI, IG: 427, legajo 31, fols. 24r–24v (Aug. 13, 1597), IG: 1957, legajo 5, fols. 56–56v (Oct. 15, 1597), IG: 744, no. 190 (Nov. 5, 1597).

50. Enrique Otte, *Las perlas del Caribe: Nueva Cádiz de Cubagua* (Caracas, 1977), 51. Linschoten's encounter is discussed in Donkin, *Beyond Price,* 327. Linschoten does not say whether he pursued the offer, but it does not appear so; see Huygen van Linschoten, "Of Certain Notable and Memorable Accidents That Happened during My Continuance in Tercera," in *Voyage of Huygen van Linschoten* (London, 1598), book II, chap. 99.

Pearls and pearl fishing figured prominently in their patronage, pointing to the significance of the industry in giving shape to European fantasies of maritime dominance.[51] *The Treasures of the Sea* was painted for Florentine Ferdinando De' Medici around 1590 by the Florence-based artist Jacobo Zucchi (Figure 11, Plate 3). The image, though fantastical in many ways (particularly its mixture of gods and mortals), is firmly located in the Americas through its depiction not only of a monkey and a parrot (associated with the West Indies) but also of the pearl-fishing practices described in some of the earliest accounts of the fisheries. Pearls' long-standing association with female sensuality is on full display, but there are visual references to the actual labor of pearl diving as well, with male bodies in indigenous-seeming carved wooden trunk canoes gathering oysters in the background. Also, among other activities, archers take aim at maritime targets while swimmers and a female holding what appear to be weights collect additional treasures from the sea. Unlike the fourteenth-century *Catalan Atlas,* which separated pearls from the bivalves that produced them, the Zucchi illustration makes a clear link between the jewel and the oysters from which they emerge. The abundance of pearls shown in shells and underfoot is perhaps an echo of tales of New World plenty. Pearls were clearly a symbol of maritime bounty and of female sexuality and sensuality, but the particulars of the painting suggest that embedded in this European fascination with the jewel was a curiosity about the types of labor that produced it.[52]

Additional paintings within the Medici collection attest to the family's fascination with pearl fishing as symbolic of overseas wealth and evocative of exotic labor regimes. The first three dukes of Tuscany followed Spain's New World explorations with interest and sought to collect items from the Americas. As Lia Markey explores in her work on the Medici collections, Ferdinando in particular expressed a curiosity about pearls and representations of their harvesting. Alessandro Allori's pearl-diver sketch and pearl-fishing scenes as well as Giovanni Stradano's image of pearl diving in a mélange of

51. Lia Markey first brought the Medici interest in pearl fishing to my attention, and I am very grateful for her help with these images. See Markey, *Imagining the Americas in Medici Florence* (University Park, Pa., 2016). Mónica Domínguez-Torres was also very generous in sharing her work and insights on depictions of pearl fishing with me. See her essay "Pearl Fishing in the Caribbean: Early Images of Slavery and Forced Migration in the Americas," in Persephone Braham, ed., *African Diaspora in the Cultures of Latin America, the Caribbean, and the United States* (Newark, Del., 2015), 73–82.

52. On early pearl-fishing practices, see Domínguez-Torres, "Pearl Fishing in the Caribbean," in Braham, ed., *African Diaspora,* 73.

Figure 11. Jacopo Zucchi, Treasures of the Sea, or Allegory of the Discovery
of America. *Circa 1549–1590. Oil on copper. Galleria Borghese, Rome.
Photograph: Scala/Art Resource, N.Y.*

various parts of the world show that the jewel was already a potent symbol of the exoticism of foreign markets as well as of the human capital required to produce the wealth of expansion. Allori's pearl diver is of indeterminate origin and is half clothed, showing a powerful masculine physique. He evokes man's power to control nature—and perhaps, through his posture of contemplation, suggests that the act of subduing nature—and the imperial enterprise itself—requires thought and care (Figure 12). Allori's painting of a far more complex scene of pearl gathering is as devoid of precise context as the sketch of the single diver (Figure 13). The image suggests empire, with semidistant scenes of somewhat frantic oyster harvesting by numerous actors in crowded boats, watched intently by many figures on shore. Those on shore focus on the cornucopias of pearl wealth emerging from conch shells.[53]

Allori's painting has echoes of the reality of pearl harvesting (it occurred in boats, by people), but, as noted, it provides little detail rooted in global practices. There are no bodies of color, and some of the participants on land suggest classical gods, placing the painting in some imagined mythos of maritime empire. Naked female bodies further add to the sensuality of the painting (and pearls' long-standing feminine overtones) and conjure the idea of empire as an assertion of masculine authority over a female nature in need of conquest and subduing. The Stradano image, on the other hand, reflects a much more detailed attention to the actual practices of pearl harvesting (Figure 14). The divers descend underwater on ropes, and the tented shacks on land call to mind early descriptions of the Caribbean pearl fisheries, as does the rendition of family groups.[54]

Beyond the private rooms of the Medici palaces and the interest their collections evince in pearl fishing as a heuristic device for contemplating overseas ventures, pearls were used in Italy in ways that echoed pearls' practical uses on the Pearl Coast and elsewhere: to negotiate fluctuating private and political fortunes. From the Caribbean to London, Italy, and beyond, pearls traveled along networks of commerce and friendship. They permitted men (and women) to take advantage of the benefits of newly connected markets while simultaneously reaffirming the durability of alliances that transcended shifting boundaries and the vagaries of that same market. Imperial governance depended upon these agents, humble and elite servants alike, to do

53. Markey, *Imagining the Americas,* esp. chapters 5 and 6.
54. For an overview of nature as female and a new early modern language of dominance and mastery, see Carolyn Merchant, *The Death of Nature: Women, Ecology, and the Scientific Revolution* (San Francisco, 1980).

Figure 12. Alessando Allori, A Pearl Diver. Circa 1570.
Black chalk on laid paper, 30.2 cm. × 21 cm. Gift of David E. Rust, 2005.147.1.
Courtesy, National Gallery of Art, Washington, D.C.

Plate 1. Enameled Sea Dragon Pendant with Baroque Pearl. Spain, late sixteenth century. Permission, The British Museum, London

Plate 2. Detail of Pearl Diving from Catalan Atlas. *Circa 1375. Permission, Bibliothèque nationale de France. The cartouche describes spells used to warn off dangerous fish. Note that the pearls are depicted as bright precious stones.*

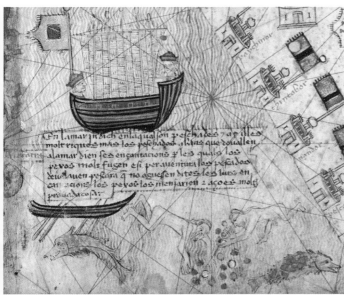

Plate 3. Jacopo Zucchi, Treasures of the Sea, or Allegory of the Discovery of America.
Circa 1549–1590. Oil on copper. Galleria Borghese, Rome.
Photograph: Scala / Art Resource, N.Y.

Plate 4. Quentin Metsys, The Moneylender and His Wife. 1514. Oil on wood, 70.5 × 67 cm. Musée du Louvre, Paris, France. © RMN-Grand Palais/Art Resource, N.Y.

Plate 5. José de Alcíbar (attributed to), "De español y negra, mulato (From Spaniard and Black, Mulatto)." Circa 1760. Denver Art Museum: Gift of the Collection of Frederick and Jan Mayer, 2014.217. Photograph courtesy of the Denver Art Museum

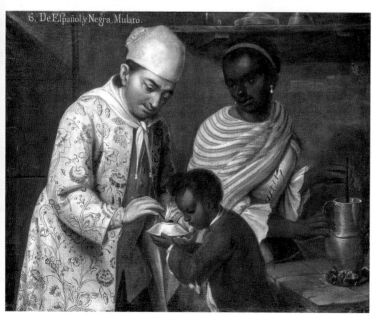

Plates 6. Lead Box (top) Containing Pearls of Varying Sizes and Shapes, Including Several Baroque Pearls (bottom), Found among the Wreckage of the Santa Margarita. *Photographs by Ron Pierson, Mel Fisher's Treasures*

Plate 7. Albert Eckhout, African Woman and Child. *1641.*
Photograph by John Lee. Courtesy, National Museum of Denmark

Plate 8. Pierre Mignard, Louise de Kéroualle, Duchess of Portsmouth. *Late seventeenth century.* © *National Portrait Gallery, London*

Plate 9. Simon Verelst, Eleanor ("Nell") Gwynn. *Circa 1680.* © *National Portrait Gallery, London*

Plate 10. Johannes Vermeer, Woman Holding a Balance. Circa 1664. Oil on canvas, 39.7 cm. × 35.5. cm. Widener Collection, 1942.9.97. Courtesy, National Gallery of Art, Washington, D.C.

Plate 11. Johannes Vermeer, Young Woman with a Pearl Necklace. Circa 1662–1665. Oil on canvas, 55 cm. × 45 cm. Post-restoration. Photo credit: bpk Bildagentur/ Gemäldegalerie, Staatliche Museen, Berlin, Germany/ Jörg P. Anders/Art Resource, N.Y.

Plate 12. Johann Georg Hinz, Cabinet of Collectibles. 1666. Oil on canvas, 115.5 × 93.3 cm. Photo credit: bpk Bildagentur/ Hamburger Kunsthalle/Elke Walford/Art Resource, N.Y.

Plate 13. Johann Melchior Dinglinger (goldsmith), Moor with Monstrous Pearl Shell. 1724. Detail of photograph by Jürgen Karpinski. Wood, lacquered, gold, silver, gold plated, enamel, precious stones, cameos, pearls, mother of pearl, 19.9 cm. × 19.4 cm. Photo credit: bpk Bildagentur/ Gruenes Gewoelbe, Staatliche Kunstsammlungen, Dresden, Germany/Jürgen Karpinski/ Art Resource, N.Y.

Figure 13. Alessandro Allori, Pesca delle Perle. *Circa 1570s. Photograph: Fototeca dei Musei Civici Fiorentini. Firenze, Museo di Palazzo Vecchio*

its bidding, but they regularly used pearls in ways that undermined imperial goals, putting forth their own divergent understandings of which boundaries mattered. In distinct settings, pearls revealed highly personal understandings of the nature of value and the assessment of worth.

A series of remarkable cases involving pearls unfolded around Cristóbal de Salazar, the secretary to the Spanish embassy in Venice in the 1570s and 1580s. These pearl and jewel deals played a role in Salazar's management of a set of alliances that stretched across considerable distances in a fractious

Figure 14. Giovanni Stradano, Pearl Diving. *Sixteenth Century.*
Pen and ink and bodycolour (white) on paper, 26.3 cm. × 18.7 cm.
The Samuel Courtauld Trust, The Courtauld Gallery, London

Iberian empire. Furthermore, these transactions revolved around men who were powerful players in the courts of Western Europe in the last half of the sixteenth century—not people for whom pearls or other jewels represented their only hope for economic or social benefit. The actors in these cases are extraordinary for their prominence—some of the most high-ranking diplomats in the Spanish imperial world, men with seemingly secure political and financial fortunes. One distinguished player was the same Spanish ambassador at the heart of the botched Gravesend pearl trade in England in the 1560s, who was posted subsequently to Venice, Don Diego de Guzmán de Silva. His protagonism in both cases suggests that pearls played an enduring role in his construction of alternate commercial and diplomatic networks. The leading figure among the diplomats in Italy involved in clandestine pearl trades was Don Enrique de Guzmán, count of Olivares, the Spanish ambassador to Rome from 1582 to 1591. (His son Gaspár de Guzmán y Pimentel would become the de facto ruler of Spain in the first half of the seventeenth century, a man whose political fortunes rose and fell on his attempts to integrate the multiple parts of the Iberian empire.) As it turned out, pearls figured in the count's calculations of how to navigate fluctuations in his personal fortunes. Additional participants were the Spanish secretary of state and war under Philip II, Don Juan de Idiáquez, and a number of archbishops, ambassadors, minor counts, and even a cardinal.

At some point during his tenure at the Spanish embassy in Venice in the 1570s and 1580s, Salazar served all of these men as a jewel broker and occasional mule of smuggled gems. No wonder that these men anxiously sought to preserve their personal fortunes and ties in this climate, as other types of affiliation seemed fleeting and unstable. Pearls—hidden under bulky tunics, sealed into secret boxes, strung and restrung in the latest fashions—traded hands among these men (sometimes at the behest of their wives) to preserve an invisible type of wealth and value: the esteem they accorded one another and their sense of their position in a rapidly changing world.

Italy at the time consisted of a complex assortment of republics, duchies, city-states, and kingdoms, all of which had their own political realities and agendas. Spain formally controlled four states (Sicily, Sardinia, Naples, and Milan) and possessed de facto control of many others. The political realities of governing these Italian territories led the Spanish to have three and sometimes four separate embassies on the Italian peninsula, Venice and Rome among them (along with Genoa and Savoy). Spain's control of its Italian territories depended on elaborate webs of patronage and favors, the burden of which rested chiefly on ambassadors, who were crucial to maintaining the authority of a distant king.[55]

Of Italy's independent states, the Republic of Venice was by far the most powerful. Its strategic location, its long-standing commercial importance, and its willingness to occasionally ally with the Ottomans made it a particularly difficult posting for the Spanish diplomats assigned there and charged with winning Venetian loyalty. As the embassy secretary, Salazar occupied a key post in the city's diplomatic and commercial web. Among his other duties, he appears to have had his finger on the pulse of the city's famous jewel trade, keeping track of stolen jewels, astute sellers, and eager buyers. He facilitated engagement between his extensive network of diplomatic con-

55. A series of political and military conquests over the course of the sixteenth century had left the Spanish Habsburgs as the dominant force in Italian affairs, a situation that would remain the case (although under increasing duress) until the death of Charles II and the end of the Habsburg line in 1700. Spain possessed de facto control of Rome, Genoa, Tuscany, Savoy, and the minor states. For Spanish Italy, see Thomas James Dandelet and John A. Marino, eds., *Spain in Italy: Politics, Society, and Religion, 1500–1700* (Leiden, 2007).

tacts and this lucrative demimonde. Salazar was perhaps little different from the diplomats with whom the Sephardic merchants dealt in London twenty years earlier. In Italy, as in London and in the pearl fisheries, expertise and private knowledge—independent action and assessment—fueled Salazar's power, much as it enabled the relative autonomy of pearl divers on the Pearl Coast of Venezuela, thousands of miles away. In his role as jewel broker, Salazar amassed intimate knowledge of his contacts' tastes and finances. Even when jewels were at the heart of his correspondence with his contacts, his exchanges contained personal and political news as well. The details of his associates' needs and concerns, their friends and possessions, placed Salazar in a powerful position. They enabled him to peer across realms of activity— the private home with its particular financial concerns, shifting political borders, and tumultuous markets.[56]

These overlapping interests are visible in an elaborate clandestine jewel trade Salazar conducted on behalf of a Portuguese cleric named Lope de Almeida. The men's correspondence suggests that trading in pearls and other jewels was a fraught activity for elite consumers. These trades enabled them to use increasingly connected markets to engage with financial and political uncertainties on their own terms but prompted them to deny this uncertainty by cloaking their arrangements in language that emphasized the permanence of friendship and allegiance.

The Almeida transaction took place in the spring of 1579, in the midst of the succession crisis that would lead to Spain's annexation of Portugal in 1580. Almeida wrote to Salazar from Lisbon to arrange the transport of jewels of considerable value from Italy to Portugal, including diamonds worth 300 ducats, sapphires worth 100 ducats, and pearls worth 30. This was a sizable sum: Salazar's entire yearly salary was only 280 ducats. Almeida provided Salazar with explicit instructions on how to transport the jewels undetected and revealed that this was not the first time that Salazar had performed such a service for him. Salazar was to dismantle a pearl necklace consisting of seven chains and a single good pearl. He could then wear the chains around his neck "as personal adornment, over your smock, and the pearl should be hidden within a stack of letters so that it is does not form a visible bump, just like your grace sent the diamond to me in Vicenzia." Once the jewels arrived in Lisbon, Salazar was to arrange their sale—an equally fraught transaction involving a web of trusted allies, including the ambassador of Mantua and three merchants, two of whom were likely New Christians, and one who was

56. AGS, Papeles de Estado de Venecia, legajo 1550, exp. 470 (n.d.).

German. A few years later, another transfer of jewels from Milan to Lisbon, via Venice and Madrid, prompted Salazar and Almeida to employ similar language as they coordinated the secret transfer of pearls and other jewels with the help of numerous dukes, ambassadors, and trusted couriers.[57]

The involvement of such merchants in the sale and distribution of Almeida's jewels reveals that these secular and religious officials were embedded in both royal and commercial channels even as they acted semi-independently of them. Almeida's closing line to Salazar in the letter arranging the initial sale in Lisbon suggests that he preferred to consider the men's dealings as affirmations of the permanence of their friendship, rather than as indications of the degree to which both men's fortunes were conditioned and shaped by the shifting market. Although an essential part of these arrangements was the complicity created by navigating and bypassing other channels for the movement of wealth, Almeida nonetheless employed rhetoric of distance from precisely these types of concerns. He closed by affirming to Salazar that "after God, I trust no one more in this matter than your grace . . . whatever state in which your grace and I find ourselves and in whatever part [of the world], may your grace count on me with the utmost confidence in matters of your happiness, and may I enjoy the same, because it would not be right for our strong and deep friendship to be subject to the laws and lunacies of the world." It would be hard to imagine a clearer articulation of the value these types of trades held for their participants. In a world in flux, characterized by unprecedented mobility and shifting borders (evoked by Almeida's reference to the two men's impermanent "states" and scattered locations), they allowed friends and associates to reaffirm the stability of their ties to one another and their approaches to cultivating and caring for what mattered to them. The "laws and lunacies" — an interesting pairing, suggesting that Almeida saw madness in proliferating regulations — that threatened to curtail the men's movements and actions were no match for their "strong and deep friendship."[58]

Comparable transactions arranged by Salazar in the 1580s were pearl sales for men acting on behalf of their wives. The anxiety that pervades their correspondence suggests that these men disliked having to sell the pearls — grateful, perhaps, for the ease with which the jewel could be anonymously turned into cash but uncomfortable with the instability of their own status that such a sale implied. These concerns are seen with remarkable clarity in

57. Ibid., legajo 1522, exp. 143 (May 5, 1579).
58. Ibid.

a pearl sale Salazar conducted on behalf of Don Enrique de Guzmán. Even a man of his stature was not immune from financial uncertainty and the attendant embarrassment. In 1583, his third year as ambassador to Rome, Olivares sought to arrange a highly secret and profitable sale of pearls through Salazar. Ten letters written over the course of more than a year reveal that the count's wish to profit from the pearls was outweighed only by his desire to keep the entire affair a secret. Olivares's preference for anonymity did not prevent him from instructing Salazar on every aspect of the sale, from the wisdom of restringing the pearls to meet Venetian tastes to negotiating with merchants, to which currency to accept in payment, to finding the right kind of buyers. Olivares demanded Salazar's absolute discretion as well as regular reports about his interactions with merchants. The count, perhaps reflecting on the pearls' quality and their dignity as jewels, wanted to sell the pearls to someone who intended to keep them rather than to resell them for a profit. This hope might reveal some perceived distinction in status between treating the jewel as a commodity—a wrought jewel in the form of a necklace—and as a resource to be assessed in terms of its cash value, dismantled, and sold separately.[59]

Perhaps the most intriguing aspect of the men's correspondence is the hint that it might well have been Olivares's wife directing the transaction and advising her husband on how to facilitate the most profitable sale. Either Olivares or his wife was intimately familiar with the market for pearls and had a keen eye for their quality and the conditions that most mattered to potential buyers, such as the degree to which the pearls on a necklace "matched." Though his wife is never referred to by name, a late letter to Salazar from the count suggests that she was indeed the *eminence gris* behind the transaction.

59. The count proved to be a powerful and contentious figure. At the time of the pearl deal he was in the middle of navigating the biggest issue of his tenure as ambassador—the papal support (political and financial) of a Spanish invasion of England, the famous and failed Spanish Armada. On Olivares in Rome, see Levin, *Agents of Empire*, 112–123. Olivares was said to have arrived in Rome with an annual disposable income of forty thousand ducats, three-quarters of which derived from his own estates and the rest of which came from the king. His initial entourage included thirty-four servants, and over the ten years he spent in Rome his household grew to more than a hundred people. They were not the only high-ranking officials in Rome to turn to pearls as a resource that year: provincial superior of the Jesuits in Rome, Claudio Aquaviva, read a letter from the provincial superior of India, Alessandro Valignano in Cochin, about the recent commission of a substantial pearl purchase. See Aquaviva to Valignano, Dec. 23, 1586, in Joseph Wicki and John Gomes, eds., *Documenta Indica*, 18 vols. (Rome, 1948–1988), XIV (1585–1588), 525–527.

In September of that year, he reported, "The countess is very satisfied and grateful to your Grace for the care with which you will arrange [the pearls'] successful sale," noting that those who criticized the quality of the pearls were only "doing their job" as they hoped to buy them. A few months later, the count continued to negotiate on behalf of his wife: "As far as what your Grace tells me that they are offering for the pearls, truth be told, the countess would prefer they give her more because they cost more in Spain than what they are offering for them. If this is because they are poorly strung and arranged, then your Grace should proceed as if this were his own matter" and restring them. It is impossible to tell whether the care with which the countess pursued the sale reflected an emotional attachment to the pearls beyond her clear financial assessment of their value. For whatever reason, she urged her husband and his associate to adhere to her own informed assessments of the jewels' worth.[60]

Like his jewel-trading peers, Olivares used networks of contacts to move his pearls from city to city, but he distinguished among the people he was willing to involve in the business and those he wanted to keep from it. At one point, the count wrote to Salazar that he could not act upon the deal until an unnamed archbishop examined the pearls and told him what to do with them. When the examination finally occurred a few months later, Olivares remained reluctant to send the pearls to Venice because of his fears concerning the reliability of the mail system. He depended on an elite ally to assure him that the trip was safe, informing Salazar that he was waiting for the go-ahead from an unspecified ambassador before he mailed the pearls to Salazar so that Salazar could unload them *(salir de ellas),* a jarring phrase that suggests Olivares's discomfort with the entire transaction.[61]

When Olivares finally sent the pearls on their way to Venice, they were in a "well-appointed and sealed box," a description that evokes the containers in which pearls were to be kept along the Venezuelan Pearl Coast; in both places, people sought secure methods of containing the jewel. The safe transport of the pearls involved an elaborate system of unwitting couriers and decoys that Olivares devised in collaboration with a network of church officials. These measures reflected more than just his fears about "all of the risks and mishaps that can occur" during the jewel's transfer; he was also desperate to conceal his identity as the seller, "because neither here [in Rome] nor there

60. AGS, Papeles de Estado de Venecia, legajo 1537, exp. 47 (Sept. 27, 1586), legajo 1538, exp. 38 (Nov. 1, 1586).
61. The phrase is used twice in slightly different form ibid., legajo 1536, exp. 30 (July 5, 1586).

[in Venice] do I want it to be rumored that these pearls are mine." His concerns again surfaced when Salazar requested permission from the count to prolong the sale: Olivares grudgingly consented but warned that he do so "with such security that no risk is run."[62]

Throughout his negotiations with Salazar, Olivares oscillated between a desire to move forward with the search and the need to control every aspect of it, urging Salazar not to be "hastier than necessary in order to obtain as much advantage as possible." At one point, Olivares urged Salazar to hold onto the pearls *hasta su sazón,* an ambiguous phrase that could mean "until the time is right" or "until their season," implying that pearl sales shifted depending on the time of year. Though the final price of the pearls concerned him, he was most adamant about keeping the sale anonymous. When Salazar suggested that the count mention the pearls to a high-ranking peer who might be interested, Olivares resoundingly rejected the proposal: "As far as the pearls are concerned, I have said nothing to Don Fernando nor would I want anyone to know that they are mine." Given the secrecy Olivares hoped to maintain surrounding the pearls' sale, it is not clear how the business concluded, only that Olivares trusted Salazar to carry out the transaction to his advantage.[63]

Olivares's pearls were not the only ones Salazar was charged with selling in 1586. That same year, one Hernando de Torres sent a small box containing valuable pearls to Salazar from Rome. In the accompanying letter, de Torres explained that the box contained two strands of pearls that he had purchased for 208 ducats and another, vastly superior strand from his wife, worth 1,000 ducats. Salazar was to act as the middleman, arranging the sale of the pearls in Venice "at the best price possible." De Torres was clearly quite eager to turn the pearls into cash: he repeated that he wanted the merchant to "make the most of the sale" and "unload" the pearls, giving the proceeds to Salazar. De Torres's letter bespeaks urgency and embarrassment: he closed his brief letter by "begging" Salazar to act on the sale as quickly as possible and with as much care "as if they were his own" while also requesting that he "forgive de Torres for the bother." In a sign of further desperation, de Torres hastily scrawled at the bottom of the page, beneath his signature, yet another reminder to sell the pearls "as well as possible" (Figure 15). De Torres wrote

62. For "well appointed and sealed box," and "neither here . . . nor there," see ibid., legajo 1537, exp. 45 (Aug. 8, 1586); for "risks and mishaps," see legajo 1537, exp. 42 (July 19, 1586); for "such security," see legajo 1537, exp. 47 (Sept. 27, 1586).

63. Ibid., legajo 1537, exp. 44 (Aug. 2, 1586), exp. 51 (Oct. 25, 1586).

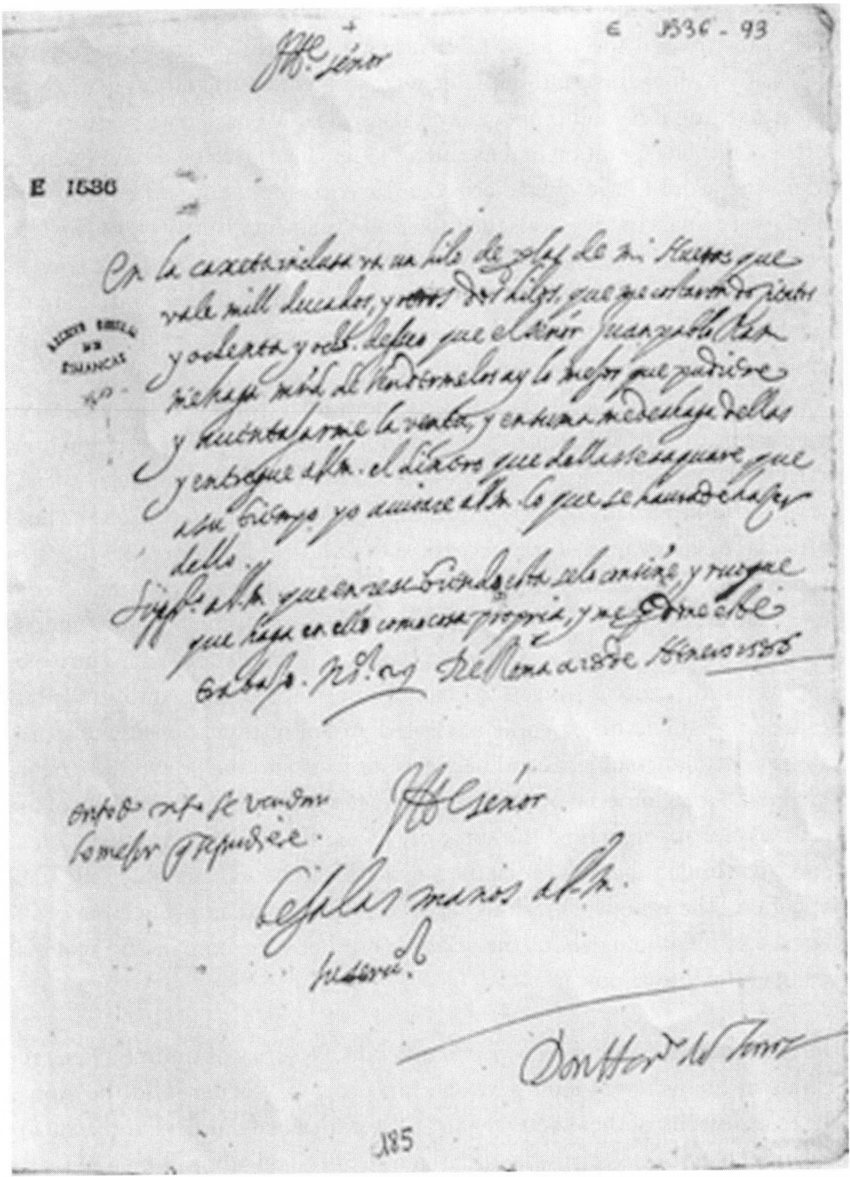

Figure 15. Hernando de Torres to Cristóbal de Salazar, Jan. 18, 1586, AGS, Papeles de Estado de Venecia, legajo 1536, exp. 93

Salazar at weekly intervals for the next two months, alternating between telling Salazar to sell the pearls "no matter what" (while also specifying the prices at which each strand of pearls were to be offered) and urging Salazar to resist selling if he could not get a certain price.[64]

The tone of desperation in these men's letters likely reflected their financial straits and would have characterized their correspondence whether or not pearls were a part of the goods they sought to sell. But pearls were indeed the good to which they turned, pointing to the remarkable utility of this jewel as a source not only of wealth but also as a token to express their own, unquantifiable assessments of the value of their alliances in the face of an expanding, ambitious, and unstable imperial state.

Whether in Venezuela, England, or Iberia, pearls loaned themselves to expressions of independence, either of individuals navigating changing imperial horizons to the best of their abilities or of networks of alliances operating outside, or partially outside, imperial channels. Pearls were a jewel whose particular qualities made them accessible to a wide range of people who then used them as vectors of commercial and political debt in ways they found beneficial. We see these contending networks in pearl dealings in the fisheries as well as in other politically charged imperial borderlands where jurisdiction over subjects and objects remained uncertain. These contested pearl dealings illuminate how people navigated an era of transition in which relationships among subjects and between subjects and the crown were being redefined. As an imperial bureaucracy emerged to harness the mobility of the era in ways that augmented the authority of an increasingly centralized state, vernacular trade practices reveal the small-scale networks on which the state depended. These networks, however, often functioned as a reflection of independent judgments about the relationship between human and material wealth and political power.

The American encounter with pearls unleashed a series of unpredictable reactions in the fisheries themselves and in pearl markets around the globe. The early lessons of these settlements—the imperfectly understood ecological component of pearl production, the role of skilled labor in their harvesting, and the difficulty their sheer variety posed to administrative attempts to tax and otherwise control their circulation—all continued to characterize this corner of the Caribbean into the seventeenth century. Even as the Antilles turned into a backwater of the growing mainland empire, the diversity and in-

64. Ibid., legajo 1536, exp. 93 (Jan. 18, 1586).

commensurability of people and of pearls meant that the fisheries continued to pose problems of governance. Their complexity forced the monarchy to confront the inadequacies of its administrative bureaucracy when it came to managing wealth. Subjects continually came up with new ways to use pearls to further their own aims, just as new names for different types of pearls proliferated along the Pearl Coast.

The unpredictability produced by pearls' abundance characterized their circulation far beyond the Americas as well. It was not just that pearls were now available in quantities and at prices that made them accessible to consumers who before the Columbian encounter had not been associated with the jewel—such as the black women bedecked in pearl necklaces who so astonished López de Gómara. It was that, even as pearls prompted royal attention and innovation as an important source of wealth and a driver of the slave trade to and within the Americas, they simultaneously encouraged the construction and maintenance of alliances that operated independently of crown supervision and the nascent imperial bureaucracy. These alternate networks spanned the Americas, Europe, and beyond, and they encompassed women and men and consumers free and unfree, elite and humble. The range of experiences and concerns of the individuals within these networks stood—as did the diversity of pearls themselves—as a reminder of the difficulty of imposing order and uniformity upon assessments of value.

MAKING "A MACHINE OF PEARLS"
IN THE SEVENTEENTH CENTURY
Custom and Innovation in Iberian Pearl-Fishing Ventures

By the turn to the seventeenth century, the Iberian crown ruled over an empire that was wealthy and wide ranging in its geography and subject base, but it was also fractured and fractious, facing severe economic and political crises within Iberia and throughout its far-flung domains. Soothsayers denounced the king and predicted end times; wars raged on distant and domestic frontiers; the Portuguese chafed at an uneasy political union they viewed as a captivity. Even as American silver poured in from mines on the mainland, it fled Iberian coffers for Spain's European creditors. What place was there, in this moment of sharpening crisis, for pearls—either the memory of their early-sixteenth-century bonanzas or the paltry harvests that continued to emerge from South American waters? Facing competition throughout its global empire as well as bankruptcies and tumult at home, the Iberian crown saw experts of various pedigrees (known as *arbitristas*) propose solutions to the financial crisis facing the empire. In the context of difficulties and schemes for recovery, pearls surfaced in plans to restore Spain's maritime wealth, either through new pearl fisheries along the Pacific coast, or in innovative approaches to harvesting oysters in the Caribbean, or in the ingenious employment of pearl divers to rescue sunken treasure from beneath the waves.[1]

Metaphorically, pearls remained symbolic not only of the wealth of empire but also of the impulse to categorize and order the chaotic wealth of the New World. *Elenco,* the term once used by Pliny to describe an elongated pearl, had, by the early seventeenth century, come to mean "index." Sebastián de Covarrubias Horozco, the author of the 1611 monolingual dictionary *Tesoro*

---

1. The literature on Spain's late-sixteenth- and seventeenth-century crisis is vast. For two fascinating case studies and an overview, see Richard L. Kagan, *Lucrecia's Dreams: Politics and Prophecy in Sixteenth-Century Spain* (Los Angeles, 1990); and Erin Kathleen Rowe, *Saint and Nation: Santiago, Teresa of Avila, and Plural Identities in Early Modern Spain* (University Park, Pa., 2011). For a discussion of *arbitristas,* see Daviken Studnicki-Gizbert, *A Nation upon the Ocean Sea: Portugal's Atlantic Diaspora and the Crisis of the Spanish Empire, 1492–1640* (Oxford, 2007).

de la lengua Castellana o Española (Treasure of the Castillian or Spanish language), offered an explicit reflection on the jewel's shifting conceptual utility, from precious pearl to an equally precious tool of categorization, a way of making sense of something large and complex: "Tables and indices of books are known as elencos, which by another name, which is the same, they call margarita, and for good reason, as there is no pearl as precious as these indices, which indicate to us, as if by pointing a finger, that which we seek, without turning every page of a lengthy book, through which we would otherwise move blindly." Pearls became synonymous with the urge toward order and mastery, the imperial impulse that their profusion in the early Caribbean provoked. Yet, pearls' long-standing association with contradictory binaries persisted; as *elenco* came to symbolize the categorization of knowledge, the *barrueca,* or baroque, would come to represent the rejection of standardization and control, the unfettered expression of independence in action and taste.[2]

In the uncertain climate of the seventeenth century, Iberian plans for, and reflections on, pearl fishing from the Pacific coast of California to Sri Lanka drew on custom and innovation, revealing an ambivalent recognition of the need for expert labor alongside the enduring hope that somehow the independence of those involved in this wealth creation — like the pearls they harvested — could be curbed through a variety of mechanisms intended to facilitate crown control. The legacy of the Caribbean pearl fisheries, the lessons learned and ignored, informed these visions and the mixture of personal and imperial initiative they reflected.

The "Great Inconveniences" of Private Practices on the Pearl Coast

Far away from the moneyed corridors of Rome's diplomatic residences, or the damp customhouses on the shores of the Thames, the Venezuelan Pearl Coast continued to be a source of frustration as well as investment for the Spanish crown, with pearls and people both circulating in ways that defied royal edict. Divers continued to live and labor under appalling conditions. The Jesuit Bernabé Cobo, traveling along the Pearl Coast in the early seven-

2. Of *elenco,* Sebastián de Covarrubias Horozco writes: "Este vocablo no es nuestro, pero usan dél en la lengua castellana, como de otros muchos, que no son nuestros, y llaman elencos a las tablas e índices de los libros, que por otro nombre, que es el mesmo, llaman margarita, y con mucha razón, porque no hay perla tan preciosa como estos índices, los cuales sin hojear todo un gran libro, nos señalan como con el dedo lo que vamos a buscar, que sin ellos andaríamos a ciegas" See Covarrubias, *Tesoro de la lenga castellana o española,* ed. Ignacio Arellano and Rafael Zafra (Pamplona, Spain, 2006), 759.

teenth century, echoed Bartolomé de Las Casas's observations from nearly a
century earlier, describing the difficult regime of pearl diving. According to
Cobo, the divers were locked into cells at night, forced to abstain from sex
and alcohol, and faced the perils of sharks and other sea creatures. Amid
these privations and dangers, divers took care to protect themselves where
they could and to seek opportunities for semi-independent commercial activities beyond the maniacal pursuit of pearls. Thus, Cobo noted that, as the
divers shucked oyster after oyster, they shielded their hands from the sharp
shells with leather gloves. Their manual dexterity preserved, the divers then
turned the refuse of their trade into profit, making spoons of shell nacre from
discarded oysters. Cobo suggested that their Spanish masters permitted them
this side activity in light of their "excessive work." The observation does more
than underscore the brutality of pearl diving, however; it points to the ongoing existence of a regional political economy around pearl production and
the trade's by-products, one in which enslaved divers participated actively.[3]

This regional political economy sustained a significant community around
pearl fishing, in spite of the residents' complaints of poverty. Cobo counted
thirty and more boats (which he described as sail-rigged and resembling
small frigates or caravels rather than the "canoes" they were called locally)
conducting pearl fishing from Margarita alone. Although Spanish officials
pointed to the challenges posed by incompliant African (and Indian) subjects, the settlements could not survive without their enslaved labor force.
The divers (and the support crews upon which they depended on land) remained the Pearl Coast's troublesome linchpin, its principal source of profits
and problems. Correspondence about the Caribbean peal fisheries preserve
snapshots of the relationships that prevailed there, creating a community in
which profoundly local dynamics vied with Atlantic and global rivalries for
primacy in shaping a regional political economy.

Spanish residents continued to complain about the autonomy of their
enslaved divers and the climate of disregard for official regulations among
the settlements' Indian, European, and African inhabitants. In the first few
years of the new century, Margarita's treasurer, Antonio Álvarez, reported
to the crown on the state of the fisheries. He noted the need for new enslaved laborers—disease had taken a serious toll the previous year, leaving
the pearl canoes unmanned—and requested five hundred "black slaves from
the Rivers and Cape Verde," four hundred of them men between fifteen and

3. Bernabé Cobo, *Historia del Nuevo Mundo . . .*, I (Seville, 1890), 132–133, 284.

twenty years of age, the rest women. He specified that Africans from Angola "are not good for this employment." Although the treasurer's memo did not expand on why Angolans were not perceived to be ideal laborers for the fisheries, it did shed considerable light on the relations among enslaved Africans in the fisheries and between enslaved Africans and their putative owners. Of particular concern was the behavior of married black women: they lived apart from the settlements and received pearls from their pearl-diver husbands, which they then auctioned off. Indeed, such was the power of these women that Spaniards suspected that young and strong black men married older women just "to have their hut and home apart [from the settlements] and so they do not have to sleep in the jail." The copious pearls to which the settlements' black women had access allowed them to indulge in all sorts of sartorial excess; they wore blouses and skirts of imported fabric and necklaces and earrings of pearls and gold, all of which, Spaniards alleged, were given to them, "not by their owners[,] but by the pearl blacks with which they do business," who bought them with untaxed pearls. Free black women were viewed to be so disruptive, the Margarita council claimed—even seducing Spaniards away from their wives in Spain—that they were banished from the island. Enslaved black men, meanwhile, caused trouble by interacting with one another, trading in pearls and generally socializing in ways the Margarita council found detrimental to the island's governance and pearl hauls. In 1612, the council in the town of Cumaná claimed that fishery slaves were "so uppity . . . that one can only expect the worst." Spanish residents often requested additional shipments of slaves, even as they bemoaned the divers' various practices, including their alleged mismanagement of the oyster banks from which (residents alleged) they harvested immature oysters.[4]

It was not only the divers who proved difficult to control, however. In 1610, the king prohibited all government officials in the Indies from trading, possessing mines or portions of mines, or acting in their own interest in the pearl fisheries. The king singled out ministers who profited personally from "canoes and black slaves" in the pearl fisheries, resulting in "great inconveniences." The unattainable goal seems to have been to keep residents of the settlements from mixing their personal agendas with their imperial responsibilities. Unfortunately for the crown, the melding of the two was critical to

4. "Expediente de Antonio Álvarez, tesorero de la Margarita, a S.M," AGI, SD: 183, ramo 2, no. 35 (1603–1605), fol. 2v (my thanks to David Wheat for sharing this document with me), fols. 11v–14r, SD: 869, legajo 6, fols. 151v–152r, 154v–154r (for blaming black divers in Rio Hacha for the decline of the fisheries).

how pearls moved locally and globally. Canoe owners and overseers who permitted black divers to engage in any number of prohibited activities were to be punished seriously, the severity of their sentences ranging from lashes to exile. Meanwhile, Margarita's treasurer complained to the crown about white slaveowners' competing with enslaved Africans for the attentions of black women. Both underscore how personal interests undermined official orders and imagined boundaries in the fisheries.[5]

Even as the Caribbean fisheries continued to vex royal authority, the crown held out hope for pearl wealth there and elsewhere. In 1612, Philip III ordered the governor of the Pearl Coast to seek the recovery and growth of the pearl fisheries by punishing those blacks, "who the others treat as captains," who refuse to locate oyster banks ("negar los ostiales"). Ten years later, seeking more profits from pearls, the crown ordered the governor of Margarita to begin fishing a new oyster bank. Meanwhile, from the Pacific coast of California to the Atlantic waters off Brazil, schemers appealed to the crown for support for their ventures, promising to produce pearls without the errors of the past. Perhaps with a few critical adjustments—a new location, a new approach to pearl harvesting, a different labor force—a regular supply of the jewel could be had without the problems that plagued the Caribbean settlements.[6]

These proposals—some of which came to fruition, some of which withered on the vine—reveal the fantasy of how the global Iberian empire was imagined to function and the reality that prevailed, as laborers and pearls moved from the Mediterranean to the Caribbean, the Pacific, and beyond. Pearl cultivation and circulation relied on individual assessment and skill; in pearl-fishing communities around the globe, as in the Caribbean, customary, vernacular practices were where expertise was accumulated and curated. The centrality of skill to the production of wealth produced independence, a barrier to crown oversight. The most important ventures, the proposals for California pearl fishing—which would continue throughout the seventeenth

5. For officials profiting illegally from pearls, see AGI, IG: 1957, legajo 5, fols. 204v, 206v, 208v (Dec. 22, 1606). For the general prohibition against officials acting in their own interest in the fisheries because of the "great inconviences" that resulted, see Archivo General de la Nación, Mexico, Reales Cédulas Duplicadas 4, exp. 104 (November 1610), fol. 112r (My thanks to Tatiana Seijas for sharing this document with me). For competition for the affection of black women, see AGI, SD: 183, ramo 2, no. 35 (1603–1605), fol. 13v.

6. For black slaves who refused to find oyster banks, see AGI, SD: 869, legajo 6, fols. 154v–154r (Sept. 9, 1612). For the crown's letter to the governor of Margarita about exploiting a new oyster bank, see AGI, SD: 869, legajo 7, fols. 163v–166r (Mar. 21, 1622).

century—demonstrate a recognition of the particular components necessary for pearl-fishing success (skilled workers) mixed with a disavowal of the importance of this human capital. This disjuncture produced predictable tensions as the independence of action and judgment—both pivotal to pearl harvesting and assessment—resulted in expressions of autonomy that challenged the success of the Pacific voyages and the authority of the crown over subjects and objects more broadly.

Custom versus Technology in the Pacific: The Case of the Cardona Company

The most well documented of the California pearl-fishing ventures was led by Tomás de Cardona and his associates, all residents of Seville, although Tomás and his nephew Nicolás de Cardona were born in Venice. The Cardona company illuminates the combination of individual enterprise and crown sponsorship that went into these expansionist forays into natural resource exploitation. The company's proposal, like similar Caribbean-focused initiatives that preceded it, built on knowledge of existing pearl-fishing practices and also introduced new ideas. The Cardonas built on the crown's willingness to turn to technology as a potential mediating factor at the tense intersection of imperial exploitation of natural and human wealth. Their initiative also incorporated a century's worth of wisdom regarding the skill of the empire's diverse—and often enslaved—subject base as well as the Spanish crown's enduring willingness to involve non-Spaniards in the imperial project.

Although the arbitrista's reforming impulse animated the Cardonas' California venture in the partners' attention to precision and accounting, disorder and independence prevailed in the execution of their endeavor. The critical players in crown-sponsored voyages to the Pacific coast were a motley crew, a testament to the role of heterogeneous influences in shaping an evolving Iberian imperial mission officially associated with orthodoxy and homogeneity. In the fortunes of the Cardonas' pearl-fishing voyages, enslaved Africans, workers drawn from around the Mediterranean, Italian entrepreneurs, European rivals, and the pearl-harvesting peoples of the Pacific coast all had a role to play. Various stipulations contained within the Cardonas contract attempted to limit the nature of these peoples' participation, but their independence won out. The divers, aware of their importance to the success of the voyage, mutinied; Dutch pirates attacked the convoy; Pacific coast denizens harvested pearls according to their custom. It was not that the Pacific's resources themselves were inferior—California oysters and pearls could rival the Caribbean's in the opinion of many visitors. It was that the laborers who cultivated them and dived for them acted as they saw fit and could not be corralled to suit the purposes of the monarchy.[7]

The Cardonas' remarkable voyages in search of pearl wealth unfolded over many decades, beginning in 1610 with a royal patent permitting Tomás de Cardona and his partner Sancho de Meras to carry their "new inventions" to fish for pearls to the New World. The contract to explore California's pearl beds was not Tomás de Cardona's first foray into either collaboration with the crown or exploration and administration of the New World. In fact, he had a great deal of experience in royal bureaucracy and was a figure at Philip III's court. Among other duties, Tomás had served as master of the Mint and bursar to the Royal Armada of the Indies. He was known to be a "practical person and experienced in journeys at sea and on land, especially in the Indies." Nicolás, who played an active role in the company's endeavors from its earliest years through the 1620s, was a seasoned navigator as well. He had enlisted in the Indies fleets in Seville in 1610, first serving as captain of a ship to New Spain and then in various capacities on behalf of the Cardona company. The Cardona venture represented the way personal and imperial ambitions could align to the potential benefit of both. As with many individuals who engaged with pearls and pearl fisheries, the men involved were motivated by the desire to both serve the king and enrich themselves while doing so.[8]

The Cardona associates put forth a plan that incorporated human expertise and technological intervention. The contract issued to Tomás de Cardona, Sancho de Meras, "and their associates" permitted the men to take six ships of twenty tons along with the people and instruments necessary for the trip, including sixty blacks (ten per ship) "for their service and that of the fisheries." The origin of the blacks is not specified, and possibly they were free men of any number of backgrounds. Their presence nevertheless points to the crown's willingness to endorse a black component of the Cardona pearl-fishing endeavor in spite of the stream of complaints about enslaved

7. On the Cardona company, see Sanford A. Mosk, "The Cardona Company and the Pearl Fisheries of Lower California," *Pacific Historical Review,* III (1934), 50–61. Although Tomás Cardona spearheaded the California pearling initiative, his nephew Nicolás became the Cardona most closely associated with the venture.

8. For the Cardona license, see "Asiento con Tomás de Cardona y Sancho de Meras y otros consortes sobre ciertos modos y nuevas invenciones y vaxeles para pescar perlas," Dec. 22, 1610, AGI, IG: 428, legajo 34, fols. 62r–69v. The background on Tomás and Nicolás de Cardona and associates are from Pilar Hernández Aparicio, ed., *Nicolás de Cardona: Descripciones geográficas e hidrográficas de muchas tierras y mares de norte y sur, en las Indias, en especial del descubrimiento del reino de California* (Madrid, 1989), xi–xii.

African divers in the Pearl Coast fisheries. The Cardona company, although it had this significant crew, presented the human labor involved in the voyage as secondary to the partner's principal contribution, which was the promise to introduce new oyster-harvesting instruments to pearl-fishing endeavors. Cardona and his partners claimed they had invented a special boat and net that would enable them to retrieve oysters from previously unreachable depths. Although the technology was new, the Caribbean fisheries clearly served as the model for the agreement between the king and the company. Their contract evoked the importance of vernacular practices in these settlements by using a word that conjured the space between de jure and de facto realities: *"costumbre,"* or "custom." The Cardona contract granted any future Pacific fisheries the same rights and privileges that obtained in Caribbean locales, specifying that in all other legal measures the company was to establish in their future fisheries "the customs that are observed in the island of Margarita and Rio de la Hacha where pearl fisheries operate."[9]

The influence of the Caribbean pearl fisheries extended beyond the king's legal stipulations concerning the future organization of Pacific pearl-fishing ventures. The Cardona company's degree of familiarity with the Caribbean fisheries, combined with their many years of Atlantic sailing experience, strongly suggests that they had spent time there. As experienced navigators of Spain's Atlantic empire, Cardona and de Meras were able to use their knowledge of the Caribbean fisheries' failing fortunes as a lever to increase the appeal of their proposal, gesturing to the precise contours of labor regimes in these fisheries and the multiple factors on which they depended. They informed the king that they had "found and discovered a new invention of instruments and boats to retrieve pearls from twenty five to fifty fathoms [150 to 300 feet] and beyond where the divers who currently fish for them have not and cannot go and will establish fisheries in those parts where there have thus far been none or they have ceased to exist because of the damage done to the black divers by sharks and other animals and excessive depths." It appears that the lessons of the importance of customary practice in the Caribbean fisheries were a bit mixed and muddled. On the one hand, the Cardonas promised that technology would replace divers and conquer the challenges posed by nature (such as dangerous sharks and the depths at which pearl-bearing oysters were found), but they nonetheless still thought divers necessary to their success.[10]

9. "Asiento con Tomás de Cardona," Dec. 22, 1610, AGI, IG: 428, legajo 34, fols. 62r–69v, esp. 62v, 63r, 64v–65r.
10. Ibid., fol. 62r.

In their description of the instruments and their utility, the Cardonas revealed detailed knowledge of the dangers facing enslaved pearl divers in the Caribbean and of the negative effect on the fisheries' productivity. The Cardonas and their associates used a series of fourteen drawings to help convince the king of the novelty and potential of their inventions. Additional sketches suggested that they framed their venture to engage with the Iberian zeitgeist of redemption and recovery alongside their promise of technological innovation. Like the arbitristas who elaborated plans for Spain's return to prosperity, the Cardonas also positioned themselves as solution providers who brought significant expertise in the field of wealth recovery. The drawings addressed the task of recovering sunken ships and removing mud from the ocean floor: the devices they depicted promised to rescue from the seabed relics of Spain's more prosperous past, such as treasure ships and their cargo. The benefit to be had from the additional use of the Cardona company's instruments was not lost on Philip III. The king stipulated that, in addition to pearl fishing, Cardona and his associates were to use their devices to search for and retrieve the silver from four galleons that had been recently lost during an Armada voyage.[11]

The drawings that the Cardona company submitted with their proposal, their contract's explicit mention of the "customs" that prevailed in the Caribbean fisheries, and the company's reliance on a diverse crew all reveal a complex bureaucratic approach to incorporating the skills and labor of varied subjects and methods in the creation of material wealth. The drawings that accompanied the Cardona file depicted different types of instruments designed to facilitate the search for pearls. Perhaps most remarkable among the Cardonas' pearl-diving innovations was a diving suit (Figure 16). The suit was designed to allow divers to descend to depths previously unreachable by humans (between 25 and 50 fathoms, or between 150 and 300 feet).[12] Whom

11. The Cardona company would also profit through this salvage work, receiving a third of whatever it managed to retrieve, with the crown and investors (meaning the people with goods on the ships) splitting the remainder. See "Asiento con Tomás de Cardona," Dec. 22, 1610, AGI, IG: 428, legajo 34, fol. 67r.

12. For a reproduction of the drawings the Cardonas submitted with their original contract, see Hernández Aparicio, *Nicolás de Cardona*. This book also includes a later, longer report by Nicolás de Cardona describing his American travels. Hernández Aparicio also provides a bit of background information on the Cardonas' associates. Very little is known about them other than that they lived in Seville and had ties of some sort to the Spanish overseas administrative bureaucracy (one was a scribe in the House of Trade, for example).

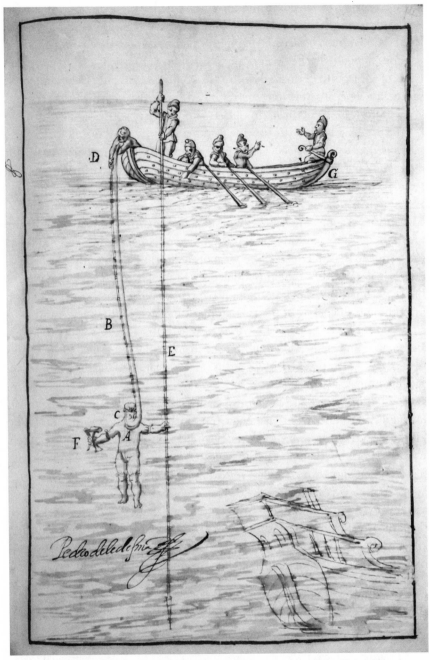

Figure 16. Diving Suit. Spain. Ministry of Defense. Archive of the Naval Museum. MS 1035/000. Treaties/Essays/Studies/Memorials. Pearl Fishery and Shipwreck Salvage. Signature of Pedro de Ledesma. 1623

did the Cardonas envision using the suit? The drawings do not reveal what they had in mind. The Cardonas undoubtedly knew of the myriad problems associated with the enslaved African divers upon whom the Caribbean pearl fisheries depended. The diving suit held out the promise of enabling distinct types of subjects to perform the critical labor of pearl diving. If the suit could protect anyone, it could obviate the need for enslaved African divers and allow Europeans to perform this labor without risk.[13]

The thinking behind the Cardona company's proposed technologies thus illustrated increasingly accurate thinking about the component parts of wealth creation. If pearls' point of genesis remained unclear at the dawn of the seventeenth century, they were no longer dissociated from their surrounding context as they had been in the fourteenth-century *Catalan Atlas,* in which they had appeared alongside rubies and emeralds, floating freely into the hands of divers beneath the waves. After a century of experimentation with pearl harvesting in the Americas, those promoting pearl wealth—individual investors and the crown—thought about pearls in context, encompassing both the key elements of their production (whether human divers or technology or both) and the needs of the keeling maritime empire that they could help sustain. Pearls were a part of a whole, a way of thinking about the relationship among the elements of empire: the lost and the yet-to-be-gained; from beneath the sea and above the waves; from the Atlantic to the Pacific; encompassing human and natural wealth.

The terms of the Cardonas' proposal and contract illuminate one vision for how these constituent elements were imagined to interact. Technology played a central role, as did skilled labor, and the Cardonas went out of their way to underscore their familiarity with the Caribbean pearl fisheries and the history of attempted mechanical interventions into this arena of wealth creation. In their explanation of the devices they would carry on their voyages, the novelty of these pearl-diving apparatuses was critical. Perhaps because of the failing record of pearl-fishing devices in the past, the Cardona contract specifically acknowledged that the devices had been tested and approved by royal officials. Persuaded that the company's instruments were indeed

13. The crews depicted in these illustrations are very small—leading to further questions about the intended use of the large black labor force the Cardonas took with them. If the black labor force was largely meant for other types of service, the illustrations would more plausibly reflect a smaller diving crew, such as the Cardonas' six designated *levantisco* (or Levantine) divers, discussed on 139.

new, Philip III gave the company exclusive permission to employ their "new method of fishing for pearls" in return for their promise to assume the cost of their explorations. The Cardonas pledged to conduct business in California for ten years at their own cost and to pay the royal fifth *(quinto)* on the pearls collected. To compensate the men for their expenses, the king granted the company the exclusive right to gather pearls with their instruments "in all the Indies," implying that they might later return to the Caribbean or employ their devices elsewhere in the Pacific.[14]

The language employed in the Cardonas' contract to address the different kinds of labor participating in their venture reveals a broad range of laborers as well as a number of administrative tools intended to manage their involvement. For example, the final terms of their contract allowed Cardona and his crew to take up to an additional "40 blacks" on their ships as "cabin boys and sailors." These black laborers were not imagined to be the sole pearl divers in whatever pearl fisheries the crew was to discover. The contract also gave the company permission to bring "six Levantine *[levantisco]* sailors to serve as divers, in spite of their being foreigners." The immediate referent of this term would seem to be the *Levant,* a word commonly used to refer to Europeans from the eastern Mediterranean; these imported workers might have had experience diving in waters close to their place of origin or in fisheries farther afield.[15]

14. "Asiento con Tomás de Cardona," Dec. 22, 1610, AGI, IG: 428, legajo 34, fol. 62v.

15. Ibid., fol. 65v; "Asiento con Tomás de Cardona," May 15, 1613, AGI, IG: 428, legajo 34, fol. 95r. On slavery in the Persian Gulf and Red Sea region, see Matthew S. Hopper, *Slaves of One Master: Globalization and Slavery in Arabia in the Age of Empire* (New Haven, Conn., 2015). An investigation in the late 1630s into the attempts of a French sailor to pass as Spanish and launch an exploratory voyage to the California coast (along with many non-Spaniards and at least one black diver) revealed that he had gone to Veracruz to find "lebantescos" to crew his ships, among them a Catalan Sicilian and a half Spaniard. A later expedition of one Pedro Porter reported on an illegal expedition to California involving French and levantisco sailors in the 1630s. For Pablo E. Pérez-Mallaína, *levantisco* refers to Greeks or inhabitants of the Venetian colonies in the eastern Mediterranean; the contemporary (1630s) reference cited above to a half Spaniard and a Catalan Sicilian as "lebentescos" seems to confirm this usage. Perhaps these Greeks or eastern Mediterranean men were harpoon fishermen or even coral divers. For the term *levantisco* as well as more information on black slaves in the Spanish navy, see Pérez-Mallaína, *Spain's Men of the Sea: Daily Life on the Indies Fleets in the Sixteenth Century,* trans. Carla Rahn Philips (Baltimore, 1998), 38–39, 55–59. For contemporary references, see "Testimonio en relacion deducido de la averiguacion que hizo Miguel Agundiz . . . ," "Testimonio de la causa

An additional feature of the Cardona contract is the insight it offers into the relationship between the skills of different subjects and perceptions of value. As the crown sought to delimit and contain the participation of the venture's crew, the terms of the Cardonas' agreement linked the presence of these laborers to precise sums of money. In recognition of the danger the levanstisco divers posed, the contract stipulated that each of them be covered by a two hundred thousand maravedi bond. The bond served to reassure the officials, judges, and president of the Royal Council of the Indies that levantiscos would not stay in American territory but would instead return to Spain at some point. The company, perhaps fearing that the divers would flee to establish their own independent pearl fisheries or sell their knowledge to Spanish competitors, required that a report of a levantisco diver's death be sworn to in person by the Cardonas and their partners in front of the officials of the House of Trade. Philip III was clearly concerned about the risky reliance on the levantiscos: six months before the company's July 1613 departure from Seville, he again specified the terms of the financial bond required to secure the return of each diver to Spain following the voyage.[16]

After numerous exchanges with the crown, in July 1613 Tomás de Cardona and his crew—including, presumably, more than one hundred black members—finally sailed from Spain with six ships under the command of one Captain Francisco Basilij.[17] In a lengthy account of the voyage submitted by

criminal . . . ," and "Relacion referente a Don Pedro Porter (1644)," in *Californiana II*, I, 545, 574, 580, II, 831. The term *buzo*, or "diver," could also refer to those seamen who were adept swimmers and could be relied on to swim under the ship and fix leaks during the voyage (Pérez-Mallaína, *Spain's Men of the Sea*, 72), but only the largest ships could afford to carry a diver, and, given the context of the pearl-fishing expedition, it does not seem likely that the term was being employed in this fashion here.

16. For Phillip III's decrees on the bond for levantisco divers, see AGI, IG: 428, legajo 34, fols. 77v–78r (Feb. 6, 1613), 87v–87r (Mar. 15, 1613).

17. A May 1613 decree reveals that Cardona and his associates played an active role in negotiating the specifics of their contract and that black labor was tremendously important to their Pacific coast venture. The company petitioned for permission to supplement its crew through a practice that the Cardonas claimed was standard; they stated that shipowners customarily took all the slaves they had on their voyages to employ them as ship's boys or apprentice seamen. The Cardona venture thus had access to (and imagined a need for) many more black laborers than their contract explicitly permitted. From the wording of the king's response (in which he granted them permission to proceed as they saw fit), it seems that the Cardonas were quite anxious about this particular aspect of the voyage. The king stated that they "pleaded with me to make sure that there is no doubt whatsoever" that they could take as many "service slaves" as they thought necessary, and he granted

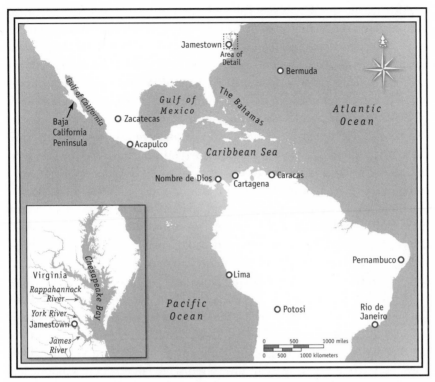

Map 3. Key Sites of Pearl Fishing in the Early Americas. Drawn by Gerry Krieg

Cardona upon his return to Spain, he reported stopping briefly in the Caribbean pearl fisheries. While there, his ships "rescued" several "blacks" from nearby Indians Cardona identified only as "Carib," scuffled with Margarita officials over their attempts to sell the "rescued" men and women into the fisheries, and tested their diving equipment.[18]

———

them permission to carry "forty or fifty" additional slaves without paying duties on them. See AGI, IG: 428, legajo 34, fols. 95r–95v.

18. For the Cardona account of this Caribbean sojourn, see "Relación de Tomás de Cardona: Descubrimiento de las perlas," 1613, AGI, Patronato Real: 20, ramo 18, no. 5, fols. 1–5v. Cardona described the armada, under the command of Captain Basilij, being attacked by "indians" in piraguas and canoes. According to Cardona, Basilij indicated that he came in peace in order to converse with and learn more about the attackers. These "carib" Indians made their living by attacking Spaniards and "ships of blacks, that come from Guinea," killing the white people aboard and enslaving the Africans. Basilij followed his erstwhile attackers to their settlements, where they found twenty-eight black men and women, for whom he paid in goods carried aboard the Spanish ships. Basilij and his crew

After leaving the Caribbean fisheries, the Cardona crew made its way to Acapulco, on the Pacific coast of New Spain. After the death of Captain Basilij in 1614, Nicolás Cardona took over as captain. With three ships and a smaller vessel carrying "soldiers and sailors" and "many black divers," the expedition sailed north from Acapulco in March 1615. During their return voyage, a Dutch pirate attacked, seizing a number of black slaves as well as many of the pearls that Nicolás de Cardona was bringing back from his travels. The pearls collected by a member of the Cardona crew, Juan de Iturbe, were the most impressive (known) haul to emerge from these North American fisheries. Presumably thanks to the labor of black divers, Iturbe gathered from a single oyster bank "fourteen or fifteen ounces of all kinds of pearls, some big ones," in only eight days and claimed that he could have gotten more had his water supply not run out. These fourteen and a half ounces — fifteen "large grains" and the rest composed of small pearls and seed pearl — proved to have a total worth of 672 pesos, taxed in Acapulco, with the royal fifth amounting to a little more than 132 pesos.[19]

But the worth assigned to the pearls harvested during the voyage was not the only assertion of value to which the Cardona ventures gave rise. The link between the labor of subjects and wealth was made clear at various times during the trip by work stoppages. At one point during the journey, the white crew mutinied in response to the divers' refusal to labor, and this mutiny left the ships vulnerable to attack. In 1632, recounting the Cardona voyages, a sailor described the situation, leaving no doubt about the independent judgment of the enslaved divers and their clear understanding of their essential presence on the voyage:

> The soldiers and Sailors mutinied because the Black Divers, having seen the Spaniards' ambition and how over a few impressive grains of pearls [the divers] brought up, [the Spaniards] wanted to kill one an-

----

then took the men and women to Margarita, where they began to dispute the duties they were to pay for the delivery of the slaves. In his request for redress to the crown, Cardona claimed that some of these "rescued" slaves had been held in captivity for many decades, and some had been born in captivity, and he noted that many were in ill health or missing limbs and ears.

19. For the account of the voyage in the wake of Basilij's death, see Report of Nicolás de Cardona to the king, in Luis Torres de Mendoza, ed., *Documentos ineditos relatives al describrimiento, conquista y organización de las antiguas posesiones españolas de América y Oceanía, sacados de los Archivos del Reino* (Madrid, 1868), IX, 54. For pearl size, see "Relación de Tomás de Cardona," 1613, AGI, Patronato Real: 20, ramo 18, no. 5, fol. 3v.

other just to take [the pearls] from them, they did not want to dive, saying that there was nothing to be had from the ocean bed, and seeing how little they had, the Sailors and soldiers mutinied.[20]

Technology aside, the importance of the divers to the success of the Cardona ventures was further evidenced by their presence in related voyages and by the monetary worth assigned to them. They were the literal embodiment of the enduring influence of the Caribbean paradigm of labor. When Nicolás Cardona sailed from the Caribbean to Acapulco and back in the course of his voyages in search of new pearl beds, sunken galleons, and whatever else he might find, he traveled with "many black divers" — key players in the transfer of skill and knowledge from one part of the Americas to another. In 1617, a prominent member of the Cardona crew, reporting the various expenses the company had incurred during this first voyage, stated that, when the Cardona flagship, the *San Francisco*, was captured by Dutch corsairs in 1615, "ten or eleven black divers, each worth more than one thousand pesos" were traveling on it. The human capital the ships carried, rather than the pearls, was where the voyage's value lay. As much as royal officials would try to objectify and commodify laborers and pearls, both resisted this type of assessment, their irregular actions and shapes attesting to the fundamental independence of subjects and of subjective assessments of worth.[21]

The idea that profit depended upon people and their practices more than pearls themselves endured and is evident in accounts of later pearl-fishing ventures in the Pacific and elsewhere. In 1618, two Portuguese entrepreneurs, Captain Gonçalo da Costa de Almeida and João Peres, advocated for the development of a pearl fishery off the coast of Brazil. Bureaucratic delays and a shortage of supplies had kept them from pursuing the endeavor in spite of having obtained royal permission. The two men lamented that they were forced to bear the high costs of "devices to get pearls" as well as the costs of

20. "Relación que dio el piloto Estevan Carbonel al Virrey de Nueva España . . . 1632," *Californiana II*, I, 339–340. He added that it was because of *"descuydo,"* or carelessness, on the part of the administrators of the Tomás de Cardona initiative that the "company and Black Divers" disbanded.

21. For an account of Cardona's voyages, see "Memorial del Capitan Nicolás Cardona al Rey . . . ," in *Californiana II*, I, 49–63 (for "many black divers," see 51). An indication of Laynes's status with the Cardona venture was his appointment as official pearl appraiser by the company, charged with evaluating the pearls gathered from the voyage and submitting them to the royal coffers ("Autos hechos por Fernando Laynes. . . . enero 1617," ibid., I, 39–40).

sustaining the divers and "other officials and people" necessary to the operation. Warning the king that further delay would only deprive the royal treasury of the great profits to be had from Brazilian waters, the two men sought
his help in procuring the necessary materials. Like the Cardonas, Costa de
Almeida and Peres were quasi-independent operators who had every intention of taking advantage of the benefits of an expanded imperial infrastructure even as they put their own vision of wealth generation at its core. The
two men even asked that the India fleet accompany them to Brazil for extra
security.[22]

Like the Cardonas, the Portuguese petitioners clearly hoped to curry and
maintain royal favor by claiming particular expertise. The two men's petition to the king identified Peres as a "master of pearls," a title that implied
familiarity with the jewel and its harvesting. But Peres's special pearl mastery
proved unconvincing. In the absence of a labor force or equipment, a pearl
fishery was unlikely to materialize. No Brazilian pearl fishery emerged, and
the crown continued to look to California, enslaved divers, and the promise
of new technology as the most likely sources of new pearl wealth.[23]

Voyages to California continued throughout the 1620s without producing either profitable pearl fisheries or permanent settlement, but written accounts of the seventeenth-century exploratory trips continued to favorably
assess the area's pearl-producing potential. Captain and cleric Diego de la
Nava, who sailed with the expedition of Francisco de Ortega (who led a voyage to the region in the wake of the Cardona ventures) to California in 1633,
described the "very good orient" of the pearls his crew received from Indians, who he said fished them out of "two and three fathoms of water." Like
Cardona before him, la Nava insisted upon the pearl fertility of the region.
Like his predecessors, he also invoked technology in his discussion of pearl
fishing, but he inverted its use, likening nature itself to a machine in his description of one spot visited on his voyage as "such a machine of pearls *[ma-
quina de perlas]* that everyone went around adorned in them."[24]

22. "Consulta sobre a pescaria das perolas do brasil," June 21, 1617, AHU, Códice 31
de Índia, 31v–32v, and "Carta de Capitão gco. da costa dalmeida e jo. peres mestre de perolas," Sept. 8, 1618, caixa 9, no. 133, n.p. There is no record of how the king responded
to the request from the Portuguese entrepreneurs.

23. "Consulta sobre a pescaria das perolas do brasil," June 21, 1617, AHU, Códice 31
de Índia, 31v–32v.

24. "Descripcion mui circunstanciada de los comederos de perlas . . . ," *Californiana II*, I, 468–479; see also "Relacion circunstanciada de los tres viages que el Capitan

Nicolás de Cardona produced a similar account, characterized by optimism and a critique of native resource husbandry. In his narrative of his voyage to the Pacific coast, he revealed his point of comparison to be Caribbean pearls. He wrote: "The oyster beds are not formed as those of Margarita island and rio de la Hacha were, but instead are found on the sandbanks in patches of twenty oysters a piece, more or less. . . . they are the size of a small plate, and full and unbroken weigh between one and two pounds." Though he conceded that the pearls brought back from California were "base," he blamed their poor quality on the indigenous practice of roasting the shells. Cardona assured the king that, "cultivating them as we do *[a nuestro modo],* they are more perfect and oriental than those of Margarita and Panamá, and more round and larger in great quantity. This has been seen to be true [of the pearls] by the said captain of the divers that retrieved them." As seen in his use of the term "oriental" to convey solely a perception of excellence, rather than an origin in the Far East, and his emphasis on the importance of particular practices ("cultivating them as we do"), Cardona unintentionally underscored how the assessment of pearls lay in subjective judgment and in the individual diver's, or harvester's, approach to removing the pearl from its shell. Context, in other words, determined pearls' value.[25]

Just as the Cardonas did not evaluate pearls in a vacuum—considering them in comparison to others and in light of how they had been harvested—neither did they pursue pearl-fishing activities to the exclusion of other imperial endeavors. Ever the imperial entrepreneurs, the Cardonas began to diversify their interests, looking to mines (terrestrial ones as opposed to underwater ones) as the potential lucrative intersection of imperial and personal ambition and natural wealth. Nonetheless, they did not give up on pearls, and in their attempts to obtain crown sponsorship they used language that evoked the words of Caribbean fishery residents nearly a century earlier, positioning pearl wealth at the top of a hierarchy of American sources of profit. In 1618, not long after their first voyage, Tomás de Cardona petitioned the crown, asking that the company's contract with the crown be modified to reflect the difficulties of the task at hand. He wanted exclusive rights to fish "both coasts of California" (referring to both coasts of the Baja peninsula). Four years later, Nicolás de Cardona sought support for additional Pacific pearl-hunting voyages, including permission to take with him

Francisco de Ortega hizo . . . ," 481. For "machine of pearls," see "Testimonio de los pedimentos y autos hechos con Francisco de Ortega . . . ," ibid., I, 291–292.

25. Torres de Mendoza, ed., *Documentos,* IX, 33–34, 54.

"all the black slaves and divers and supplies and necessary items" from the mainland. Thinking broadly about the human capital of Iberian domains, he further requested permission to do business with the inhabitants of Panama, who would supply him with ships and "slave divers" for the endeavor.[26]

Some twenty years later, a Spanish explorer named Pedro Porter offered an explicit reflection on the centrality of skill to pearl fishing and the enduring significance of Caribbean labor paradigms in producing pearls. In his account of his Pacific voyage in the 1640s, Porter noted that the difficulty of getting pearling operations up and running lay, not in the land, but in the labor. California Indians were "in general excellent divers" but "could not be forced to dive because they never submit [to such pressures]" and were too lazy to dive of their own volition. By way of explaining his dismal pearl haul so far, Porter claimed that the best pearls were to be had far from the coast, and that "with some divers from Margarita and Rio de la [H]Acha . . . I do not doubt

---

26. "Memorial de Nicolás de Cardona al Rey," *Californiana II,* I, 49–50, "Memorial de Nicolás de Cardona: 1618," I, 79; AGI, IG: 450, legajo A5, fols. 114–114v (1618). For "all the black slaves and divers," see "Autos hechos por Nicolas de Cardona: Julio 1622," *Californiana II,* I, 113. Pearl fishing and underwater salvage work were not the sole specialties of the Cardona company. Tomás de Cardona was clearly a man with many irons in the fire, all of them relating to the administration of national patrimony and natural wealth. Over the course of his life, Cardona maintained his interest and involvement in the exploration and exploitation of other natural American industries — and he frequently presented his ideas to the king. At some point in the 1620s, he submitted a petition to the king containing his ideas on how to increase and maintain the royal patrimony; in 1626, a royal decree named Cardona the official mine administrator. Four years later, a similar decree appointed him to a supervisory post in Spain's olive oil industry. Nicolás, meanwhile, traveled extensively around Spain in the king's entourage in the mid-1620s. Like his uncle Tomás, Nicolás was a student of the natural mineral potential of the New World, and pearls were never his sole American interest: in the 1630s, he served in numerous mines in various capacities, looking for valuable metals. For more on California pearl-fishing endeavors, see Peter Gerhard, "Pearl Diving in Lower California, 1533–1830," *Pacific Historical Review,* XXV (1956), 239–249. Micheline Cariño has also written extensively on pearl fishing in Baja California; see, for example, Micheline Cariño, "Mito y perlas en California (1530–1830)," *Sociales-Humanidades: Revista del area interdisciplinaria de ciencias sociales y humanidades,* no. 2 (1990), 53–59; and Cariño and Mario Monteforte, "De la sobreexplotación a la sustentabilidad: Nácar y perlas en la historia mundial," *Periplo sustentable,* XII (2007), 88–131; and Cariño and Monteforte, "Episodes of Environmental History in the Gulf of California: Fisheries, Commerce, and Aquaculture of Nacre and Pearls," in Christopher R. Boyer, ed., *A Land between Waters: Environmental Histories of Modern Mexico* (Tucson, Ariz., 2012), 245–276.

that great wealth would be found." He remained optimistic about the region's pearl wealth, claiming that, "if all the people of New Spain were divers, they could all fish for pearls." This was a remarkably explicit articulation of the dependence of imperial wealth upon the skilled labor of subjects.[27]

Global Reflections on People and Profit: Pearl Fishing along the Venezuelan Pearl Coast and in the Indian Ocean in the Seventeenth Century

The importance of labor to wealth creation emerged in accounts of pearl fishing from regions far beyond the California coastline. Throughout the Iberian imperial world, pearl profits from the Pacific to the Caribbean and the Indian Ocean continued to be explained or lamented in terms of the behavior of the laborers and subjects involved. The jewel remained a potent symbol of maritime dominance and attracted investment and attention long after other commodity trades had eclipsed the jewel as sources of profit. The difficulties that surrounded pearls' cultivation and distribution served again and again to remind the crown that imperial approaches to the management of wealth depended on small-scale approaches to wealth husbandry. Complex political ecologies — influenced by the natural world and human behavior — produced pearls; these interlocking relationships fascinated and frustrated observers.

This attention to the variety of factors at play in pearl production is evident in the account of pearl fishing on Margarita in the 1630s written some years later by visiting Englishman Thomas Gage, a Dominican friar (later Puritan). The pearl fisheries, in Gage's telling, were marked by disparities: the excessive wealth and power of the canoe owners and the contrasting abasement of the enslaved and yet an uncontrollable and equalizing circulation of the jewel. His 1648 work explored the entire panorama of pearls' fraught jour-

27. For his assessment of California's indigenous divers and the possibilities of greater pearl profits with Caribbean divers, see "Carta de Pedro Porter al Virrey Conde de Alva . . . 1651," *Californiana II,* II, 896–897; for "if all the people of New Spain," see "Memorial del Almirante D. Pedro Porter Casanate," ibid., II, 765. Positive impressions of the California coast's pearl wealth continued throughout the 1680s. In 1684, Jesuit priest Father Eusebio Francesco Kino wrote to the duchess of Aveiro to report on their efforts and noted that officials in Mexico awaited pearls in payment of the mission's expenses but that the fathers were occupied in building fortifications and houses rather than in fishing for pearls — although he acknowledged that there were many to be had (and further repeated the critique of native harvesting of pearls). See Father Eusebio Kino to the duchess d'Aveiro, Dec. 8, 1684, in Kino Papers, box 1 (1680–1687), HM 9976 (fac.), fol. 4, Huntington Library, San Marino, Calif.

ney from seabed to market, painting a portrait of industry undermined from within and without by forces local and distant. He marveled at the contrasts embodied in the trade (reminiscent of Pliny's account of the many binaries present in pearls' appeal): not only the display of extravagant mastery and abject degradation in the settlements but also the primacy of local conditions and yet the power of distant markets embodied by the regular threat of corsairs.[28]

The extreme and yet unstable hierarchies of power in the fisheries drew Gage's attention: he laid out a world in which value was inextricably tied to ability. He pointed to the "many rich merchants who have thirty, forty, or fifty blackamoor slaves only to fish pearls out of the sea about the rocks." This description suggests that the luxury of so many slaves working for one man was an important part of the narrative of pearls, a component of their perceived value. However, the owners' control was not absolute. Even as he used language that likened the divers to beasts of burden, Gage noted that the divers' skill forced a measure of independence from their masters as well as concessions to their welfare. He wrote, "These Blackamoors are made much of by their masters, who must needs trust them with a treasure hidden in the waters, and in whose power it is to pass none, a few, or many of those they find." Because they produced such valuable wealth and controlled its circulation, they were treated accordingly. In this observation, Gage echoed the accounts of many visitors to the settlements, all of whom recognized that the nature of labor at sea influenced the experience of bondage on land. The dependence of Spaniards on these enslaved laborers shaped their treatment of the divers as they hoped for higher pearl harvests: "I have heard some that have thus dealt in pearls say that the chief meat they feed their Blackamoors is roast meat which maketh them keep their wind and breath longer in the water." The centrality of these laborers to the economy of the Pearl Coast and the prosperity of its Spanish residents shaped the divers' experience of enslavement, guaranteeing careful attention to their diets even as they suffered the many privations associated with the labor regime.[29]

Many of the pearls harvested by these divers stayed in regional markets, flowing into Cartagena, where Gage described an entire street dedicated to "pearl dressers" where the jewels were "refined and bored." Although

28. J. Eric S. Thompson, ed., *Thomas Gage's Travels in the New World* (Norman, Okla., 1958), 97–98.
    29. Ibid., 97.

local practices shaped regional pearl circulation, however, so, too, did the demands of distant markets and authorities, which sent pirates and traders of all sorts to the fisheries and nearby settlements, seeking pearls by means fair or foul. Gage observed how the threat of foreign predators shaped life on the Pearl Coast. He noted that, when the ships left the Pearl Islands each July, bearing pearls worth "threescore or fourscore thousand ducats" each, they were "reasonably well manned, for the Spaniards much fear our English and the Holland ships." As Spain's rivals entered the Caribbean in increasing numbers in the early seventeenth century, attacks on Spanish ships and settlements increased, with pearls disappearing any number of ways in the ensuing pandemonium. Gage recounted a 1637 attack on a ship sailing for Cartagena from Margarita. Pursued by an English ship from Providence Island, the Spanish vessel managed to make an escape when two rival Dutch ships set upon the English attackers. The Spanish ship made for shore and succeeded in hiding some of its cargo on land before burning the vessel. At this point, however, new threats emerged. When a crew arrived from Cartagena to recover "the pearls hid in the wood . . . they were not the third part of what was in the ship." Pearls collapsed distance, both by evoking faraway places in the imagination and by convening far-flung contenders for wealth in their sites of production.[30]

As Gage reflected on the violent and contentious dynamics of the Caribbean pearl fisheries, halfway across the world a young man witnessed similar complexities in pearl-diving communities in the Indian Ocean. Across the global Iberian imperial world, pearls and pearl fishing provided lessons in the complexity involved in husbanding the wealth of empire. The author of the report, a Portuguese official named João de Ribeiro, published his nostalgic account of Sri Lankan pearl fishing around 1680. Ribeiro spent nearly two decades (from 1640 to 1658) working for the crown in the Estado da Índia, as Portugal's eastern empire was known; his chronicle highlighted the immensity, wealth, and romance of the industry and trade in pearls. Perhaps the dominant note of his elegiac description of large-scale and lucrative pearl-fishing operations was the heterogeneity of the people and tastes involved. Ribeiro located pearl fishing within a precise place, the Gulf of Mannar, detailing how the industry looked and smelled and sounded there, from the vast seas of boats and divers to the putrefaction of rotting oysters, to the impact of seasons and the hustle bustle of the market. Yet, at the same time, Ribeiro

30. Ibid., 97, 98.

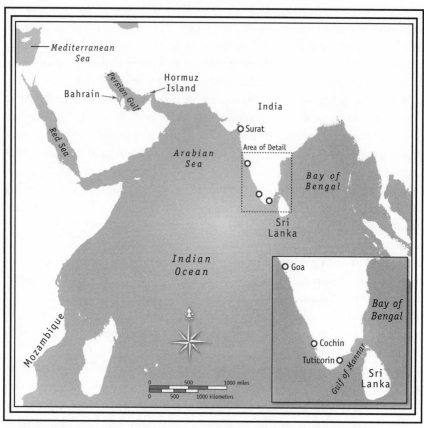

Map 4. Key Sites of Pearl Extraction in the Indian Ocean. Drawn by Gerry Krieg

invoked nearly as powerfully the influence of distant tastes and markets on the desire for this jewel and its circulation far beyond its place of harvesting.[31]

When Ribeiro penned his account in the 1640s, the Indian Ocean pearl fisheries had long been associated with pearl wealth but also with squandered opportunities because of the coast's never-ending labor disputes and the battles among rivals for control over the region's human and natural wealth. At the time of the work's publication some forty years later, his description

31. João Ribeiro, *The Historic Tragedy of the Island of Ceilão,* trans. P. E. Peiris, (Colombo, 1948). See also João Ribeiro and Fernão de Queiroz, "The Final Dreamers," in John Clifford Holt, ed., *The Sri Lanka Reader: History, Culture, Politics* (Durham, N.C., 2011), 176–181.

of long-ago splendor and wealth was particularly plangent, as much of the Estado da Índia had slipped from the Portuguese crown's grasp.

In Ribeiro's account of riches lost, pearls stand out as being subject to the interests of many people and forces. This was not an inaccurate characterization. Across the Gulf of Mannar from Sri Lanka, in the pearl-fishing town of Tuticorin, long-standing tensions between religious figures and secular administrators grew sharper at the turn to the seventeenth century, a reflection of the unusual demographics and religious politics of the Indian Ocean pearl fisheries. The early-sixteenth-century conversion of the pearl-fishing Paravas to Catholicism stands as an excellent example of how the various arms of empire could facilitate and frustrate one another. By 1601, twenty resident Jesuits ministered to twenty churches, three-quarters of them on the coast. In Tuticorin, the Jesuits operated a successful seminary where they gave classes in Tamil, Portuguese, and Latin. The power of the Jesuits in the Indian Ocean pearl fisheries remained a continual source of tension in these settlements, however, as they squabbled with local Muslim authorities as well as Portuguese secular and religious authorities for control of the pearl fisheries' residents and products.[32] In spite of the Jesuits' substantial influence, control of the region's inhabitants and resources remained impossible. By the early seventeenth century, the Iberian crown expressed concern about the decreased pearl hauls from the region's fisheries. Complicating material concerns were political and administrative problems: conflicts among Portuguese officials and ecclesiastical authorities as well as power struggles with local authority figures plagued the region. Meanwhile, the Dutch and English threatened Ormus, near the lucrative Persian Gulf pearl fisheries, while the shah of Persia adroitly manipulated the envoys from the two competing European powers and at one point even seized for himself the massive pearl horde kept by the Portuguese on the island of Bahrain.[33]

32. For an overview of the rise and fall of the Estado da Índia, see A. R. Disney, *A History of Portugal and the Portuguese Empire: From Beginnings to 1807*, II, *The Portuguese Empire* (Cambridge, 2009).

33. Stephen Neill, *A History of Christianity in India: The Beginnings to AD 1707* (Cambridge, 1984), 242–243, 353; *LM*, VII, doc. 81 (Livro 14, fols. 158–159), [n.d., post 1614]. The authors of the letter urged the king to do his best to further his relationship with the shah of Persia for the safety of Ormus and the entire Estado da Índia. For Dutch incursions onto the Coromandel Coast, see *LM*, III, doc. 630 (Livro 9, fol. 25), Feb. 6, 1616. For more on increased competition in the Estado da Índia, see P. E. Pieris with R. B. Naish, *Ceylon and the Portuguese, 1505–1658* (Delhi, 1920).

These regional challenges, in addition to the problems of overfishing, the need to discover new oyster beds, and rampant smuggling, all drew royal attention. In the winter of 1610, the king complained to the viceroy about the lower-than-expected tax haul from the Estado da Índia, owing at least in part to low returns from the pearl fisheries, and urged him repeatedly to take measures to restore the fisheries to their earlier, lucrative levels of production. In the Indian Ocean pearl fisheries, as in the Caribbean, the overriding concern as expressed in extant official correspondence was the mobility—in other words, the independent movement—of people and products. Crown and church officials sought to impose order upon these settlements by containing the subjects living within them and the objects—pearls—they produced. For example, in 1610, the king wrote the Indian viceroy about the possibility of encouraging "the Christians from the fishery coast" to relocate across the Gulf of Mannar to Ceylon (Sri Lanka). The king phrased this wish in terms of benefits to the Parava, with regard to both their pearl-fishing industry and their political situation: such a move would liberate them from the influence of the local Muslim ruler of Madurai. The king did not fail to note that such a development would also be beneficial to the royal treasury and for regional diplomacy, allowing the Portuguese to better fund the defense of their fortress in Mannar. Indeed, he went to on to predict that this relocation would address the problem of recently diminished profits from the pearl fishery; the disturbances *(inquietações)* among the area's Christians (an ambiguous phrase that might have referred to European Christians or Indian converts) would cease with the move to Ceylon.[34]

It was in this context that a fourteen-year-old Ribeiro arrived in Sri Lanka in 1640 and rose to the rank of captain over the course of his nearly twenty years there. His depiction of pearl fishing off the island's coasts suggests that the conflicting interests that had prevailed in Tuticorin for decades continued to characterize pearls' harvesting and sale across the Gulf of Mannar and that this fraught environment formed a critical part of the jewel's allure.

Ribeiro assigned pearls a separate section in his memoir. Although he identified cat's-eye, rubies, sapphires, and topazes as "the four most valuable

34. *LM,* I, doc. 3 (Livro 1, fol. 27), Feb. 26, 1605, doc. 19 (Livro 1, fol. 119), Jan. 13, 1607, doc. 102 (Livro 3, fol. 31), Jan. 23, 1610, doc. 117 (Livro 3, fol. 37), Feb. 20, 1610. See also *LM,* I, doc. 18 (Livro 1, fol. 115), Jan. 12, 1607, in which the king argued that, without the island of Ceylon, the pearl and aljofar fisheries could not be sustained. On excitement over news of new oysters, see *LM,* I, doc. 19 (Livro 1, fol. 119), Jan. 13, 1607. On concern that the lack of pearl harvests contributed to low revenues from Estado da Índia, see *LM,* I, doc. 102 (Livro 3, fol. 31), Jan. 23, 1610.

kinds of stones sought for in this Island," he also identified the "treasures of the sea" as "no whit inferior." He further emphasized that "the fishery of pearls . . . helps to ennoble the name of the Island no less than the rest." The logic behind Ribeiro's ordering of Sri Lanka's many sources of wealth reflected more than the perceived material qualities of the goods involved or their monetary worth. His account of the island's pearl trade suggests that he placed pearls and pearl fishing in a separate category, not because they were held in less esteem, but because of the politics of labor and resource husbandry that surrounded their cultivation. He provides a window into Iberian perceptions of the components of empire that included attention to labor regimes and ecologies and to the relationship between local distribution patterns and the effect of global markets.[35]

One of the defining characteristics of both Caribbean and Indian Ocean fisheries was the scale of labor and capital the industry required. Ribeiro described a regime of precision and complexity, one that operated on a rigid seasonal schedule (likely a reflection of the monsoons that swept the region from June to September) and that pulled thousands of people into the production of this good and its distribution. He conveyed the visceral, physical realities of the fisheries as well as the power of the market to mobilize large-scale operations. Ribeiro opened his account by emphasizing merchants' command of human and material wealth in the outfitting of pearl-fishing vessels.

His descriptions of the vast fishing fleets and their crews underscores the level of resource mobilization that producing pearls required. The work that went into pearls' harvesting and the complex risks and rewards of the market for the jewel could encompass entire families and villages and defined the relationship they had with the lands and seas that surrounded them. At the onset of the pearl-fishing season in early March, an enormous surge in activity occurred, as merchants "Moor and Gentile and also Christian" equipped between three and five thousand *champanas* (small boats) to carry out the work. A single merchant might outfit "one to four boats, some more, some less," and occasionally "two or three" merchants would join forces to share the expense of a single boat if they could not afford more. It is not surprising that merchants occasionally teamed up to lessen the costs associated with this industry: the boats they financed were large, carrying "as a rule ten to

35. João Ribeiro, "The Pearl Fishery in Ceilão," in Ribeiro, *The Historic Tragedy of the Island of Ceilão . . .*, trans. P. E. Pieris, 4th ed. (New Delhi, 1999), 70–73 (quotations on 70).

twelve sailors each with a master, and up to eight divers." In addition to the divers, the pearl trade counted on boat builders, as well as the beggars and merchants and food sellers that flocked to markets where pearls were sold. The pearl-fishing crews themselves composed a decent-sized navy. Taking the low end of Ribeiro's estimate—three thousand champanas—and assuming that two-thirds of this number were financed by individual merchants and a third as collaborative ventures between two or three men, there were at least thirteen hundred merchants investing in the trade, at least thirty thousand sailors, and twenty-four thousand divers.[36]

In the Indian Ocean, the sources of order and disorder in the fisheries emanated from the natural world as well as the human one. The season began precisely: "On the 11th of March at 4 o'clock in the morning a signal is given by the firing of a gun by the Captain of the four boats; all start for the sea and cast anchor at the spot selected for fishing in," in waters approximately thirty to forty-five feet deep. Each diver stayed underwater for what Ribeiro described as "the space occupied in saying two *credos*" (somewhere between one and two minutes, a lengthy but not improbable amount of time), and, once his bag was full, two sailors in the boat would hoist him back up to the surface. As in the Caribbean, it was an exhausting labor regime: "The moment his head emerges from the water another diver plunges to the bottom, and in this same fashion they all go down turn and turn about." Teams of three boats would move up and down the coast, gathering thousands of oysters. They were accompanied by safety convoys consisting of three to four "rowing boats" owned by each merchant "to prevent [the pearl fishing boats] being disturbed by pirates." The workday would continue until "four o'clock in the afternoon, when at a signal from another gun they sail back, each making for the point of land where he has to unload." Unlike the Caribbean pearl fishers described by Gage, the Sri Lankan divers Ribeiro witnessed were not enslaved. Nonetheless, the essential aspects of the labor regime were so similar that the contours of the divers' autonomy resembled each other. Ribeiro noted "that as soon as the diver enters the boat he is at liberty (till the other who is at the bottom comes to the top) to open with his knife all the oysters that he can, and whatever he finds inside is his; and similarly with the rest." In the Gulf of Mannar as in Venezuela, divers had considerable control over the pearls they harvested.[37]

36. Ibid.
37. Ibid, 70–71. For a modern perspective on the depths that free divers are able to reach and the length of time they can hold their breath, see Adam Skolnick, "Free Diver

Political loyalty to the crown as reflected by payment of material goods (pearls) resembled tribute more than taxation. The variability of the pearl fishery's payments to the crown reflected not only the fluctuation of the harvest but also the contingent nature of the compact itself. It was not only access to pearls — shaped from the moment of their discovery by the nature of the labor that harvested them — that affected the bureaucracy intended to structure the material and political relations around the jewel. The subjective quality of any given pearl also played a defining role. Ribeiro's description of what happened after the oysters were opened underscores this point. He noted that each year's pearl harvest was variable, and "some years the pearls are better than in others"; consequently, boat owners would make a yearly decision "and settle upon the royalty which they are to pay to His Majesty for the fishery."[38]

Ribeiro's account serves as a reminder that this human bustle depended upon the exploitation and destruction of living creatures and that the people involved in pearl fishing paid close attention to the seasonality and physicality of their sustaining industry, just as they did to the politics of the fishing crews and the changing demands of the market. Once the oysters were assembled on shore, the process of putrefaction began. Ribeiro wrote: "The place where they are piled is half a league to leeward of where the people assemble, in consequence of the evil smells which hover around the spot; for the sun causes the shells to open, and an immense quantity of flies which they breed gathers around. The fishery continues in this fashion every day from the 11th of March to the 20th of April when it closes, and they go on piling the oysters one over the other."[39]

In addition to being a vast and noxious-smelling industry, the Indian Ocean pearl fishery was a collaborative one that generated quite a din. Of the boats' arrival on shore, Ribeiro wrote: "The noise which is made every day on the shore during the two hours the unloading lasts, is astonishing. Two planks are run out with a quantity of baskets, and the sailors divide into two parties, one filling them and the other carrying them away." Ribeiro points to the many people (far beyond boat owners and divers) who were drawn into the pearl-fishing indus-

Natalia Molchanova Descends for Fun, Then Vanishes," *New York Times*, Aug. 4, 2015. Today's most accomplished free divers can hold their breath for three to five minutes on a deep dive; see Joel Gunter, "Freediving: The Lure of the Deep," *BBC News*, Aug. 5, 2015.

38. Ribeiro, "The Pearl Fishery in Ceilão," in Ribeiro, *Historic Tragedy*, trans. Pieris, 70.

39. Ibid., 72.

try. "A host of young men and lads from the neighborhood also come to assist in the work," he wrote; "they receive no payment but each one steals what he can." Ribeiro's description of the Sri Lankan fishery captured the overlapping circuits that shaped pearl circulation. Local boys scrapping for whatever they could get their hands on, boat owners trying to keep a watchful eye on divers, the divers themselves, and merchants from far and wide—all played a role in the movement of pearls from seabed to private possession.[40]

The theme of mobility and flux that characterized the trade runs throughout Ribeiro's account, whether he is discussing activity at sea or on land. It was a trade characterized by movement and connection, not just because it linked labor regimes at sea with practices on land but also because it linked different areas on the island to one another and the island itself to global markets. After unloading their boats, Ceylon's pearl-fishing vessels "put back to sea and sail away from the spot to where the Fair is held, leaving the oysters abandoned and unguarded." Ribeiro marveled at the human and material wealth this open market brought together, recalling "all the business men" who came to the fair "where they collect every kind of merchandise which our discoveries trade in with the nations of Europe and the whole of Asia." These traders came bearing "gold, silver in bars and wrought, all kinds of precious stones, amber, perfumes, carpets, *meleques,* money, with the rarities of all the provinces of the world, in such a fashion that if there is anything anywhere on which one can spend money and time in seeing it, it is this great fair." Pearls existed at the heart of this glorious bazaar; they functioned as a vehicle for precise explorations of the global tastes, labor regimes, and commercial and religious practices that created wealth.[41]

The religious diversity that was cause for such trouble in the pearl-fishing town of Tuticorin on the other side of the Gulf was a source of wonderment to Ribeiro. Pearls emerged from this heterogeneous and exotic world, and it was clearly part of their allure. At the regional fair, "Christians, Jews, Moors and Gentiles" gathered: "Here everything is bought and sold which each one would like to take to his own country—not only pearls, but everything on which profit can be made." The opportunities this trade presented were many and varied, accessible to a wide range of people. Ribeiro noted: "The sailors, divers, lads, and young men—and they are beyond counting—all are busy selling what they steal; many go about buying and others who have

40. Ibid., 71–72.
41. Ibid., 72.

their own shops or merchandise and goods also join in the buying, each one making his own profit." Like the pearl trades in Spanish America, what "profit" looked like to any one of these participants in the market is unclear.[42]

From independent "lads" who stole their pearls to the "large merchants" who bought pearls in conglomerated batches, Ribeiro shows the various types of practice and participation that composed the early modern market for pearls. He suggests that buyers small and large were aware of variegated markets for the jewel and structured their behavior accordingly: "Those who buy in small quantities sort the large from the small pearls and the various grades of the latter; but it is all sold together to the large merchants at a great profit." In the range of practitioners with a stake in the trade and the overlapping networks that saw to pearls' further distribution, the nature of the pearl industry did not vary so much from the Coast of Venezuela to the shores of Sri Lanka.[43]

After the fair concluded, the shipowners returned to the piles of shells to take stock of what remained after the putrefaction process. Ribeiro described the dismantling of the shells and the division of remaining pearls into nine different qualities. Each category's worth depended upon a subjective appraisal by wholesalers reflecting the quantity and quality of the harvest. It is also worth pausing at Ribeiro's assessment of "minute" (seed pearls, or *aljofar*) and baroque pearls:

> By the time the pearls are cleaned, almost all have been disposed of and the earnest money paid according to the agreement which had been made out by the brokers. The baroque pearls are sold for a much smaller price. . . . The minute pearls which fall from the sieves are left on the sand, and in the rainy season the poor in the neighborhood come to the beach with trays and expose the sand to the air; when it is dried by the wind they collect what they call the botica. A great quantity of this is sent to this kingdom and also to other parts, and the natives sell it very cheap.

There is a contradictory element to Ribeiro's simultaneous emphasis on the rich, complex, ungovernable diversity of the production and trade in pearls and his attention to the themes of categorization and specialization. As in the Caribbean, the pearl fisheries in the Gulf of Mannar were characterized

42. Ibid.
43. Ibid.

by disorderly cacophony as well as by a definition of "profit" that was highly subjective and measured by varied and interlocking local practices and distant tastes.[44]

Ribeiro's account illuminates the division of various types of labor that accompanied the growth of these global markets and the various acts of collaboration and obfuscation that moved goods among them. In the absence of a consistent exchange mechanism to measure and contain pearls' value, the trade hinged upon subjects' independence of action and of judgment—both of which were exceedingly difficult for governing officials to control, whether at sites of pearl production or distribution. Pearl fisheries, and the pearls they produced, functioned and moved in response to locally determined hierarchies and patterns as much as they responded to imperial directives.

How had more than 150 years of proliferating networks of pearl distribution and consumption shaped Iberian imperial approaches to pearls, this jewel that had occupied pride of place in Spanish and Portuguese maritime forays at the turn of the fifteenth century? In Portugal's dwindling eastern empire, pearls allowed for reflection on past glories, such as Ribeiro's. In the Spanish Atlantic, the Pearl Coast, once the treasure of the Indies, was a source of constant complaints and paltry harvests by the end of the seventeenth century. Foreign predators caused "losses" and prevented boat owners from taking their canoes to the fisheries; Pearl Coast officials begged for "aid" to "clean" the coast of these pirates.[45] The Spanish crown depended ever more on the mainland's production of agriculture and specie for profits while Spain's imperial rivals encroached on the Caribbean and controlled the trade in enslaved labor upon which colonial endeavors depended.[46]

44. Ibid., 73.

45. For complaints about "losses" occasioned by pirates and the request to "aid and clean" the Pearl Coast, see AGI, Casa de la Contratación: 120, no. 5, fol. 1 (Sept. 2, 1664). For excitement about a brief recovery of pearl banks, see "Real provisión para que el gobernador de Venezuela y su teniente en Santa Ana de Coro, cumplan un auto sobre pesquería de perlas, 1667," AGI, Casa de la Contratación: 122, no. 10.

46. Reliant on the mainland trades in specie, hides, tobacco, and cacao (which by the mid-seventeenth century would represent half of all Venezuelan exports) and other agricultural products, the economy of Venezuela was ever more deeply tied to the trade in Mexican silver, obtained in exchange for cacao beans in New Spain—and then used to purchase slaves in Caracas. Nearly thirty-four thousand slaves are estimated to have arrived in Venezuela from 1641 to 1714. See Alex Borucki, "Trans-imperial History in the Making of the Slave Trade to Venezuela, 1526–1811," *Itinerario,* XXXVI (2012), 29–54,

Pearls, however, persisted, both in the imperial imagination and as a source of investment and sporadic rewards for individual investors and the crown. Pearls continued to draw the attention of profit seekers—corsairs in the Caribbean, feuding adventurers and missionaries on the California coast, so-called Chinese divers *("buzos Chinos"),* and provincial adversaries on the coast of New Spain—but the real wealth of the pearl fisheries by the late seventeenth century was its expert labor force. With few oysters to harvest, skilled Guayquerí divers were sent to search the ocean floor for shipwrecks in the Bahama Channel, while African divers from Panama were redeployed in similar efforts in Pacific waters. Pearls were no longer central to an imperial economy, but pearl fishing and pearl fishers represented the global range of the Iberian world and its dependence on the participation of diverse peoples in acts of resource husbandry.[47]

A remarkable indication of imperial recognition of pearls' distinctive and

----

esp. 30 (Table 1) and 33, for estimated slave arrivals in Venezuela. Borucki, David Eltis, and David Wheat, in "Atlantic History and the Slave Trade to Spanish America," *American Historical Review,* CXX (2015), 433–461, note that "bullion production alone averaged 8 million pesos annually from 1696 to 1700" from Span's mainland colonies (435).

47. For *"buzos chinos"* (Filipino divers) near Acapulco, see Archivo General de la Nación, Mexico City, General de Parte 15, exp. 36, fols. 28v–30v. For more on Asian slaves in New Spain, see Seijas, *Asian Slaves in Colonial Mexico: From Chinos to Indians* (Cambridge, 2014). For Guayquerí divers in the Bahamas, see AGI, Casa de la Contratación: 853, no. 3 (1659): "Autos de Jorge de Salazar y Antonio Gonzalez, indios naturales de Isla Margarita y buzos, con el gobernador de nao Juan de Somovilla Tejada, sobre que les pagase el buceo que hicieron en el casco de la Almiranta de galeones que se perdió en Las Mimbre." A few years before the case brought by Salazar and Gonzalez, the abovementioned Indian divers who sued for payment for their labors, the governor of Margarita received a royal order to supply "40 Guayquerí Indians, the best on the island" to dive the wreck of a ship that had sunk in the Bahamas passage. If this could not be done, he was ordered to make up the numbers in "blacks." In the end, the governor complied, sending for all Guayqueríes and "other naturals" (or Indians from elsewhere), which resulted in thirty-five divers, to whom he offered "twenty *pesos peruleros* to each one for the sustenance of their families." He also reported buying "five blacks, good divers," on the royal account. For Africans' diving wrecks in Panama, see AGI, Audiencia de Panamá: 21, ramo 9, no. 54 (Mar. 14, 1655). The divers were later credited with rescuing "3 million and all the artillery and other things." For corsairs near the Caribbean fisheries in the late seventeenth century, see AGI, Casa de la Contratación: 120, no. 5 (Nov. 13 1664). There are many accounts of late-seventeenth-century voyages to California contained in *Californiana II,* I. See also Juan Cavallero Carranco, *The Pearl Hunters in the Gulf of California, 1668: Summary Report of the Voyage Made to the Californias by Francisco de Lucenilla,* ed. and trans. W. Michael Mathes (Los Angeles, 1966).

enduring resistance to imperial oversight came in the reissue of the body of laws governing the Indies in 1681. The *Recopilación de leyes de los reynos de las Indias* gathered in four volumes all existing laws related to the governance of the American colonies and organized them into thematic categories. These categories represented a major improvement over the chronological order in which the crown had until then kept the many thousands of colonial laws issued in the previous two centuries. In these regulations, pearls appear along-side chapters on the regulation of gold and silver, which unlike pearls had not generated their own corpus of laws concerning municipal organization.[48]

The 1681 *Recopilación* charted the changing dynamics in the pearl fisheries over two centuries and reflected a prolonged effort in containment as the crown struggled to impose order on the mixture of subjects and objects in these settlements. The laws included in the *Recopilación* reveal the imperfect coexistence of a recognition of de facto social and labor realities in the pearl fisheries and a persistent desire to assert de jure control over the material wealth produced there, expressed through fiscal measures. The critical role of human expertise and subjective judgment in pearl harvesting was only ever imperfectly acknowledged in law.

The forty-eight laws concerning pearl fishing contained within the 1681 *Recopilación* span the two preceding centuries, from the reign of the Catholic Monarchs Ferdinand and Isabella through the reign of Philip IV (though, re-markably, it includes no laws from the reign of Carlos II, who came to power in 1665—perhaps a reflection of the increasingly dire straits in which the monarchy found itself). Most of the legislation, however, came into being in the late sixteenth or early seventeenth century, the problematic decades when pearl fishing along the Pearl Coast had made a limited recovery but social and labor practices remained vexing to royal officials.

Even as categorization remained critical to the crown's approach to con-trol over the settlements' people and products, the laws recognized the influ-ence of the subjects who lived in the settlements. The evolving contours of fishery life were laid out in detail in the section of the *Recopilación* devoted

48. See *Recopilación de leyes de los reynos de las Indias* (1681), 4 vols. (facs. ed., Madrid, 1973); Francisco Dominguez Compañy, "Municipal Organization of the Rancherías of Pearls," *Americas,* XXI (1964), 58-68. Compañy asserts that the silver and gold mines "did not create, like the pearl-fisheries, a local administrative organization of their own" (58). He argues that, even though the laws concerning precious metal mines did indeed provide for the establishment of neighboring Indian towns, they did not have a municipal administration comparable to the pearl fisheries, which was designed with the particular character of these settlements in mind (58-59).

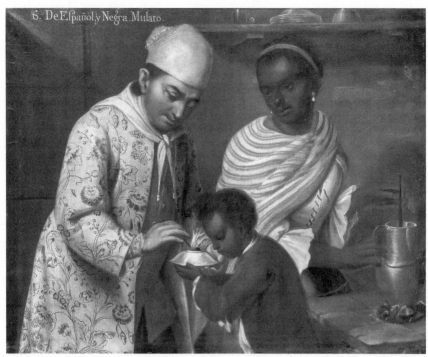

Figure 17. José de Alcíbar (attributed to), "De español y negra, mulato (From Spaniard and Black, Mulatto)." Circa 1760. Denver Art Museum: Gift of the Collection of Frederick and Jan Mayer, 2014.217. Photograph courtesy of the Denver Art Museum

to the *rancherías de perlas* (pearl-fishing settlements). The creation of a section of the *Recopilación* devoted to physical settlement structure (as the rancherías represented) reflects this desire to contain the unruly settlements and underscores the focus on the human wealth at the heart of the fisheries. This section tracked the complex labor dynamics in the fisheries—and implicitly, through the repeated attempts to control and discipline the laborers in the settlements, the changing workforce and increasing importance of enslaved Africans to the fisheries' continued existence.[49]

The body of laws concerning the crown's fiscal presence in the fisheries, as measured by the assessment of the quinto, however, revealed very little recognition of the industry's underlying realities. The section on pearl taxation was divided between laws specifying the importance of separating pearls into their distinct categories and assessing them accordingly, as if they could

49. *Recopilación*, II, Libro IV, Titulo XXV, 134-140.

be separated from the messy realities that produced and distributed them. In their frequent correction of existing practices, centuries of legislation gave the lie to the notion of objectivity when it came to pearl assessment. Various laws addressed the frequency with which officials improperly categorized pearls, underassessed them, carried them out of the fisheries without paying the quinto, or failed to supervise them properly. In other words, the fisheries' free and enslaved inhabitants continually undermined imperial oversight in word and deed.

The prevailing concern in all sections addressing the pearl fisheries in the *Recopilacíon* is the undesirable but unstoppable mixture of subjects and objects, of people and products in these settlements. In the quest for order and categorization around pearls and pearl fisheries, the *Recopilación* offers a legislative prefiguring of the ordering impulse that came into full flower in the *casta* paintings of the eighteenth century—in which pearls were put to various uses as a part of these visual attempts to categorize and describe the qualitative nature of the Spanish colonies' burgeoning multiracial populations (see Figure 17, Plate 5).[50]

Even if law never completely kept up with practice in the fisheries, the crown's approach to labor supply in pearl-fishing ventures in Atlantic, Pacific, and Indian Ocean waters revealed broad participation by subject peoples in the crafting of an empire that was both locally determined and profoundly shaped by the global horizons of the Iberian empire. The 1681 *Recopilación* made no mention of "Chinese" divers in New Spain or the employment of expert Guayquerí divers and African divers in underwater salvage endeavors, but the incorporation of these actors and their expertise represented an acknowledgment, in practice if not in law, of the centrality of skilled subjects to the creation of early modern wealth.[51]

50. Ibid. On casta paintings, see Magalí M. Carrera, *Imagining Identity in New Spain: Race, Lineage, and the Colonial Body in Portraiture and Casta Paintings* (Austin, Tex., 2003).

51. *Recopilación*, II, Libro IV, Titulo XXV, 134–140.

: 5 :

"REGARDLESS OF GENDER, CLASS, COLOR, AND CONDITION"

Pearls in Private Possession around the Iberian Imperial World

Alongside accounts of the hustle and bustle of pearl production in the Caribbean, Pacific, and Indian Oceans, records of pearl trades over the course of the seventeenth century point to similarly complex approaches to the custodianship of wealth. In the first few years of the century, in the growing port of London, royal jeweler Arnold Llul was rumored to be buying Portuguese pearls from a ship anchored in the Thames, while a boat captain named Richard Crewe seized pearls from a German-manned boat and delivered them to the former ambassador to Spain at his private home. In 1601, crew members recalled Francis Drake's delivery of a haul of pearls of dubious provenance to the queen just a few years earlier. Meanwhile, in Lisbon, English spies intercepted news of the shipping of pearls and other valuables between Cochin and Portugal's capital city. When a Spanish flagship, the *Santa Margarita,* sank in 1622 carrying a small lead box with sixteen thousand untaxed pearls in it, or when a Spanish merchant, en route to India, died in Mozambique that same year with valuable pearls sewn into the sleeve of his shirt, these types of circulation networks were often neither legal nor illegal. They were the independent actions that gave form and function to drafty imperial infrastructures characterized by limited powers of enforcement. They reflected people's perceptions of markets and value—of alliances as well as of material goods—and the actions they took to maintain and pursue them.[1]

From the harbors of Lisbon and London to the vibrant Pacific and Caribbean port towns of Lima and Cartagena, to the green hills and hidden coves of Galicia, to the ship holds of India-bound Portuguese carracks, pearls illuminate how people curated and thought about wealth, approaches that some-

1. For Drake, see E 133/10/1486 (November 1601), TNA. For Llul, see HCA 30/840/262, fols. 667-669, TNA. For pearls between Goa and Lisbon, see SP 89/3, fols. 23-24, 26-30, 39-40 (Jan. 10, 12, August 1601), TNA. For pearls brought to the house of Richard Crewe, see E 134/5Jas/Mich 41 (Sept. 4, 1607), TNA.

times intersected with and sometimes diverged from imperial policies. Even if pearls as an aggregate source of imperial wealth had diminished, global demand for them meant that they circulated more widely and, likely, in greater numbers among a broader selection of consumers than before. Indeed, by the turn to the seventeenth century, pearls moved so freely and in such numbers that the crown stopped trying to regulate their use through sumptuary laws. In 1602, a decree issued by Philip III intended to address "the great excesses and excessive expenses that have prevailed in our kingdoms" in both male and female dress. The decree referenced earlier similar laws and prohibited all people, regardless of "gender, class, quality, and condition," from wearing items of clothing decorated in any fashion with gold, silver, pearls, *aljofar* (seed pearl), or stones. Yet, barely a decade later, the crown reversed its decision. In 1611, "desiring to provide for and remedy the great excess that has existed of late, in these kingdoms," the king ordered that his council institute measures designed to eliminate such profligacy and prevent it from consuming "the wealth of our subjects and citizens on superfluous and excessive things." Although prohibiting many different types of decorative items, ranging from bed curtains and carriage decorations to diamond jewelry, the decree allowed that "women may freely wear any strands and ropes of pearls" along with a variety of other pearl decorations.[2]

Pearls were embedded in the wider social and material contexts of the communities through which they moved, tokens of belonging within intricate webs of personal ties. Whether as currency or adornment, pearls flowed along networks of mutual obligation. They trace delicate skeins of interdependence that linked diplomats with sailors, divers with corsairs, Pacific Ocean ship captains with Caribbean merchants, mothers in Spain with daughters in America, and cities' most humble residents with their most wealthy.

Procuring "Pearls as Big as Garbanzos": Gondomar in Galicia and Distributing the Wealth of Empire

Far from damp customhouses on the shores of the Thames or the docks of Lisbon and Seville, the small Iberian harbor town of Baiona hosted a lively

2. RAH, Salazar y Castro, N-25, fols. 266–269; RAH, Jesuitas, 7.176, "Pragmática," 1611. Juan Sempere y Guarinos discusses Spain's shifting sumptuary laws in *Historia del lujo y de las leyes suntuarias de España,* ed. Juan Rico Giménez (Valéncia, 2000). Although absolute numbers of pearl hauls are elusive, there is abundant and wide-ranging evidence (discussed over the course of this book) of new attention to sites of pearl production around the world and of strong global demand for exotic specimens—hence my conclusion that pearl distribution shifted and the available supply of pearls grew.

trade in gemstones and other goods, delivered from the holds of India ships and distributed to sundry consumers. It was in Baiona, which possessed one of the coast's best harbors, that a local power broker and international diplomat named Diego de Sarmiento, the count of Gondomar (1567–1626), presided over the unloading and dispersal of overseas treasure that sailed into the town's sheltered waters.

The power of a well-placed individual to exercise personal judgment in the execution of official duties was perhaps heightened in Iberian port towns at the turn of the century, given the enhanced legal confusion brought about by the Iberian Union. Since its annexation by Spain in 1580, Portugal had largely maintained its existing administrative structure, rendering more difficult than ever before any royal attempts to streamline the movement of goods between global markets and Iberian ports. The abolition of some customs controls at strategic points along the Spanish and Portuguese border led to such an increase in commercial traffic into Lisbon that customs procedures were re-established in 1592. The simultaneous existence of distinct and sometimes contradictory Spanish and Portuguese protocols meant that pearls (among other items) could get lost between the claims of competing authorities.

Protestant and Catholic anxieties about Spain's brief mid-sixteenth-century union with England had receded in the face of the far greater concerns posed by Spain's inheritance of Portugal's vast territories and enemies. In addition to the threat and cost of occupation, warfare, and blockades by Iberia's global rivals, the immense distances and lengthy, dangerous travel times between the Estado da Índia and Portugal complicated attempts at royal oversight, as did the legacy of Portuguese rule in the Estado.[3] Portuguese policy regarding the taxing of precious stones had been remarkably lax throughout the sixteenth century, only beginning to tighten in the early years of the seventeenth century. Years of minimal authority allowed purchasers of

---

3. The Dutch seized northeast Brazil from the Portuguese in 1630 and held it until 1654; and Spanish-Dutch hostilities of their eighty-year war resumed in 1621 after a twelve-year truce. The Estado da Índia referred to the eastern Portuguese empire, beginning at Mozambique and extending to Macao, with its center at Goa, as the viceregal capital. The normal schedule of the *Carreira da India* fleets was to leave Lisbon in late March or early to mid-April, arriving in August or September at Goa or Cochim. The ships would then stay only three or four months before leaving in December or January for the return trip to Europe, arriving in Lisbon in July or August after stopping in the Azores. For a further discussion of this pattern, see Francisco Bethencourt and Kirti Chaudhuri et al., eds., *História da Expansão Portuguesa*, I, *A formação do império, 1415–1570*, ed. Maria Fernanda Alegria et al. (Lisbon, 1998), 83.

valuable stones and pearls to avoid declaring them when they left India on Portuguese ships. Although the crown specified that pearls, seed pearls, and other precious stones be placed in locked boxes and under the charge of the ship captains (similar to regulations imposed, fruitlessly, on the Caribbean fisheries), such measures failed to prevent the flow of material goods through myriad semi-official channels. Merchants trafficking in pearls frequently failed to pay taxes on precious stones traveling to Lisbon from India, in spite of the king's very clear directives about how to control this lucrative trade.[4]

The crown attributed the difficulty of controlling the trade in precious stones at least in part to the diversity of the population living in India: each distinct community had developed its own ways of subverting or otherwise ignoring Portuguese imperial authority. In 1607, Philip III went so far as to abolish the post of *corretor môr da pedraria* (chief gem broker, *pedraria* meaning precious stones, a category that included pearls) because it was such a competitive and contested position and demanded such a high level of skill and responsibility that it was difficult to find appropriate candidates. In 1616, Philip III attributed a large part of the illegal trade between India and Europe to the activities of foreigners and *"homens de nação"* (literally, "men of the nation," a term that referred to people of Jewish descent) who lived in Goa but trafficked illegally in stones, smuggling them through Hormuz for sale in "Venice, Turkey, France, Italy, and other parts." The king accused the merchants of cheating the royal treasury by setting the prices so high that resi-

---

4. On provisions for safe and legal transport of precious stones and pearls, see AHU, Índia, caixa 1, doc. 103 (Mar. 17, 1611). On minimal control over precious gems (diamonds, for example, were not taxed until the 1640s), see João Teles e Cunha, "Hunting Riches: Goa's Gem Trade in the Early Modern Age," in Pius Malekandathil and Jamal Mohammed, eds., *The Portuguese, Indian Ocean, and European Bridgeheads, 1500–1800: Festschrift in Honour of Prof. K. S. Mathew* (Kerala, India, 2001), 271, 281. For more on the participants in and routes of the Indian gem trade, see George Winius, "Jewel Trading in Portuguese India in the XVI and XVII Centuries," *Indica*, XXV (1988), 15–34; Nuno Vassallo e Silva, "Jewels and Gems in Goa from the Sixteenth to the Eighteenth Century," in Susan Stronge, ed., *The Jewels of India* (Bombay, 1995), 55–56. Regarding the king's concern about the correct transportation of precious stones and that taxes were not being paid, see *LM*, III, doc. 514 (Livro 8, fol. 151), Feb. 14, 1615; AHU, Índia, caixa 5, doc. 163 (Dec. 23, 1615). On the failure of these provisions to be enacted, thus hurting the royal treasury, see *LM*, III, doc. 685 (Livro 9, fol. 140), Mar. 5, 1616, doc. 763 (Livro 9, fol. 344), Mar. 15, 1616. See also James C. Boyajian, *Portuguese Trade in Asia under the Habsburgs, 1580–1640* (Baltimore, 1993), 43, 48, 68.

Map 5. Key Iberian Pearl-Trading Ports. Drawn by Gerry Krieg

dents of Goa (presumably tax-paying ones) could not afford them and by selling the bulk of their stones in lucrative foreign markets.[5]

This administrative confusion left a lot of space for personal, locally established authorities to flourish in the pearl fisheries themselves and in Iberian distribution hubs. So it was in Baiona, where, under the frequent threat of corsair attacks, Gondomar oversaw the unloading of ships, juggled the often demanding requests for exotic goods from friends, and accommodated the visits of the royal jeweler, all while reporting on his duties to the king as a faithful servant of the crown.

5. AHU, Índia, caixa 1, doc. 103 (Mar. 17, 1611); *LM*, III, doc. 765 (Livro 9, fol. 342), Mar. 16, 1616. On the post of *corretor môr*, see *LM*, I, doc. 26 (Livro 1, fol. 175), Jan. 18 1607.

Baiona lay at the heart of Iberian administrative confusion, nestled on the border between Spain and Portugal. Gondomar grew up on the Spanish side, in the eponymous town of Gondomar, Galicia, not far from the Portuguese border. His aristocratic lineage and title—lord of Gondomar and Tui (Tui is a Spanish border town that sits on the banks of the river Minho that separates it from Portugal)—led him to a position of responsibility for the Galician coast. Throughout the 1590s, Gondomar oversaw the defense of Galicia's port towns and was rewarded with the perpetual governorship of Baiona's fortress of Monte Real, overlooking the town's excellent harbor. First as a port official in charge of supervising the arrival of ships and merchandise into Galicia's harbors and later as the Spanish ambassador to London, Gondomar came into frequent contact with pearls and had ample opportunity to shape their distribution through official channels and private ones. His careful attention to customs procedure, on the one hand, and his willingness to distribute riches from the Indies among his friends and contacts, on the other, reveal the intersection of individual approaches to wealth distribution and crown approaches to the same.[6]

A well-connected diplomat (much as Cristóbal de Salazar had been in Venice), Gondomar helped distribute global goods—pearls among them—to jewelers and merchants, women and men. The valuable cargo brought in by the ships that docked in Baiona attracted interested buyers from far and wide, including emissaries from the royal court and Portuguese merchants coming from Lisbon to make purchases. A sign of Baiona's importance as a well-known unloading point for riches from the Indies was the presence on at least two occasions of the king's jeweler, Petijuan Vergel, who arrived in

6. Baiona's port possessed an excellent Atlantic pedigree: the *Pinta,* one of the ships from Columbus's exploratory convoy, was said to have returned in 1493 after its voyage to the New World. The town's port also played an important role in Galicia's maritime activity in the late sixteenth and early seventeenth century, serving as a frequent harbor for ships returning from the Indies, a target for hostile English corsairs, and even the launching point of a ninety-eight-ship Spanish armada that gathered in Baiona in 1596 before sailing for Ireland in an attempt to join forces against the English. For a specific discussion of Baiona's fortifications and susceptibility to English attacks, as well as the Irish armada, see José Ramón Soraluce Blond, "Las fortificaciones de Galicia durante el reinado de Felipe II," in Antonio Eiras Roel, ed., *El reino de Galicia en la monarquía de Felipe II* (Santiago de Compostela, 1998), 183–186. For biographical information on Gondomar, see *Oxford Dictionary of National Biography Online,* s.v. "Sarmiento de Acuña, Diego," by Glyn Redworth, http://www.oxforddnb.com/view/article/69257.

the port town to weigh and classify the precious stones unloaded from the ships—and presumably to get the best specimens for the royal jewel house.[7]

Pearls were far from the only goods sought and distributed in Baiona. They were embedded in material contexts of exotic wealth; ship holds were floating cabinets of curiosities, containers of the range of the wealth produced by maritime empire. Pearls and pepper, evoked as symbolically destructive agents by French essayist Michel de Montaigne in the 1570s, lay side by side amid monkeys and rugs, diamonds and bedposts. The logic of their presence, jumbled together below deck, can be explained only by the private whims and fantasies of people such as those with whom Gondomar did business in Baiona. The consumer demand for goods large and small, humdrum and eclectic, that fueled this redistribution of goods throughout global markets and private households cannot be understood without a careful look at the individual motivations of private buyers—motivations informed by personal friendship as well as material yearnings. In Gondomar's distribution of these goods through circuits of friendship and mutual obligation, we see how estimations of skill shaped his and his contacts' assessment of worth and their perception of the basis of his jurisdiction over the material wealth that passed through his hands.

Gondomar's letters to Philip III chronicle his attempts to supervise the arrival of goods into port, an intimate process that required eyewitness attention to the behavior of all involved. A phrase that Gondomar employed in one of these letters to the king, "hand-sized," referring to small goods that were easily smuggled, underscores the power that individuals could exert over the movement of wealth. There were many such opportunities in Baiona. Just as pearls were embedded in rich contexts of exotic valuables below deck, in port towns of varying sizes the unloading of the vessels carrying these cornucopia took place amid the quotidian commotion of church attendance and the mayhem of the market. Pearls scattered to locations near and far, never to be seen again. On more than one occasion, Gondomar complained of Portuguese robbing the ships in the night and of contraband being smuggled into neighboring houses, disappearing into private hands and homes in the port and in the hinterland, moving along networks of consumption that stretched from the sea to the interior.[8]

7. RBM, II/2239, doc. 21 (Mar. 12, 1603). For Petijuan Vergel in Baiona, see RBM, II/2110, doc. 120 (Feb. 9, 1604), II/2239, doc. 73 (May 18, 1604).
8. RBM, II/2239, doc. 21 (Dec. 12, 1603). Gondomar was not all that successful in

Gondomar sought to keep this kind of chaos at bay, imbuing his duties as harbormaster with the religious imperial mission. In December 1603, Gondomar described the arrival of four vessels in Baiona's harbor, an occasion celebrated with a solemn church service arranged by Gondomar himself. In his account of the event, he emphasized his personal authority and wisdom in organizing the day's actions and tone. He led the church attendance and the subsequent order in which the boats were to be unloaded:

> I arranged things so that yesterday we all went, the Portuguese and myself, to the main church of this town, and after having said a mass with great devotion to the Holy Spirit I went with them [the Portuguese] to the ship São Roque and I informed them that they were to turn over to me all items that in Portugal they call "hand-sized," which are stones, pearls, seed pearl, amber and musk, and other valuable items that are easily made-off with and hidden, and because of this danger and because they are such valuable cargo it seemed wise to begin with them.

It is easy to imagine the days' hubbub and excitement: a town in its finery, piety colliding with curiosity about the riches that lay waiting in the harbor while residents worshipped in the church's pews. When the townsmen at last traipsed down to the docks and began unloading the carracks' cargo, their eyes must have grown wide at the sight of the treasures contained within. But Gondomar's account conveyed none of this, opting instead to emphasize his skill in imposing order on a potentially chaotic process:

> Each man happily wrote down for me which items belonged to him and which were destined for others. I took down the names of those who were to receive the goods, and in my presence and that of the tax administrator of this kingdom . . . who is anxious to increase the tax yield and is a highly satisfactory individual, I say Sir that in our presence and that of the ships' officials each man turned over his jewels and all of them came with [identifying] marks, and as we continued to take

preventing contraband; in a letter from his son later that same year, he was told of a house in the neighboring town of Tui where prodigious amounts of contraband were found (RBM, II/2110, doc. 90 [Dec. 17, 1603]). The following year, two letters to Gondomar from associates in neighboring towns described "a great disorder" that accompanied the unloading of ships in the harbor of Vigo and marked irregularities and theft during the unloading. See RBM, II/2110, doc. 46 (Jan. 13, 1604), II/2115, doc. 1 (June 27, 1604). A year later, Gondomar complained to the king about the difficulties of preventing smuggling from Portuguese ships docked in Baiona; see RBM, II/2115, doc. 72 (July 11, 1605).

inventory, the Portuguese [unclear in original] of the ship and my own shared the task of placing [the jewels] in chests and turning the keys over to the keeper of the safe.

Perhaps most remarkable is his assertion that these men "happily" complied with Gondomar's wish to draw up lists of recipients of the ships' treasures, conveying a nearly machine-like order and level of cooperation between Gondomar, the townspeople, the unnamed tax administrator, and the ships' crews as well as men acting in his employ ("my own" men, in his account). Gondomar was proud of his efforts to categorize and control the movement of these goods. He highlighted the essential components of the process, compliant laborers and extensive physical mechanisms for storing the goods, writing, "Afterwards we placed seals on top of the locks with the rubrics of both of the men, as well as my own, and in this manner we dispatched with the goods aboard the São Roque . . . and [today] . . . for more security [the keeper of the safe brought me the key] and as I said, the chests being sealed, I had them brought to my lodgings where I believe they are finally secure." Gondomar's account had the effect of emphasizing the potential of one man's diligence (in this case, his) to succeed where an inefficient bureaucracy tended to fail: "I thought I ought to advise your highness of all of this and say that God be praised, because this has all gone so pleasantly and smoothly that the Portuguese themselves are saying that they do not recognize themselves." In a letter to the king a month later, the count again referred to how well this particular unloading of ships had gone: "According to some aged Portuguese men, we unloaded and registered more [pearls and seed pearl] than are harvested by Lisbon's customs." The comment smacks of provincial rivalry with the capital city but also points to a common perception that Lisbon's customs practices were far from perfect.[9]

The records of Gondomar's time in Baiona reveal that the imperial was personal. His skill and diligence assured orderly processes in the port of Baiona; the same qualities entitled him in his own eyes and those of his contacts to exercise personal jurisdiction over the goods to which he had access. Gondomar's use of his official status as port supervisor to participate in private networks of commodity exchange points to the intersection of personal judgment and royal policy in patterns of early modern wealth distribution.

The multiple people with whom Gondomar conducted private business operated at once on a global imperial scale and on an intensely local one. Their

9. RBM, II/2239, doc. 19 (Feb. 18, 1603), doc. 21 (Dec. 12, 1603).

letters are vivid glimpses of commercial appetites stimulated by exotic goods but made sense of through reference to intimate relationships, local hierarchies, and the household cupboard. The empire fueled the material imagination; but the custodianship of this wealth depended upon local ties, local knowledge, and local perceptions of skills and status. Gondomar's privileged access to the riches of overseas empire was not lost on his associates, who frequently asked the count to procure all kinds of items for them. Gondomar did not always respond with the alacrity they expected. One Pedro de Toledo berated the count in a 1604 letter: "You have not seen fit to respond to my letters, as if I were not your most [loyal] servant." He had just recently arrived in "his corner [of the world]," and "they were in need of everything." A second contact asked for a blanket from India for his bed and a bezoar stone for his health. Yet another wrote to Gondomar to say that, "since he was going to his good homeland to visit the ships," and since the ships "usually" arrived with a better selection of certain goods that he desired, could the count please bring him several items from the holds?[10]

In echoes of the dealings of Spanish diplomats in Italy thirty years earlier, some of Gondomar's contacts in Baiona claimed to be conducting business on their wives' behalf. One Juan de Tassis asked Gondomar very apologetically (and laying the blame for the burdensome request on his wife) to procure some diamonds and a small monkey from the ships arriving in Galicia. Pearls, in particular, might have been the avenue by which women sought to engage with the promise and allure of the wealth of maritime empire. The following year, Don Gaspar Rivera y Villagra wrote to Gondomar, mentioning, "Once again, my wife requests fifty pearls, and asks that they be of good quality and as big as garbanzos." Sometimes women wrote Gondomar on their own with requests for jewels and other items. In January 1604, one Isabel de Prada beseeched him to purchase high-quality pearls for her through a contact, likely a merchant. It is clear that, like her male counterparts, she assessed the value of material wealth through its link to human expertise and networks of mutual respect and obligation. She seems to have conducted regular business with Gondomar. After updating him on the result of a recent transaction, she wrote: "Though it be terribly forward of me I beg your grace to purchase for me six ducats of pearls from Gonçalo Mendez, the heaviest and best available, preferably pierced pearls but if not, then the others, and forgive me your Grace this [extravagance] of wanting

10. RBM, II/2128, doc. 40 (May 24, 1604), doc. 26 (Feb. 18, 1604), II/2110, doc. 28 (Oct. 17, 1603).

something so expensive and prestigious as it will be coming from such a hand." De Prada wrote of pearls matter-of-factly, measuring them by their worth (ducats) and utility (drilled, presumably to facilitate stringing), but the request was embedded in implicit and explicit assessments of the people who procured them: the (presumably) merchant Gonçalo Mendez and Gondomar himself. Pearls, as "hand-sized" goods, were linked to the quality and connections of the person who handled them. Furthermore, her attention to the weight of the pearls, her preference for their being pierced, and her invocation of a "best" type of the jewel implies a consensus about what a good pearl was while also revealing an acknowledgment of the inherent variety of the jewel.[11]

Another woman who requested pearls (among other jewels) from the count, Leonor Sarmiento, might not have given much thought to the distant origin of the baubles she was requesting. However, she certainly knew the name of the town where they landed: in 1605, she wrote to Gondomar asking for certain items she needed to repair some pieces of jewelry, including a pair of pearl earrings. She knew that the count had access to the best supply, even specifying that "the replacement stones come from Baiona."[12]

As the records of Gondomar's supervision of port towns suggest, there was a great deal of room for individual enterprise amid vast, imperfect imperial structures. The use and exchange of pearls among families, friends, and business associates point to contextual assessments of value. The personal political economies that pearls illuminate were often, if not always, at odds with official assessments of the jewel, which tried to remove them from their context and assign arbitrary financial worth to them. Vernacular vocabularies for pearls, and the vernacular practices they reflected and reveal, captured pearls' value in any given situation far more effectively than numeric abstraction. Imperial approaches to pearls—at sites of consumption as well as sites of production—were much more effective if they incorporated personal expert knowledge and the realities of local exchange economies. Gondomar bridged this gap. He was proud of his efficacy as a royal official and aware of

11. RBM, II/2171, doc. 120 (Dec. 17, 1603), II/2110, doc. 147 (Feb. 22, [1604]), II/2150, doc. 68 (Jan. 22, 1604).

12. RBM, II/2130, doc. 155 (Feb. 14, 1605). Pearls were not the only jewels that women dealt in; a letter from one Doña Eloisa de Ribera y Estéfano to the merchant Pablo de Meneses in 1607 about a variety of her orders and the status of her credit included her admonition to the merchant that her sister be able to select the bediamonded buckles that she found most pretty; see RAH, Salazar y Castro, A-80, fol. 284 (Dec. 8, 1607).

how much his success depended upon his knowledge of local tastes and customs and his willingness to reaffirm personal as well as imperial allegiances.

"Merchants and Businessmen Don't Tend to Register These Things": Pearls in Private Possession and Imperial Bureaucracies

Another striking illustration of the inadequacy not only of customs controls but of categories of legal and illegal trade comes from the 1620s, in the remarkable saga of a Spaniard who died on the East African coast in unclear circumstances. Born in a small mountain town in the Pyrenees, the merchant Pedro Pérez de Medina had traveled far from Iberia on numerous occasions by the time of his death. A veteran of multiple trips to the West Indies, he set sail once again in the spring of 1623, this time heading east rather than west. After bidding farewell to his wife and sons in Seville, Pérez de Medina made his way to Lisbon. From there, he embarked on Portugal's India fleet, bound for Goa. He did not make it, however. Several months after the harrowing voyage began, the fleet with which Pérez de Medina was traveling took shelter on the coast of Mozambique. Maybe the Spaniard ventured too far from the camp; maybe he got drunk and into a fight; maybe his body gave out after many grueling months at sea. Somehow death found him far from home and far from where he had made the fortune he was carrying eastward: valuable pearls sewn into the sleeves of the shirt he was wearing when he died. If he was murdered, his assailant had no idea of the Spaniard's hidden jewels, which were discovered only after his body was found. We cannot know what Pérez de Medina intended to do with his pearls or how he hoped to market them. Perhaps he was carrying Caribbean pearls to Goa with the intention of reselling them as native to the region, thereby capitalizing on the long-standing appeal of pearls deemed "oriental." In spite of the changes in the global market for the jewel—with millions of pearls from the Caribbean and elsewhere made newly accessible to consumers through recently established commercial routes—the imagined superiority of material products from an "orient" associated with luxury consumption persisted and shaped European assessments of pearls. But this historical association of goods from the "orient" with high quality was challenged by the exoticism of a new era; it is also possible that Pérez de Medina intended to exploit the jewels' origin rather than disguise it, selling them as unusual specimens from a far-off land. Either way, in one of the many letters sent to Philip IV from bureaucrats involved in the case of the deceased Spaniard's pearls, there is an explicit mention of the pearls being found without any proof of the dry ports (that is, the on-land customs barriers) through which they had "doubtless" passed. They had likely come from another Iberian city, most likely Seville, just shy of two hundred miles from Lisbon, the major market for incoming Caribbean pearls and, significantly, Pérez de Medina's home.[13]

Regardless of their origin, over the next several years these pearls became the subject of complex epistolary battles between the Spaniard's widow and sons and Portuguese secular and religious authorities. Each contender for the pearls' worth had distinct ideas about who should pay for and profit from the hazards of empire. Portuguese officials determined that the pearls were unregistered (meaning that Pérez de Medina had not wanted to advertise his possession of them or pay a fee for shipping private cargo), and, with no clear legal proof of ownership, many people with various loyalties fought to claim them after their initial discovery.[14] The lengthy disputes over the pearls revealed the porous, imperfect nature of the imperial administrative bureaucracy, whose failings Pérez de Medina hoped to exploit and to which, ironically, his family turned in the wake of his death. Extant records suggest that the family prevailed. The last scrap of evidence concerning the saga was a hasty scribble by Philip IV, written in 1640. In response to an earlier plea from Pérez de Medina's sons—who claimed they were suffering "many infinite necessities" and needed the profits from their father's jewels to survive—the king ordered that the matter be resolved.[15]

13. For records of Pérez de Medina's early trips to the Indies, see AGI, Casa de la Contratación: 5266, no. 2 (Feb. 26, 1601), 5310, no. 10 (Jan. 2, 1610). For documents pertaining to his death and its aftermath, see AHU, Moçambique, caixa 1, doc. 44 (Mar. 26, 1624). For a selection of the letters exchanged between Goa and Lisbon regarding Pérez de Medina's pearls, see AHU, Moçambique, caixa 1, doc. 49 (Aug. 7, 1625); ANTT/LM (Livro 23, fol. 307, no. 153), Apr. 5, 1626 (Livro 24, fols. 31-32, no. 153), Feb. 18, 1627 (Livro 24, fol. 275, no. 85), Mar. 31, 1627 (Livro 24, folio 277, no. 86), Apr. 2, 1627.

14. AGI, Casa de la Contratación: 5310, no. 10 (Jan. 2, 1609–Dec. 31, 1609). For more on the pearls' fate, see ANTT/LM (Livro 24, fols. 31-32, no. 153), Feb. 18, 1627. See also ANTT/LM (Livro 24, fol. 275, no. 85), Mar. 31, 1627 (Livro 24, fol. 277, no. 86), Apr. 2, 1627 (Livro 25, fol. 304, no. 141), Apr. 3, 1628, (Livro 27, fol. 357, no. 170), Apr. 6, 1630. From the earliest days of the Carreira trade between India and Portugal, the Portuguese monarchy permitted *liberdades,* or "liberties," to many passengers aboard the carracks; these allowed the holder to ship small quantities of commodities on his own account and avoid paying taxes in Goa or Lisbon. It is not surprising that Pérez de Medina would have wanted to avoid paying for the privilege of transporting something he could easily hide. See Boyajian, *Portuguese Trade,* 39.

15. AHU, Índia, caixa 18, doc. 32 (Feb. 17, 1635). The king's first response to this letter is attached to the sons' petition; a second letter is found in *LM,* 21-A (no folio provided), in the catalog guide to the *Livros das Monções;* see "Carta de El-Rei para o Vice-Rei da

The case of the Spaniard's jewels did more than underscore the imperfections of imperial bureaucracy; it also pointed to the subjective, shifting nature of value. The stated worth of Pérez de Medina's pearls reflected a knot of hopes, expectations, and realities rather than any fixed material qualities. As the pearls languished in a strongbox somewhere, their assessment grew astronomically in reflection of private hopes, family tragedies, and the internecine wrangling that characterized the governing infrastructure of Portugal's waning eastern empire. The pearls were first estimated to be worth two hundred cruzados (a Portuguese unit of currency equivalent to the Spanish *ducado*), but later estimates valued them at fifty thousand and two hundred thousand cruzados. To put these conflicting numbers in perspective, two hundred cruzados bought about two quintals (one quintal equaled roughly 112 pounds) of pepper in 1631, whereas fifty thousand cruzados amounted to one quarter of the value of an entire ship's worth of stones and other precious commodities (including twenty-two boxes of diamonds and three chests of semiprecious stones, among other things) that were seized in the Lisbon harbor in 1639.[16]

By way of further comparison, consider the wealth contained in a small lead box that sank with the Spanish *Santa Margarita* the year before Pérez de Medina's death (see Figure 18, Plate 6). Just 3.5 by 5.5 inches, this box contained sixteen thousand pearls of tremendous variety, some drilled, some not, some miniature and irregular, a handful extraordinarily large and lustrous. There was no indication that any taxes had been paid on the box. The pearls might have come from Panama or from the Caribbean, but, in any event, they put Pérez de Medina's smaller haul in perspective.[17]

Índia, Assinada pela Duquesa de Mântua," Mar. 16, 1640, *Boletim da Filmoteca Ultramarina Poruguesa*, XIII, 2, doc. 129, 748. For tension in handling the Pérez de Medina pearls and the king's reminder to clearly state what was going on in these types of matters, see "Carta de El-Rei para o Vice-Rei da India, Conde de Linhares," Lisboa, Apr. 6, 1630, ibid., VII, 2, doc. 228, 528.

16. For early modern currency equivalencies and the Portuguese cruzado, see Mark Häberlein, *The Fuggers of Augsburg: Pursuing Wealth and Honor in Renaissance Germany* (Charlottesville, Va., 2012), 7. For original and revised estimates of the pearls' worth, see AHU, Moçambique, caixa 1, doc. 44 (Mar. 26, 1624), and ANTT/LM (Livro 24, fols. 31–32, no. 153), Feb, 18, 1627. For pearls being worth two hundred thousand cruzados and the king's suggesting they be used for the aid of the Estado da Índia, see ANTT/LM (Livro 23, fol. 307, no. 153), Apr. 5, 1626. On the 1639 seizures, see Boyajian, *Portuguese Trade*, 208, 253 (appendix A).

17. On the pearls found in the small lead chest recovered from the wreck of the *Santa*

Figure 18. Lead Box (top) Containing Pearls of Varying Sizes and Shapes, Including Several Baroque Pearls (bottom), Found among the Wreckage of the Santa Margarita. *Photographs by Ron Pierson, Mel Fisher's Treasures*

Pérez de Medina's story points to the role of private, clandestine initiative in expanding intercontinental trade. These types of dealings were not legal, but they were the bread and butter of maritime commerce nonetheless. At one point during the lengthy struggle to determine the rightful claimants of the Spaniard's pearls, the Portuguese viceroy in India said as much. Writing to another official, the viceroy stated that he saw "no justice" in returning Pérez de Medina's pearls to his heirs because they had been smuggled to begin with. The case was hardly unusual, he continued: "Merchants and businessmen don't tend to register these things." The viceroy's comments indicate that Pérez de Medina's jewel dealings were business as usual. Just as he acknowledged that it was par for the course for independent travelers to carry out sub-rosa commercial dealings beyond the purview of the imperial bureaucracy, he seemed to scoff at the notion that such individuals could then turn to that very same bureaucracy they had skirted for redress when their dealings went awry. Justified or not, his sentiments were misguided. It was precisely this kind of imperfect back and forth that gave the imperial infrastructure its form and function, from the ships that carried men, merchandise, and frantic letters to the religious brotherhoods that managed intestate cases to the government officials from Goa to Lisbon and Madrid who busied themselves with the particulars of the case.[18]

Cases similar to Pérez de Medina's suggest that the Portuguese viceroy was not incorrect. Portuguese merchants in Amsterdam moved pearls of uncertain provenance between buyers and even in small numbers to India, such as two fourteen-carat pearls sent to India from Lisbon by one Bento Henriques de Pas. In 1627, Portuguese New Christian merchants sold a string of pearls for eight hundred gilders, another example of the near anonymity of many pearl trades. Mobility, the movement of people and products across borders, bothered officials in charge of gatekeeping, but there was little they could do about it. Flux and exchange were simultaneously essential to the wealth of these emerging empires and the crux of their woes.[19]

People whose lives or deaths got caught in imperial webs, such as Pérez

Margarita, see Associated Press, "Thousands of Pearls Found in Shipwreck," *Washington Post*, June 15, 2007.

18. ANTT/LM (Livro 24, fols. 31–32, no. 153), Feb. 18, 1627.

19. Notarial Archives relating to the Portuguese Jews in Amsterdam before 1639, 611A (film 330), fols. 368v–369, and Notarial Archives 633, fols. 129–129v, both in Stadsarchief, Amsterdam (I am grateful to Henriette Rahusen for sharing her extensive database of Dutch merchant transactions, including references to these notarial records); *LM*, III, doc. 514 (Livro 8, fol. 151), Feb. 14, 1615.

de Medina, provoked intense interest in their wanderings and global connections. When Inquisition officials in Lisbon interrogated jeweler Cristovão Raus, they asked him repeatedly about his own birthplace and travels as well as those of the stones with which he worked. Felipe Escudo, a jeweler working in Goa, came under similar scrutiny in 1620, suspected of aiding the Dutch and English. So, too, did jewel merchant Jacques de Coutre, a Flemish adventurer whose extraordinary life received a great deal of publicity and attention in the 1620s. By the seventeenth century, pearls were associated with the allure of distant markets and foreign practices, eastern or otherwise. They represented the romance and promise of empire, and they traveled in pockets and coat sleeves and lead boxes, on prize ships, in massive hauls by pirates, and with enterprising merchants. Jewelers and goldsmiths in need of pearls could buy them from ship captains or sailors passing through town — or, as Gondomar's record of service in Baiona attests, from well-connected customs officials. The innumerable, unknowable decisions that went into individuals' calculations about which risks to take and how best to cultivate wealth could align with, or diverge from, crown-sponsored approaches to managing the riches of empire. People's misadventures with pearls illuminate the moments when these distinct understandings of wealth husbandry collided with one another, shaping expectations and practices.[20]

Amassing Capital in Lima and Cartagena: Pearl Use among Prisoners of the Inquisition

Alongside major hubs for pearls such as the Iberian ports of Lisbon and Seville, or the towns near their sites of production in the Gulf of Mannar or in the Caribbean, there were many smaller markets served by circuits of exchange that kept pearls moving among consumers of many distinct backgrounds. The variegated nature of these pathways comes to life in the records

20. For the Cristovão Raus case, see ANTT, Inquisição de Lisboa, Processo 5586. These questions by Inquisition officials are highly reminiscent of the interrogation of Portuguese merchants in London in 1567, discussed in Chapter 3. On Escudo, see *LM*, VI, docs. 5 and 6 (Livro 12, fols. 8, 9), Mar. 18, 1619, Feb. 6, 1620. On Jacques de Coutre, see Peter Borschberg, ed., *The Memoirs and Memorials of Jacques de Coutre: Security, Trade, and Society in 16th- and 17th-Century Southeast Asia*, trans. Roopanjali Roy (Singapore, 2014). For jewelers' purchase of pearls from ship captains, see Additional Manuscripts 14027, fols. 13–19 (1593), BL; SP 46/78, fol. 194 (Jan. 1, 1632), TNA. For sailors and captains of ships selling pearls to interested goldsmiths, see "Bills of Sales of Pearls to Various Goldsmiths, and Expenses, 1593," Add. MSS 14027, fols. 13–18, BL; SP 46/78, fol. 194 (Jan. 23, 1632), TNA.

of Inquisition procedures from the colonial centers of Lima and Cartagena. The Inquisition prosecutions that wreaked havoc on these and other Spanish American communities in the 1630s and 1640s reflected the Iberian crown's distrust of networks that operated independently of sanctioned channels and challenged royal authority over human and material resources.[21] The Holy Office targeted communities believed to be undermining Spain's commercial and religious hegemony through devious practices. In particular, the Portuguese communities (particularly merchants) in the Spanish New World—widely perceived as being predominantly New Christian and thus religiously suspect—suffered as a result. Lima experienced this wave of Inquisitorial attention from 1630 to 1635 and Cartagena from 1634 to 1640.[22]

21. On the Cartagena tribunal, see Fermina Álvarez Alonso, *La Inquisición en Cartagena de Indias durante el siglo XVII* (Madrid, 1999); and Anna María Splendiani et al., eds., *Cincuenta años de inquisición en el ribunal de Cartagena de Indias, 1610–1660*, II, *Documentos inéditos procedentes del Archivo Histórico Nacional de Madrid (AHNM), libro 1020, años 1610 a 1637* (Santa Fe de Bogotá, 1997). On the Lima tribunal, see René Millar Carvacho, *Inquisición y sociedad en el virreinato peruano* (Santiago, 1998); and Paulino Castañeda Delgado and Pilar Hernández Aparicio, *La Inquisición de Lima*, II, *(1635–1696)* (Madrid, 1995). Between 1570 and 1635, the Lima Inquisition charged 1,046 people, 790 of whom were punished and twenty-nine condemned to burn to death. The decades surrounding Portugal's break with Spain in 1640 saw a wave of persecutions of Portuguese communities in the Spanish Americas. See Teodoro Hampe-Martínez, "Recent Work on the Inquisition and Peruvian Colonial Society, 1570–1820," *Latin American Research Review*, XXXI, no. 2 (1996), 49.

22. For a discussion of Portugal's New Christian community in the sixteenth and seventeenth centuries, see Daviken Studnicki-Gizbert, *A Nation upon the Ocean Sea: Portugal's Atlantic Diaspora and the Crisis of the Spanish Empire, 1492–1640* (Oxford, 2007). The prosecution of Portuguese communities began with the Portuguese Inquisition in Portugal and Brazil in 1619–1620 and continued in Lima and Cartagena. The Castilian Inquisition led prosecutions in Madrid (1623–1645), Mexico City (1639–1646), and Seville (1655–1660). In Lima, where Inquisition prosecutors believed they had discovered a plot *("gran complicidad")* of global dimensions, shopkeepers and minor peddlers represented more than half of the Portuguese merchants seized by the Inquisition in the 1630s and 1640s. The preponderance of merchants did not fairly represent the Portuguese presence in the New World—the Portuguese population in the Spanish-American territories numbered between five thousand and seven thousand, and many were neither merchants nor prosperous. That the Inquisition seized a great deal of wealth from the merchants they prosecuted suggests that financial as well as religious considerations lay behind the tribunals' zeal. The Lima Inquisition, for example, was nearly bankrupt in the 1620s, but, thanks to the wave of prosecutions in the 1630s, the tribunal seized goods worth several million pesos, a sum so vast as to sustain the tribunal's operation until the Inquisition's

Inquisition documents underscore the futility of efforts to regulate pearl movement, ownership, and use. The violent and destructive bureaucratic invasion of prisoners' lives, and the resulting attempts of Inquisition officials to enumerate and impose imperial order upon the accused's possessions as well as their family and business associates, revealed material wealth to be embedded in complex and wide-ranging webs of alliance. In both Lima and Cartagena, pearls came from all over by way of all kinds of networks. From the sea floor to enslaved divers' hands and the private homes of free women of color, pearls' widespread presence might first suggest that there was nothing remarkable about them, but it is precisely this near omnipresence of the jewel that deserves attention. Many people owned pearls of varying quality for countless reasons. They provided small stores of capital to many, serving as a kind of insurance against a changing world. Despite the many varieties of pearls seized from prisoners, Inquisition officials failed to use any of the nuanced, descriptive terms for different types and qualities of pearls that were employed in the fisheries. Instead, their basic, blunt language served to highlight how the real value of prisoners' pearls lay in the practices and networks that procured and exchanged them.

Pearl deals alone did not generate these Inquisitorial trials, though they figured prominently in them. Large quantities of pearls sometimes occupied pride of place in the inventories of major merchants, but they also appeared in smaller quantities in the possession of Pacific pilots moving between ports and in the homes of former slaves. In preserving these patterns of pearl circulation, the Inquisition records provide perspective on 150 years of reports of pearls' unchecked circulation along the Pearl Coast and elsewhere in the Americas.[23] Pearls were not just fished by enslaved Africans; pearls were also

---

abolition in the nineteenth century. For a brief discussion of these trials, see Studnicki-Gizbert, *A Nation upon the Ocean Sea,* 167. There are many lengthier treatments of the trials; Alfonso W. Quiroz Norris, "La expropiacion inquisitorial de cristianos nuevos portugueses en Los Reyes, Cartagena y Mexico, 1635–1649," *Histórica,* X, no. 2 (December 1986), 237–303, and Irene Silverblatt, *Modern Inquisitions: Peru and the Colonial Origins of the Civilized World* (Durham, N.C., 2004), are just two of many works that have discussed the spate of prosecutions in the 1630s and 1640s.

23. Such reports from the Venezuelan Pearl Coast are discussed in earlier chapters; numerous chroniclers remarked on pearl use among the inhabitants of the Spanish colonies. See, for example Thomas Gage's description of Mexico City inhabitants: "A hatband and rose made of diamonds in a gentleman's hat is common, and a hat-band of pearls is ordinary in a tradesman. Nay, a blackamoor or tawny young maid and slave will make hard shift, but she will be in fashion with her neck-chain and bracelets of pearls, and

owned by them. Some people who possessed pearls were invested heavily in the labor system that enabled pearl diving—the slave trade—while others might have gotten no closer to the fisheries than the docks and streets of Cartagena where the jewel moved freely. Pearls were often items of adornment, giving added value to cherished objects that could then be pawned or sold; they sometimes were collected alone, as useful to sailors and seamstresses as they were to monarchs, albeit in different quantities. Often, loose pearls (from small quantities to as much as fifteen ounces, or nearly a pound) appeared in individuals' inventories along with other crafted jewels, suggesting that they were valued as trade items and as a substitute for cash.[24]

These practices came to light as a result of the questionnaire administered to all Inquisition prisoners. As standard procedure when possessions were confiscated, each prisoner was asked to list the material goods he or she owned as well as any outstanding debts, which in both Cartagena and Lima often involved pearls that had been bought, sold, or pawned. The frequency with which pearls were pawned by people who were unable to obtain credit by any other means demonstrates that pearls were well suited to a practice that reflected the uncertainty of the age. People's fortunes could alter, for better or for worse, in new and abrupt ways. Pearls—small, accessible, almost untraceable—helped people to survive this changeability.[25]

Pearl use and possession, as glimpsed in Inquisition records, suggest that anyone could profit from pearls and that the measure of this profit defied easy definition. Pearls were unencumbered by association with gendered patterns of consumption or predictable sentimental significance. Women and men alike bought and sold pearls in all sorts of combinations and numbers; prior ownership by particular individuals seems to have had no lasting detrimental effect on their appeal. Indeed, the very range of people who could and did obtain them was likely central to their appeal. The Inquisition records show how New World practices with pearls corresponded to nuanced relationships and networks of belonging and obligation. These networks of exchange and alliance stand in contrast to artwork of the period, which often paired pearls

---

her ear-bobs of some considerable jewels" (quoted in Gridley McKim Smith, "Dress," in Evonne Levy and Kenneth Mills, eds., *Lexikon of the Hispanic Baroque: Transatlantic Exchange and Transformation* [Austin, Tex., 2013], 113).

24. Such instances of pearl possession are contained in Inquisition records held in the Archivo Histórico Nacional in Madrid. Below I discuss such findings from the Lima and Cartagena tribunals.

25. On merchant credit networks and pawning, see Studnicki-Gizbert, *A Nation upon the Ocean Sea,* 96–110.

with dark skin to illustrate idealized and hierarchical relationships or to depict fantasies of New World wealth and abundance.[26]

Pearls' utilitarian value can be seen in the language Inquisition officials used to describe them and in the jewel's matter-of-fact circulation at Inquisition auctions. That Inquisition officials did not bother to employ some of the qualitative categories that existed to assess pearls (instead categorizing them solely by their weight) suggests that in this context they were viewed, not as jewels per se, but as a commodity whose value to the crown could be easily quantified. It is impossible to know whether those people who purchased pearls seized from prisoners and sold at Inquisition auction did so out of sentimental attachment to the jewels, but it is unlikely. Indeed, there is no indication that there was either stigma attached to buying a prisoner's pearls nor any sense of sympathetic custodianship. Consider, for example, the case of the wife of a certain Juan de Biengol, who bought just a portion of the chain of pearls that had once belonged to the merchant Amaro Dionis Coronel. Though his chain of pearls originally weighed eighty grains and eight ounces, Biengol's wife bought a part of the chain weighing only eight ounces and five-eighths. Who knows what she intended to do with the pearls: perhaps make a smaller bracelet from what had been a necklace? Or fashion a smaller necklace for a child? Or simply use the loose pearls—sold to her by weight, rather than as wrought jewelry—as cash? In any event, she did not purchase the chain of pearls in the state in which Coronel owned them, suggesting that the transaction was not motivated by sentimental reasons. Residents of Lima and Cartagena—men and women, rich and poor—used pearls of varying quality in the course of their attention to the ups and downs of their lives. They served as part of a material portfolio of mobile wealth, their value symbolic and economic in ever-changing and inextricable ratios.[27]

Pearls did not exist in a vacuum but were embedded in the industries that sustained their production and encouraged their consumption. In both Cartagena and Lima, pearl possession among people prosecuted by the Inquisition was closely linked to the slave trade that supplied the labor that harvested pearls and that created the fortunes of the traders who amassed them.

---

26. Many scholars in different fields have discussed these themes. See, for example, Joseph Leo Koerner, "The Epiphany of the Black Magus circa 1500," on blackness as a device to illustrate difference and to emphasize binaries, in David Bindman and Henry Louis Gates, Jr., gen. eds., *The Image of the Black in Western Art*, III, *From the "Age of Discovery" to the Age of Abolition*, Part 1, *Artists of the Renaissance and Baroque*, new ed. (Cambridge, Mass., 2010), esp. 15.

27. AHN, Inquisición 4794 (Tribunal de Lima), exp. 64, fols. 3–4v.

One of the Lima tribunal's wealthiest victims was the cosmopolitan merchant and pearl trader Manuel Bautista Pérez, prosecuted and eventually executed for Judaizing. Bautista Pérez began his career as a merchant with the profits he made from a single slave shipment in 1618, the cost of which he had shared with his uncle in Lisbon. When the slaves were sold in Lima, each man made a profit of 406 pesos for each African sold, and Bautista Pérez's net gain once the sales were completed was 50,000 pesos. The money from this venture allowed him to launch a successful career as a merchant in Lima.[28]

Bautista Pérez's pearl dealings went hand in hand with his business of importing slaves. He said as much at one point during his trial, when he referred to "other delayed bills pertaining to blacks and pearls and other things," grouping these "things" together as if they were closely related. Bautista Pérez's discussion of the various pearls in his possession revealed that most of his contacts were from Cartagena, an unsurprising admission given the city's proximity to the pearl fisheries. His business delivering slaves to the region would have easily dovetailed with his trade in pearls, either directly through island merchants and vendors or through the jewel market in Cartagena. The links between the slave trade and the trade in pearls extended beyond the jewels purchased with profits from the sale of enslaved Africans. Francisco Rodríguez de Solís, a slaveowner prosecuted by the Cartagena Inquisition, owned one man named "Manuel Angola" whom he identified as a "pearl borer" and who, along with his tools, was valued at auction at 250 pesos.[29]

Both Rodríguez de Solís and Bautista Pérez dealt in commodities other than pearls as well, but pearls of all sorts occupied an important place in Bautista Pérez's commercial portfolio. At the time of his arrest, he possessed numerous and distinct types of pearls, whose value reflected not just their perceived monetary worth but also the networks of obligation that linked the merchant to pearl buyers and sellers throughout the Americas. Bautista Pérez confessed to keeping in a desk in his house a chain of pearls weighing thirty ounces and worth more than four thousand pesos—an extraordinary sum. He owned this valuable pearl necklace jointly with one Bernabé Sancho, a silversmith residing in Cartagena, who had sent him the neck-

28. Linda A. Newson and Susie Minchin provide a bibliographic essay on Manuel Bautista Pérez in *From Capture to Sale: The Portuguese Slave Trade to Spanish South America in the Early Seventeenth Century* (Leiden, 2007), appendix F, 325–330.

29. AHN, Inquisición 4794 (Tribunal de Lima), exp. 20, fol. 5v, 4822 (Tribunal de Cartagena), exp. 8, fol. 19v.

lace via a certain Juan Rodríguez. Bautista Pérez, Sancho, and a third man were also co-owners of another batch of pearls, most of which Bautista Pérez had already arranged to sell to diverse buyers. Bautista Pérez's chain of suppliers was similarly wide ranging, reflecting the reach of Iberian markets that spanned the Atlantic and Pacific Oceans. One Melchor Polo, identified in the records as a "pilot from the south sea," reported that a certain Pedro Rodríguez Duarte had given him three large chains of pearls in Panama City to bring to Lima. In Lima, he was to deliver the shipment to Rodríguez Duarte himself or his business partner Bautista Pérez.[30]

Bautista Pérez's many pearl dealings encompassed various kinds of debts. Some extended beyond his activity as a wholesaler—which generated one set of obligations—to include pawned pearls, which embedded him in a distinct set of social and economic alliances. An example of the imperfect interface between the administrative aims of the Inquisition and the local realities it sought to alter were the difficulties of undoing these alternate networks of obligation. Inquisition officials faced the daunting task of returning confiscated goods to all those people who had pawned them to the suspect. It proved exceedingly difficult to untangle these small-scale but wide-ranging and complex strands of personal and financial indebtedness. Among his other possessions, Bautista Pérez told Inquisition officials that he had a strand of pearls in a large box in his house, which a man named Fernando de Espinosa had pawned to him for the sum of 1,008 pesos. Bautista Pérez also acted as a broker and warehouse of sorts for acquaintances who invested in varying quantities of pearls. Among his many possessions, he kept in an ebony and marble desk a thirty-ounce strand of pearls belonging to Juan Rodríguez Duarte; two lighter strands of pearls (each weighing about half this amount); a strand described as having been treated by mastic (probably meaning lacquered, one of the uses to which mastic could be put); a little string of pearls on black velvet that weighed only three ounces; and a little piece of paper containing a small amount of seed pearl. In the larger portfolio of Bautista Pérez's extensive holdings and activities, pearls are easy to overlook; yet the diversity of the pearls in his possession point to the myriad relationships and assessments that lay at the heart of his private practices of wealth hus-

30. Ibid., exp. 20, fols. 1r–8v, 12r–12v, 34r–35v, 42r–42v, 88r–88v. On Bautista-Pérez, see Newson and Minchin, *From Capture to Sale*, 15; Silverblatt, *Modern Inquisitions*, 150; and Studnicki-Gizbert, *A Nation upon the Ocean Sea*, 96–98. The Panamanian pearls likely came from the pearl-fishing grounds off that coast; see AHN, Inquisición 4794 (Tribunal de Lima), exp. 64, fol. 3, exp. 13, fols. 8r–9v.

bandry. Behind (or awaiting) each separately stored collection of pearls — the tiny seed pearl, the delicate chain wrapped in black velvet, the larger chain pawned to him by a male contact — lay a distinct purpose, buyer, and seller. The sudden crises, the intimate affections, the grand plans that motivated the movement of this type of wealth in the hands of a large-scale merchant (like Bautista Pérez) remain just off screen, beyond the historian's view. Indeed, they remained beyond the view of the Inquisition officials carrying out the inventories in which they appear, either because of a lack of interest or an inability to track down the stories behind their presence in the possession of prisoners. Nonetheless, the appearance of these diverse pearl holdings in the web of Inquisition prosecutions illuminates the intersection of individuals' small-scale political economies with the imperial machinery of human and material wealth husbandry.[31]

The accounts of Antonio Gómez de Acosta shed additional light on the ways pearls linked residents of Pacific and Atlantic port towns and served purposes both commercial and personal. Gómez de Acosta possessed many pearls when his goods were seized in 1635, most of them acquired as part of business deals he conducted with various associates. One of the items in his possession was a box full of pearls, including some simple strings of the jewel as well as rosaries and a brooch, "all of pearls." Some of these items had been given to Acosta by one Lope Días de Leron, resident of Cartagena, with instructions to give them to a certain Manuel Henriques to sell in Lima. Acosta also possessed, courtesy of one Amaro de Oniz, "a chain of thick pearls in a box from Panama" whose weight he was unsure of. Acosta described a complicated pearl transaction: he claimed that he had asked Oniz to provide him with the pearls so that he could loan them to one Diego de Zúñiga, who needed them to "adorn a boy" (presumably for a religious ceremony). Zúñiga later returned the pearls to Gómez de Acosta as promised. The pearls

31. AHN, Inquisición 4822 (Tribunal de Cartagena), exp. 11, fols. 1–2v. See also Castañeda Delgado and Hernández Aparicio, *Inquisición de Lima*, 219, for difficulties of sorting out debts and credits owed by imprisoned merchants; the tribunal also had to recognize the creditors of those condemned. The Lima Inquisition estimated the goods of prisoners at 1,204,174 pesos, but, once food expenses and debts were paid, the tribunal only netted 367,710 pesos, or 30 percent of the original estimated worth of prisoners' goods (226). Another instance of seed pearl treated with mastic is seen in the inventory of the goods of Manuel de Fonseca y Enríquez — among his numerous jewels and pearls were two pearl bracelets and a necklace of "mastic-treated" pearls, which he said belonged to his mother-in-law. See AHN, Inquisición 4822 (Tribunal de Cartagena), exp. 9, fol. 6r.

were still in Acosta's possession because they were "safer" with him, he said, than with Oniz.[32]

Many of the pearls circulating in Lima and Cartagena were of poor quality and possessed in small quantities, suggesting they were valued less for ornamental purposes than for the social and economic debts they could pay or incur. The Portuguese merchant Simón Correa, for instance, possessed many pawned jewels at the time of his arrest, including earrings, clips, and brooches fashioned with pearls. These were modest jewels; Inquisition officials described one set of his earrings as made with "very old pearls." Matias Rodríguez Delgado, identified as Portuguese by Inquisition officials, worked as a silversmith and said he "bought and sold things" for a living. He had in his possession a little piece of paper containing pearl and emerald earrings and a note saying that an unnamed tailor had pawned them to him for an unspecified sum. One Baltasar Gómez de Acosta, Antonio's nephew, owned a paltry selection of pearls, which were deemed "undrilled, black and bad" and weighed only seven and a half ounces, suggesting that he cannot have sought them or kept them for aesthetic reasons. These "rough pearls" had some value to him, no doubt reflecting the relationships they facilitated, through trade, pawning, barter, or the like. It seems unlikely that Gómez de Acosta intended to turn these ragged pearls into jewelry, but surely he could have traded them for something—a favor, a meal, information, if not material goods or specie—on Cartagena's variegated market. Perhaps the pearls came from a stray ship chased ashore by pirates and their primary allure was their proximity to danger and the mere fact that they had been scavenged. Once again, the appeal of pearls of all qualities forces us to consider just what exactly it meant to profit from the jewel in these distinct and distant locales.[33]

In Cartagena, the possessions of wealthy merchant and slave trader Juan Rodríguez Mesa further demonstrate the ways pearls embedded their owners in webs of mutual obligation that connected residents to one another and to distant markets. Among Rodríguez Mesa's pearl holdings were seven chains of mediocre pearls *(medio rostrillo)* in a small chest that he was to sell on behalf of Rafael Gómez and one Captain Andres de Blanquesel. It is impossible to know what interests led these men into this joint venture; they might have

32. AHN, Inquisición 4794 (Tribunal de Lima), exp. 66, n.p. [fol. 3]. Gómez de Acosta was *reconciliado*, or reconciled, meaning that he faced minor punishments but was not put to death.

33. Ibid., exp. 15, fols. 13r–17v, exp. 21, fol. 11, exp. 57, fol. 39v, exp. 23, fol. 5, exp. 59, fol. 1v.

crossed paths as a part of slave-trading ventures in Angola or through Rodríguez Mesa's ties to Lisbon or Amsterdam. Like the assorted pearl holdings among prisoners of the Lima Inquisition, the origins and intended destination of these pearls remain unknown, but the holdings stand as a reminder of the personal and private approaches to wealth management within a larger framework of global imperial commerce.[34]

Luís de Vega, a diamond dealer from Lisbon, owned a little piece of paper in which there were folded just six or eight grains of pearls, some of them undrilled. Similarly opaque are his reasons for doing this small side trade in pearls. Perhaps someone used them to pay a debt and he hoped to turn a profit on them by taking advantage of Bautista Pérez's numerous contacts. Bautista Pérez had acted as a broker for him before: once for a batch of pearls and, on another occasion, for the sale of a black slave. In a third instance, he had supervised the sale of some dresses belonging to Vega's wife. At the time of his arrest, Vega claimed that Bautista Pérez owed him for the proceeds of one of these transactions. Pearls, in these instances, functioned—alongside enslaved human beings and clothing—as just another commodity trade, a vehicle for value, an item of exchange that reaffirmed personal and business ties.[35]

The commitments forged around pearl deals included women, revealing their participation in these commercial and social circuits. In a desk in Bautista Pérez's house he kept a strand of Panamanian pearls weighing eight or nine ounces, pawned to him by one Doña Catalina de Zurbarán for three hundred pesos. Many of the jewels in Simón Correa's possession at the time of his arrest belonged to women. One had pawned "a little bit of gold with seven emeralds and seven pearls" to him for cash; another, an image of the Immaculate Conception made with small pearls. Yet another had consigned eleven "little pieces" of gold, each one decorated with a baroque (meaning misshapen) pearl.[36]

Women, like men, used pearls in a variety of ways. People wore them as jewels, used them as economic investments, and at other times exchanged

34. AHN, Inquisición 4822 (Tribunal de Cartagena), exp. 7, fols. 5r–6v, 216r. *Rostrillo* was a specific term that described tiny pearls (six hundred per ounce) commonly used to decorate images of Mary and saints. There were different qualities of rostrillo, and *medio rostrillo* referred to pearls so small that there were twelve hundred of them per ounce. See the Real Academia Española's online version of the *Diccionario de la lengua española*, s.v. "rostrillo," http://dle.rae.es/?w=diccionario.

35. AHN Inquisición 4794 (Tribunal de Lima), exp. 4, n.p.

36. Ibid., exp. 15., fols. 13r–17v.

them as symbols of enduring affective ties. The wife of Sebastián Duarte, Bautista Pérez's brother-in-law, possessed her own pearls that fell into both of these categories. In addition to eleven slaves, Duarte himself owned many jewels, including diamond and ruby rings and numerous pearl chokers (necklaces). His wife also owned pearls, he confessed, but she kept her pearls separately. Duarte testified that his wife owned "some jewels of diamonds and pearls and some rich pearls *[perlas ricas]* in a chain that she brought from Castile that her mother gave her when she came to this kingdom and was a part of her dowry." His description of her jewels suggests that both husband and wife distinguished between pearls with particular sentimental value and those that they considered investments.[37]

For people of Spanish or African origin, freeborn or born into servitude, rich or poor, pearls were both accessible and easy to pawn in times of hardship. Enrique Paz de Melo, for example, listed many valuable pawned jewels in his possession, pearls among them, but he did not limit himself to high-quality items. He identified one of his pearl necklaces as having been pawned by "a mulatta lady"; it weighed just an ounce and was valued at only four pesos. Indeed, for the free women of color accused by the Inquisition of witchcraft, pearls appear to have played a prominent role in the accumulation of capital. The records of the goods seized by Cartagena Inquisition officials from "various black women" reveal that almost all of the sixteen women owned pearls embedded among their other valuables. One of them, Juana Gramaxo, owned a necklace consisting of gold beads and an image (presumably religious) with six pearls. The necklace was eventually auctioned off to one Antonio del Castillo. Theodora de Salzedo, a "free black woman," owned bedding and two necklaces made of beads (some of them gold), two large coral bracelets, eight gold earrings featuring two small jewels with a "few little pearls" on them, and some separate pearl earrings. (De Salzedo's pearls, likely regionally sourced, formed part of an impressive Atlantic commodity inventory: in addition to her jewels, she also owned cloth from Rouen and Guinea, a chest from Flanders, and taffeta, among other things.) Angelina de Nava, identified as a "woman from Guinea," also owned a small choker of little pearls along with her own slave and a few other possessions. Dorotea de Palma's possessions consisted almost entirely of linens, but she also wore a

37. Ibid. exp. 13, fols. 1r–3v: "Iten dixo que su muger tiene algunas joyas de diamantes y perlas que truxo de Castilla y unas perlas rricas que le dio su madre quando se vino a este rreyno que una cadena y se hallava en poder de su muger y que tanbien constara por la carta de dote que se hizo."

beaded gold necklace from which hung a green cross as well as three pearls adorning an image of the Immaculate Conception. The sheriff responsible for seizing de Palma's goods, "finding nothing but the necklace and her bustier of black taffeta," removed the necklace from her neck and confiscated it, too. Juana de Ortensia, described as a "free colored woman," had few items—bed sheets, a pillow, some livestock—but, in addition, she owned two pairs of small gold earrings with three pearls. Ana Suaréz de Zaragoza (first identified as a free black, then as a creole from Zaragoza), one of the wealthiest women brought in on charges of witchcraft, possessed numerous pearl items: a necklace with small pearls, earrings with pearls, and an image of Our Lady with pendants made of pearls.[38]

These Inquisition accounts preserve just a glimpse of the immeasurable private calculations that made imperial economies hum with the movement of licit and illicit goods. They also remind us that any single archival source can offer only a fragmentary picture of these individuals' lives. Incomplete and tantalizing, these accounts hint at what lies just beyond our frame of vision: the motivations that led a man from a Pacific port town to an Atlantic entrepôt; the concerns that motivated many residents of Lima and Cartagena to collect modest numbers of assorted jewels; the religious convictions and aesthetic experiences that informed their taste in bejeweled crucifixes or gifts for their religious brotherhoods. Pearls loaned themselves well to these kinds of nearly invisible and ungovernable transactions; there was a logic to their movement between markets, but it remained largely beyond the purview of imperial authorities.

In general, practices with pearls called attention to the independent movements of subjects and objects—pearls could be in the hands of a royally appointed governor operating relatively close to an imperial capital, or sewn into an unfortunate traveler's sleeves, or traded on the streets of Lima—with which imperial laws were always chasing to catch up. Patterns of pearl use also underscore their accessibility. They were used not just by the wealthy

38. Ibid., exp. 57, fol. 39v, 4822 (Tribunal de Cartagena), exp. 2, n.p. For context on the role these *"morenas horras"* (free black women) played in Spanish Caribbean society, see David Wheat, "Nharas and Morenas Horras: A Luso-African Model for the Social History of the Spanish Caribbean, c. 1570-1640," *Journal of Early Modern History,* XIV (2010), 119-150. Wheat states that at least thirty thousand captives arrived in Cartagena in the 1580s and 1590s, including roughly ten thousand women (130). Tamara J. Walker, in *Exquisite Slaves: Race, Clothing, and Status in Colonial Lima* (Cambridge, 2017), considers the relationship between aesthetic adornment and status in the region.

Figure 19. Albert Eckhout, African Woman and Child. *1641. Photograph by John Lee.*
Courtesy, National Museum of Denmark

and powerful or to adorn black bodies in art that sought to describe the nature of different types of subjects and global locales. They were in fact used by women of color and traded by subjects of all backgrounds, wealthy and poor. Consider, for example, the iconic rendition of a Brazilian black woman by the Dutch artist Albert Eckhout, in contrast with the patterns of pearl use preserved by Inquisition documents (Figure 19, Plate 7).[39]

In Eckhout's 1641 depiction of an African woman and child in Brazil, pearls adorn the body of the woman and naturalize her presence in the Americas, further linking the wealth of the land and the labor of her body to the wealth of maritime empire. There is no hint of the complex alliances that produced pearls and that pearls helped to maintain among women of color and their neighbors. In contrast to pearls' role in the fantasy rendered by Eckhout, in which pearls serve to objectify a type of subject, pearls figured in actual practices of wealth husbandry throughout the Americas. These practices reveal diverse subjects playing an active role in the creation and custodianship of value. African women, like European women, owned and pawned pearls in lively economies of obligation and accumulation throughout American port towns and beyond. Their practices of wealth management did not differ in meaningful ways from their non-African counterparts. Pearls' accessibility and anonymity enabled early modern subjects around the globe to engage in practices of wealth management that were deeply embedded in the social (and, at sites of pearl production, natural) worlds in which they lived. These worlds often intersected with—but did not always align with—emerging imperial visions of wealth husbandry focused on orderly relationships among people and goods.

39. On Albert Eckhout, see Rebecca Parker Brienen, *Visions of Savage Paradise: Albert Eckhout, Court Painter in Colonial Dutch Brazil* (Amsterdam, 2006). See also her essay, "Albert Eckhout's *African Woman and Child (1641):* Ethnographic Portraiture, Slavery, and the New World Subject," in Agnes Lugo-Ortiz and Angela Rosenthal, eds., *Slave Portraiture in the Atlantic World* (Cambridge, 2013), 229–255, which offers further reflections on Eckhout's ethnographic portraits as expressions of early modern natural history practices and the colonial impulse to categorize and control subject populations. Other than noting that pearls and particularly coral were common in representations of the personification of Africa (245), she does not spend much time on their significance in the portrait.

: 6 :

"A FEW MORE OR LESS MAKE NO DIFFERENCE"

Accounting for Pearls in Northern Europe in the Seventeenth Century

As pearls continued to illuminate Iberian imperial approaches to maritime empire into the seventeenth century, they caught the imagination and attention of state actors and quasi-independent entrepreneurs throughout northern Europe as well. As empires moved to objectify profit and regulate the role of subjects in new ways, pearls continued to serve as a useful index — an *elenco,* in Spanish — of the private calculations that diverse subjects made about the worth of the relationships that structured their lives. Pearls had been long eclipsed as a source of profit by other commodity trades, but their deceptively simple beauty, their complex and mysterious origins, and their powerful association with mastery of the seas allowed the jewel to remain a powerful heuristic device for the expression of ideas about mutability, profit, and the nature of different places and peoples around the world. Throughout northern Europe's expanding monarchies and on frontiers domestic and distant, pearls illuminate diverse parties' thinking about the creation and expression of wealth. And there was no better symbol of the diversity of tastes and practices to which pearl use attested than the *barrueca,* or baroque, pearl: a pathology of nature transformed into art, a signifier of the independence of taste and the ungovernable diversity of the world.[1]

Pearls and "the Assuredness of the Commodities": Early English Visions for Virginia

In the early seventeenth century, as Iberian entrepreneurs scouted new fisheries along the coasts of Brazil and California and stood guard over existing ones as best they could, English rivals encroached on the Ameri-

---

1. On the baroque as a pathology, see Mabel Moraña, "Baroque / Neobaroque / Ultrabaroque: Disruptive Readings of Modernity," in Nicholas Spadaccini and Luis Martín-Estudillo, *Hispanic Baroques: Reading Cultures in Context* (Nashville, Tenn., 2005), 241–281, esp. 242.

cas. Pearls' symbolic association with maritime glory and their popularity in global commodities markets assured them a place in English imaginings of these new territories. In northern European imperial blueprints for Atlantic empire, as in Iberian ones, pearls loaned themselves to meditations on wealth creation and its component parts.

In the years following Elizabeth I's death in 1603, the English crown transitioned from a haphazard approach to Atlantic endeavors, one that relied heavily on the semi-independent ventures of slave traders and pirates-cum-knights such as Francis Drake and John Hawkins, to a more methodical and long-term policy of settlement and colonization. A mixture of private and crown investment, the Virginia joint-stock company received its charter from James I and VI in 1606. The Council of Virginia made the case for the new settlement by noting "the assuredness of the commodities," a hopeful note sounded by numerous reports from visitors to the region.[2]

Pearls figured prominently in early accounts of Virginia's natural bounty. Virginia pearls, the council noted, "though discolored and softened by fire for want of skill in the naturals to pierce them," were found "in great abundance," in addition to less glamorous items such as "pitch, soap-ashes, timber," and other goods. Council member George Percy recalled happening on an abandoned campground and fire, where the English party ate "very large and delicate" oysters and observed others, unharvested, lying "on the ground as thick as stones." They opened some and found pearls "in many." John Smith recounted with interest that one group of Indians showed him "the manner of their diving for mussels, in which they find pearls," and George Summers observed that "there are many large pearls in that country and a great quantity of coral." Ralph Hamor recounted with care the diplomatic purposes served by a pearl necklace exchanged between Powhatan and an English envoy. According to William Strachey, "The lakes have pearls it cannot be doubted, for we ourselves have seen many chains and bracelets worn by the people, and we have found plenty of them in the sepulchers of their

2. The Council of Virginia, "A True and Sincere Declaration . . ." (circa 1607), in Edward Wright Haile, *Jamestown Narratives: Eyewitness Accounts of the Virginia Colony: The First Decade, 1607–1617* (Champlain, Va., 1998), 367. There are a number of excellent accounts of these early decades of exploration. For a few examples, see Mark G. Hanna, *Pirate Nests and the Rise of the British Empire, 1570–1740* (Chapel Hill, N.C., 2015); James Horn, *A Kingdom Strange: The Brief and Tragic History of the Lost Colony of Roanoke* (New York, 2010); Karen Ordahl Kupperman, *The Jamestown Project* (Cambridge, Mass., 2007); Peter C. Mancall, *Hakluyt's Promise: An Elizabethan's Obsession for an English America* (New Haven, Conn., 2007).

kings." But, in English eyes, this abundance of pearls was wasted. As with Spanish assessments of indigenous pearl-harvesting practices in the Caribbean and along the Pacific coast of North America, English assessments of Virginia's potential included reports on pearl wealth that relied heavily on perceptions of native mismanagement of this particular natural resource. Building a case for the superiority of English husbandry of this new land and its abundance, Virginia Company members condemned native practices of pearl harvesting and drilling. Strachey lamented natives' treatment of pearls, writing that the pearls they gathered were "discolored by burning the oysters in the fire and deformed by the gross boring." English industry, in contrast, could render pearls profitable along with the Chesapeake's numerous additional resources.[3]

These English accounts equated value with skill—a narrative that could bolster imperial claims to resource management. Gabriel Archer, describing the pearl mussels in the kingdom of Wynauk, remarked on a particularly impressive pearl necklace he had seen worn by one werowance. The necklace was a rich rope ("a chain of pearl about his neck thrice double"), made of pearls "as big as peas." He guessed that the necklace itself would have sold for three or four hundred pounds "had the pearl been taken from the muskle [sic] as it ought to be." In skilled English hands, pearls could be properly removed from the fleshy bivalves that produced them, nature's bounty transformed through husbandry. It is not as surprising to find the Virginia Council include "2 Pearl-drillers" alongside surgeons, saltmakers, coopers, joiners, and other artisans in their list of skilled tradesmen desired for the new settlement. The cultivation of pearl wealth was an economic and symbolic indica-

---

3. The Council of Virginia, "A True and Sincere Declaration," 367, George Percy, "Observations Gathered out of a Discourse of the Plantation of the Southern Colony of Virginia by the English, 1606 . . . ," 90, Percy "A True Relation of the Proceedings and Occurents of Moment Which Have Hap'ned in Virginia . . . ," 501 (for Percy's also noting the pearls he and his party gained after having "ransacked their temples . . . and carried away their pearls, copper, and bracelets wherewith they do decore their kings' funerals"), John Smith, "A True Relation of Such Occurrences and Accidents of Note as Hath Hap'ned in Virginia since the First Planting of that Colony . . . ," 147, George Somers, "Letter to Salisbury, 15 June 1610," 445, Ralph Hamor, "A True Discourse of the Present Estate of Virginia" (circa 1615), 831, 832, William Strachey, "The History of Travel into Virginia Britannia . . . ," 688, all in Haile, ed., *Jamestown Narratives*. Keith Pluymers discusses English attitudes toward natural resource use in Virginia in "Atlantic Iron: Wood Scarcity and the Political Ecology of Early English Expansion," *William and Mary Quarterly*, 3d Ser., LXXIII (2016), 389–426.

tor of success in extending control over the people and products of the New World.[4]

As the Virginia Company surveyed the Chesapeake, some 650 miles from the North American coast dreams of pearl wealth also informed early English activity on the island of Bermuda. There, local and distant stakeholders understood skilled labor to be critical to the creation of pearl wealth. The arrival of English interlopers on Bermuda caused alarm among Spanish officials, wary of new competition for Atlantic pearl wealth. Two years after an English ship first wrecked on the island in 1609, Don Francisco de Varte Cerón, the president of the Board of Trade, wrote to the Council of War in Madrid, reporting that the Englishmen had "landed at Bermuda for the purpose of settling it and fishing for pearls" and "talked much of the great wealth of pearls at that island." There was cause for concern: de Varte assured his contact "that there are large pearl fishing grounds there and that, as they have never been fished, the pearls are of extraordinary size and quality." (Indeed, inhabitants of Margarita and Rio de la Hacha repeatedly sought licenses to extend their operations to the island.) In 1613, the Spanish Council of War warned Philip III that, if Bermuda were to be left unprotected, the English would claim it. Not only was its location ideal as an Atlantic refuge, it was also important because "the pearl oyster beds reported to exist in that island may become lucrative to the royal treasury." Later that fall, the Spanish Council of War reported two hundred Englishmen living on Bermuda in rough dwellings, which suggested "they have gone there merely to essay the pearl fisheries, as another Spanish Captain did this spring."[5]

Early English reports from the island, which emerged shortly after its permanent settlement by Virginia Company members in 1612, confirm that Spanish fears were not unfounded. They emphasized the pearl-producing capacity of the island's outlying oyster banks and the potential profit to be had from the jewel. An October 1613 report to the Spanish ambassador in London from a Spaniard held captive in Jamestown noted that Bermuda was "rich in amber and pearls, of which they say they have in very few months sent to this kingdom more than fifty thousand ducats in value, counting the

4. Gabriel Archer, "A Relation of the Discovery of Our River from James Fort into the Main, Made by Captain Christofer Newport . . ." (circa 1608), 113, and Council of Virginia, "A True and Sincere Declaration," 371, both in Haile, ed., *Jamestown Narratives*.

5. Quoted and translated in Henry C. Wilkinson, "Spanish Intentions for Bermuda, 1603-1615," *Bermuda Historical Quarterly*, VII (1950), 52 (May 24, 1611), 67 (July 6, 1613), 72 (Sept. 1, 1613).

ounce at a moderate value." Central to the production of this wealth were the divers that harvested the pearls. Not long after arriving on the island in 1616, Governor Daniel Tucker of Bermuda sent a ship to the Lesser Antilles to "trucke . . . for . . . negroes to dive for pearls"; it returned with "an Indian and a Negroe." Contemporary Spanish reports claimed that, although the English were alarmed by the danger posed by sharks, they had already found numerous pearls in shallow water that sold in England for "40 reales each pearl," and they were redoubling their efforts and "hope in deeper water to find more of them and larger ones." This was a collaborative effort: "For this purpose they take out with them some famous divers." Spaniards found the news doubly worrisome since the same divers were to be employed in salvaging the wreck of a Spanish fleet. As Shakespeare's play *The Tempest*, first produced in 1611, brought images of corpses with pearls for eyes to London audiences, conversations about pearl fishing on Bermuda reveal that adventurers were thinking explicitly about the living components of Atlantic wealth production, dependent upon the skilled exploitation of the natural world by New World subjects.[6]

"A Great Quantite of True and Orient Pearles Have Bin Transported beyond the Seas": Pearls and the Mayhem of the Markets

The Virginia Company's visions of Chesapeake pearl wealth failed to come to fruition, likely forgotten amid the dire circumstances that nearly brought an end to the Virginia settlement. In Bermuda, pearl fishing also failed to take hold as an industry, along with some of the grander hopes for the island's future, such as silk-producing mulberry trees and spiders as well as sugar and wheat cultivation. Although the future wealth envisioned by sponsors of both Virginia and Bermuda settlements in their earliest days reflected Iberian rivalries and English hopes of establishing lucrative exotic commodities trades,

6. Don Diego de Molina to Don Alonso de Velasco, May 28, 1613, in Haile, ed., *Jamestown Narratives*, 748; Philip D. Morgan, "Virginia's Other Prototype: The Caribbean," in Peter C. Mancall, ed., *The Atlantic World and Virginia, 1550–1624* (Chapel Hill, N.C., 2007), 374, 375, 377; J. H. Lefroy, *Memorials of the Discovery and Early Settlement of the Bermudas or Somers Islands, 1515–1685*, 2 vols. (London, 1877–1879), I, 115–116 (for "negroes to dive for pearls"); Wilkinson, "Spanish Intentions," *Bermuda Historical Quarterly*, VII (1950), 88 (May 14, 1614). Gondomar's report to Philip II, in which he notes early English pearl-harvesting success near Bermuda, is translated and published in Alexander Brown, *The Genesis of the United States*, 2 vols. (Boston, 1890), II, 683. On early Bermuda pearl hopes, see Michael J. Jarvis, *In the Eye of All Trade: Bermuda, Bermudians, and the Maritime Atlantic World, 1680–1783* (Chapel Hill, N.C., 2010), 19.

inhabitants of both places soon turned their attention to tobacco and the construction of enduring settlements. Meanwhile, the English East India Company, founded in 1600, developed along different lines as a successful commercial venture with a steady trade in pearls. By the end of the second decade of the seventeenth century, East India Company traders shipped pearls to and from Eastern markets and England. These commercial patterns reflected pearls' enduring potency as a symbol of maritime empire and exotic locales even as their long-standing earlier association with the wealth of the Far East continued to loosen.[7]

The East India Company paid careful attention to the demand for pearls in Indian markets, as did individuals who paid for the privilege of shipping their own specimens on company ships. One Mr. Castleman offered to sell the company pearls twice in a two-week period in the 1620s. Meanwhile, a "Treasurer Bateman" "on his own adventure" sent "two pendant pearls" to the Indies. In 1624, the company considered the offer made by an individual named Mr. Leate to sell "divers fair pear pearls," but "the Court, according to their accustomed manner, would be sudden in contracting for jewels, but would first take advice, and then give answer at the return of their ships."[8] Some people paid for the privilege of shipping their goods on company ships, but some did not. In the words of one man who got caught shipping unregistered pearls aboard a company ship, there were many people who "indulged in private trade in a small way, not prejudicial to the Company." Pearls were particularly susceptible to this kind of "private trade."[9]

7. Jarvis offers a helpful, brief summary of the early years of Virginia and Bermuda settlement in *In the Eye of All Trade,* 12–32.

8. For Castleman, see Court Minutes of the East India Company, Mar. 11–18, 1625, *CSP,* VI, no. 82, 40; for Bateman, Mar. 8–12, 1628, *CSP,* VI, no. 624, 482; for Mr. Leate, June 16, 1624, *CSP,* IV, no. 471, 290. For Sir Thos. Roe to Thos. Kerridge at Surat, Dec. 2, 1617, *CSP,* III, no. 209, 81. For pearls coming back from India, see Court Minutes of the East India Company, Jan. 19, 1619, *CSP,* III, no. 552, 237 ("pearls to be sent back to Surat"), Jan. 22, 1617, no. 557 ("The Small pearls not to be brought back if they can be sold for not above 20 or 30 per cent. loss").

9. A Court of Committees, Oct. 30, 1625, in Ethel Bruce Sainsbury, ed., *A Calendar of the Court Minutes etc. of the East India Company, 1635–1639* (Oxford, 1907), 112. English officials in Batavia wrote to the company of a "small box of diamonds and pearls belonging to Elias Wood"; see Thos. Brockedon, Hen. Hawley, and John Goninge to the East India Company, Feb. 24, 1624, *CSP,* IV, no. 415, 251. Court minutes reveal that "it was also observed that the embroidered pieces, also the ruby and pearl refused by the Company, are gone on some private man's account"; see Court Minutes of the East India

The East India Company relied on pearls for diplomatic as well as commercial purposes. In 1624, it received a report that "the particular commodities vendible in these parts which the Company should send are cloth of gold and silver, a pair or two of great fair orient pearls, by sale of which to regain their friends in the King's court." "Orient" pearls could refer to high-quality pearls from any number of sources. In 1625, a company agent inquired after the jewels sold recently to an Indian client and was particularly curious about the impression that a "Scotch pearl" had made on the buyer. The appeal of unusual pearls — and an indication that baroque pearls in particular had come to represent the diversity of the world — is further indicated by the Spanish king's wish to send "baroque pearls from the Castilian Indies" to the "king" of Persia in 1626.[10]

Pearls' increasing association with distant, exotic markets in the age of expanding maritime empires did not come without a cost. Their association with mutability and the uncontrolled flow of subjects and objects created anxiety among those who perceived the increased accessibility of the jewel as a threat to their profession and status. This unease surfaced in the late 1620s in a petition from London's Worshipful Company of Goldsmiths. The goldsmiths offered a reflection on the challenges posed by new patterns of pearl circulation, linked in the growing market town of London, as in pearl fisheries around the globe, to the ungovernable movement of people across borders of various types. In spite of their guild's tendency to procure their wares from different sources, in 1629 the city's goldsmiths offered an explicit articulation

———

Company, Mar. 26, 1624, *CSP*, IV, no. 435, 262; see also *CSP*, Apr. 2, 1624, IV, no. 437, 263. One Mr. Wylde was "warned to Court" because of an undeclared "parcel of pearl" found shipped to him; see Court Minutes, East India Company, Sept. 11–18, 1633, *CSP*, VIII, no. 489, 457. One Mr. Heynes engaged in "private trade at the waterside" and confessed (among other things) that a Mr. Gibson "sent home a parcel of pearl"; see Court Minutes of the East India Company, Oct. 30, 1635, in Sainsbury, ed., *Calendar of the Court Minutes,* 112. See also, concerning pearls belonging to a Mr. Gove, A Court of Committees, Oct. 21, 1640, ibid., *1640–1643* (Oxford, 1909), 101, Oct. 30, 1640, 104, May 19, 1641, 164.

10. For "a pair or two of great fair orient pearls, by sale of which," see Thomas Kerridge to the East India Company, Nov. 15, 1624, *CSP*, IV, no. 677, 442. For the query about the impression a "Scotch pearl" made on a potential buyer, see May 7, 1625, *CSP*, VI, no. 130, 65. For "baroque pearls" to the shah (called "king" in the document) of Persia, see "Presente au Rei de Persia," Jan. 22, 1626, AHU, Códice 31 de Índia, caixa 14, no. 8. For another document on gifts for the shah of Persia, see "do que entregou dom garcia e Silva . . . ," Apr. 23, 1626, AHU, Códice 31 de Índia, caixa 14, no. 108.

of the risks and concerns engendered by this flux. The goldsmiths' immediate concern was the presence of what they called "counterfeit" pearls, a term whose early modern meaning encompassed both the notion of being wrought or fashioned as well as the more familiar and negative meaning of having been forged with the intention to deceive. The goldsmiths requested that the king address the circulation and abundance of pearls through an edict banning the fabrication and importation of "counterfeit pearles, stones, and jewels, and of guilt *[sic]* and coulord studs of brasse enamel." They objected to the social fluidity that accompanied the recent proliferation of goods. In an accusation that conveyed an overwhelming, if imprecise, sense of invasion by people and pearls, the goldsmiths urged the king to restrain the "brokers, foreigners, [peddlers] and other interlopers" from "meddling" with their trade by dealing in lesser jewels. The influx had led to sumptuary abuses, the petition stated, but animating the goldsmiths' complaint was their worry about the challenge to their jurisdiction over this kind of material wealth. Too many people, "Englishe as Strangers," were making jewels, and too many people were wearing them "gewdally [that is, gaudily]."[11]

By making pearls accessible to a wide range of consumers, "foreigners" and "interlopers" diminished their significance and value to the elite consumers upon whom the goldsmiths—and the nation—relied. As they argued, "It is not onely a great dishonor to the state of this Land and the nobilitye thereof but also great losse and hindrance to the common weale." Pearls, at sites of consumption as well as sites of production, were embedded in con-

---

11. Records of the Goldsmiths' Company: Company Minutes Q, part 2, and Company Minutes R, part 1: Sept. 5, 1629, fol. 159, Goldsmiths' Hall, London. My thanks to David Beasley for his assistance with these records. London's population grew at an impressive rate during the first few decades of the sixteenth century. Between 1550 and 1630, London's population quadrupled, increasing from fifty thousand to two hundred thousand, and, by 1650, it had become the second largest city in Europe after Paris. On the increase in English overseas trade and a growing domestic market, see Keith Wrightson, *Earthly Necessities: Economic Lives in Early Modern Britain* (New Haven, Conn., 2000), esp. chap 7. On London's growing population, see Linda Levy Peck, *Consuming Splendor: Society and Culture in Seventeenth-Century England* (Cambridge, 2005), 17; and Jean E. Howard, *Theater of a City: The Places of London Comedy, 1598–1642* (Philadelphia, 2007), 1. On immigration and industry, see Lien Bich Luu, "Aliens and Their Impact on Goldsmiths' Craft in London in the Sixteenth Century," 43–52, and John Styles, "The Goldsmiths and the London luxury trades, 1550 to 1750," 112–120, both in David Mitchell, ed., *Goldsmiths, Silversmiths, and Bankers: Innovation and the Transfer of Skill, 1550 to 1750 . . .* (London, 1995).

cerns about the relationship between the creation and display of wealth and the political economy of the nation.[12]

The proliferation of pearls of uncertain origin disrupted long-standing social and economic hierarchies. The goldsmiths worried that "counterfeits" were now so commonly worn that the elites were beginning to lose interest in "real" specimens whose value hitherto had never been questioned. "Counterfeit pearles," brought into the realm by unspecified bearers along unspecified routes, were disrupting the jewel's association with a "true and wight" beauty that was held to reflect their "oriental" origin. The goldsmiths lamented that pearls were "now held in less esteeme than ever" because they were "so deceiptfully made, garnished sett, guilt, collored and enameled that they cannot well bee discerned from true and wight pearles and stones and such goldsmiths worke as aforesaid. And . . . excel the true and orient pearles and jewels worne by the royal mjty. and divers honorable Ladyes of this kingdome." The petitioners' fears about the jewels' diminished esteem were inseparable from their distrust of the proliferation of the commercial routes by which pearls reached England. The goldsmiths suggested that the influx of inferior pearls was mimicked by an exodus of superior ones: "And it is [also] probable that since the wearinge of such counterfeite hath bin exhibited a great quantite of true and orient pearles have bin transported beyond the seas and in liew thereof the said counterfeit imported."[13]

The goldsmiths were not wrong about the ease with which pearls moved across borders. Shifting European alliances meant new possibilities for trade as well as new constraints because of the increasingly close communication among markets. In 1635, the president of the East India Company in Surat signed the Convention of Goa that established a Portuguese-English alliance in Asia, thereby opening Portuguese ports and markets to English merchants. Yet, that same year, despite pearls' popularity, the company was not able to sell its pearl holdings. Following a September 1635 auction, company records noted: "No offer made for divers parcels of pearl put up for sale." Earlier that same year, company officials gave the order "to pack up the remainder of the pearls for Surat"—implying that they had a surfeit of the jewel in London. In February 1636, hoping to avoid having pearls and other jewels "lie dead in the Company's hands," it decided to employ a "skilful lapidary" to inventory, evaluate, and sell the "pierced pearls" and other items. If he failed to do so,

12. Records of the Goldsmiths' Company: Company Minutes Q, part 2, and Company Minutes R, part 1: Sept. 5 1629, fol. 159.

13. Ibid.

the "unpierced pearls" were to be sent back to Persia, where it was believed they could be sold for profit. If a merchant was willing to assume the risk of loss or theft, there was little to prevent him (or, more rarely, her) from transporting pearls to wherever he might find a buyer.[14]

Even if pearls were not selling well in Asia, there were other markets for Europe's supply of the jewel. Entrepreneurial individuals, working in concert with an expanding state, found pearls to be their entry point into global commodities markets. In the 1630s, for example, a team of brothers based in London and Moscow traded pearls between the two cities. In 1634, George Read wrote from Moscow, where he had traveled with the Muscovy Company, to his "kinde brother Robert" in London. Anxious that their uncle had not yet responded to an earlier request for "forty [more] pounds worth of purle [sic] by the next Shipping," George again expressed his wish for impressive quantities of the jewel; he stood to make a fair profit from them, because "[pearls are] very deare in this country and there is none to be had but what the merchants bringe out of England." Indeed, a voracious appetite existed for pearls in Russia in the early seventeenth century, where they accounted for 25 percent of all imports. Though pearls sold in Russia were usually represented as coming from the Indian Ocean and Persian Gulf, they were most frequently sold into Arkhangel by Dutch merchants — which likely meant New Christians of Portuguese origin, who had access to pearls from various locales. The Read brothers' pearls could have come from any number of sources, foreign or domestic. The quantities of pearls in which they dealt are as remarkable as their many possible origins. What ocean reef or

14. A Court of Sales, Sept. 25, 1635, 99, A Court of Committees, Feb. 12, 1636, 156, and A Court of Committees, Mar. 23, 1636, 168, all in Sainsbury, ed., *Calendar of the Court Minutes, 1635–1639*. Perhaps the most important of these changing policies was the alliance signed by the Portuguese with the English in Goa in 1635, effectively ending English aggression in maritime Asia. This was the first of a number of treaties (1642, 1654, and 1662) that would solidify and strengthen the Anglo-Luso alliance. For an overview, see A. R. Disney, *A History of Portugal and the Portuguese Empire: From Beginnings to 1807*, 2 vols. (Cambridge, 2009), 169–170. For a summary of England's expansionist agenda in the aftermath of the war-torn 1640s, see Joyce E. Chaplin "The British Atlantic," in Nicolas Canny and Philip Morgan, eds., *The Oxford Handbook of the Atlantic World, c. 1450–c. 1850* (Oxford, 2011), 219–234. See also Geoffrey Parker, *Global Crisis: War, Climate Change, and Catastrophe in the Seventeenth Century* (New Haven, Conn., 2013), chaps. 11 and 12. Steve Pincus in *1688: The First Modern Revolution* (New Haven, Conn., 2009) also considers the notion of England's "interventionist state" (6) emerging in the seventeenth century as England was in the throes of rapid change.

river bottom harvests produced their forty pounds of pearls? The lead box lost with the *Santa Margarita* at sea in 1622 weighed only five pounds, most of it the box itself (see Chapter 5). Which hands pulled the Read brothers' pearls from the bivalves that produced them? Which set of concerns, technologies, and laws worked in point and counterpoint to get these pearls to London so they could be transshipped to Moscow? It is impossible to know, and that was, in part, their appeal. A tiny pearl could conjure a whole world of exotic geographies, labor regimes, and permutations of political and religious power.[15]

Pearls evoked the promise of fortunes to be made in distant markets flush with consumers whose appetites for them could only be imagined—and those appetites could be imagined to be enormous, as shown by the thousands shipped aboard the *Santa Margarita* or those amassed in London for resale in Moscow by the two enterprising brothers. But pearls' association with the foreign exotic had a downside: the ease with which they changed hands and moved across borders threatened those people invested in maintaining such demarcations, whether imperial officials or guild members such as the goldsmiths. Pearls symbolized the possibilities and variety of a newly connected world, its mayhem and its magic.

"Glory by Your Own Pearls": Custom, Commerce, and the Crown in Scotland and Sweden

Pearls gave rise to conversations about the component parts of wealth husbandry on domestic frontiers as well as on distant ones. Centralizing and expanding monarchies—Swedish and British as well as Spanish and Portuguese—found that discussions about the nature of jurisdiction bloomed in this arena of natural resource cultivation.

As pearls of all origins traveled to all sorts of consumers around the globe, it is unsurprising that a domestic frontier of river pearl production caught the attention of the English crown. Whereas in Virginia and Bermuda joint-stock companies facilitated the spread of imperial authority over Atlantic resources, pearls included, in Scotland royal attempts to harness river pearl production relied on the granting of monopolies and their enforcement by

15. For Russia's pearl market in the early seventeenth century, see B. N. Floria, "Torgovlia Rossi so stranami Zapadnoi Evropy v Arkhangel'sle (konets CVI—nachalo XVII v.)," *Srednie veka*, XXXVI (1973), 129-159, esp. 146-147. I am grateful to Chester Dunning for the citation and translation. For the Read brothers' carrying pearls to "Muscovy," see SP 46/127, fol. 278 (June 27, 1634), TNA.

crown officials. In the 1620s, royally appointed commissioners carried the concerns and approaches of the metropole to a discontented periphery with its own customs of pearl management. In this polycentric monarchy, as in Iberia, the royally sponsored endeavor collided with local practices of pearl harvesting, revealing a fierce and tenacious vernacular understanding about the relationship between skill, wealth, and political power. When resistance and widespread political upheaval forced a controversial royal agent appointed to oversee Highland pearl production to flee to Sweden in the 1640s, he used pearls as his entryway into Swedish politics and commerce. Here, too, his interference with patterns of pearl harvesting—a long-standing arena of local resource use and a point of entry into a lucrative, if dangerous, global commodities market—surfaced many similar tensions and debates.[16]

After king of Scotland James VI succeeded to the English throne (where he ruled as James I) in 1603, "civilizing" the borders of the empire—including the Scottish Highlands—remained one of his top priorities. In establishing political hegemony over outlying regions within Britain and Ireland, the Stuart crown took aim at many local customs deemed to be subversive of (or antithetical to) crown authority. River pearl fishing fell into this category. As it turned out, however, the relationship between crown authority and local custom was not a linear hierarchy. An encroaching royal bureaucracy, its presence made visible through divisive imperial officials, could and did prompt careful considerations of the limits and nature of authority over wealth management. The clash over Scottish pearl fishing illuminated competing networks for resource management and distribution as well as the ambitions of individuals who sought to make their own fortunes in the space between crown oversight and local control.[17]

16. On polycentric monarchies, see Pedro Cardim et al., eds., *Polycentric Monarchies: How Did Early Modern Spain and Portugal Achieve and Maintain a Global Hegemony?* (Brighton, U.K., 2012); and J. H. Elliott, "A Europe of Composite Monarchies," *Past and Present,* no. 137 (November 1992), 48–71.

17. Jane H. Ohlmeyer, "'Civilizinge of Those Rude Partes': Colonization within Britain and Ireland, 1580s-1640s," in Nicholas Canny, ed., *The Oxford History of the British Empire,* I, *The Origins of Empire: British Overseas Enterprise to the Close of the Seventeenth Century* (Oxford, 1998), 126–127. The intervention coincided with the king's attempt to address the kingdom's financial woes and solidify Scotland's commercial reorientation from the Netherlands to England. See T. M. Devine, *Scotland's Empire, 1600–1815* (London, 2003). I am particularly grateful to Dr. Thomas McKean of the University of Aber-

The crown's interest in reforming Scottish pearl-harvesting practices dated to 1620. That year, the Privy Council of Scotland responded to an order from James I to address the "fisheing and seeking of pearlis in the watteris of this kingdome." The directive contrasted the potential benefits of proper royal governance with individual and, by implication, collective, Scottish mismanagement. Pearls, a "commoditie quhilk [which] being rightlie used wauld prove honnorable to the cuntrie and beneficiall to his Majestie," had been neglected for many years or fished out of season, bringing more harm than profit. The king's objections to customary patterns of pearl fishing notwithstanding, altering Scottish practice would prove difficult. Skilled labor and knowledge protected local practitioners from crown incursions, as did geography itself. River pearl fishing in Scotland was highly independent: because pearls were found in relatively shallow rivers, rather than oceans, and pearl fishing required very little equipment and no craft, any man (or, for that matter, woman) could search for pearls.[18]

In recognition of the limits of his authority, the king looked to enlist regional power brokers in the endeavor. Acting on the king's orders, the council appointed a handful of elite landholders from Highland districts to oversee pearl fishing in the rivers within their jurisdiction. The commissioners were empowered to nominate or grant licenses to pearl fishers in their districts and to seize all pearls fished illegally and to punish the offenders. In spite of the concession to the local stature of these men, the very act of appointing commissioners asserted the preeminence of crown initiative in matters concerning the district's natural wealth and its management and distribution.[19]

As in expansionary assessments of pearl-fishing practices in the Atlantic and the Pacific, the notion of proper custodianship of natural wealth informed justifications for imperial intervention and fueled resistance to these efforts. The royal intervention targeted Scottish independent approaches to pearls at the moment of harvesting and at the moment of circulation; in other words, it sought control over local engagement with pearls as a product of the natural world as well as control over pearls as a commodity. The council reclassified pearl fishing as an activity reserved for "speciall personis of skill and experience," rather than recognizing river pearl fishing as a central

---

deen for walking me around the River Ythan and explaining a great deal of Scotland's historic tensions over river management, especially in the Highlands.

18. *RPCS*, Jan. 30, 1621, XII, 408.

19. Ibid.

element of Highland communities' livelihoods. The new policies were also couched in language commonly used for natural resource protection. In the Highlands, pearl fishing was to be carried out only during summer months, and all pearl fishers were to submit the best pearls of their haul to the king's commissioners before selling the rest as they saw fit. In direct contradiction to that policy, however, the act sought to reduce the pearl fishers' remaining economic independence by prohibiting merchants from buying pearls from anyone but the designated commissioners.[20]

The controversy generated by a particularly disruptive commissioner illuminated the competing imperatives that obstructed James VI's regulatory experiment. Robert Buchan, a Scottish trader with an extensive commercial background, became a pearl commissioner in 1622. Buchan's individual ambitions seem to have outweighed his desire to serve the crown, and his pursuit of his own interests did more to aggravate than facilitate the relationship between the king and his remote subjects. Charged with subordinating individual enterprise and local custom to royal prerogative, Buchan needed the cooperation of the very people and communities whose practices his presence threatened. The task he faced—mapping the sites of pearl production and the participants in this local industry—infringed on the autonomy and privacy of communities through which he moved, creating a heightened sense of shared identity in his wake.[21]

Noting that Buchan would encounter "some dangeir" in fulfilling his duties, the council ordered that he be allowed to appoint local figures to "tak him in thair saulf gaird and gif him all assistance" during his stay in their towns. Straining regional hospitality was hardly the only way Buchan alienated the people whose labors he was charged with supervising. Upon assuming his post, Buchan appeared before the Lords of Council and promised that "anes [once] or twyse everie yeir he s[h]all gife up to the clark of his Majesties Counsell ane roll of names of the personis whome he is to imploy in the fisheing of pearlis, togidder with the nomber, quantitie, and value of

20. Ibid.

21. *RPCS*, June 27, 1622, XII, 751–752. For a discussion of Buchan's commercial career, see Steve Murdoch, "The Pearl Fisher: Robert Buchan 'de Portlethin' in Sweden, 1642–1653," *Journal of the Society for Northern Studies*, XL (2007), 51–70, esp. 53–54. Buchan's appointment is quoted and discussed in the introduction to *RPCS*, IV, xxiv–xxv. Buchan fits Jane H. Ohlmeyer's term "imperialist," which she employs in her essay, " 'Civilizinge of Those Rude Partes,' " in Canny, ed., *Oxford History of the British Empire*, I, *The Origins of Empire*, 124–147.

the pearlis that s[h]albe ta[ke]ne be tham, and quhat [what] pryceis he gevis for the same." His attempts to render vernacular practice legible to the state through enumeration not only failed but also prompted revealing rejections of these interventions. Pearl fishers refused to turn over their pearls to commissioners and sold them instead to whomever they pleased; they also declined to identify themselves to authorities as demanded and generally made life miserable for Buchan.[22]

Buchan was far more successful in chronicling his woes than he was in imposing orderly practices of pearl harvesting and circulation on an ungovernable populace whose practices he condemned as commercially and environmentally harmful.[23] In the early 1630s, he railed against the Highland pearl fishers who, rather than submitting their hauls to the appointed royal commissioners, instead sold pearls "to all persons at their pleasure and to strangers for small advantage," causing "the broode of the pearl" to be "spoyled." He claimed that the monopoly was no longer proving profitable to him because so many people were now fishing for pearls in violation of his authority. Buchan's complaints were more than just a personal rant against an unruly population. He also drew attention to the fallibility of crown approaches to extending central authority over distant people and products. Large-scale mechanisms for harvesting wealth for an ambitious crown could not succeed without the support of local custom. Buchan's interference prompted an articulation by the aggrieved pearl-fishing communities of their own view of the proper relationship among subjects, natural wealth, and the crown. In a 1631 complaint against Buchan by residents of his jurisdiction, the petitioners accused him of claiming to serve the king's interests but in fact advancing only his personal ambition. The petition suggested that it was perhaps local power brokers (identified as merchants and burgesses), accustomed to managing pearl wealth themselves, who resented Buchan's inter-

22. *RPCS,* June 27, 1622, XII, 752.

23. Buchan received significant payments from both James I and his son and successor, Charles, for pearl deliveries. See *RPCS,* May 30, 1625, I, 290, July 25, 1626, 366. See also "Precept," Oct. 25, 1626, and "To the Exchequer," June 14, 1630, in *The Earl of Stirling's Register of Royal Letters: Relative to the Affairs of Scotland and Nova Scotia from 1615 to 1635,* I and II (Edinburgh, 1885) (hereafter cited as *Stirling*), I, 85, II, 449. As late as 1630, Buchan remained invested in the region's continuing integration into the empire, lobbying for improved roads between the north and south of Scotland and continuing to supply the king with regional gems. See *"To the General Convention,"* June 14, 1630, in *Stirling,* II, 449.

vention the most. Buchan was interfering with "a commodity 'whiche hes bene ever heiretofore customablie reaped by the burrowis' . . . to the prejudice of all others of the lieges." As the petitioners made clear, Buchan's meddling threatened the political ecology of these Highland communities, one in which pearls played a critical role in structuring the customary political relationship between political units ("burroughs") and their "lieges," or lords.[24]

As in the Caribbean, local custom stymied imperial designs that did not take into consideration the power and knowledge contained in vernacular practices. In 1632, Charles I abolished Buchan's monopoly, but Buchan continued to petition the council throughout the decade for services rendered and pearls delivered as well as for the continuation of his appointment. In 1634, the Scottish Privy Council ruled definitively against him and declared: "Libertie grantit to all his Majesteis subjects, especiallie the free burrowes, to fishe and take pearle in all the rivers of the kingdom at thair pleasure." The council's ruling affirmed that pearl fishing was an act of resource husbandry that was best managed by residents, not crown interlopers.[25]

But Buchan did not give up. In the tumultuous, war-wracked early decades of the seventeenth century, he was able to take advantage of widespread European interest in resource husbandry and flee the hostile climate of Scotland for Sweden, taking with him his alleged expertise in pearl fishing and other natural industries. Buchan was one of many Scots to establish themselves in Scandinavia in the seventeenth century, and family connections (a cousin had served in the Swedish army) enabled him to gain the ear of Axel Oxenstierna, Sweden's governing chancellor under Queen Christina (r. 1644-1654). Over the course of slightly more than a decade, Buchan reported on his progress

24. For Buchan's complaint, see *RPCS,* March 1631–April 1632, IV, 296; for the petition of complaint against Buchan, see *RPCS,* July 26, 1631, IV, 669. A second nearly identical petition was presented to the council the following year; see *Stirling,* July 31, 1632, II, 613. The word "stranger" in this period usually referred to people deemed foreign, or non-British. It is impossible to know exactly what it meant here, but it seems possible, given the market, that non-British merchants from London were coming to Scotland to buy pearls. For more on the term "stranger" in early modern Britain, see Laura Hunt Yungblut, *Strangers Settled Here amongst Us: Policies, Perceptions, and the Presence of Aliens in Elizabethan England* (New York, 1996). On rivers and their influence on the extension and limitations of colonial authority, see April Lee Hatfield, *Atlantic Virginia: Intercolonial Relations in the Seventeenth Century* (Philadelphia, 2007).

25. For the revocation of Buchan's monopoly, see *RPCS,* July 31, 1632, IV, 548, Jan. 26, 1633, V, 540; "To the Counsell," May 14, 1634, in *Stirling,* II, 757. For "libertie grantit," see *RPCS,* Nov. 6, 1634, V, 398.

and woes to Oxenstierna—and when he found himself at odds with Oxenstierna, he appealed directly to Queen Christina herself.[26]

Swedish aims in the decades immediately following the Treaty of Westphalia in 1648 were strongly nationalist, including policies intended to reclaim aristocratically held lands for the state. Buchan's interventions into traditional natural industries (such as pearl fishing) on behalf of the crown reflect this impulse to consolidate state control of human and natural resources. His letters to Swedish royal officials show that his pearl expertise was just one part of the large skill set of master manipulator of nature and its bounty. Salt panning, the jewelry and tapestry trades, sheep husbandry, and shipbuilding were just some of the industries in which Buchan took an interest. He was ecumenical in his investments, an eager pursuer of all improvement-minded projects that involved resource use and allocation.[27]

26. See Murdoch, "The Pearl Fisher," *Journal of the Society for Northern Studies,* XL (2007), 51–52, for the circumstances of Buchan's flight. More than once he made the case for bringing skilled Scottish pearl fishers to Sweden from his homeland. Buchan also relied on Scots based in Sweden for various types of help during his time there. For bringing Scottish pearl fishers to Sweden, see Buchan's letters 2686 (Apr. 9, 1643), 2690 (July 31, 1643), 2691 (July 31, 1641), 2695 (Sept. 26, [1643]), 2703 (n.d., 1643/1644), AOSB, vol. E575, Swedish National Archives, Riksarkivet. Buchan's letters cited throughout this chapter are addressed to Axel Oxenstierna, various members of Sweden's governing council, the Riksråd, and, occasionally, to the queen herself. Photographs and translations of the letters were made available to me by Steve Murdoch, and I am very grateful for his generous help.

27. The increase in state control of resources included the growth of the Swedish army as well as the consolidation of iron ore mines and waterworks. For Buchan's connections in Sweden, see Murdoch, "The Pearl Fisher," *Journal of the Society for Northern Studies,* XL (2007), 57. Alexia Grosjean estimates that, of the approximately thirty thousand British troops that fought for Sweden during the Thirty Years' War, more than twenty-five thousand were likely Scots; see Grosjean, "Scotland: Sweden's Closet Ally?" in Steve Murdoch, ed., *Scotland and the Thirty Years' War, 1618–1648* (Leiden, 2001), 151. See also Grosjean, "A Century of Scottish Governorship in the Swedish Empire, 1575–1700," in A. Mackillop and Steve Murdoch, eds., *Military Governors and Imperial Frontiers, c. 1600–1800: A Study of Scotland and Empires* (Leiden, 2003), 53–78. For a brief summary of Sweden's political fortunes in the seventeenth century, see Björn Wittrock, "The Making of Sweden," *Thesis Eleven,* LXXVII, no. 1 (May 2004), 45–63, esp. 50–52. Janken Myrdal, in "Food, War, and Crisis: The Seventeenth-Century Swedish Empire," in Alf Hornborg, J. R. McNeill, and Joan Martinez-Alier, eds., *Rethinking Environmental History: World-System History and Global Environmental Change* (Lanham, Md., 2007), 70–99, considers how Sweden's constricting economy fueled competition for resources, particularly woodlands (with consequences for mining).

Map 6. Select Northern European Sites of Pearl Extraction and Commerce.
Drawn by Gerry Krieg

In Sweden as in Scotland, Buchan attempted to link local practices of labor and distribution with North Sea circuits of human and natural wealth distribution as well as with global markets for luxury goods. An experienced merchant and student of commodities markets, Buchan presented his intervention in Sweden's pearl production as an endeavor that would simultaneously form part of domestic resource husbandry while also allowing the crown to benefit from a global market for pearls that prized exoticism. His experience in Sweden was not unlike his experience in Scotland, characterized by optimism and profits, but also by conflict and difficulty with pearl fishers—and pearl consumers—who resented Buchan's abrasive meddling on behalf of an aggressive crown. One notable perspective on the depth of the

networks he disturbed came from the reaction of a Gothenburg grandee and
his wife, who sent strongmen to prevent Buchan from fishing in rivers near
the town. Buchan's complaint about their actions reveals the intimate connection between local production and consumption practices:

> I am stayed from fishing of pearls in some places, especially by Major
> Isaacson's house and rivers within 3 miles from Gothenburg. He sent
> his servant to me, having two of his castle soldiers with me, and inhib-
> ited me from further fishing of his rivers within his bounds. The two
> rivers are very rich. The Queen's Majesty would take not small pleasure
> to see her own pearls taken etc. The Major's lady causes fish the river
> and ties all pearl rings to her hands.

In this arena of wealth husbandry, the practices of river fishermen could not
be divorced from the consumption patterns of landed women and their own
perceptions of their claims to the fruits of the lands and waters that surrounded them.[28]

During his time in Sweden, Buchan played adeptly with pearls' complex
association with the allure and threat of foreign lands: pearls might draw
people to Sweden in search of them, but this influx of people could drain
the country of resources even as it added to Sweden's renown. In the early
1650s, Buchan evoked pearls' long-standing association with the Far East
when he judged three "pendent Swedish pearls" to be "no less valuable than
the eastern [kind]." The fine quality of pearls could increase Sweden's commerce: "In most years not only the abundance of pearls but also their in-
fertile shells will undoubtedly draw foreigners to you, to the benefit of the
kingdom." He also warned that the quality of Sweden's pearls could work
against the crown, however, if this important resource was left unattended.
In 1643, Buchan condemned the popularity of pearl fishing: "Now everyone
wants to fish for pearls, even though it is more harmful than profitable." That
same year, Buchan noted the popularity of pearl fishing as well as the pervasive anxiety about the dissolution of borders and the flux of people across
them: "As long as H R M [Her Royal Majesty] does not make a general prohibition within Sweden's borders to the effect that no one may or dare in
person fish for such until the enterprise has been proven to have the right to
do so, [so long] shall such absurdity cause great damage in more ways than

28. Letter 2703 (undated, 1643/1644). Murdoch, "The Pearl Fisher," *Journal of the Society for Northern Studies*, XL (2007), 51–70, provides an overview of Buchan's entrepreneurial activities and difficulties in Sweden.

YE [Your Excellency] can imagine." The specter Buchan conjured was of domestic resources squandered, of pearls left to disappear into the hands of foreigners who were quick to seize opportunities that Swedes ignored. In the early 1650s, he offered an explicit condemnation of the local networks that undermined royal control of the jewel:

> I have found a very large number of rivers which are most productive of pearls. They are inexhaustible, and their productiveness was made known first of all by me. The citizens of Gothenburg, who have no re-gard for either the advantage to, or glory of their own country, are daily enriched, [and] share in the fruits of my labors, not with the Queen or the princes of the kingdom, but with foreigners and strangers.

Despite the difficulties, however, Buchan promised that pearls would bring Sweden's crown fame and fortune. To Oxenstierna he wrote:

> A hundred ages to come the Crown of Sweden shall have glory by your own pearls, noblemen, ladies, gentlemen, and all sorts pleasure and commodiously. . . . My humble petition and desire is that all pearls to be taken in time coming may be presented to your sacred Majesty, that your Majesty may be once furnished with your own pearls; and let the finders and fishers thereof be paid for their pains as custom be in other kingdoms.

Even here, Buchan's attention to hierarchies is visible in his distinction be-tween "noblemen" and "all sorts" as well as the intriguing reference to "find-ers" and "fishers" as separate categories. The reference to the "custom" of other kingdoms adds additional power to Buchan's use of pearls as a way of thinking about, or indexing, relationships among subjects and between sub-jects and the crown in Sweden and "in other kingdoms."[29]

As in Scotland, Buchan's Swedish adventures seem to have produced more angry pearl fishers than pearls. In spite of his own failures as an agent of crown authority, however, his efforts on behalf of the monarchy did, in some ways, reaffirm the legitimacy of royal authority. A 1654 letter from two

29. Letter 2684 [circa 1652], 2699 [circa 1643] (Buchan could not resist asserting that this insight on the inevitable interest of foreigners in Sweden's pearls was so valuable that "I think more cannot be asked of me"), 2690 (July 31, 1643), 2691 (July 31, 1643), 2701 [n.d., post-1651], 2703 [n.d., 1643/1644]. The concern about population movement and the leaching of Sweden's wealth must be considered in light of the human and material costs of the Thirty Years' War.

Swedish pearl fishers to the new king, Karl X (who ascended the throne after Queen Christina abdicated), stated that there were too many men fishing for pearls in Sweden (in Småland and some in Västergotland), and they wanted authorization to send these people on their way.[30]

The push and pull of external and internal forces continued to shape the global market for pearls into the seventeenth century. As consumers around the globe sought unusual specimens from distant rivers and seas, local men — and women — resisted attempts to expand crown purview to the management of this arena of wealth husbandry. In these disputes over pearl harvesting and management, it became clear that authority emanated from distinct sources. In the case of Robert Buchan, his contentious career is most interesting for what it illuminates about the power of local relationships to delimit crown authority over natural wealth.

"At Present There Are No Baroques at All in the Country": *Wealth, Virtue, and Variety in Mid-Century England*

Contrasting views of how best to manage wealth, which were revealed through conflicts over pearl fishing in Scotland and Sweden, surfaced somewhat differently in England, where foreign visitors, armchair naturalists, and assorted consumers of pearls employed the jewel to ponder the nature of value, the wealth of the nation, and the impermanence of good fortune. Pearls prompted considerations of stability and mutability as well as the shifting significance of origin.

Midcentury inquiries into the location and nature of pearls reflected renewed interest in England's domestic resources as well as the birth of new scientific practices and understandings of political economy and wealth. This mid-seventeenth-century strain of inquiry is visible in the research that German-born polymath Samuel Hartlib conducted on pearls throughout the 1650s. Hartlib's interests, like those of Robert Buchan, reflected a widespread interest in improvement and global commerce. Curiosity about the natural world was inextricably linked to the profusion of new global goods. Whereas Buchan focused on pearls and pearl fishing as they could transform relationships to nature and power, however, Hartlib focused on pearls for what they might reveal about transforming nature itself.[31]

30. This letter is discussed in Murdoch, "The Pearl Fisher," *Journal of the Society for Northern Studies,* XL (2007), 67.

31. Hartlib's inquiries into pearls reflected the general trend (by the so-called Hartlib Circle), inspired by Francis Bacon, to seek out improvement on all fronts: natural history,

Hartlib's papers included numerous descriptions of global locales, and it is clear that much of his knowledge of pearl production and the international market for the jewel derived from these sources.³² He also corresponded with gentlemen scholars who shared his interests. In January 1659, Hartlib received a letter from John Beale titled "A Disquisition concerning Pearle-Bearing Shellfish." This text described pearl fishing in great detail (including the seasons when it occurred), focusing on the customs of the "Paravians." The context was comparative: in this same account, he mentioned hearing of "exceeding greate muscles in Spaine and the West Indyes" as part of a discussion of theories that suggested the larger the mussel, the greater the pearl. The jewel also surfaced in domestic improving discourses that Hartlib consulted as well as in travel narratives. In one undated manuscript in Hartlib's papers, written by John Bulmer, pearls appear alongside other improvement projects as part of the author's general aim "to find out all sorts of *Mines* and *Minerals,* and to direct the *working* of them according to their severall Natures and Qualities." Pearls' potential to benefit the state seems to have warranted their inclusion in the text. In addition to an investigation of pearl fisheries, the author surveyed "*Engins* either offensive or defensive for the *Warres*" as well as projects for deepening harbors, recovering goods from sunken ships without diving, and draining fens. There were also "diverse Rivers in *Scotland* wherein diverse Pearles have been, and are to be found."

the economy, and morality. Carl Wennerlind argues that "the scientific revolution played an integral role in the making of the Financial Revolution"; see Wennerlind, *Casualties of Credit: The English Financial Revolution, 1620–1720* (Cambridge, Mass., 2011), 4. For more on the Hartlib Circle, see Mark Greengrass, Michael Leslie, and Timothy Raylor, eds., *Samuel Hartlib and Universal Reformation: Studies in Intellectual Communication* (Cambridge, 1994). See also Thomas Leng, "Epistemology: Expertise and Knowledge in the World of Commerce," 97–116, and Fredrik Albritton Jonsson, "Natural History and Improvement," 117–133, in Stern and Wennerlind, eds., *Mercantilism Reimagined.* Leng explores the "information economies that underpinned both trade and natural philosophy" (100).

32. Hartlib's collection included a printed booklet titled *The Moderate Intelligencer: Impartially Communicating Martial Affaires to the Kingdome of England,* no. 160, Apr. 6–13, 1648, 39/2/74/1A–6B. This work surveyed global political divisions and commodity trades and attests to the prestige that access to gem trades brought the Iberian crowns. The text noted the early dominance of the trade by the Portuguese at Hormuz and the mecca market of Goa, "wherein the Orientall Pearls are fished; and where is managed all the traffick for Diamonds, and other precious stones, which have heretofore made the Court of Madrid so pompous, and full of glittering" (1262). See *The Hartlib Papers,* published by HRI Online Publications, Sheffield, 2013, http://www.hrionline.ac.uk/hartlib.

Pearls, in the author's mind, were considered alongside mines and precious metals as natural wealth that could and should be harvested.[33]

Hartlib also followed and carried out his own experiments with the jewel, a reflection of his alchemical interests and the era's preoccupation with transformation. The role of the word "oriental" in Hartlib's correspondence — not a fixed location but rather an idealized, and theoretically attainable, quality — illustrates this point well. These themes appear in a letter Hartlib wrote to Robert Boyle, relaying a story about a young German baron who schemed with a Frenchman about how to make money while both were held in a Parisian prison. According to Hartlib, the baron allegedly sent "his man" to a goldsmith, where he purchased "seven or eight ordinanary *[sic]* pearls, of about twenty-pence a piece, which he put a dissolving in a glass of vinegar." Once they were dissolved, "he took the paste, and put it together with a powder (which I should be glad to know) into a golden mould, which he had in his pocket, and so put it a warming for some time upon the fire; after which, opening the mould, they found a very great and lovely oriental pearl in it, which they sold for about two hundred crowns, although it was a great deal more worth." "Oriental" conveyed only quality, not origin. The transformative power of the experiment did not end with pearls; Jones's source claimed that, after making this pearl, the baron threw a bit of powder into a pitcher of water and after four hours discovered that it had made "the best wine, that a man can drink."[34]

In this anecdote, pearls' transformative powers were physically experi-

33. John Beale, Discourse on Pearle-Bearing Shellfish, January 1659, *Hartlib Papers,* 25/17/1A-16B (quotation on 25/17/2A), Printed Note, John Bulmer on Minerals and Other Discoveries, undated, 8/36/1A.

34. Samuel Hartlib to Robert Boyle, Oct. 22, 1659, *Hartlib Papers.* In many of Hartlib's correspondences about pearls, we see a glimpse of the personal, furtive interactions that helped such knowledge and secrets travel among London's cognoscenti (and that were reminiscent of the clandestine dealings of Spanish diplomats in Italy a century earlier). Deborah E. Harkness, in *The Jewel House: Elizabethan London and the Scientific Revolution* (New Haven, Conn., 2007), considers these private channels of communication in the sixteenth century. A spirit of secrecy and alchemical intrigue informed even communication about recipes. A 1655 Ephemerides collection included a note that "one Capit. Hues or Huys" was reported to have "a most rare Medecin Universal for all diseases made out of pearles gold and quicksilver." "But the preparation requires two years. The dosis hee sels for 10 shillings. It cures in once or twice taking or not at all. . . . Hee hath also an Art of making true Iewels and shewed one of them to Mr. Boyle but would not more hereafter. Hee lives obscurely and uncertainly and goes abroad only at night." See Ephemerides 1655, Part 4, Aug. 13–Dec. 31, 1655, *Hartlib Papers,* 29/5/55A.

enced. Even if it remained impossible to transform a number of mediocre pearls into one excellent one, pearls could transform that with which they came into contact: a person's fortunes, for example, or, in this case, a bad wine into a better one. After relating the story, Hartlib seemed to joke about it, saying that he wished he had some of this powder "that we might try, whether we could make the like pearls and wine."[35] A few months later, an Irish nobleman (and nephew of Robert Boyle) wrote to Hartlib about his ongoing experiments in pearl fabrication. He lamented that "the secret of making one great pearle of many little, is very weake." He had heard of the German baron and his pearl-producing attempts and remained hopeful that "at last by many experiments some curious or other in England or elsewhere may find it out." In the meantime, he went on to inquire about Welsh pearls, wondering "whether the pearles, that have lately been found in Wales, be found in ordinary Oisters or no, and what sort of Pearles those are that have been seen in mussells shells, as also whether those and the Scotch perles are found in rivers or in the sea." Pearls continued to be the point of entry for in-quiries into natural relationships as well as social ones. Attempts to produce pearls, to locate and describe them, and to manage their circulation revealed the interworkings of natural environments just as they revealed the warp and the weft in the social fabric of the communities that harvested them.[36]

Pearls thus appeared in many contexts: from tracts on distant markets and unfamiliar locales to treatises on domestic improvement and wealth genera-tion. But the paradox is that, although pearls were increasingly drawn into the quest for knowledge (often as an extension of dominion and power over land, peoples, and nature), mystery remained central to their identity and appeal. It was not only that the genesis of pearls remained unknown; it was also that their association with market forces and the movement of people and products among them imbued dealings in the jewel with secrecy and a frisson of danger. The proximity to illicit frontiers could be invoked by a con-versation with a Frenchman in a jail cell, or a discussion of exotic "Paravian" divers, or by reference to domestic frontiers, such as Scotland.

Pearls' association with illicit dealings is evident in Hartlib's attention to

35. Hartlib to Boyle, Oct. 22, 1659, *Hartlib Papers*. But then, as if with a shrug and a chuckle, Hartlib dismissed these pursuits as follies; in his next line, he wrote, "The great society, which is said to have far greater matters, is like to break forth next week." Follow-ing this seeming dismissal, the conversation about the German baron and his experiment continued.

36. For the Irish nobleman's letter, see R. Jones to Hartlib, Dec. 13, 1659, ibid., 44/9/1A–1B.

the correspondence of the alchemist Joachim Polemann. Among Hartlib's papers were letters from Polemann in German beseeching a contact for assistance in procuring Scottish pearls. Polemann hoped to "get them directly from Scotland and buy them there so that the London merchants will have no profit from the business." In the tradition of prominent men doing business with pearls, Polemann asked his contact to conduct this business with great secrecy. He wrote, "I request that my Lord says nothing to anyone about what I have written here with regard to the Scottish pearls, and that I have made enquiries about them." It is unclear why he wanted to keep the transaction secret, perhaps out of some embarrassment with the commercial nature of the deal or fear of price gouging by pearl merchants. Hartlib's subsequent letter to another contact on Polemann's behalf suggests that both explanations are possible. It is worth noting Hartlib's emphasis on his "philosophical" friend, as if to give Polemann more cachet as an intellectual than as a mere consumer: "Sir you would very much oblige mee if you or your Frends could favour mee with your truest and best Directions about Scottish Pearls that are of a yellow colour. I mean whether and where good stores of them may bee had at London? Especially of the bignes of a pease beane or of a small hasel-nut. Item. At what price they may bee had?" He further wondered whether the jewel could be obtained without involving the middlemen associated with the major London market. He asked "whether it were not better to have them bought up in Scotland itself that the gaine gotten by the Merchants at London may bee saved? A Philosophical friend of mine, desires most earnestly to have a certain and full information from the hands of him, who subscribes himself ever Sir Your must humble and unfeigned Friend to serve You." Polemann continued to attempt various improving techniques with these Scottish pearls. At one point, he experimented with a process for heightening their whiteness by pouring water over them and letting them sit for many days; the results disappointed. Polemann did not give up hope, writing: "It is certain that the secret of the baron in Paris, of making large pearls from small ones, is far, far better than this refining of the Scottish ones. My Lord will want to do his best, as will I, to obtain this secret." Polemann was, in the end, highly disillusioned with this water technique, but he vowed to persist.[37]

37. Copy Extracts in Hands of Hartlib and Scribe ?, Polemann to ?, Sept. 26, 1659–Jan. 2, 1660, *Hartlib Papers,* 16/1/29A–31B (original text is in German; this translation is by Steve Murdoch), 16/1/30B; Hartlib to contact [perhaps John Evelyn], Sept. 24, 1659, *Hartlib Papers,* Additional MSS 15948, fol. 66B, BL.

Hartlib and his contacts feared rival networks even as they confirmed their own secret alliances. Concerns about the new and fluid connections linking markets, people, and places endured from one century to the next, and these anxieties continued to coalesce around pearls. What was once believed permanent could dissolve. Impermanence—the transformation of one nature into another, for better or for worse, was at the heart of alchemical inquiries. The same spirit guided experiments that sought to transform the unprofitable into profit and that prompted queries into the nature of the physical body and the body politic.

Just a year after Hartlib's correspondence with Polemann, a glimpse of the commercial world Poleman feared can be seen in the correspondence of two Portuguese Sephardic merchants, David Gabay and his Amsterdam-based partner Manuel Levy Duarte.[38] Gabay had come to London to assess the market for pearls; his partner, Levy Duarte, was one of the principals in a jewelry business in Amsterdam. The two men were less interested in natural transformations of the jewel than in the political transformations that shaped their availability and appeal. Gabay's presence in London reflected the political shifts of the previous decade. Cromwell's readmission of the Jews in 1655 linked London's burgeoning pearl and jewel trade to the global merchant networks of Portuguese New Christians based in Amsterdam, and Charles II's 1662 marriage to Catherine of Braganza (one manifestation of the increasingly secure Luso-British alliance) further brought the people and products of the Portuguese empire to the forefront of English consciousness.[39]

Pearls were at the heart of the jewelers' concerns: Gabay reported to Levy in 1660 that he at last had "a better basis to give the information, you re-

38. I am grateful to Edgar Samuel for his help researching David Gabay and other members of the Sephardic merchant community in London and Amsterdam. Samuel published a translation of Gabay's letter (along with a transcription of the original); see "David Gabay's 1660 Letter from London," in The Jewish Historical Society of England, *Transactions: Sessions 1973–1975*, XXV and Miscellanies Part X (London, 1977), 38–41. The original manuscript is in section 334, no. 667, fols. 606–607, Archive of the Portuguese Jewish Community of Amsterdam, Gemeentearchief Amsterdam (hereafter cited as GAA).

39. The readmission of the Jews and the advent of Sephardic merchants to London furthered the Luso-English alliance that had already been solidified by numerous treaties throughout the 1630s, guaranteeing English access to eastern markets once controlled by the Portuguese. The Portuguese sought to further their alliance with Britain to protect domestic sovereignty in their struggle for independence from Spain. That domestic peace could be bought with imperial prizes is clear in the dowry that accompanied the marriage of Catharine of Braganza to Charles II in 1660, which included Tangiers and Bombay.

quested in your letter, about the prices of pearls and the kind you can buy here, and also how much each kind of pearls by the ounce cost." Gabay's findings suggest that it was no wonder that Polemann and Hartlib feared the jewel's high prices and sought ways to improve the quality of inferior specimens. Pearls were at the height of their popularity, particularly the ungainly, irregular pearls that Spaniards had deemed *barruecas*, or "baroques," more than 150 years earlier. Such was their popularity, Gabay reported, "that at present there are no baroques at all in the country."[40]

In Gabay's reference to his collaboration with a jewel broker, we glimpse the variety of actors who played critical roles in the pearl markets. He wrote, "I went with a broker all this week, trying hard to discover them and we couldn't find any quantity anywhere, because whatever stock there had been sold readily." He gestured to the range of networks of people who bought pearls for diverse purposes: baroque pearls were scarce on the ground "except in the house of some wholesalers *[drogistas]*, where I found them priced from £10 to £12 sterling. They are expensive and not worth bothering about." Pearls were not the only business of Levy's; Gabay promised to "give good attention to all your commissions whether in baroques or diamonds of which there was an abundance."[41]

Gabay's description of the demand for pearls gestures to a world just off stage, the world of self-fashioning. Consumers in London used pearls just as they did in Lima and Cartagena: to align their personal fortunes with shifting imperial horizons and domestic politics. The market fluctuations, Gabay asserted, reflected the political upheavals of the day, and he predicted a strong demand for pearls now that the court had returned. "Be patient, because you have no other choice," he counseled Levy, while reassuring him that "there should be a demand for pearls, which will enable you to attain your objective, because this Court is ennobled by many lords and gentlemen, who used to be retired on their estates during the King's absence." Gabay confidently wrote, "Now, with his Restoration they will once again frequent the Court and, because of this, all the ladies are buying jewels, in order to visit the palace." Pearls were at the top of this list: "The broker told me that if he had a pearl necklace costing as much as £1,500 sterling, he had a Countess who would buy it." From sites of production to sites of consumption, women played powerful roles in moving pearls within and between markets, from Cartagena

40. Samuel, "David Gabay's 1660 Letter from London," Jewish Historical Society of England, *Transactions*, XXV and Miscellanies Part X, 38–39.

41. Ibid., 39.

to Sweden to London. Gabay further observed that consumers paid according to the size of the pearls they purchased and that the possession of pearls reflected their owners' socioeconomic identity: "People of substance," Gabay specified, wanted pearls "of four grains upwards." Although he asserted that "the middling sort *[mediocras]* of women do not wear [pearls or] jewels of any kind," contemporary inventories (discussed below) tell a different story, one that echoed the findings of Inquisition officials half a world away. In London, those who did buy pearls wanted only the best: "With diamonds as with pearls they must be perfect." But what did "perfect" mean? Apparently, given their scarcity, the irregular beauty of the baroque.[42]

Gabay's letter, when considered alongside contemporary art and correspondence, suggests that, by the end of the seventeenth century, pearls were linked in the popular imagination to women's political identity and their perceived virtue and worth. A contemporary of Gabay's, the Italian count Lorenzo Magalotti, echoed this observed link between pearl wearing and gendered performances of virtue. Magalotti was a Tuscan autodidact who traveled to London and toured England in 1668–1669 in search of general knowledge and making the acquaintance of scholars. He highlighted pearl use in his meditation on the qualities of English women. He noted that "their style of dressing is very elegant, entirely after the French fashion." London's women were more interested in "in rich clothes (which are worn of value even by women of the lowest rank) than in precious jewels, all their expense in the latter article being confined to pearls, of which they wear necklaces of very great price; consequently, pearls are in great esteem and request in England." In Magalotti's account, as in David Gabay's letter, pearl use was the public display of a modest engagement with the world, and pearls figured in their general reflections on the nature of the body politic. Consumption of the jewel was linked to gendered political and moral virtue.[43]

There are many examples of pearl use in paintings that echo Gabay's and Magalotti's associations of the jewel with the presence or absence of feminine virtue. Pearls were also put to other purposes in contemporary artwork: they could be used in portraiture as a way to highlight black skin, to exhibit an

42. Ibid. The rest of Gabay's letter touches upon personal matters and negotiations between London's Jewish community and the crown.

43. Lorenzo Magalotti, *Travels of Cosmo the Third, Grand Duke of Tuscany, through England, during the Reign of King Charles the Second (1669)* ... (London, 1821), 399–400. For an account of Magalotti's trip, see Eric Cochrane, *Florence in the Forgotten Centuries, 1527–1800: A History of Florence and the Florentines in the Age of the Grand Dukes* (Chicago, 1973), 231–316, esp. 256–259.

excellent technique for creating a perfect white hue, or to evoke Catholicism. In England, as elsewhere in northern Europe, portraiture from these capitals of the jewel trade reveals pearls' prominence as both a symbol of wealth and a reflection of the supposed nature of those whose bodies they adorned.[44]

In the context of rising debates about luxury and consumption and concern about the increased visibility and political prominence of women in the aftermath of the tumult of the English Civil War and Protectorate, pearls' natural, reflective beauty could absorb the dueling fantasies of women as controllable and uncontrolled.[45] In depictions of courtesans at the court of Charles II, pearls are central to visual explorations of sexual accessibility and political mobility. They are used to play with boundaries between the physical body and the body politic in ways that suggest that, like the bodies that wore them, they were far from stable repositories of value or virtue. In these portraits, the changeability of pearls' value is suggested by their association with women who had only recently ascended to power and with subjects—female and enslaved—who could be purchased. Pearls were accessible, like the subjects who wore them.[46]

44. For pearl symbolism in portraiture, see E. de Jongh, "Pearls of Virtue and Pearls of Vice," in *Simiolus: Netherlands Quarterly for the History of Art,* VIII (1975–1976), 69–97. Also see Marcia Pointon, *Brilliant Effects: A Cultural History of Gem Stones and Jewellery* (New Haven, Conn., 2009), chap. 4. A line from Shakespeare's *Two Gentlemen of Verona* (1592–1593) suggests an early link between pearls and black bodies and casts women's desire for pearls as sexual: "But pearls are fair; and the old saying is 'Black men are pearls in beauteous ladies' eyes" (5. 2.11–12). I am grateful to Diana Scarisbrick for the reference. On images of black bodies, New World industry, and the English imperial imagination, see Catherine Molineux, "Pleasures of the Smoke: 'Black Virginians' in Georgian London's Tobacco Shops," *WMQ,* 3d Ser., LXIV (2007), 327–376.

45. Charles II's return to the throne and its attendant return of court culture and a revival of the luxury goods market represented in some ways a triumph for England's aristocracy. England's growing commercial power and the opportunities provided by the nation's expanding empire, however, coupled with the prominent mixing of social classes that characterized his reign gradually eroded the exclusive privileges previously enjoyed by England's elite. These portraits reflected an emergent court culture that celebrated female sensuality and sexual power in the context of the shifting norms of gender behavior that had occurred during and after the English Civil War. See Patricia Crawford, "The Challenges to Patriarchalism: How did the Revolution Affect Women?" in John Morrill, ed., *Revolution and Restoration: England in the 1650s* (London, 1992), 112–128; and Kim F. Hall, *Things of Darkness: Economies of Race and Gender in Early Modern England* (Ithaca, N.Y., 1995), 9; Wrightson, *Earthly Necessities,* esp. chapters 8, 9, 10.

46. The erosion of the markers of different kinds of subjects was at the heart of the

Pierre Mignard's portrayal of one of Charles II's most famous mistresses, the duchess of Portsmouth, Louise Renée de Kéroualle, highlighted her French origins (the source of public distrust and derision) and her influence at court (Figure 20, Plate 8). She was known for her conspicuous displays of wealth, intended to advertise her power over the king. The young female slave, wearing a pearl collar and proffering coral and a conch shell full of pearls, gazes adoringly at her mistress. The offering links the slave's identity as a symbol of imperial expansion to the maritime jewels of pearls and coral. The sea in the background further alludes to maritime empire, and may also represent the duchess's foreign roots. Her pearl earring, connected in a straight visual line to the conch shell full of pearls, further connects female subjugation to the enslavement of the young girl. The pearls here suggest the duchess's slavish devotion—whether to luxury or to the king—by linking them to the enslaved child. The pearl collar on the female slave, worn as a choker rather than as a necklace, further suggests the blurring of the line between pearls as adornment and pearls as symbols of slavery. As the enslaved child stares at her mistress, wearing and offering pearls as signs of her affection, the duchess stares at the viewer, wearing pearls and offering her own sexual allegiance, highlighted by the provocative placement of the conch shell full of pearls, to the beholder.[47]

---

lament of a minister who criticized women in a 1674 harangue. Decrying the "excess of apparel" among English women, he complained that "the proud and haughty stomacks of the daughters of England are so maintained with divers disguised sorts of costly Apparel" that "there is left no difference between an honest Matron, and a common Strumpet." See *Coma Berenices; or, The Hairy Comet: Beign a Prognostick of Malignant Influences from the Many Blazing Stars Wandring in Our Horizon* (London, 1676). For more on consumption patterns, see Peck, *Consuming Splendor.*

47. Hall reprints and discusses this painting in *Things of Darkness,* 251–252. See also Susan Dwyer Amussen, *Caribbean Exchanges: Slavery and the Transformation of English Society, 1640–1700* (Chapel Hill, N.C., 2007), 67. On Louise Renee de Kéroualle's status as Charles II's favorite mistress and her political power, see Nancy Klein Maguire, "The Duchess of Portsmouth: English Royal Consort and French Politician, 1670–85," in R. Malcolm Smuts, ed., *The Stuart Court and Europe: Essays in Politics and Political Culture* (Cambridge, 1996), 263. There are a number of discussions of the use of pearls in depictions of black subjects in David Bindman and Henry Louis Gates, Jr., gen. eds., *The Image of the Black in Western Art,* new ed., 5 vols. (Cambridge, Mass., 2010–2014); see, for example, III, *From the "Age of Discovery" to the Age of Abolition,* Part 1, *Artists of the Renaissance and Baroque,* 153–155, on black and white contrasts in cameos, and in III, Part II, *Europe and the World Beyond,* 226, on pearls as manacles.

Figure 20. Pierre Mignard, Louise de Kéroualle, Duchess of Portsmouth.
Late seventeenth century. © *National Portrait Gallery, London*

Figure 21. Simon Verelst, Eleanor ("Nell") Gwynn. *Circa 1680.*
© *National Portrait Gallery, London*

Consider also Simon Verelst's painting of another of Charles II's mistresses, Eleanor "Nell" Gwyn (Figure 21, Plate 9). The painting uses pearls to highlight mobility and sensuality; they are a changeable jewel for a woman of changeable status. The pearls the humble-born Gwyn wears in the painting, combined with her sideways glance, suggest coy and disingenuous modesty, rather than fixed and unchanging qualities. Pearls are central to this bold depiction of the sexuality that defined the consort's public images. Pearls hint at unrestrained sensuality and the fantasy of domesticating an exotic and wild nature—in this case, of the woman portrayed.[48]

Useful in visual explorations of mutability and the instability of social status, pearls in practice circulated in quantities and qualities that affirmed much the same thing. They were a jewel for changing fortunes, with no fixed value and no inherent worth that could be easily monetized. Pearls demanded contextual information to shed light on their origins or use. As many observers had pointed out around the globe, a pearl or a strand of pearls could be had for a fortune or for a song.

Because of this variability in price and quality, pearls were a useful way of marking the purchaser's evolving social and economic fortunes. London diarist Samuel Pepys used them in just this fashion, purchasing increasingly expensive pearls for his wife as his career flourished. Pearls also surface in his diary in stories of unusually valuable specimens, their extravagance serving to illuminate the nature of particular people and places.

In 1660 (at the start of his career as a naval administrator), Pepys noted a modest pearl purchase he made for his wife, a necklace that cost him £4 10s., seemingly a concession to a bad mood of hers: "In the evening my wife being a little impatient I went along with her to buy her a necklace of pearl." But the purchase was not just "for her encouragement" but also "because I have lately got money, having now about 200£ in cash beforehand in the world." For the naval administrator as much as for his wife, the pearls were a mark of prosperity. Four years later, pearls again surfaced in his diary as a marker of status—and, significantly, as a point of his wife's engagement with the world of commerce. In April 1666, he noted that his wife was "mighty busy about" a pearl necklace. The previous year, Pepys had promised to buy her such a necklace for £60. Having noted that his net worth was nearly £6000, he revised his estimate of what he was willing to pay up to £80. Both Pepys and his wife Elizabeth took the necessary steps to conclude the purchase. He noted that he asked "in two or three places the worth of pearles," but, a few days later, it was his wife who carried out the plan. He wrote, "At noon dined

48. See Hall, *Things of Darkness,* esp. chap. 5, "'An Object in the Midst of Other Objects': Race, Gender, Material Culture." Her reproduction and discussion of Nell Gwynn is on 170-171. For an exploration of the black presence in London, see Catherine Molineux, *Faces of Perfect Ebony: Encountering Atlantic Slavery in Imperial Britain* (Cambridge, Mass., 2012). The anxieties over the role of black slaves in English society would be given further visual expression by William Hogarth in the next century; see Molineux, "Hogarth's Fashionable Slaves: Moral Corruption in Eighteenth-Century London," *English Literary History,* LXXII (2005), 495-520; Hall, *Things of Darkness,* 244.

alone, my wife gone abroad to conclude about her necklace of pearle." She returned with "a necklace with three rows, which is a very good one." Elizabeth Pepys later assessed her "stock of jewells" at £150, suggesting that this necklace represented her most valuable possession. She clearly knew where to purchase pearls in the city, and both she and her husband were comfortable with her carrying out this transaction on her own. It was not her act of buying the pearls — as an agent in the market — that discomfited Pepys; it was the thought of how, once purchased, the pearls left her vulnerable to the external gaze. In December of that year, he worried when she returned home from a play in the evening, wearing the necklace and accompanied only by one other person. He feared, presumably, that the jewel would catch a thief's eye. Pearls brought engagement with the outside world through the commercial transactions they facilitated and the attention — often predatory — their beauty drew.[49]

Pearls also surfaced in Pepys's diary in reflections on value that had nothing to do with his personal purchases. In a 1662 dinner conversation that included (among others) Edward Backwell, the prominent London goldsmith and financier (who once charged the king £1,800 for a pearl necklace for Catherine of Braganza), Pepys noted that the men discussed the charitable customs of Catholic countries. Specifically, they discussed a story from Paris in which the grain shortage of the previous year had been so great that, during "a collection made for the poor, there was two pearls brought in, nobody knew from whom (till the Queen, seeing them, knew whose they were, but did not discover it), which were sold for 200,000 crownes." The story, apocryphal though it might have been, reveals pearls' ability to absorb fantasies about the nature of governance and the intersection of public and private virtue, with personal generosity in this instance enabling public welfare. Extraordinarily expensive pearls as indicators of status and worth again surfaced in Pepys's account in 1667, when he recorded that Charles II had given to Frances Stuart, duchess of Richmond, by way of unsuccessfully wooing her, "a necklace of pearl of about £1,100" upon her first coming to the court. As with the story of the French pearls, the stated value of the necklace said less about the quality of the jewels than of the mores and desires of those

49. Samuel Pepys, *The Diary of Samuel Pepys . . .*, ed. Henry B. Wheatley, 2 vols. (New York, 1946), Sept. 5, 1660, Apr. 23, 28, 30, Dec. 17, 1666, Feb. 23, 1667/8, I, 160, II, 188, 190, 191, 377, 808. A net worth of £6,000 was quite a sum — he noted that his brother-in-law was about to take a position at sea that would bring him one hundred pounds a year (Apr. 28, 1666, II, 190).

who dealt with them. Pearls' worth was relative and contextual; they could be meaningful at £4, at £80, and at £1,100.[50]

The ungovernable range and variety of pearls—their inextricable dependence upon subjective assessments of their past, present, or future utility—can be seen in the monetary evaluations of pearls assessed by London's Court of Orphans.[51] These records place Pepys and his wife firmly in the middle of a continuum of pearl holdings by late-seventeenth-century London tradesmen (and women). In these inventories, pearls abound in all quantities and qualities. The records reveal next to nothing about what physical qualities determined the monetary worth assigned to each pearl or batch of pearls, but they say a great deal about who owned pearls. Ironmongers, drapers, vintners, tallow makers, merchants, widows, and goldsmiths bought, sold, drilled, and possessed pearls of all origins and qualities, from the most humble to the grand. They were held and traded alongside other jewels, in large and small batches, in boxes, in drawers, loose, strung, in multiple and single stands. They were "Scotch" and "oriental," and sometimes no origin was noted at all. Quantity was no indicator of quality: a few choice specimens were often worth more than hundreds of pearls. From seed pearls to parts of pendants to multistranded necklaces, the sheer range in executors' judgments of pearls' monetary value attests to the jewel's resistance to evaluation. At the same time, this scope underscores pearls' accessibility and subjective utility to a wide range of London buyers.[52]

50. On Backwell's sale of a pearl necklace, see David Mitchell, "Documentary Insights into the Jewellery Trade in London during the Seventeenth Century," unpublished paper, 2006, courtesy of the author; Pepys, *Diary,* ed. Wheatley, Sept. 18, 1662, Apr. 26, 1667, I, 478, II, 499.

51. London's Court of Orphans handled the cases related to the children of freedmen of the city. The records, including the Orphans' Inventories, [1600]–1773, series CLA/002/02, cited below, are held at the London Metropolitan Archives.

52. In spite of their popularity, pearls would lose part of their appeal as new faceting techniques enhanced the appeal of hard gemstones at the end of the seventeenth century. For diamonds' rising popularity in this period, see Gedalia Yogev, *Diamonds and Coral: Anglo-Dutch Jews and Eighteenth-Century Trade* (Leicester, U.K., 1978), 89. On stone-cutting techniques, see Edgar Samuel, "Gems from the Orient: The Activities of Sir John Chardin (1643–1713) as a Diamond Importer and East India Merchant," *Proceedings of the Huguenot Society,* XXVII, (2000), 351–368. On the shifting role of goldsmith-bankers, see Luu, "Aliens and Their Impact on Goldsmiths' Craft in London," 43–52, Styles, "Goldsmiths and the London Luxury Trades," 112–120, and Stephen Quinn, "Balances and Goldsmith-Bankers: The Co-ordination and Control of Inter-banker Debt Clearing in

A few examples from the inventories make these patterns clear, as assessors tried to tally and quantify the pearls they encountered. The precision with which they counted most of the pearls in the inventories was markedly futile. A necklace composed of 131 pearls was valued at £65, while two distinct pearl necklaces were assessed at just £3 12 s. What perceived differences warranted such a price differential? There might have been a major difference in the quality of the strands, or perhaps the valuations reflected one knowledgeable executor and one who cared little for pearls. In only a handful of instances (usually in the estates of wealthier individuals) do the additional insights of the inventory elucidate the role pearls played in larger patterns of material loss and acquisition. The pearl holdings of Jonathan Dawes, a major merchant, suggest that pearls were just one way in which he engaged with global sources of wealth, from cloth and ginger to investments in "Guinea" and "India" voyages. Dawes's estate amounted to more than £33,000. Amid this extraordinary wealth and the range of its sources, he also had several different kinds of pearls in his possession. These included "one bagge of seed pearle cont. 208 oz at 2 [8] p ounce" worth £20 16s. These loose pearls, measured by the ounce, were clearly in a different category from his necklace composed of 51 pearls assessed at £50 or his bracelet "of pearle, gold and diamonds" valued at £10. A similarly clear distinction between pearls intended for different purposes is seen in the 1678 assessment of the estate of James Burkin, a clothmaker. Whereas he owned one pearl necklace worth £9, he also had 440 "small pearle," totaling £11, which he likely used for embroidery.[53]

The estates of goldsmiths reveal a similar range in pearls and are reminiscent of Inquisition inventories in showing pearls' utility in practices of debt management and pawning. The 1672 estate of John Marlow included numerous pearls, including necklaces made up of pearls worth just a few pounds to highly valued single-strand necklaces. The 1679 estate of Phillip Traherne totaled nearly £1,000 and included an array of pearls somewhat haphazardly

Seventeenth-Century London," 453–476, in Mitchell, ed., *Goldsmiths, Silversmiths, and Bankers*.

53. John Wall left his daughter Anne a pearl necklace composed of 131 pearls, valued at £65 (CLA/002/02/01/0878, 1672). For the two pearl necklaces held by a John Hobby, assessed at just £3 12s., and a selection of what must have been very modest jewels, including a pearl pendant, that all together was valued at only 17s., see CLA/002/02/01/1070, 1675. For Dawes, see CLA/002/02/01/0809, June 27, 1672. All of these pearl-containing items paled in comparison to the most expensive jewel in Dawes's possession, a breast jewel, covered in diamonds, worth £230. For Burkin, see CLA/002/02/01/1314, 1678.

mixed in with other jewels of middling value. Present in "a little box" were "10 Scotch pearls . . . and a small pearle" along with other loose diamonds, rubies, and garnets. The entire assemblage amounted to no more than £10. More "scotch" pearls were found in "the other drawers," where Traherne had six ounces of seed pearl as well as "a parcell of old scotch pearle and odd stones." Along with a few other stones and a diamond, assessors put these pearls at £16 44s. In another cabinet of sorts, Traherne had "15 small pearles on a stringe" along with assorted "crosse" dollars, "guilt spoons," and a silver watch. Kept in a "large showe glass" were several four- and five-strand pearl necklaces (including seed pearl) with coral, amber, and white cornelian necklaces, all valued at just over £5 8s. Traherne also dealt in pawned goods: assessors noted "money lent of [several] rings—watches and gold."[54]

Goldsmith Charles Everard's estate was comparable to Traherne's. Although his account was burdened by many "desperate" and "doubtful" debts, his total jewel holdings were significant: the jewels in his "foreshop" totaled slightly more than £2,400. Pearls, great and small, figured prominently, from a pearl necklace composed of 124 pearls worth more than £50, to assorted necklaces (including one with a mix of large and small pearls worth £20), to "40 odd pearles" worth £30, several "ragg pearles," including some of "gold and emerald on a paper," and "1 pearle round loose in a box" worth £6. Whereas Everard's pearls warranted no discussion of origin, Scottish pearls as distinguished explicitly from "oriental" pearls appeared in the 1680 inventory of John Keech. Keech's extensive jewel holdings included many pearls (some of them pawned; he had loaned out £3 5s. to one Mr. Kirk

---

54. Marlow's shop held many jewels, among them a necklace containing 48 pearls at £65 and another necklace of a single strand with no pearl count at £70. Far less impressive were a four-stranded necklace consisting of 384 pearls, worth 11£; two necklaces composed of two strands each, the first containing 137 pearls, worth £35, and the second with 13 more pearls, worth less than half that amount at £16. Most humble of the bunch were two necklaces of seed pearls, worth £2 and £3, respectively. He also possessed "od pearle and stones" valued at £9 even and "ragged small pearle and some smooth pearle abt. 3 oz ¾" valued at £7. He clearly sold pearls to all sorts of buyers. The pearls were amid many other jewels—diamonds, amber beads, amethysts, and coral rubies—and his shop holdings amounted to £1,138.16.6 (CLA/002/02/01/0812, Dec. 14, 1672). For Traherne, see CLA/002/02/01/1526, Sept. 3, 1679. Pearl pawning took place at the highest levels in seventeenth-century London. When Henrietta Maria, wife of the beheaded Charles I, died in 1669, Sir Thomas Bond had in his possession several valuable pearls that she had offered as security against a £7,500 loan; this included two pearls that weighed nearly fifty carats each. On the pearls held by Sir Thomas Bond, see Mitchell, "Documentary Insights," 17.

"upon pearles"). His jewels alone amounted to just more than £1,639. Pearls, in general, did not represent a large proportion of his wealth. They also varied a great deal in quality. A parcel of "round browne pearls about two grains a peece" were worth £5; he also had twenty-three "scotch pearls," all of them together worth just £3 and "28 round Scotch pearle" at just over £4. His "Scotch button pearles" were also assessed at £3, but the "4 fine large scotch pearles abt 10 graines a peece" were assessed at £12. Far more valuable was the "necklace of orientall pearle" made of 57 pearls "of abt. 5 granies a peece" and worth £60. But not all "oriental" pearls were created equal: Keech also owned "28 round orientall pearle abt 4 granies a peece" that were assessed at a total of £14.[55]

Amid the general reconsideration of value evidenced in the founding of the bank of England in 1694 and the 1696 recoinage, the notion of pearls as a fixed repository of wealth loosened even further. The futility of trying to assign a fixed value to pearls can be seen in a 1697 account of pearl-fishing practices that appeared in the travel narrative of one John Fryer, a former English East India Company surgeon. Appended to his account of pearl fishing in the Persian Gulf was a chart that listed pearl weights alongside their corresponding prices and a guess of how many of each size would be useful in "the wearing" in London. The desire to impose order on this disorderly jewel persisted—but a note at the bottom of Fryer's chart stating that "a few more or less make no difference" suggests an increasing recognition of pearls' maddening qualities. When it came to pearls, attempts at abstract precision, in the end, were misguided.[56]

This proliferation of pearls was equaled by the innumerable paths and assorted individual traders who moved them from market to market. It is impossible to know where or how the pearls contained in the Court of Orphans inventories and goldsmiths' estates came into their owners' hands. In Lon-

55. For Everard, see CLA/002/02/01/0333, undated. For Keech, see CLA/002/02/01/1744 (a–e), Aug. 24, 1680.

56. John Fryer, *A New Account of East India and Persia, Being Nine Years' Travels, 1672–1681*, ed. William Crooke (London, 1915), II, 367–368. On the recoinage, see Joyce Oldham Appleby, *Economic Thought and Ideology in Seventeenth-Century England* (Princeton, N.J., 1978), chap. 8. See also Perry Gauci, ed., *Regulating the British Economy, 1660–1850* (Farnham, U.K., 2011). It is worth noting that this was the era in which price currents emerged; pearls had no place in a world of such financial precision. On price currents, see John J. McCusker, "The Demise of Distance: The Business Press and the Origins of the Information Revolution in the Early Modern Atlantic World," *American Historical Review*, CIX (2005), 295–321.

don, pearls might arrive through East India Company traders and sailors, Sephardic merchants, or individuals who happened to have access to the jewel through their own connections to networks of production and distribution. This last possibility was the case with a young and ambitious Scotsman named Duncan Campbell who found himself in London in 1671 in need of cash. Campbell sought to render his relationships profitable. He wrote to his brother back in Scotland of his plight, complaining that "I am dayly looking for ane opportunity but as yett [doe] gatt non." He turned to pearls. He asked that his brother "doe me ye favore to send to ye highlands to ye. Laird of [Mcnabb] or any whom you are best acquant. with thereabouts to buy all ye. pearls they Can gett up and doune ye. Cuntery, especially ye biggest and brightest." Pearls allowed Campbell to bridge his past and his present, turning his childhood connections into a material good that might give him some literal and metaphorical purchase in a new city. From the Highlands, the pearls were to travel to Edinburgh and then to London through several trusted contacts. Once in London, Cambell would move from intimate networks to less familiar ones. He wrote, "I have mynd to sell [the pearls]. to ye Jews for they buy ym all here." Campbell might have sold his pearls to Jewish merchants, or to London goldsmiths, or to private citizens like Pepys and his wife. He might have emphasized their origins in the Highlands or obscured it; the pearls could be whatever he, and his buyer, needed them to be.[57]

A decade earlier, one of the "Jews" Campbell invoked might well have been David Gabay, who would have taken the pearls back to his employer, Manuel Levy Duarte, in Amsterdam. Levy Duarte relied on many suppliers such as Campbell for his pearls. His ledgers span more than thirty years of commercial activities, and, over the course of these decades, pearls came and went through his hands in a variety of ways: in bulk, in small batches, and as necklaces. They traveled to and from India and many places in between. Levy Duarte's dispassionate accounting of pearl purchases and sales situates the jewel in the context of a global commodities market formed by broad participation of individuals and networks across Europe and the East and West

---

57. Campbell concluded his letter by saying, "In this doeing you shall oblidge me very much and shall ingadge me to serve you in as much here and more if it lay in my pours [that is, powers]. I hope you will doe this busyness, with ye. first occasione to yt." Firmly embedding this business within the context of intimate family responsibilities, he signed off, "Your loving brother Duncan Campbell" (Duncan Campbell to his brother, the Laird of Glen Orchy, Nov. 25, 1671, GD/112/39/117/15, National Archives of Scotland, Edinburgh).

Indies. The ledgers also attest to pearls' presence as both integrated in and separate from other commodity trades. Whereas rubies, emeralds, and sapphires were all bundled into one category, the rate of profit on pearls was distinct, a remarkable recognition of the jewel's unusual qualities.[58] Levy Duarte dealt in many goods in addition to pearls—his ledgers record paintings, tobacco, emeralds, sapphires, coral, rubies, garnets, ambergris, wrought jewels, unworked stones, and even sheets of an atlas. Pearls were a part of his commercial profile but stood alone, usually purchased and accounted for separately from other goods.[59]

Pearls of all qualities and sizes passed through Levy Duarte's hands, from perfect single specimens to rough pearls and seed pearl *(aljofar)*. On more than one occasion he recorded the sale of single pearls that he had fashioned into jewels. The different financial language that he used to discuss their purchase and sale suggests the different perceptions—and likely uses—of these various pearls. For the larger batches of (presumably) less remarkable pearls, Levy Duarte talked about size and weight and, often, rates of exchange. For purchases or sales of one or two pearls, he used descriptive, evaluative lan-

58. Manuel Levy Duarte was the child of two Portuguese Sephardic parents; his mother was born in France and his father, in Portugal. His family background prepared him well for commercial life, particularly the jewelry business. This connection was strengthened when he joined forces with Jacob Athias, a fellow Sephardim who had been born in Brazil during the Dutch occupation. The two friends and partners married two sisters, the daughters of a prominent Amsterdam jeweler, and with their dowries established their own jewelry business in 1660 in Amsterdam's Jewish quarter. Their business was both a "household and merchant jewellers'" business, meaning that they sold to private buyers and wholesalers. See Edgar Samuel, "Manuel Levy Duarte (1631–1714): An Amsterdam Merchant Jeweller and His Trade with London," Jewish Historical Society of England, *Transactions and Miscellanies*, XXVII (1978–1980), 11–31 (quotation on 11). Samuel speculates that pearls' natural variety and consumers' desire to string together pearls of matching sizes meant that dealers had to carry larger quantities of the jewel. He writes, "Since pearls are usually sold in matched and graded strings or, at the very least, in Paris, the dealer must carry a larger stock than with the other gemstones, and this hints that a higher profit margin would have been necessary to finance it" (17).

59. Manuel Levy Duarte's ledgers are part of the Archive of the Portuguese Jewish Community of Amsterdam, GAA. They span the 1660s through the 1690s. In 1660, for example, Levy Duarte wrote to a cousin of having received from one Mr. Del [monte?] a *boçeta*, or sack, with eight hundred pearls in it, measuring a quarter grain (a grain being equal to a quarter of a carat, or a twentieth of a gram), in two piles; the entire batch appears to have been destined for further transportation and sale (Ledger #691, section 334, fol. 613).

guage. Along with the Scottish pearls were those sold by "Yndianos" (people who had spent time in the Indies) who came to Amsterdam to unload their wares. He also bought various goods from "English India" *("India da Ingla-terra")* and Venezuelan specimens from Sephardic contacts on Curaçao in the Caribbean. Levy Duarte followed pearl prices in Venice; on other occasions, he bought "a pearl from a Fleming," from "a stranger," and from "a man from the Hague" *(uma pérola dum framengo; um estrangeiro; um homen da Haya)*. All of these private relationships played an important role in Levy Duarte's pearl dealings. In Levy Duarte's ledgers, pearls linked goldsmith bankers and diplomats with independent traders; the world of art with the world of finance; the activities of widows with the multi-market assessments of powerful investors; the private enterprises of individuals with the imperial fortunes of Dutch and English East India Companies. The variety of pearls — Scotch, East Indian, West Indian — that Levy Duarte purchased and sold was equaled by the variety of people who contributed to their comings and goings.[60]

The reality of the networks of Levy Duarte's suppliers contrasted markedly with contemporary visions for the orderly conduct of trade and resource husbandry. Juxtaposed with the many vendors, drillers, and purchasers of pearls in Levy Duarte's and contemporaries' records of pearl circulation, the illustration by Dutch artist Caspar Luyken (after Jan Luyken) of a single male pearl driller, *De Peerelgaater* (pearl borer), in *Het menselyk bedryf* (The book of trades), published in Amsterdam in 1694, seems like pure fantasy (Figure 22).

The depiction of the pearl borer suggests the orderly assignment of such a task to a European man, who worked in a studio. The taxonomic impulse toward order and categorization prevails, utterly at odds with how pearls moved from global sites of production to imperial coffers and private possession. In reality, pearl drillers, like pearl buyers and sellers, had varying profiles. European women and African men drilled pearls on commission and outside studios. Levy Duarte, for example, made numerous payments to one female *"corredora,"* or broker, named Ruts. She was also referred to in the ledgers as the "widow of Vercuil." She bored pearls for Levy Duarte on

60. Ledger #677, fol. 747 ("Yndianos"), #691, fol. 24 ("English India"), #858, fols. 310 ("stranger," "man from the Hague") and 388 ("Fleming"), GAA. In 1692, Levy Duarte oversaw the sale of some "pearls from Curaçao" to one Benjamin Brandão that he had obtained from one S. Vaz Nunes, a contact perhaps of Levy Duarte's nephew Gabriel Levy, who lived on the island; he sold him eleven more ounces of rough *(refuzos)* pearls the following year. These were likely Venezuelan specimens.

De Peerelgaater. 81

Ô gaauwe koopman soekt en bied, Naat Peereltie, dat jesus hiet.

Een Schat van onwaardeerlyk goed,
Leid onder 't slecht, godvrugtig leeven,
Gelyck de schone Peerel doed,
Die met een Oester is omgeeven:
Als 't buitenst' afvald door de Dood,
Dan word hy in Gods licht ontbloot.

Figure 22. Caspar Luyken, after Jan Luyken, De Peerelgaater. Etching.
From Het menselyk bedryf *(The book of trades) (Amsterdam, 1694).*
Permission, Rijksmuseum, Amsterdam

Figure 23. Johannes Vermeer, Woman Holding a Balance. *Circa 1664.*
Oil on canvas, 39.7 cm. × 35.5. cm. Widener Collection, 1942.9.97.
Courtesy, National Gallery of Art, Washington, D.C.

several occasions but also sold jewels to him in 1690. She was not the only
woman to appear in his ledgers; women also sold him tablecloths and nap-
kins. Nor was she the only person contracted to drill pearls; Levy Duarte paid
one Francisco Renders, identified as a goldsmith, for the service.[61]

Although a product of a very different genre to that of the *Book of Trades,*

61. Ledger #691, fol. 14, GAA.

Figure 24. Johannes Vermeer, Girl with a Pearl Earring. *Circa 1665.*
Mauritshuis, The Hague. Photography: Margareta Svensson

a similarly distorting illustration of pearl use is offered by a far more familiar
Dutch artist of the period, Johannes Vermeer. The varied paths that pearls
took into and out of Levy Duarte's possession ask us to look differently at
some of Vermeer's most iconic renditions of pearls and their imagined female
bearers (see Figures 23 [Plate 10], 24, and 25 [Plate 11]). Given that women
were involved with pearls at all stages of their journey from sea or riverbed
to market, it seems possible that the artist employed pearls as a symbol of the

Figure 25. Johannes Vermeer, Young Woman with a Pearl Necklace.
Circa 1662–1665. Oil on canvas, 55 cm. × 45 cm. Post-restoration.
*Photo credit: bpk Bildagentur / Gemäldegalerie, Staatliche Museen,
Berlin, Germany / Jörg P. Anders / Art Resource, N.Y.*

material wealth in which women took an interest and could, and did, procure through their own initiative. In Vermeer's paintings, pearls play a role
in a narrative of engagement with the global exotic, even as they also embodied the inscrutable, private motivations of the women who wear them.
Vermeer famously plays with the boundary between domestic and external
worlds; early modern patterns of pearl use suggest that their practical asso-

ciations with precisely this duality might have shaped their prominence in his works.[62]

In each of the three paintings shown here, the artist might well have drawn the pearls as part of a larger allegorical meaning. As jewelers' ledgers, diarists' accounts, travelogues, inquisition records, and private letters have shown, however, women did procure and pawn and sell pearls in all sorts of circumstances around the world. They were more than mere adornment: they were often the link that enabled women to engage with wealth produced in local waters and in distant markets without leaving the domestic sphere. With these practices in mind, we can look in new ways on the place of pearls in Vermeer's artistic reflections on the boundaries between the private, internal world and the world beyond the home, considering how pearls evoked female engagement with the outside world as much as a letter in a woman's hands, her bold gaze of self-regard in the mirror, or her frank meeting of the viewer's eyes.

Pearls' prominence at the intersection of the most private calculations and judgments—whether shifting personal financial fortunes, aesthetic tastes, or long-standing relationships with local land- and seascapes—and the allure and exoticism of distant peoples, places, and markets is seen in a poem published in the late 1630s (though written a decade earlier). The poem underscores the private, intimate nature of river pearl fishing as well as the way a fierce global demand for the jewel transformed the act into a dangerous challenge to commercial and social hierarchies. The poem was written in Scotland in the early 1620s, as Robert Buchan fought his way through Highlands pearl-fishing communities. It appeared in an Edinburgh newspaper in 1638, just a few years before Buchan fled across the North Sea to Sweden. The poem portrays pearl fishing as sensual yet fraught and highly competitive. There are clear echoes of the classical associations of pearls with sex and illicit activities as laid out by Pliny. Pearl fishing was, in the Highlands as elsewhere, an act that literally immersed the individual in local context at the same time that it exposed them to fast-flowing currents of water and commercial avarice:

62. For more on Vermeer, see Renzo Villa, *Vermeer: The Complete Works* (Milan, 2012); and E. de Jongh, "Pearls of Virtue and Pearls of Vice," *Simiolus: Netherlands Quarterly for the History of Art,* VIII (1975–1976), 69–97. Susanah Shaw Romney reflects on some of these qualities in *New Netherland Connections: Intimate Networks and Atlantic Ties in Seventeenth-Century America* (Chapel Hill, N.C., 2014), 1–4.

Then off our shoes we drew
And hose, and from us we our doublets threw,
Our shirt-sleeves wreathing up, without more speeches,
And high above our knees we pulling our breeches,
In waters go, then streight mine arms I reach
Unto the ground, whence cleverlie I fetch
Some of these living pearled shells, which do
Excell in touching and in tasteing too,
As all who search, do by experience try,
And we oftimes; therewith I loudlie cry.
Good Master *Gall*, behold I found a pearle,
A jewel I assure you for an Earle.
Be silent, said good *Gall*, or speak at leasure,
For men will cut your throat to get your treasure.[63]

When the pearl fisher rolled up his pants and shirtsleeves and waded into a river, personal ambition intersected with market forces in risky ways. Plying rivers and streams for jewel-carrying mussels, Scottish pearl fishers participated in an unmediated and personal engagement with (and conquest of) nature and its bounty. The pearl fishers' silent, skilled plumbing of the river's depths in search of nature's bounty was a vital encounter between man and nature. The evocative descriptions of the fisher's entrance into the water climaxes with his discovering a pearl inside a shell, a moment that causes him to "loudlie cry" with joy. But the act contained a challenge to the power of a literally cutthroat market for the jewel, which the distribution of wealth was supposed to align with political hierarchies ("A jewel I assure you for an Earle"). The poem's emphasis on the intimate physicality of the act of fishing underscores its illicit nature. The pearl fisher has taken something that does not belong to him; he has challenged the order imposed by a powerful market for the jewel and its distribution of wealth along hierarchies of power. The personal act posed a challenge to larger political and economic forces. While pearl fishing by individuals was neither legal nor illegal, this grey area of individual engagement with increasingly commodified natural resources

63. The stanza is taken from a poem entitled *The Muses Threnodie; or, Mirthful Mournings on the Death of Mr. Gall . . .* , published in Edinburgh in 1638 (but composed circa 1621) by Henry Adamson. A new edition with historical footnotes was published by James Cant in 1774 in Perth. I am grateful to Susan Payne, Mark Hall, and Mark Simmons at the Perth Museum and Art Gallery for the reference.

served to highlight the competing economic interests that shaped emerging regulations concerning wealth production and distribution.

Amid the strains of continual warfare and the tremendous innovation in approaches to resource distribution that the demands of seventeenth-century conflicts inspired, northern European governments relied on ever more defined mechanisms for the generation and management of natural, material, and human wealth. As imperial approaches to money and wealth crystallized in formal institutions and practices, the range of pearls gave opportunities for people to exercise their own independent understandings of these relationships that produced wealth. The irregularity of pearls and the riot of judgments about their worth rendered them useless as stable repositories of value. However, these same qualities and the two centuries of curiosity pearls unleashed about the political ecologies of labor and resource husbandry made them an enduring heuristic device for exploring the nature of empire.

By the end of the seventeenth century, pearls had become an inconsequential element of imperial calculations of wealth—not only because of their financial insignificance compared to other commodity trades but also because of their inherent incommensurability and the importance of context in the assessment of their value. As pearls were relegated to categories of their own in jewelers' ledgers, they also became synonymous with the diversity of global practices and places, of people and tastes. This global range of local practices reveals the persistence of the small-scale actions and judgments that helped to refine the form and function of early modern empires.

Yet the apparent chaos of independent action and assessment that characterized pearl production and circulation was not, in fact, a gross outlier of imperial practice but rather essential to it. Dutch political theorist Samuel Pufendorf offered a characterization of late-seventeenth-century monarchy that was itself baroque. In a testament to the transformative power of irregular vernacular practices, he observed that "irregularity of the form" of monarchical government was "legitimated by public law or custom."[64]

If the category of the baroque emerged to contain the irregularity of pearls,

---

64. This insight is not my own; it belongs to Antonio Feros in his essay "Governance," in Evonne Levy and Kenneth Mills, eds., *Lexikon of the Hispanic Baroque: Transatlantic Exchange and Transformation* (Austin, Tex., 2013), 141–144. Feros quotes Pufendorf as stating that the main characteristic of a monarchical government was its "'irregular form' *(respublica irregularis)*, a type of government in which 'we do not find that unity which is the essence of a state completely established, not because of a disease or fault in the administration of the country, but because the irregularity of its form has been as it were legitimated by public law or custom" (141).

an experiment in linguistic abstraction employed to try to shape perception and regulation of value, irregularity in form and function was, of course, not confined to pearls alone. As Pufendorf observed, this ungainly back and forth between practice and law characterized early modern governance itself. The core challenges that generated the use of the word "baroque" in the pearl fisheries were the core challenges of the era—containing and managing an immensely varied world. Given the ubiquity of the conceptual problem that gave the term its utility in the Caribbean pearl fisheries, it is no wonder that "baroque" spread as a useful category of analysis in the centuries that followed, long after its debut on a small island in an archipelago and a world in transformation.[65]

65. For a thought-provoking treatment of the link between linguistic and economic abstraction, see Blair Hoxby, *Mammon's Music: Literature and Economics in the Age of Milton* (New Haven, Conn., 2002).

Rescuing "That Tired Irregular Pearl from Such Lengthy Isolation"

By the end of the seventeenth century, pearls and pearl fisheries from the Caribbean to the Indian Ocean to the rivers of northern Europe were embedded in sprawling imperial enterprises and proliferating networks for the distribution of people and products along global pathways. This complexity was increasingly acknowledged to be part of pearls' appeal. The potency of pearls in the European imagination can be seen in three distinct artifacts from the mid-seventeenth century, one produced in Germany, one in England, and one in Denmark.

The first is an illustration of global pearl-fishing practices from 1637, which appeared in a treatise on pearls called *Margaritologia*, created for the prince of Bohemia in 1637 by Malachias Geiger (1606–1671) (Figure 26). The text, a consideration of the use of Bavarian pearls for medicinal purposes, points to the utility of pearls as both a natural resource of interest to monarchies eager to engage with domestic and global commodities markets and as an entry point for reflections on the diversity of labor practices and resource husbandry around the globe.[1]

Geiger's illustration, contained within a work devoted to pearls, underscores the importance of context in assessments of pearls' worth. All of the friction that surrounded pearl production—from unruly enslaved divers in the Caribbean to sparring pearl-fishing communities in the Indian Ocean to aggrieved yeoman in Scotland and Sweden—might have diminished the pearl hauls to which European officials were able to lay claim, but these conflicts produced the knowledge about distinct approaches to this arena of wealth production depicted, if in a somewhat garbled fashion, by Geiger. From left to right, Indian fishers use wide nets to gather the oysters; West Indian divers use sticks with net baskets for the same purpose; below, divers descend with baskets to the ocean floor in the Persian Gulf; and Scottish pearl fishers use sticks to dislodge mussels from a river bottom.

As Germans contemplated the worth of river pearls in the context of global markets and labor practices, an artisan in London offered a material reflection

---

1. Malachias Geiger, *Margaritologia; sive, Dissertatio de Margaritis* . . . (Munich, 1637).

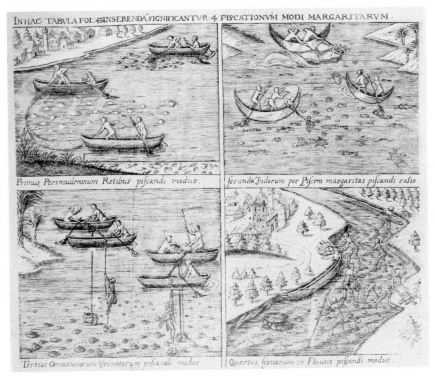

Figure 26. Four Modes of Pearl Fishing. From Malachias Geiger,
Margaritologia; sive, Dissertatio de Margaritis . . . *(Munich, 1637)*

on the jewel's enduring association with the romance of the seas. Sometime
in the 1640s in the west end of the city, a jeweler buried his stock-in-trade.
Amid rough-hewn diamond and ruby rings, an extraordinary watch chiseled
from an American emerald, and delicate wrought-metal necklaces, lay the
little bauble pictured below (Figure 27). The image shows a miniature hatpin in the form of a boat; the vessel's masts, rigging, and pennant are made
of gold, and a baroque pearl forms its hull. The jewel is a remarkable double
emblem of maritime expansion—the boat that plied the waves built from a
pearl that emerged from beneath them. The irregular contours of the baroque
pearl that forms the body of the boat echo the irregular paths that pearls traveled on their journey from seabed to private possession.[2]

2. The Cheapside Hoard, an assortment of Tudor and Jacobean jewelry, was buried
sometime between 1640 and 1666 under property that was part of the holdings of the
Worshipful Company of Goldsmiths. The Cheapside district of London had long been

If the baroque boat stands as the embodiment of the intersection of a jeweler's personal imagination with imperial maritime fantasy, the 1666 rendition of a curiosity cabinet by Georg Hinz offers an additional rich perspective on the place of pearls in the imagined and objectified political economy of the era (Figure 28, Plate 12). Though at first glance the objects in the cabinet seem to be assembled haphazardly, they in fact attest to the emergence of a new maritime order and pearls' place within it.[3] Pearls are juxtaposed with the other maritime symbols of coral and shells but also shown alongside a newer source of maritime profitability. Echoing the Drake Jewel discussed in Chapter 3, pearls in this imagined Danish cabinet are suspended from the medallion commemorating Denmark's 1661 possession of the trade fort at Christiansborg on West Africa's Gold Coast. In the emerging plantation-driven economy of the Caribbean and the Atlantic world, imperial wealth rested ever more on the labor of enslaved Africans, a trade that was increasingly objectified and naturalized. The inclusion of the medallion as a token of Denmark's involvement in the transatlantic slave trade reflected this continuing process by placing a symbol of the trade in objectified bodies alongside other natural tokens of imperial prowess. The imagined cabinet also reflected the desire to

---

associated with the jewelry trade, but by the 1620s the area as a goldsmiths' center was in deep decline. See Hazel Forsyth, *The Cheapside Hoard: London's Lost Jewels* (London, 2013), 21–22. The English Civil War might have been the immediate motivation for the jeweler's decision to bury his wares. Kris Lane offers another plausible hypothesis based on a jewel theft from an East India Company ship in *Colour of Paradise: The Emerald in the Age of Gunpowder Empires* (New Haven, Conn., 2010), 120–124.

3. On curiosity cabinets, natural knowledge, and visual representation, see José Ramón Marcaida and Juan Pimentel, "Dead Natures or Still Lifes? Science, Art, and Collecting in the Spanish Baroque," in Daniela Bleichmar and Peter C. Mancall, eds., *Collecting across Cultures: Material Exchanges in the Early Modern Atlantic World* (Philadelphia, 2011), 99–115. Renditions of curiosity cabinets (and still life paintings, as the authors point out), like collecting itself, recall Paula Findlen's insight that collecting became a form of business in *Possessing Nature: Museums, Collecting, and Scientific Culture in Early Modern Italy* (Berkeley, Calif., 1996). This is quite explicit in the Hinz cabinet with the object that references the slave trade (115). Bleichmar and Mancall also look to the work of Jean Baudrillard, who argued that "objects become part of a collection when they are no longer in use, that is, when they are stripped away from their ordinary function and turn into mere possessions. In other words, their functional aspects, according to Baudrillard, yield to the subjectivity of the collection, which not only modifies their meaning but also adds new dimensions to it" (104). Pearls, in collections or lying in a moneylender's studio as depicted in the Metsys painting discussed in Chapter 2, were just waiting to be put to some new use, their functionality on hold.

Figure 28. Johann Georg Hinz, Cabinet of Collectibles. 1666.
Oil on canvas, 115.5 × 93.3 cm. Photo credit: bpk Bildagentur/
Hamburger Kunsthalle/Elke Walford/Art Resource, N.Y.

contain the products and profits of trade as routes and consumers proliferated. In spite of their relative insignificance within a larger world of imperial
commerce in the seventeenth century, pearls belonged in such meditations
on wealth and trade both because of their lingering associations with the
wealth of seaborne empire and because they continued to prompt migrations
of labor and capital and imperial and personal investment.[4]

In prose and in art, pearls opened the door to reflections on the nature
of empire. They did the same in practice for many people around the globe.
Whether creatively transformed into jewels or used in innumerable, unfath-
omable ways by private consumers, pearls expressed the unquantifiable and
unpredictable range of human longings and desires, imagined and enacted.
All sorts of records, from testimonies before the Inquisition to the records
of London's Court of Orphans, document pearl ownership and attest to the
inaccessible, private calculations behind peoples' assessments of value. Artistic expressions of this independence of imagination to which pearls' loaned
themselves is seen in the transformation of baroque pearls into spectacular
jewels.

This variety of pearls drew attention to the variety of tastes; pearls offered
a way of exploring the diversity of the world—a cornucopia that both fascinated and overwhelmed. The wonder provoked by the myriad possible participants, origins, and landscapes that produced pearls is best seen in the
1676 account of global pearl production and tastes written by the prominent
French jeweler Jean Baptiste Tavernier. Tavernier offered a holistic approach
to the jewel, chronicling the political economies that attended pearl production in fisheries around the world in addition to the preferences that characterized distinct markets for the jewel. He observed how much money pearl
fishers in the Indian Ocean had to invest in order to participate in the harvest
as well as the tributes demanded of local rulers and the presence of pirates
in pearl-fishing waters. He emphasized the difficult labor and seasonal unpredictability that characterized pearl harvesting and the variability of the
market for the jewel. Tavernier also recognized the ultimate mystery that sur-

---

4. James Delbourgo, "Slavery in the Cabinet of Curiosities: Han Sloane's Atlantic
World" (2007), http://www.britishmuseum.org/PDF/Delbourgo%20essay.pdf. On collecting and the slave trade, see Kathleen S. Murphy, "Collecting Slave Traders: James
Petiver, Natural History, and the British Slave Trade," *WMQ*, 3d Ser., LXX (2013),
637–670. The fort at Chistiansborg was established first by the Swedes in 1652 and then
taken over by the Dutch in 1660, before becoming Danish a year later. See Pernille Ipsen,
Daughters of the Trade: Atlantic Slavers and Interracial Marriage on the Gold Coast (Philadelphia, 2014), 23.

rounded the appeal of any given specimen. There was no accounting for taste: "Each has its price, all being saleable," he noted. Exoticism and mobility gave pearls their appeal. They sailed with ease between distant markets, and even the "leaden-coloured" pearls from the West Indies would find their home. East Asian markets were, in his estimation, the most discerning: "Fine jewels ought not always to be taken to Europe, but rather from Europe to Asia, as I have done, because both precious stones and pearls are esteemed there very highly when they have unusual beauty." Tavernier noted the existence of northern European pearls but affirmed that they could not compete with those produced in more exotic locales: "Although necklaces are made of them which are worth up to a 1000 *écus* and beyond, they cannot enter into comparison with those of the East and West Indies." That Tavernier's account of Indian fisheries shared space with his reflections on Scottish and West Indian pearls is not surprising; pearls from all these places intermingled in jewelers' ledgers and private homes. In his comprehensive accounting for global pearl fashions, he noted the general popularity of round, lustrous pearls of good "water" (or color) but otherwise eschewed all qualitative descriptive categories—except for the term *baroque,* which he used as a shorthand for the unpredictability of taste. Only the consumers of India, less discerning than others in his estimation, would accept these irregular varieties.[5]

In addition to commenting on pearl tastes and practices, he acknowledged that such a range and complexity of opinions meant that some pearls could not be bought or sold; they meant more to their owners than money could buy. Some pearls were beyond price, their value based in assessments of worth that could not be monetized. He offered as an example some extraordinary Eastern pearls that could not be purchased from their adoring owners no matter the price offered or the influence of the potential buyer. Pearls' appeal was as varied and unpredictable as the people who harvested, traded, and wore them.

Tavernier's account affirmed the lessons of two centuries of pearl circulation throughout global markets; pearls were infinitely varied in their natural state, and their worth could not be fixed for purposes of taxation or other-

---

5. Jean Baptiste Tavernier's report appeared in print in French in 1676 and shortly thereafter in an English translation. See Tavernier, *Travels in India . . . ,* ed. and trans. V. Ball, 2 vols. (London, 1889). See Book II, chap. XX, "Concerning Pearls and the Places Where They Are Fished for," II, 107–115, esp. 108–109, and chap. XXI, "Concerning the Manner in Which Pearls Originate in Oysters, How They Are Fished for and at What Seasons," II, 116–122.

wise. The price of a particular pearl or strand of pearls was a negotiation between buyer and seller, its beauty always in the eye of the beholder. Pearls *qua* pearls—in inventories with no additional information about their provenance—would mean little or nothing; they were a jewel that could not be quantified. Without context and expert knowledge, pearls could not be cultivated or evaluated. It took the independent judgment of private buyers and sellers or the skill of artisans to cultivate the jewel and transform it into a precious good. Pearls thus underscore the inherent subjectivity of value.

What do we learn from the history of pearls in the sixteenth and seventeenth centuries that we could not learn about the early modern era through a different lens? Pearls do not change our understanding of the trajectories of imperial fortunes, of the cycles of competition and warfare, of disease and encounter and violence and exchange that transformed the Atlantic world and bound together the people and products of the globe in the early modern era. Nor does the importance of pearls lie in the challenge their history poses to our understanding of the role of specie in imperial economies. Their significance is in what they reveal about the relationship between small-scale political economies and large-scale imperial approaches to the generation and management of profit. They also bring our attention to points of continuity in an era of change. Even as the revenue pearls generated ceased to be a major source of imperial profit, their power in people's hands changed very little, partly because they reflected, not a fixed monetary value, but a host of associations that expanded alongside imperial trade.

In addition to the cachet that pearls accrued as symbols of the exotic in a newly connected world, pearls represented the possibility of engaging with shifting commercial and political frontiers on independent terms. Accessible and easy to hide, pearls enabled people to pursue personal ambitions in ways that both made use of the emerging architecture of empire and flouted it. The movements of pearls map the challenges that continued to define the limits— financial, political, physical—of the imperial state and, in many places, the gulf between de jure and de facto realities.

The relationships pearls facilitated ask us to consider the limitations of historiographies that assign significance according to capital flows. Extant official records of pearl shipments between markets are few and far between, and only fragmentary records of pearl pricing and flow in the sixteenth and seventeenth centuries remain. Such data, however, even if it were available, would fail to convey the story of the jewel's significance. The unofficial pathways along which pearls traveled were where the jewel's value resided. Pearls come in and out of focus randomly in the historical record, their presence preserved in private letters, incomplete court cases, inventories, and records of people prosecuted for reasons that often had little do with the pearls themselves. There were times—such as along the Pearl Coast of Venezuela in the early sixteenth century—when pearls were at the center of major imperial initiatives. Sometimes, as along the rivers of Scotland or Sweden, they were the products of smaller-scale experiments in the extension of royal jurisdiction. But always these varied records offer a glimpse—as if out of the corner of an eye—of a rich and deep level of engagement by people of all backgrounds, around the globe, with questions of wealth generation and management.

A consideration of how individuals used pearls reveals the myriad actions and results that could qualify as "profiting" from a relationship with a material good. In this respect, the study of pearls offers a new perspective on early modern commodity trades, one that tracks a trajectory of meaning based on personal assessment of webs of connectivity rather than market fluctuations.[6] Indeed, the prevalence of clandestine pearl trading asks us to consider the relationship between extralegal transactions and state formation. People who staked their own claim to pearls at sites of production and consumption were less smugglers than participants in the crafting of a porous and imperfect web of regulation intended to control the movement of people and products between realms. In the fragmentary evidence of such transactions, we see how people and communities took recourse in nature and its products in their attempts to engage with developing markets and emerging governing bureaucracies.[7]

6. My approach builds on the insights of the classic work of Arjun Appadurai, ed., *The Social Life of Things: Commodities in Cultural Perspective* (Cambridge, 1986), and Pierre Bourdieu, *Distinction: A Social Critique of the Judgement of Taste,* trans. Richard Nice (Cambridge, 1979).

7. In thinking about the relationship of action to political identity and belonging, the book also engages with scholars of the nature of Spanish polity formation, such as Tamar Herzog (whose most recent work, *Frontiers of Possession: Spain and Portugal in Europe and the Americas* [Cambridge, 2015], builds on her earlier work in its consideration of border formation) and Regina Grafe (who has written extensively on polycentric monarchies and the construction of the Spanish state, including her monograph, *Distant Tyranny: Markets, Power, and Backwardness in Spain, 1650–1800* [Princeton, N.J., 2012]). Pamela H. Smith explores the link between authority and knowledge of nature in *The Body of the Artisan: Art and Experience in the Scientific Revolution* (Chicago, 2004).

Following pearls from Caribbean oyster banks to pearl fisheries in the Gulf of Mannar, from the private rooms of Spanish diplomats in London and Rome to the manor houses of the Scottish Highlands allows commonalities in conversations about value to emerge. In the microhistories traced by *American Baroque,* imperial edicts intersect with personal initiative, local knowledge of seasonal water temperatures and the sonic landscapes of oyster beds with the imperatives of global markets and continental armies. At sites of pearl cultivation and distribution around the globe, individual stakeholders in the enterprise of empire used pearls in ways that reflected their understandings of worth—their own, that of pearls, that of the people with whom they did business. Their alliances formed rival networks of jurisdiction over wealth that posed meaningful challenges to the authority of the crown. It was this human capital—its knowledge of tides and reefs and rivers banks, of merchants' marks and the preferences that prevailed in Moscow versus Lima—that consistently reasserted the power of subjects themselves to facilitate and foil imperial efforts at wealth husbandry.

Two centuries after the spectacular production and destruction of the Caribbean pearl fisheries, what was the place for pearls amid the ungovernable din of global markets, bodies, labor systems, geographies, religions, fashions, and tastes? The American profusion of the early sixteenth century was long gone, but this early glut had upended the market for the jewel, unleashing an enduring and widespread interest in the diversity of form and function that pearls had come to symbolize. This diversity extended beyond the natural range of the jewel itself—from *barruecas* to *caconas*—to the types of labor regimes that produced pearls, the myriad interests and technologies and circuits that shaped their movement, and the numerous geographies in which they could be found. The chorus of voices asserting dominion over the jewel, this riot of judgments and opinions, was the maelstrom of interactions unleashed by the American encounter.

The term *baroque,* as this book suggests, came to denote outlandish and

---

Susan Scott Parrish also considers the relationship between expertise, natural history, and authority in *American Curiosity: Cultures of Natural History in the Colonial British Atlantic World* (Chapel Hill, N.C., 2006). Examples of works that explore the intersection of extralegal transactions and state formation in the Indian Ocean and Atlantic context, respectively, are Eric Tagliacozzo, *Secret Trades, Porous Borders: Smuggling and States along a Southeast Asian Frontier, 1865–1915* (New Haven, Conn., 2005); and Mark G. Hanna, *Pirate Nests and the Rise of the British Empire, 1570–1740* (Chapel Hill, N.C., 2015). Shannon Lee Dawdy also discusses the illegal and extralegal components of empire in *Building the Devil's Empire: French Colonial New Orleans* (Chicago, 2008).

excessive expression because of how pearls were used in the hands of people around the globe. Human practice was central to the emergence of this new, expansive understanding of the term. The irregularity that characterized the trade in pearls illuminates the lived experience of empire on jurisdictional, commercial, and personal levels. Scholars have emphasized the baroque space as one of superabundance and waste, but the proliferation of pearls can be seen instead as a sign, not of waste, but of creation, as enabling participation in the elaboration of the political economy of the era.[8]

By tracking the relationship between vernacular approaches to pearls and the aims and abilities of emerging imperial bureaucracies, *American Baroque* moves away from a view of the baroque as a reflection of a binary: either a baroque imposed from above or a baroque revised from below during the centuries of colonial rule. Neither a hard-and-fast representation of the opposition to colonial rule nor, as Chilean critic Hernán Vidal characterized much scholarship on the baroque, a representation of "the *angst* of the established order before chaotic trends that may bring it to fragmentation and demise," the irregularity of the baroque was central to the creation of the new world order of the early modern era. The early modern history of pearls, for its part, restores some of the practical, historical complexity that gave the term its power, beyond its role as a curious material vehicle for the expression of artisanal ingenuity through the creation of fantastical jewels. In the image below,

8. In his review of José Antonio Maravall's work on the baroque as a historical construct (Maravall, *Culture of the Baroque: Analysis of a Historical Structure,* trans. Terry Cochran [Minneapolis, Minn., 1986]), J. H. Elliott cautioned against the temptation to make aesthetic generalizations based on social and political practice: "It is hard enough to find common denominators in the infinitely complex and varied Europe of the seventeenth century, and harder still to make convincing connections between the aesthetic and literary sensibility of an age and its political and social organization." Nonetheless, as decades of scholarship on cultural production of the baroque from art and literature scholars have shown, the baroque as "a question of form" and the history of Latin America are deeply intertwined. Hernán Vidal quotes J. H. Elliott in "Aesthetic Categories as Empire Administration Imperatives: The Case of the Baroque," in Nicholas Spadaccini and Luis Martín-Estudillo, eds., *Hispanic Baroques: Reading Cultures in Context* (Nashville, Tenn., 2005), 20–51 (quotation on 21). The original Elliott review, titled "Concerto Barocco," appeared in the *New York Review of Books,* Apr. 9, 1987. On the baroque as a question of form, see the introduction, "Technologies of Transatlantic Exchange and Transformation," in Evonne Levy and Kenneth Mills, eds., *Lexikon of the Hispanic Baroque: Transatlantic Exchange and Transformation* (Austin, Tex., 2013), 5–6. On the legacy of the term for Spanish science, see Marcaida and Juan Pimentel, "Dead Natures or Still Lifes?" in Bleichmar and Mancall, eds., *Collecting across Cultures,* 99–115.

a provocative vision of the nature of wealth emerges from a baroque pearl (Figure 29). The figure of an enslaved boy, his hands manacled behind his back, embodies and—through its dependence on a natural, baroque pearl for its realization—naturalizes the violence that produced pearls and, indeed, much of the wealth of empire.[9]

Although pearl fishers, buyers, and sellers rarely characterized their actions in such a way, engaging with pearls carried an inherent statement of independence. Pearls were an inscrutable jewel, and their value in any given situation remained beyond the purview of administrative bodies. Pearls' value owed something to their physical qualities, but what they did not reveal was equally as important. Their round, simple perfection elided the irregular circumstances not just of their creation but also of the irregular paths they traveled once harvested. Pearls could mean one thing and its opposite; they absorbed the fantasies and hopes of their owners and those who gazed upon them. They were worth the favor that needed trading, the networks that the seller had access to, the privately assessed scale of advancement that their purchase or sale signified to the people involved. The chaotic implications of this subjectivity—the inherent ungovernability of the independent gaze— were embedded in the appeal of the baroque.

A baroque pearl left alone could be nearly worthless, or, as French jeweler Tavernier suggested, synonymous with unrefined tastes. But in the right hands, such as those of famed Dresden goldsmith Johann Melchior Ding-

9. See Severo Sarduy, "El barroco y el neobarroco," in César Fernández Moreno, ed., *America Latina en su literatura* (Mexico, 1973), 181. The trend of this binary in some scholarship on the baroque is discussed in the Editors' Note for both Alejo Carpentier, "The City of Columns," and Carpentier, "Excerpt from 'Questions concerning the Contemporary Latin American Novel,'" in Lois Parkinson Zamora and Monkia Kaup, eds., *Baroque New Worlds: Representation, Transculturation, Counterconquest* (Durham, N.C., 2010), 241–243. As Vidal points out in "Aesthetic Categories as Empire Administration Imperatives," in Spadaccini and Martín-Estudillo, eds., *Hispanic Baroques*, this vernacular / imperial dichotomy can also be found in art criticism of the baroque; he contrasts Wolfflin's conception of the baroque, based in the "micro-dimension of everyday life," with Arnold Hauser, who located baroque art in Counter-Reformation efforts of the Catholic Church (22–23). In his survey of scholarship on the concept of the baroque, Vidal characterizes a wide range of commentary on the baroque as tracing this type of flamboyant disintegration (22). He argues that the baroque "as a category of imperial administration is obviously located in the consent area in the application of violence" (30). On the baroque as "decorative excess" and the extreme, see David R. Castillo, "Horror (Vacui): The Baroque Condition," in Spadaccini and Martín-Estudillo, *Hispanic Baroques*, 87–104.

Figure 29. Brooch of an African. By a German jeweler (Dresden).
Circa 1680–1720 (Baroque). The Walters Art Museum, Baltimore

linger, a baroque pearl could be transformed into an essential component of a valuable jewel—in this case, a symbol of the wealth created by African bodies (Figure 30, Plate 13). In the statue shown below, the servant's ebony body glistens no less than the jewels that adorn him or the proffered tray of pearls. It is an image of double subservience, drawing the viewer's attention both to the "Moor" who offers his services as a purveyor of wealth and to the shimmering symbols of imperial dominance that bedeck him. Unlike the enslaved figure fashioned from a baroque pearl pictured above, this figure is not passive; the Moor's body conveys motion and power, asking the viewer to reflect on the magnificence of whomever commands him. The figure's bearing and posture also raise the possibility that he is delivering jewels that he himself harvested. Given European familiarity with the labor regimes that produced pearls, this may indeed be the artisan's intention.

By the end of the seventeenth century, the appeal of pearls was their association with the relationships that lay at the heart of the imperial project: the push and pull between order and disorder, between containment of subjects and objects and unfettered movement of both across borders, between subjectivity and objectivity. The infinite variety of paths and purposes to which pearls could be put—a reflection of the infinite variety of human taste and judgment—shaped the emergence of the term *baroque* as a descriptor for aesthetic and administrative complexity. The myriad paths of pearls from seabed to the hands of diverse consumers charted the shifting borders and new encounters that redefined the early modern world. Their ubiquity in art of the period attests to their utility in representations of the possibilities of a new era, from the promise of maritime wealth to feminine power and virtue to the subjecthood of enslaved Africans. The qualities that made pearls so difficult to control as a commodity and so useless in an increasingly precise financial sphere made them a potent component of visual explorations of the nature of an increasingly complex world.

Pearls were simple, and they were complex; like people, pearls offer infinitely varied expressions of a single unifying identity. It was the baroque that came to symbolize this duality: "a way of living the unity-diversity of the world," in the words of Martinican writer and philosopher Édouard Glissant. The enduring lesson of the Caribbean pearl fisheries is that the baroque was more than a misshapen pearl; it was the complex knot of relationships, coerced and collaborative, that produced the wealth and knowledge upon which the imperial endeavor depended. Pearls were a potent by-product of this enduring and evolving encounter, and as such they continued to command attention, even as imperial authorities invested in more lucrative trades

Figure 30. Johann Melchior Dinglinger (goldsmith), Moor with Monstrous Pearl Shell. 1724. Detail of photograph by Jürgen Karpinski. Wood, lacquered, gold, silver, gold plated, enamel, precious stones, cameos, pearls, mother of pearl, 19.9 cm. × 19.4 cm. Photo credit: bpk Bildagentur / Gruenes Gewoelbe, Staatliche Kunstsammlungen, Dresden, Germany / Jürgen Karpinski / Art Resource, N.Y.

and turned from taxonomies of pearls to taxonomies of people. Pearls' symbolic and economic worth were inextricably intertwined and could not be measured in an account book. Instead, pearls' power lay in their evocation of the interlocking relationships — among humans and between humans and the natural world — at the heart of empire.[10]

10. Édouard Glissant, *Poetics of Relation,* trans. Betsy Wing (Ann Arbor, Mich., 1997), 79.

ESSAY ON SOURCES

PRIMARY SOURCES

My interest in pearl fishing in the Caribbean began when I came across a document in the Archivo General de Indias in Seville, Spain (the Spanish empire's colonial archive), describing the labor regime of Caribbean pearl diving. It soon became clear that situating the production and circulation of this jewel in context would take me not only throughout the Caribbean but far beyond it. As the book argues, this arena of American colonial expansion was embedded from its earliest years in networks of labor and commerce that were regional, Atlantic, and global. As I traced the paths of pearls and people into and out of the pearl fisheries, I realized that the project would not evolve in a single imperial context.

Since beginning to work on this project, I have sought pearls in archives in Spain, Portugal, England, Scotland, the Netherlands, and Venezuela. If I had greater language skills and infinite time and resources, global archives from India to the Midde East and East Asia would surely yield interesting stories about pearl use in these regions, long centers of their own thriving trade in the jewel. My focus on the Caribbean and Atlantic worlds reflects both the constraints of time and training and my interest in how the encounters of the post-Columbus era shifted patterns in the trade.

The logic behind my archival peregrinations is not only that merchants and consumers from these regions purchased Caribbean pearls—although they did—but also that the history of pearls could not be told through a reliance on official accounts of their production or merchant accounts of their purchase and sale. Much like the jewel itself, records about pearls are varied and hard to find. In many ways, the most complete record of pearls' popularity and abundance in the early modern period is the immense body of sixteenth- and seventeenth-century artwork depicting the jewel—pearls bedeck men and women in secular and religious settings around the globe, pointing to a lively trade in the jewel and its popularity worldwide.

Archival sources on pearls are incomplete and irregular in their reflection of pearls' particular qualities and the related difficulty of keeping track of them. Pearls easily evaded taxation; jewel merchants avoided announcing valuable shipments of the jewel when possible; individual owners of pearls did not always, or often, advertise their valuable possessions. As the microhistories recounted in this book indicate, when people sold pearls, they often sought to do so in secret, for reasons about which we can only speculate. The stories of who used pearls and how they used them appear in the interstices of imperial archives, in community archives, in travel accounts and the writing of early royal chroniclers, in incomplete personal letters and diaries, and in the odd merchant ledger. They emerge in discussions of production, of consumption, of regulation, and of diplomacy. Often they surface in the most interesting ways in discussions about something else entirely—such as Inquisition records or court cases about local scandals. It is not uncommon to find records of pearls in the bureaucratic aftermath of shipwrecks and unexpected deaths, when survivors and investors suddenly had a reason to register the loss of goods whose presence they had preferred not to declare when they assumed they would reach their destination.

Concretely, even as I failed to find clear accounting of Caribbean pearls' yearly production and distribution, I was drawn to other types of evidence. Scattered among Seville's notarial and imperial archives, and in the invaluable source compilations produced by historians such as Enrique Otte and H. Nectario María, was evidence of pearls' utility and prominence in many different kinds of transactions. Concerns about pearls' abundance and their scarcity led to court cases about oyster harvests, American officials' constant litany of complaints about life and labor in the fisheries, council deliberations about specie shortages, and royal letters concerning the distinct uses of particular types of pearls. Evidence from archives around Spain and elsewhere in Europe further complicated the story of pearls, suggesting that the jewel's worth encompassed more than could be recorded in a ledger. In the Spanish state archives in Simancas, pearls surfaced in correspondence between anxious diplomats who used the jewel in times of duress. Inquisition records in Lisbon and Madrid underscored pearls' accessibility and illuminated the networks of local contacts and global merchants that moved pearls from household to household, pawned and sold and gifted, between neighborhoods and across oceans. I followed these global pathways alluded to in Iberian records to repositories elsewhere in Europe: private letters, East India Company files, and independent merchant books in Edinburgh and Amsterdam and London. Along the way, material artifacts and portraiture in all these cities provided a reminder of the deep consumer hunger for the jewel and its mutable symbolism.

Alongside these journeys to archives and museums across Europe, I talked with many people, from Scottish jewelers who explained complexities of pearl coloring and river-pearl poaching to marine biologists and gemologists who discussed the intricacies of pearl formation. The remarkable staff of the

Mel Fisher Museum in Key West, Florida, taught me about pearl restoration and showed me more varieties of baroque pearls than I had ever laid eyes on. Finally, I was able to go to Venezuela to visit the Pearl Islands themselves. The harshness of the land, the clarity of the water, the density of the mangrove swamps, and the proximity of the mainland made the calculations of unsupervised enslaved divers, pearl-hungry and parched traders, and besieged Guayqueríes that much easier to imagine.

Over the course of this sleuthing, my methodology often felt haphazard— looking for low-hanging fruit, searching for pearls in indices and finders' guides—but over time I realized the significance of this seemingly haphazard distribution of records concerning the jewel. Pearls ended up scattered so randomly throughout the imperial archives and beyond them because that was how they moved in the early modern period: people alternately engaged with imperial bureaucracies and avoided them. The bureaucracies themselves were nascent and imperfect, their approach to tracking the movement of people and products across realms still being honed through trial and error. Pearls' random distribution, the absence of consistent major records of their production and movement across borders, *was* the story.

SECONDARY SOURCES

More works than I could possibly list have critically influenced my thinking and writing about pearls, but five books in particular served as models of creative and informed risk taking and provided enduring inspiration as I grappled with my disparate pearl evidence. Christopher S. Wood's *Forgery, Replica, Fiction: Temporalities of German Renaissance Art* (Chicago, 2008) made me think differently about the evolving significance of origin in the early modern world and its link to the imagination. The changing relationship between an artifact's place of fabrication and its appeal and the role of the artisan in creating meaning were of profound significance for me as I considered how people thought about pearls, their alleged provenance, and their worth. Wood's work led me to Pamela H. Smith's *Body of the Artisan: Art and Experience in the Scientific Revolution* (Chicago, 2004), which furthered my thinking about the role of skilled individuals in the creation of value and the prominence of the natural world in expressions of subject identity. Mark Mazower's *Salonica, City of Ghosts: Christians, Muslims, and Jews, 1430–1950* (New York, 2004) provided a thrilling model of how to tell a long durée history encompassing world history in the story of a single subject. The combination of erudition and imagination in Stephen Greenblatt's creative biography of Shakespeare, *Will in the World: How Shakespeare Became Shakespeare*

(New York, 2004), made me think in new ways about the limits of historical knowledge and what a scholar can responsibly do to imagine a world just beyond the borders of what the documents allow us to say with certainty. My interest in how pearl dealings provide a fleeting glimpse of what lies almost entirely out of view—the subjective judgment contained in the independent gaze, so central to peoples' perceptions of the value of pearls—drew a great deal of inspiration from Greenblatt's book. As I began to investigate the ecological elements surrounding pearl harvesting, Pekka Hämäläinen's *Comanche Empire* (New Haven, Conn., 2008) caused me to reflect on political ecologies and holistic understandings of how communities husbanded human and natural wealth.

To the extent that *American Baroque* is a commodity study and a consideration of consumption practices, I am indebted to many excellent works that situate their subject in rich contexts of production, distribution, and consumption. Many such studies have explored the social, economic, and political contexts of material goods' circulation in order to illuminate the history of the commodity at the heart of their inquiry. Particularly helpful in thinking about the movement of goods and consumer appetites in the context of the shifting early modern world were Craig Clunas, *Superfluous Things: Material Culture and Social Status in Early Modern China* (Cambridge, 1991); Paul Freedman, *Out of the East: Spices and the Medieval Imagination* (New Haven, Conn., 2009); Amy Butler Greenfield, *A Perfect Red: Empire, Espionage, and the Quest for the Color of Desire* (New York, 2005); and David Hancock, *Oceans of Wine: Madeira and the Emergence of American Trade and Taste* (New Haven, Conn., 2009). Perhaps the only natural and highly valued product that rivaled pearls as a reflection of the era's fascination with variety was the tulip. The phenomenon of "tulipmania" is more familiar to most people than the story of pearls, even though tulips' heyday was far briefer and the flower was less useful and certainly less portable. For an excellent recounting of the tulip craze, see Anna Pavord, *The Tulip: The Story of a Flower That Has Made Men Mad* (London, 1999). Lisa Jardine in *Worldly Goods: A New History of the Renaissance* (New York, 1998) and Ina Baghdiantz McCabe in *A History of Global Consumption, 1500–1800* (London, 2014) offer rich overviews of the changing early modern context of consumption.

For the role of consumption and cultural identity in a medieval Iberian context, see Barbara Fuchs, *Exotic Nation: Maurophilia and the Construction of Early Modern Spain* (Philadelphia, 2009). Brian Cowan looks at the rise of English coffee consumption and coffeehouse culture in the seventeenth century in *The Social Life of Coffee: The Emergence of the British Coffeehouse* (New

Haven, Conn., 2005). Jonathan Eacott considers the relationship between empire and trade regulation in *Selling Empire: India in the Making of Britain and America, 1600–1830* (Chapel Hill, N.C., 2016). Michael Ziser considers the cultural power posed by a particular commodity in "Sovereign Remedies: Natural Authority and the 'Counterblaste to Tobacco,'" *William and Mary Quarterly*, 3d Ser., LXII (2005), 719–744. For a consideration of the relationship between commodities and state power in modern times, see, especially, Sven Beckert, *Empire of Cotton: A Global History* (New York, 2014), and Michael T. Klare, *Resource Wars: The New Landscape of Global Conflict* (New York, 2001).

A growing body of literature approaches commodity trades with a deep appreciation of the natural habitats that produce them, focusing on the relationship between resource exploitation and political and commercial hegemony. Signal contributions include Peter E. Pope, *Fish into Wine: The Newfoundland Plantation in the Seventeenth Century* (Chapel Hill, N.C., 2004), which introduced me to the notion of "vernacular industries"; Jennifer L. Anderson, *Mahogany: The Costs of Luxury in Early America* (Cambridge, Mass., 2012); and Marcy Norton, *Sacred Gifts, Profane Pleasures: A History of Tobacco and Chocolate in the Atlantic World* (Ithaca, N.Y., 2008). The latter two are stellar commodity studies that offer rich social and cultural histories of the worlds that produced the goods in question. Kris Lane, *Colour of Paradise: The Emerald in the Age of Gunpower Empires* (New Haven, Conn., 2010), is a model of precision and broadmindedness in its re-creation of local context in global perspective. Additional examples of Latin American environmental history and commodity chains are, for example, Shawn William Miller, *Fruitless Trees: Portuguese Conservation and Brazil's Colonial Timber* (Stanford, Calif., 2000), and his *Environmental History of Latin America* (Cambridge, 2007); Steven Topik, Carlos Marichal, and Zephyr Frank, eds., *From Silver to Cocaine: Latin American Commodity Chains and the Building of the World Economy, 1500–2000* (Durham, N.C., 2006); and Daviken Studnicki-Gizbert and David Schecter, "The Environmental Dynamics of a Colonial Fuel-Rush: Silver Mining and Deforestation in New Spain, 1522 to 1810," *Environmental History*, XV (2010), 94–119. My attempt to write a social and cultural history of pearls in *American Baroque* draws inspiration from all these works, each of which furthered my thinking about the centrality of commodity chains to social relations in an early American context over the long durée. I depart from these books to the degree that *American Baroque* is more pointillist in its approach—owing to a combination of my source base and my own magpie-like intellectual orientation. I focus on pearls to illuminate the human networks that then eclipse the jewel as the focus of the story. These human webs of obligation, knowledge, and belonging, as much as pearls themselves, inform my understanding of the baroque.

In its emphasis on the fundamental importance of peoples' connection to the natural world and its products, *American Baroque* reflects both renewed attention to climate change in the early modern period as well as to the link between shifting political and economic geographies and control of the natural world. Other works that take a similar approach include Vera S. Candiani, *Dreaming of Dry Land: Environmental Transformation in Colonial Mexico City* (Stanford, Calif., 2014); Hämäläinen, *The Comanche Empire;* Fredrik Albritton Jonsson, *Enlightenment's Frontier: The Scottish Highlands and the Origins of Environmentalism* (New Haven, Conn., 2012); J. R. McNeill, *Mosquito Empires: Ecology and War in the Greater Caribbean, 1620–1914* (Cambridge, 2010); Alan Mikhail, *Nature and Empire in Ottoman Egypt: An Environmental History* (Cambridge, 2011); Geoffrey Parker, *Global Crisis: War, Climate Change, and Catastrophe in the Seventeenth Century* (New Haven, Conn., 2013); Christopher L. Pastore, *Between Land and Sea: The Atlantic Coast and the Transformation of New England* (Cambridge, Mass., 2014); and John F. Richards, *The Unending Frontier: An Environmental History of the Early Modern World* (Berkeley, Calif., 2003).

American Baroque also builds on the wide-ranging and growing body of literature focused on the relationship between the expansion of commercial circuits, global trade, and curiosity about nature. I found the following works on the cultural context of knowledge production to be particularly helpful: Harold J. Cook, *Matters of Exchange: Commerce, Medicine, and Science in the Dutch Golden Age* (New Haven, Conn., 2007); Richard Drayton, *Nature's Government: Science, Imperial Britain, and the "Improvement" of the World* (New Haven, Conn., 2000); Richard H. Grove, *Green Imperialism: Colonial Expansion, Tropical Island Edens, and the Origins of Environmentalism, 1600–1860* (Cambridge, 1995); Paula Findlen, *Possessing Nature: Museums, Collecting, and Scientific Culture in Early Modern Italy* (Berkeley, Calif., 1994); Deborah E. Harkness, *The Jewel House: Elizabethan London and the Scientific Revolution* (New Haven, Conn., 2007); and Lorraine Daston and Katharine Park, *Wonders and the Order of Nature, 1150–1750* (New York, 2001).

Although the book ranges beyond the bounds of the Iberian imperial world, it emerges from a unique Iberian cultural context. The many works of Regina Grafe and Tamar Herzog—especially Grafe, *Distant Tyranny: Markets, Power, and Backwardness in Spain, 1650–1800* (Princeton, N.J., 2012), and Herzog, *Defining Nations: Immigrants and Citizens in Early Modern Spain and Spanish America* (New Haven, Conn., 2003)—were particularly helpful as I thought about how inhabitants of the Spanish and Portuguese empires understood their political identities on scales small and large. On scientific practice in the Iberian world, see Antonio Barrera-Osorio, *Experiencing Nature: The Spanish American Empire and the Early Scientific Revolution* (Austin, Tex., 2006); Daniela Bleichmar, *Visible Empire: Botanical Expeditions and Visual Culture in the Hispanic Enlightenment* (Chicago, 2012); Daniela Bleichmar, Paula De Vos, Kristin Huffine, and Kevin Sheehan, eds., *Science in the Spanish and Portuguese Empires, 1500–1800* (Stanford, Calif., 2008); Jorge Cañizares-Esguerra, *Nature, Empire, and Nation: Explorations of the History of Science in the Iberian World* (Stanford, Calif., 2006); and María M. Portuondo, *Secret Science: Spanish Cosmography and the New World* (Chicago, 2009). These scholars, among others, have worked forcefully to counter the long-standing legacy of the Black Legend that still shapes historiography on the Spanish and Portuguese empires and that portrays these powers as backwaters of scientific learning and progressive thought. On the origins and legacy of the Black Legend, see Richard L. Kagan, "Prescott's Paradigm: American Historical Scholarship and the Decline of Spain," *American Historical Review,* CI (1996), 423–446.

In its consideration of pearls as wealth, *American Baroque* also engages with a wide-ranging literature on the financial transformations of the era, beginning with the work of scholars of the Spanish Americas who have grappled with the significance of the empire's silver outputs and the political and economic costs of the wealth produced in the sixteenth century. See Earl J. Hamilton, *American Treasure and the Price Revolution in Spain, 1501–1650* (Cambridge, Mass., 1934); Stanley J. Stein and Barbara H. Stein, *Silver, Trade, and War: Spain and America in the Making of Early Modern Europe* (Baltimore, 2000); and Elvira Vilches, *New World Gold: Cultural Anxiety and Monetary Disorder in Early Modern Spain* (Chicago, 2010).

J. H. Elliott towers over the field of scholarship on early modern Spain; like all scholars of anything touching upon the early modern Iberian world, my own work is deeply indebted to his oeuvre. Given my particular interests in the intersecting British and Iberian spheres, his consideration of the British and Spanish empires in *Empires of the Atlantic World: Britain and Spain in America, 1492–1830* (New Haven, Conn., 2006) served as an inspiring model of comparative history. Scholarly discussions of Habsburg fortunes have occurred in large part separately from discussions of the era's evolving political economy focusing on developments in the Anglo and Dutch worlds, in spite of the increasing scholarly emphasis on "entangled" histories. See the forum, "Entangled Empires in the Atlantic World," *American Historical Review*, CXII (2007), 710–799. One study that does consider the larger European context is Mauricio Drelichman and Hans-Joachim Voth, *Lending to the Borrower from Hell: Debt, Taxes, and Default in the Age of Philip II* (Princeton, N.J., 2014), which looks at how Spain's economic fortunes embedded the empire in a series of economic and social relationships throughout Europe.

To craft the book's considerations of communities that engaged deeply with pearls, either at sites of production or in the distribution of the jewel, I have read widely about different types of networks. *American Baroque* defines networks in a capacious fashion to include small communities of friends, families, or enslaved laborers as well as diplomatic circles and religious orders. These networks often operated along nearly imperceptible circuits, their participants' precise motivations and concerns remaining largely invisible. Excellent scholarship on early modern Sephardic communities proved particularly useful as I made sense of merchant networks. Exemplary works include Daviken Studnicki-Gizbert, *A Nation upon the Ocean Sea: Portugal's Atlantic Diaspora and the Crisis of the Spanish Empire, 1492–1640* (Oxford, 2007); Francesca Trivellato, *The Familiarity of Strangers: The Sephardic Diaspora, Livorno, and Cross-Cultural Trade in the Early Modern Period* (New Haven, Conn., 2009); Sarah Abrevaya Stein, *Plumes: Ostrich Feathers, Jews, and a Lost World of Global Commerce* (New Haven, Conn., 2008); and Gedalia Yogev, *Diamonds and Coral: Anglo-Dutch Jews and Eighteenth-Century Trade* (Leicester, U.K., 1978). Each of these authors considers distinct moments in the history of the Sephardic diaspora and various commercial and trade practices that operated outside state-sponsored commercial activities. *American Baroque* also looks to networks of resource mobilization and heterogeneous trading practices, such as David Parrott, *The Business of War: Military Enterprise and Military Revolution in Early Modern Europe* (Cambridge, 2012), and Philip J. Stern, *The Company-State: Corporate Sovereignty and the Early Modern Foundations of the British Empire in India* (Oxford, 2011).

Lastly, my contention that the seed of the conceptual utility of the term "baroque" lay in the knot of Caribbean encounters echoes the findings of many scholars who have focused on the uniquely American history of the concept. Beginning with the classic work of José Antonio Maravall, *Culture of the Baroque: Analysis of a Historical Structure*, trans. Terry Cochran (Minneapolis, Minn., 1986), I began to think about how pearls' global pathways in the early modern period might have shaped the conceptual influence of the term. Irlemar Chiampi in *Barroco y modernidad* (Mexico City, 2000) explores the baroque as an aesthetic and cultural crucible that lay at the heart of modernity and was uniquely American in its characteristics. Severo Sarduy, in his essay "El barroco y el neobarroco," in César Fernández Moreno, ed., *America Latina en su literatura* (Mexico City, 1973), characterizes the baroque space as one of wasteful excess. In contrast, *American Baroque* considers the innumerable pathways of the era's millions of pearls to be a sign of global engagement on a microhistorical level with the elaboration of value — in short, a space of creation rather than dissipation.

As the transnational and non-national perspectives have long had a role in scholarship on the baroque, this book seeks to build on, rather than break with, this traditional emphasis on the concept's relevance for Latin America, seeking global commonalities in the negotiations this particular natural resource engendered. Lois Parkinson Zamora and Monika Kaup offer a useful overview of the role of the transnational / non-national in discussions of the baroque in literary (and art historical) criticism in Zamora and Kaup, eds., *Baroque New Worlds: Representation, Transculturation, Counterconquest* (Durham, N.C., 2010). Additionally, Nicholas Spadaccini and Luis Martín-Estudillo, eds., *Hispanic Baroques: Reading Cultures in Context* (Nashville, Tenn., 2005), provide numerous useful perspectives on new directions in scholarship on the baroque since Maravall. Evonne Levy and Kenneth Mills, eds., *Lexikon of the Hispanic Baroque: Transatlantic Exchange and Transformation* (Austin, Tex., 2013), consider the cultural components of the Hispanic baroque in their rich collection of essays on key concepts in the Spanish Atlantic world. Roland Greene's *Five Words: Critical Semantics in the Age of Shakespeare and Cervantes* (Chicago, 2013) proved invaluable for thinking about the relationship between language and practice in the early modern era, and particularly for the relevance of the vernacular during this period.

Working seriously within as well as across these multiple arenas of scholarship has been critical to this book's argument about early modern political economy and the nature and influence of the baroque. In particular, the book underscores the resonance of the concept for thinking about the tension between chaos and order in the wake of the American encounter. As baroque pearls — and all pearls — represent a beautiful, irregular by-product of an unwanted penetration of the oyster, *American Baroque* considers the complex and rich encounters generated by the accidental European and African intrusion into the Americas. Both conceptual and rooted in fine-grained archival history, *American Baroque* incorporates the insights of scholars working in disparate fields to trace a path that links macro-level cultural and political elaboration to small-scale decision making by individuals.

Alongside my argument about the importance of small-scale approaches to wealth husbandry is a historiographic point about the global context in which the post-Columbus Americas took shape. The early modern encounter in the Caribbean was from its first moments deeply shaped by distant peoples and practices as well as by local context. This complexity and diversity of influences characterized the early Americas far beyond the pearl fisheries. In its inclusionary and multi-scale approach, the book offers a vision of a dynamic early modern world in which conversations about the nature of belonging and value, of people and products, bypassed imperial—and historiographic—boundaries.

INDEX

Page numbers in italics refer to illustrations.

MIX
Paper from
responsible sources
FSC® C013483